Jung

and the
OUTSIDE
WORLD

Jung
and the
OUTSIDE
WORLD

Barry Ulanov

CHIRON PUBLICATIONS • WILMETTE, ILLINOIS

Library of Congress Catalog Card Number: 91-26662

Printed in the United States of America.
Editing and book design by Siobhan Drummond.
Cover design by Michael Barron.

Library of Congress Cataloging-in-Publication Data:

Ulanov, Barry.
   Jung and the outside world / Barry Ulanov.
      p.   cm.
   Includes index.
   ISBN 0-933029-58-6 : $16.95
   1. Jung, C. G. (Carl Gustav), 1875-1961 – Influence.   2. Archetype
(Psychology) in literature.   3. Archetype (Psychology)
4. Psychoanalysis and religion.   I. title.
BF109.J8U53   1992
150.19'54 – dc20   91-26662
                                                                              CIP

ISBN 0-933029-58-6

FOR ANN

CONTENTS

FOREWORD BY ANN BELFORD ULANOV —————— ix

CHAPTER 1 JUNG'S OUTSIDE WORLD ————— 1

CHAPTER 2 AUTOBIOGRAPHY ————— 5

CHAPTER 3 RELIGION ————— 10

CHAPTER 4 EASTERN RELIGION ————— 46

CHAPTER 5 MYTH ————— 52

CHAPTER 6 LITERARY THEORY ————— 81

CHAPTER 7 THE NOVEL ————— 121

CHAPTER 8 POETRY ————— 164

CHAPTER 9 THE OTHER ARTS ————— 184

CHAPTER 10 PHILOSOPHY ————— 205

CHAPTER 11 *COMPLEXIO OPPOSITORUM* ——— 244

INDEX ————— 247

FOREWORD

Much has been written on Jung's life and Jung's work. Little has been written on the effect of the man's work on other thinkers and artists of talent and depth. We read here, in my husband's book, of the responses to Jung of people of the stature of Eliade, Gebser, Beckett, Toynbee, Tippett, Zaehner, Bachelard, Muir, Hughes, Joyce, Musil, White, Broch and many others. With prodigious scholarship, Barry makes accessible the work of theologians, philosophers, poets, composers, novelists, painters, filmmakers, literary critics, and what they say, both positive and negative, about Jung's ideas and his influence on their own creative work.

This book is thus a whole library. The reader can look up a philosopher, a theologian, a novelist, a poet, a painter, and see how Jung touched him or her. It is astonishing to see how many people Jung's work did touch, and what sort of people. Even where the criticism of Jung comes harshly, the critic has had to reckon with Jung as a "problem thinker" who forces others to think about central things most people try to forget – evil, identity, madness and sanity, purposiveness and purposelessness, imagination, soul.

Barry makes clear from his selection and discussion that Jung's perception of the objectivity of the psyche – the collective unconscious – stands out as the signal influence. Next would come the transformation of the self and, in particular, in relation to what we experience of the transcendent. Finally, the alchemy of the two sexes catches many. They see that anima and animus, in the mystery of the meeting and interpenetration of these archetypal elements, open onto the crucial events of integration.

All the authors included here circle around and around Jung's notion of the collective unconscious. Whatever they call it – the *Ursprung*, primordium, ever-present time, imaginative territory, common human ground (although not untouched by differences in background, history, ethnic group), the mystery of the whole, the founding symbols – this reality draws them to Jung and into his ideas. There they find hope for the present and for the future. This hope, poignant and robust, survives the horrors of our century, which the authors, given their large sensibilities, suffer and articulate in their poems of war and death, their music of black slave blues and AIDS destruction, their paintings of unconscious monsters, or their religious meditations on the brute facts of evil. Here, in this "objective psyche," this life that we all share, dwell archetypal images that bespeak human emotions, aspirations, the stuff from which myths are drawn, things that speak to us of what is all but unspeakable but always deeply felt. Here is where our roots go down into a shared history of soul to reach an inheritance that both precedes individual consciousness and is, at the same time, its nutriment. From this depth, the life of imagination springs; to this depth, it always returns, to circle around and around the complexity of opposites to do the destructive and constructive work of the arts. These authors show us that we can find in Jung's idea of the collective psyche a place for religious belief and a reality that makes possible a life of the spirit.

A true sense of self, the transformation of the self, all these people seem to agree, come only in relation to the primordial unconscious. An ego-centered life can then give way to a spiritual discipline – and they seem to say this whether or not they adopt a religious idiom. A bigger self can then take over the running of a life, and one can live in touch with "perpetual plenitude," open to the hidden soul in persons, in things, in matter itself. The arts as a whole and each one individually work at the alchemical transformation of our egos into a unity shared with all selves and with the world. The soul, as Bachelard puts it, grows cosmic roots. Unconscious depth unites with conscious purpose as imaginatively – with the help of these authors – we sense the goal of completeness.

Some of these authors are fascinated by Jung's idea of our double-sexed nature. We carry in us, as Barry puts it, "a great well of otherness" that looks at life from a departure point opposite to that of our conscious identity. Patrick White, in particular, shows a genius of insight into a world gathered and formed from separate and mixed, from opposed and shared sexual identities, from the point of view of his female characters and then from his male characters and all the alternations that occur within the same persons. This achievement of meeting and matching – the *coniunctio* of masculine and feminine – is shown not to be some esoteric, once-and-for-all acme of development, but a here-and-now imaginative possibility for persons brought together and persons altogether within themselves. It is a joining and maturing of identities that changes our perception of reality, enabling us really to see, to see into the daimon within that beckons to us through this other point of view and seeks to usher us into that abiding other world manifest here, now, in our daily lives.

Barry's own views run as leitmotifs through this capacious work and give, I think, new insight to Jung. Neither an adorer nor a defender, neither caviling nor attacking, he sees Jung as the great chronicler of the collective unconscious, its historian, its transcriber. Jung was scrupulous in reporting what he saw welling up from the archetypal world of the unconscious. His inner daimon drove him to gather all he could of this primordial world. In addition, Barry makes us see again that, for Jung, only by finding one's own myth can one overcome conflicts, including them, absorbing them, in a sense of self. Thus and thus only do we participate in that central *complexio oppositorum* that characterizes the self as the centering archetype of the collective unconscious.

Barry gives us, through the lens of Jung's work, a sense of being itself looking to find and bring into heightened consciousness its wellspring of images and symbols, the life of the soul. We glimpse, through his presentation, the intercessory strength of being. It is there for the taking. It wants to be taken and lived through us in all our multiplicities, in all our antideterministic sprawl. In this presentation of Jung through the lens of many and talented authors, Barry leaves us with a sense of Jung's large contribution to culture, one which enlarges our own sense of being and brings us to confront the largeness of being itself.

Ann Belford Ulanov

CHAPTER 1

JUNG'S OUTSIDE WORLD

I t is not easy to place depth psychology among the disciplines of learning. At various times in its short history, its practitioners have made claims for it as a science, while almost as often strong arguments have been raised against such claims by people like the philosopher Karl Popper. For Popper, depth psychology cannot be a science. Its assertions, he says, are unfalsifiable. They command belief rather than proof. They suggest a religion rather than a science.

Others, sometimes within the precincts of depth psychology, sometimes outside, have proposed that we look at depth psychology as at least as much an art as a science. Their case has much to recommend it. The writing skills of Sigmund Freud certainly support it. So does the critical acumen of Otto Rank, nourished by a large acquaintance with literature, or the sensitivity to the arts of Heinz Kohut, or the imaginative response to children of the Lewis Carroll of psychoanalysis, D. W. Winnicott. But the pre-eminent example of depth psychology as a humanistic discipline is surely the work of C. G. Jung.

Jung's work makes a case not for one discipline, but for many disciplines brought together through one sensibility. Jung's capacity to take in and use the insights, data, and speculations of philosophy, theology, anthropology, literature, and historiography in his work as an analytical psychologist almost matched his appetite to keep track and make sense of everything that found its way into the human unconscious. It is an astonishing reach, matched often enough by the grasp to make Jung almost larger than life, greatly respected by many, harshly objected to by others.

What is remarkable about Jung's achievement is that, art or science, respected or castigated, it is still very much with us. It is not only followed, with whatever narrowing or enlargement, by analytical psychologists trained in Jungian centers around the world, it is looked upon seriously, drawn upon usefully, a source of inspiration to people in each of the areas where Jung himself touched down. There are, then, two worlds of Jung, the inside world of analytical psychology and the outside world of the disciplines apart from psychology where he so often ventured, and ventured productively, from which he learned so much, and which learned so much from him.

It is the purpose of this book to give some fair indication of the size and substance of the outside world affected by Jung as it affected him. The size of that world is huge, as the following pages suggest, and the quality of mind and sensibility engaged in it high. One finds strong influences in it, lessons learned, so to speak, from the master, and strong arguments, ranging from polite demurrer to violent repudiation. But whether in acceptance or rejection, pleased or troubled dialogue with Jung, there is no mistaking his presence in the works and careers charted in these pages. Jung is very much alive in this outside world, a constant and significant figure in the lives of writers and painters, musicians, theologians and philosophers, scholars of myth and comparative religion, literary theorists, historians, and historiographers.

There are more people in Jung's outside world than I have been able to include in this book, more who have made noteworthy use of his work in theirs. But the group that I have assembled here is a goodly company, a representative one, and one that misses few of consequence, I believe, whose writings about their encounters with Jungian ideas are available in English or whose works, if they are in the arts, are generally available.

Those who are familiar with Jung will find the people dealt with here more accessible than they would be without that familiarity. Jung's thinking, his special vocabulary, his characteristic movement in and out of system and structure, will inevitably become more familiar, more understandable, more engaging. In many ways, the novelists, poets, theorists, and scholars who have responded so strongly to Jung bring him much more sharply into view. We may not always accept what we find in the refractions and resonances of Jung in these people, but, positive or negative, our judgments will be more securely founded, our responses better tutored, our sense of Jung and his achievement considerably enlarged.

What abides in this meeting of Jung and the outside world is an irreducible complexity. Jung understood this in the nature of the psyche; it is what drew him to so many areas and procedures and sets of materials in analysis; it is what drew so many in so many different disciplines to examine his work and to make use of it. One cannot altogether separate Jung from the methods of the sciences, for he was trained to use them and did so where he thought them apposite and his own equipment adequate. Nor should we fail to recognize the inclination of the artist to see persons, things, and events in all their parts and as much as possible not to lose sight of the parts. Finally, we should hesitate to sum up such a complexity, whether of the man or the ideas, in any one term, such as *mystic* or *mystical*, whether meant to praise or to dismiss.

A 1973 entry in the journal of Mircea Eliade speaks to the point and suggests something of the complexity and richness of the meeting between Jung and the outside world. "According to the Freudians, as well as to many others, C. G. Jung is a 'mystic,' " Eliade writes. "They claim that he improvises, imagines, generalizes, etc. I find it offensive to say that about a man who took the trouble to analyze sixty-seven thousand dreams, those of his patients as well as of his collaborators, before proposing his own theory on dreams."[1]

"No invidious distinctions" is Eliade's point and mine. Jung is not a mystic in quotation marks, which is to say, credulous about what purports to be religious experience, because he observes and analyzes so carefully what goes on in that domain, in himself as well as in others. Nor is he a psychological positivist, because he gathers so much material from the world of the psyche, his own as well as others', and looks for verification of his findings wherever he can find it.

Complexity is the governing texture of Jung's inside and outside worlds. The approaches to it are those of the arts and sciences and any other speculative or analytical discipline that can be gathered up under the rubrics and procedures of depth psychology. A whole is not often grasped this way; Jung proposes no tidy definitions of human nature. What we have, in this complexity, is not an anarchic proliferation of parts, vaguely linked by one man's interest. Rather we have a history of consciousness and the unconscious reaching farther back into primordial beginnings than anyone before Jung had thought to look. The history traced is tantalizing in its fullness, reassuring in its respect for oddments of the human imagination often dismissed as disreputable.

The complexity of this world of consciousness and the unconscious is such that its parts keep moving in and out of each other. Thus it is that one can take up its informing disciplines in almost any order and find one's way among them. There is one radical reality that holds the parts, or at least some of them, together: the mediating sensibility of the inquirer, the speculative intellect, the analytical forces of the psychologist, the novelist, the theologian, the musician, the painter,

---

[1]Mircea Eliade, *Journal III 1970–1978*, trans. T. L. Fagan (Chicago: University of Chicago Press, 1989), pp. 90–91. Eliade's rumination on Jung's interpretation of the *puer eternus* is very much to the point of this book — its "mythology must be completed by a yet insufficiently elucidated 'ontology'. . ." (p. 102).

the poet, the philosopher. In the presentation of Jung in the outside world that follows, I begin with autobiography. I begin, in other words, where Jung ends. But Jung's ending is a grand beginning, for as he says in the retrospective last moments of his autobiography, "clouded" in old age, fulfilling the "archetype of the old man who has seen enough," there remains a balancing fact: "The more uncertain I have felt about myself, the more there has grown up in me a feeling of kinship with all things."[2] That is the complexity and the simplicity of Jung and the outside world.

---

[2]C. G. Jung, *Memories, Dreams, Reflections*, ed. Aniela Jaffé, trans. Richard and Clara Winston (New York: Pantheon, 1963), p. 359.

CHAPTER 2

AUTOBIOGRAPHY

In *Memories, Dreams, Reflections*, Jung says straightforwardly, "My life is what I have done, my scientific work; the one is insepa-rable from the other." The work on the outside reflects the man on the inside, "for commitment to the contents of the unconscious forms the man and produces his transformations." James Olney in his valuable work on "The Meaning of Autobiography," *Metaphors of Self*, agrees and more than agrees. He finds the "private images" and the "projected career" joined as never before to produce what is for him Jung's most considerable book, his "fullest statement." What Olney does with the book itself is impressive. He makes the case for Jung's story, Jung's myth of himself, "a myth about divine spirit in human form," and for the process of individuation, that process which involves "the psyche realizing itself, becoming aware of itself," not only in terms of the tale told and the observations made in the autobiography, but in the *Col-lected Works*, all of them, every last word of them. Both, he says, and says persuasively, "project metaphors of Jung's moment-to-moment becoming."

Olney reinforces his judgment with the example of the poet Yeats. Like Jung, Yeats goes far beyond the limits of ego-consciousness in gathering the materials of his own myth – "the fantas-tic myth called *A Vision*" – from his "ghostly instructors" who in count-less ways, not the least of them direct dictation, spoke to him out of the *anima mundi* or *spiritus mundi*, as Yeats called it. Soul or spirit of the world, Great Mind, collective unconscious, objective psyche – whatever we choose to call it, we are speaking in metaphors. Olney's term is "metaphors of self" and it fits not only Jung but the six other figures brought together with him as tutelary examples of the autobio-graphical genre and its metaphorical substance.

Montaigne is the figure who is most insistently coupled with Jung by Olney, for the rigor of his critical examination of himself in his essays and the unquenchable impulse to self-renewal inherent in the criticism. But Cardinal Newman, who works "under cover of another

discipline" as Jung does, is not far removed from these two, nor is the
T. S. Eliot of the *Four Quartets*. And the others considered, writers of
"autobiography simplex," George Fox, Charles Darwin, John Stuart
Mill, have their connections with the same kind of examination and
renewal of self. What is particularly interesting is the role assigned
Jung. He is to be seen, in effect, as definer and referee of the task and
the achievement, if only to measure an even greater preoccupation
than his with self: "not even Jung, who is largely responsible for developing the concept in modern psychology, has ever given himself so
intensely to the question of selfhood as G. M. Hopkins. . . ."

Olney makes a distinction between autobiographers of the single
metaphor – Fox, Darwin, Mill, sometimes Newman – and of the
double – Montaigne, Jung, Eliot, Newman on occasion. Each of the
first group had "his daimon, his personal genius and guardian spirit, a
dominant faculty or function or tendency that formed a part of his
whole self and from which there was no escape, even had he wished it."
For the second group, the daimon "can only be described as the self,
the whole self, as it turns out, "symbolically complete" in the metaphors of Montaigne's essays, Eliot's *Quartets*, and Jung's autobiography. It is a whole "revealed to be greater than the sum of all its various
parts" as such parts appear in Fox, Darwin, Mill, and Newman. Jung
did not invent the terms of discussion here, but surely the understanding of "daimon" that informs it owes at least as much to him as to the
pre-Socratic philosopher Heracleitus, whose dark wisdom – "Man's
character is his daimon" – Olney cites.

Olney makes sense of Fox and Darwin by comparing them to
Montaigne and Jung, to note, for example, the "single and partial"
appeal, the narrowness for all the attractive qualities of the first, the
"unsophisticated" nature of the second, his lack of "perspective awareness" about himself. To understand Newman's "growth . . . from merely
notional to intensely real assent," we must not only make sense of
"assent," the grammar of which Newman wrote in his most significant
philosophical work, but see the growth as "a process not altogether
unlike 'individuation' " in Jung's usage. To fix Mill's character in our
minds, it is useful to invoke Jung's function types, to call attention to
the way one "is always developed at the expense of its opposite," to
underscore Mill's rejection of intuition, deficiency of feeling, and
attraction to thinking modes, especially those that emphasize the general, abstract, and rational. The discussion of Eliot is deepened by
allusion and explication out of Jung, for Olney sees the poet as one who
"treats his own experience as representative and symbolic, [and]
resolves and merges those dualities of consciousness and the unconscious, of the individual and the race, that have long attracted and
teased the minds of psychologist and philosopher." In Eliot's *Four*

Quartets, there is a process of multiple mirroring that brings with it a fullness of self, recognized, "realized . . . revealed." Experience recalled in Montaigne-like ways yields perspective and pattern and "gives the poem its Jungian sense of being a summary repetition in the individual of the evolution of consciousness in humanity to the present epitomizing moment."

Olney's own sensitivity to Jung, demonstrated again and again in the remarkable gathering of quotations from the collected works to bulwark and enlarge the material from the autobiography, gives his reading of the *Quartets* in these terms a persuasive logic, or at least does so for those who have similar understanding of Jung. "Putting the matter in Jung's language," he explains, "one might say that *Four Quartets* is the autobiography not of ego-consciousness alone, though of course the portrait includes that, nor of the external person and his acts, but of the whole psyche and self." What the poem offers is "a whole self . . . not a partial self . . ." What it represents and symbolizes is "not the private self of T. S. Eliot," yet it emerges from that self, "raised out of" it, filtered through it and beyond it. "Whatever Eliot may have been as a man, the limitation of wholeness implied in psychological 'typing' seems not to obtain for the poet in his work: he, or the voice of the poem, is simultaneously introverted and extroverted, adapted alike to the world of the senses and the realm of intuition, equally sensitive in thought and in feeling, conscious of everything in the world and of nothing more than of the self as it becomes conscious."

Olney manages very well in what he acknowledges as a "lonely" task, trying to hold down to critical, psychological, philosophical earth the autobiographical genre, about which so little of value has been written. Although he thinks we can never "have the experience in consciousness that the autobiographer had" and as a result may never know what he was "in his deepest and inaccessible self," Olney has brought us very close to that experience and the self which undergoes it. We see, especially with Jung, Montaigne, and Eliot, the psyche realizing itself, or at least the symbols of symbols that Jung talks about in the myth-making process that Olney accounts psychological explanation. The reality of the personal myth is all but palpable. In its terms the assumption that man can "complete the intention and creation of his God" and in his creative acts "put the stamp of perfection on the world by giving it objective existence" seems less brazen, less an act of pride. We understand how Olney can say in the last long paragraph of his treatment of Jung that the "*Collected Works* might equally well — better, one might say — be entitled *Essays; or, The Making of C. G. Jung*. It is not so much an *Opus Scientificum* — for, given the subject, it could never be that — as it is a large and complex metaphor for all that he and he alone knew about the process of becoming a self—i.e., his unique self, a heritage and an experience."[1]

In attempt to deal with British autobiography in the twentieth century, Brian Finney's *The Inner I* adds to our understanding of Jung's importance in the genre. Finney has chosen, as he says, to use the theories of Freud and Jung—"though sparingly"—because so many autobiographies of this era "are heavily indebted to them for their entire outlook and presuppositions." Jung once again figures as a point of comparison, for he is not only a theorist of autobiography but a practitioner. The construction of personal myth as a way of gathering some sense of the "interior self" has obvious Jungian sources, as does the feeling of freedom to omit whatever the autobiographer would like to do, "as Jung, for instance, does with abandon in *Memories, Dreams, Reflections.*" Jung is cited in the treatment of Herbert Read's *The Innocent Eye* as understanding, as Read does, the Garden of Eden as " 'an ever-present archetype of wholeness' to which the self can return in later life for renewal by a process of reintegration." Jung on childhood and the life-cycle helps us understand Laurie Lee; his definition of the artist makes Richard Church's childhood autobiography accessible in a special way as we see the work of art like a child growing out of its

---

[1]James Olney, *Metaphors of Self: The Meaning of Autobiography* (Princeton: Princeton University Press, 1972), pp. 105–106, 108, 23, 39–40, 157, 198, 211, 241–244, 261, 274, 306, 311, xi, 128n., 149. This quotation from Jung's autobiography is from the end of chapter VII, "The Work," p. 222. It is clearly a statement that comes with age. As A. O. J. Cockshut says in the introduction to his splendid examination of *The Art of Autobiography in 19th and 20th Century England* (New Haven: Yale University Press, 1984), "the autobiographical process begins with a long barely conscious process of inner assimilation. A journalist, even if he happened also to be a gifted autobiographer, could hardly write a convincing autobiographical account of the incident which he reported brilliantly yesterday. But thirty years later perhaps he might." Thus, Cockshut concludes, "there is a particular interest in knowing the age at which autobiographers wrote. No doubt it is an obscure sense of the autobiographer's need for these years of assimilation that makes the idea of an autobiography written by a very young person seem faintly ridiculous." The size of the autobiographical event is handsomely drawn by the phenomenologist William Earle in *The Autobiographical Consciousness: A Philosophical Inquiry into Existence* (Chicago: Quadrangle, 1972), where he stresses the subjectivity of the experience: "I am not and cannot be an object for me; no object I can apprehend can be me. I am therefore absolutely nonobjective; and if the 'world' is taken as an 'objective world,' or a world of things and events that are objective, I can never be a member of that world" (p. 54). In autobiography at the level at which Olney confronts it, which Jung surely exemplifies, we meet again and again the phenomenon of what Earle calls "an enacted relationship" in which the gap between the past and the present is somehow "bridged by the self that presided over both occasions," the remarkable achievement of memory. "Nothing like it is to be found in the physical world, and . . . it is clear that no purely physical or physiological mechanism can account for it" (pp. 160–161). It becomes each time it is brought alive, I think, what Henry James called an "act of life"; it became the center of Jung's explorations whenever he could make it such. That is what drew so many in the "outside world" to him.

mother, "or rather out of what Jung calls the unconscious 'realm of the Mothers.' " The father-imago or archetype is a "potent presence" in the autobiographical Yeats. Osbert Sitwell's father, important in his life as in his brother Sacheverell's and his sister Edith's, is described in Jung's typology as a neurotic introvert who "shuts himself up with his complexes until he ends in complete isolation." John Osborne, playwright turned autobiographer, invokes Jung's suggestion that children are often led unconsciously to try "to compensate for everything that was left unfulfilled in the lives of their parents."

Personal myth or fable inevitably figures in a number of autobiographies. Christopher Isherwood directly acknowledges Jung in his attempt in *Christopher and His Kind* "to explore one's personal sexual mythology and identify one's sexual archetypes." With or without acknowledgment, Jungian ideas and feelings, if not an explorative technique drawn from Jung's work, turn up in the "shadow self" who is Forrest Reid's "ideal companion" and in the large presence of the collective or racial unconscious in Edwin Muir's autobiography, as in his poetry, where the "ancestral" or "millennial" dream is given such compelling articulation.

In the last two chapters of Finney's book, "The Spiritual History of the Self" and "The Double Perspective: The Self and History," Jung appears as an unmistakable mover and shaker of ideas, although acknowledged directly only at the beginning of the first of these. There Finney says simply enough that in his examination of modern "autobiographical accounts of the self it is fitting that [he] should have resorted to the terminology of analytical psychology which has revolutionized our conception of human nature in the course of the century." Presumably he means Freud as well as Jung. That would not bother Jung, nor would the reminder that follows, that what we call "self" or "psyche" today could be understood as "continuous with what was called the 'soul' for centuries. . . ."[2] Nobody worked harder than Jung to link modern psyche to ancient soul. No one had more respect for metaphors of self.

[2]Brian Finney, *The Inner Eye: British Literary Autobiography of the Twentieth Century* (New York: Oxford University Press, 1985), pp. 15, 23, 68, 124–125, 135, 152–156, 158, 184, 188, 195, 203, 207. A related volume is Jeffrey Mehlman's *A Structural Study of Autobiography: Proust, Leiris, Sartre, Lévi-Strauss* (Ithaca: Cornell University Press, 1974), insistently Freudian and Lacanian, but with an epigraph from, and at least the distant presence of, Bachelard that the opening words reflect, namely Mehlman's "concern . . . to elaborate a *structure*: a self-regulating series of transformations of a constant system of relationships." Jungians should be interested.

CHAPTER 3
RELIGION

J ung's various writings about religion over the years emboldened some, annoyed others, and perplexed many. Although he did not speak as a believer with an identifiable creed, he clearly took religion seriously, knew its issues well and respected them, and saw as a "fact" its pivotal importance in the second half of life to those brought up within its precincts. There is a famous statement in *Modern Man in Search of a Soul*, calling "attention to the following facts":

> I have treated many hundreds of patients, the larger number being Protestants, a smaller number of Jews, and not more than five or six believing Catholics. Among all my patients in the second half of life – that is to say, over thirty-five – there has not been one whose problem in the last resort was not that of finding a religious outlook on life. It is safe to say that every one of them fell ill because he had lost that which the living religions of every age have given their followers, and none of them has been really healed who did not regain his religious outlook. [1]

A British clergyman and academic, sometime editor of the *Hibbert Journal*, G. Stephens Spinks sounds a fervent amen to these facts in his examination of what he calls "the peculiar dilemma of the 20th century." For him, it is a "pre-occupation with the realm of things," which has made ours "an extrovert society trying to live either without beliefs about God, Nature and Man," or left us "living surreptitiously and furtively, on the vaguely understood beliefs of earlier and introverted forms of society whose convictions we have rejected on the superficial levels of consciousness."

Spinks's examination in *The Fundamentals of Religious Belief* is not merely emboldened by Jungian ideas but deepened. He is caught by Jung's insistence that "the most significant part of our experiences cannot be put into words," the reasons, as Spinks reads Jung, "why

---

[1]C. G. Jung, *Modern Man in Search of a Soul*, trans. W. S. Dell and C. F. Baynes (New York: Harcourt, Brace, 1933), p. 229.

purely intellectual attempts to express the nature of religion (which is intimately concerned with experience) give rise to such misunderstanding." He has followed Jung closely on the life of the symbol and the rooting this gives the life of modern man "in his ancestral past." He writes lucidly and thoughtfully about archetypes and the collective unconscious. He is caught by Michael Fordham's description of Jung as, at least at first, an archaeologist and sees him as "a supreme arbiter of primitive pictorial art and mythology, which he was able to correlate with the dreams and fantasies of his patients."

Spinks's response to Jung as a religious thinker is enthusiastic, but never fawning. Without rancor or simplistic repudiation, he turns away from scientistic readings of religious experience, from Freud and all whose reading of religion fails to recognize that "Religion is not concerned to draw a tidy intellectual picture of Reality, for the sufficient reason that religion does not believe that reason comprehends all." The conclusion is inescapable: "Religion will never be able to outgrow the mythological as science claims the ability to do. Reality evades a fully rationalistic explanation and there are elements in human experience which cannot be adequately dealt with in logical terms."

Spinks is a notably sympathetic reader of Jung and shrewd in drawing materials for a kind of religious apologetic from Jung's work alone as well as from his collaborations with the physicist William Pauli and the mythographer C. J. Kerenyi. An example of his effective use of Jung is in making a distinction between "a limited *certainty*" and "*certitude* which is a more comprehensive truth. . . ." Certitude is provided by what Spinks calls "corroborative probability," offering a truth very differently established from scientific truth. "It was to this condition of 'certitude' that Jung seemed to have been referring," he says, "when in a B.B.C. television programme – Face to Face – he was asked by Mr. John Freeman, 'Do you believe in God?' To which Jung answered quite simply – 'I do not believe, *I know*.' "[2] The exchange is famous in Jungian annals. No one, as far as I know, has made better use of it or lifted it more effectively from the tufts and wisps of gossip. If one thinks of this famous rejoinder as expressing certitude, and just that, it becomes much less mysterious or tricky than it has often been thought to be, even as, in its own simple, blunt way, it describes mystery.

Reducing Jung to catchphrases and simple summation is all too easy to do, especially in a religious context. Gai Eaton, in his generally fair-minded and tidy little book on Eastern tradition and modern

[2]See G. Stephens Spinks, *The Fundamentals of Religious Belief* (London: Hodder and Stoughton, 1961), pp. 28, 70, 75, 96, 138–139, 182.

thought, *The Richest Vein*, cites Jung several times accurately enough, but the citations are too brief; without any footnote apparatus or other indication of sources, the disputations and refutations that follow become little more than expressions of annoyance and perplexity. To say, for example, that "Jung's Unconscious is a decidedly ambiguous and ill-defined term" is to carp at Jung for the use of a word which has had a long and troubled history, at least from the time of the Romantics in the late eighteenth and early nineteenth century to the present. It is no more easily run to earth in Coleridge or Wordsworth, in Eduard von Hartmann or Freud, than it is in Jung. All of us who have been constrained to use it, after fruitless attempts to find substitutes, can understand Eaton's discomfort but not his laying particular blame upon Jung, who possibly did more to give texture and detail to our understanding of the territory of the unconscious than anyone before him.

In a discussion of the understanding of consciousness in the Upanishads, Eaton quotes Jung: "Consciousness is derived from the Unconscious." That is the extent of the quote, and while it leads to a felicitous few words on consciousness or intellect in Indian philosophy and a parallel insight in Meister Eckhardt, the effect is exactly the kind of ambiguity and poor definition of which he has accused Jung. A similar criticism can be made of his truncated presentation of individuation and Jung's use of Taoism in his attempt "to show the man of our time the way back to the source of his powers." The "comparison," he explains, "must not be pushed too far, nor must Jung's confession of his indebtedness to the teachings of Taoism be taken as evidence that his psychology is in line with these teachings." This is surely saying too much, as it is again in his discussion of Jung's notion of individuation to question whether Jung's psychology "offers a real technique" for a kind of descent into Hell, "whereby the inferior possibilities of a particular state may be exhausted," as well as for a "subsequent return." The criticism assumes claims on Jung's part which are never made. Jung may be open to serious objection for establishing connections between ancient worlds and modern ones that are not securely tied together, perhaps because they cannot be. We are in the realm of religious mystery, where those dartings and dodgings, for which Spinks has spoken so well, may be all the apparatus of understanding we will be given. Eaton himself says it very well at the end of this highly condensed discussion. Speaking of Jung's provisions for "descent into the darkness," where we may "meet in strange shapes, all that we have neglected in our one-sided lives," he acknowledges that Jung "has certainly restated in modern terms a very ancient doctrine and demonstrated the necessity for a reorientation of consciousness if we are to come into possession of our integral humanity."

Eaton says all of this more felicitously in his presentation of the teasing textures and provocative condensations of the Zen koan, which he calls "chief among the techniques for baffling the mind and arousing the intuitive powers. . . ." He defines the koan as "some totally illogical problem, to which quite obviously there is no reasonable answer. . . ." Zen Buddhism sets its monks to puzzling over the insoluble, to working out in their mixture of patience and physical exhaustion, of ingenuity and bafflement, the vision or state of intensified awareness that Zen calls satori. Here Eaton's use of Jung is very much to the point – of Zen Buddhism and of Jungian thought.

> The meaning of this practice is sufficiently clear. The Koan is the image of life itself, which in terms of reason, must always present a completely insoluble problem. But because we are always cheating and trying to solve human problems by some short cut – generally by an act of violence – we need to be reminded that such problems are not given us to solve, but to live through and to live out, until the problem itself is shattered and falls away. C. G. Jung has said that, in most cases, a neurosis cannot be cured; it can only be transcended. And the same applies to every problem, of which the Koan is a representation in miniature. The mind, struggling to find a solution, rushes from one extreme to the other; it takes counsel from a confusion of voices. . . . But the only real solution is to admit that there is none, within the terms of the situation from which the problem arose, and to live through the consequences of that "impasse." Life presents a dilemma to which every final answer is the wrong one. Very well, say the teachers of Zen; then on with the dilemma.[3]

Jung would surely not be displeased with that appropriation of his understanding of the treatment of neurosis to the world of the koan. It is a fair exchange. It makes the devilishly paradoxical nature of the koan more accessible to those who have some sense of the nearly complete contradictions and necessarily incomplete solutions of the neurotic psyche, while it offers some sense of the psyche in general and its neurotic accents in particular to those who have some grasp of Zen Buddhism.

Those who have made the most significant use of Jung's work in religion, it seems to me, are those who have been most responsive to the elements of paradox and antinomy in his thought. Such people are not put off by the lack of easy prescription and cure. They recognize

[3]See Gai Eaton, *The Richest Vein: Eastern Tradition and Modern Thought* (London: Faber, 1949), pp. 85, 43–44, 86, 67, 113. This book and several others that deal with Eastern religion are treated in this chapter rather than the next because the questions they raise seem to me to be of importance for an understanding of Jung's approach to religion generally rather than for his specific use of Eastern materials.

that religion is not itself a scientific discipline, however much it may be able on occasion to use the procedures, findings, and insights of one science or another. An example is the handbook of pastoral care prepared by a German physician, Theodor Bovet, for both ministers and laymen, *Lebendige Seelsorge*, translated for its sense rather than its literal meaning in English as *That They May Live*. Jung is a major exhibit in Bovet's chapter on the nature of the human. He draws a characterology from the four function types—thought, feeling, intuition, and sensation—and defines the spiritual "aspect" of the human person on the basis of the archetypes of the collective unconscious. The economy of these pages on the psychic and spiritual aspects of the person is exemplary. It is not only the terseness and clarity that are so impressive, but the insistent avoidance of reductionist simplification, a rare achievement where the function types are used. These are not the final words for any pastor or layman looking for guidance in the world of character and spirit, but they are unusually serviceable summaries, even for those who know the material well. They make persuasive Bovet's employment of Jungian structures as a scaffolding for theological understanding.

Understand, Bovet tells us, this is not an attempt to present a psychology of primitive religion; it is a linking of every kind of religion with the archetypes of the collective unconscious, "for with these religious figures the pastor has to deal at every turn." The point is that "God never shows himself to men unveiled; the *deus revelatus* is at the same time always a *deus velatus*." As one cannot look at the sun except through a smoked glass, which breaks the vision into facets, so one must first approach God through the facets which are the archetypes. Thus the origin of the "gods." "But the more mature Man becomes, the more directly does God reveal himself to him; in the terms of our analogy the facets are ground flat, and the picture becomes clearer." A strong caution here is the reminder "that Jung himself was never tired of stressing that none of his statements referred to the transcendent or to God as such, but only to the images which men make of him, or which, to speak more precisely, emerge from their collective Unconscious."[4]

So much of Jung is an elaborate thinking aloud, a transcript of his inner life, that there are bound to be contradictions, confusions, leaps, bounds, digressions that leave even the sympathetic reader at a loss for understanding and provide the unfriendly critic with rich material for attack. This is especially true in the area of religion. Even so warm a supporter and explicator of Jung as the priest Josef

---

[4]Theodor Bovet, *That They May Live*, trans. J. A. Baker (London: Darton, Longman & Todd, 1964), pp. 24–53. The quotations are from pp. 47–48.

Goldbrunner sees Jung as teaching "his patients how to feel at home in the house of the soul," and then unhappily confining them to it: "the door to transcendence is barred."[5] To say that is to confine Jung to one moment in his long conversation with himself and to forget that Jung sees transcendence as the way out of neurosis. Transcendence in the treatment of psychic dysfunction may not be a reaching toward mystical experience, but neither is it a refusal of the "breakthrough into a higher sphere" that both Goldbrunner and another friendly critic, the philosopher E. W. F. Tomlin, see Jung keeping himself and his patients from achieving. For Tomlin, Jung's reading of the union of conscious and unconscious arrests religion "at the threshold of reflective consciousness . . . it is a mere substitution of sign for symbol. The symbol is exhausted and the sign points nowhere." The only answer to this dead end in Jung, from Tomlin's perspective, is the suggestion that "at the end of his life Jung underwent a genuine religious experience or conversion, and that he liberated himself from the psychologism which, despite his efforts to shake free of it, had persistently dodged his thought."

This sort of criticism is not unreasonable if one is looking in Jung for a creed, an assertion of values *tout court*, which makes everything subservient to the life of the spirit. It is much like blaming novelists and playwrights for all the evil acts of their villains and esteeming them for the virtues of their heroes and heroines, identifying the writers unalterably with their characters. Jung may or may not have undergone a late conversion, may or may not have achieved the certitude that Spinks identifies in his famous "I know" in the Freeman

[5]See Josef Goldbrunner, *Individuation: A Study of the Depth Psychology of Carl Gustav Jung*, trans. Stanley Godman (New York: Pantheon, 1956), p. 1. Goldbrunner's fine, brief work came a few years after the classical exposition of Jungian ideas from a Catholic point of view by the Dominican priest Victor White, *God and the Unconscious* (Chicago: Regnery, 1953). Jung's foreword to Father White's book stresses what is an unmistakable fact for both psychologist and priest: "No art, science or institution which is concerned with the human being will be able to avoid the effect of the development which the psychologists and the physicists have let loose, even if they oppose it with the most stubborn prejudices" (p. xxv). In White's words, "as soul (Psyche – the subject of psychology) is subject to the action of the living organism (*Bios* – the subject of biology) so the living organism (*Bios*) in its turn is subject to the action of nature (Physis – the subject of physics and chemistry)" (p. 120). It is a point to which White returns eloquently in *Soul and Psyche: An Enquiry into the Relationship of Psychotherapy and Religion* (New York: Harper, 1960), with particular conviction and clarity in the chapter on "Health and Holiness," where he outlines a "view of health as a harmony of *Physis* or nature" with ancient roots and a modern understanding contributed by depth psychology. The last words of a book greatly influenced by Jung are worth quoting: "For depth-psychology has already gone far, as we have seen, to offer us a better understanding and appreciation of our very 'doxies,' and of their healing relevance to the inmost needs of our soul – or psyche" (p. 216).

interview. But Jung wrote as a depth psychologist, with some pretension at least to scientific objectivity. I see him less as a scientist than as a gifted humanist, but one with a positivist bias. He sought to present verifiable evidence for his speculations and conclusions, even those which were simply way stations in the course of his journey through himself. These were the things he met in the journey, met in himself, in his patients, and in his restless rooting through the records of the past, in alchemical documents, in the religious and philosophical classics of East and West, in every visual and verbal tracing of the primordium that he could find, ancient or modern.

It does not follow, as Tomlin suggests, that for Jung archetypes are "confined to the unconscious" or that he fails to understand that archetypes "belong to the spiritual as well as to the psychic world," and concomitantly, that "the latter are the shadows of the former." Tomlin, in effect, calls for a theological or philosophical conclusion from Jung, one that Jung did not see himself as equipped to make or as appropriate to the form in which he recorded his experiences, those of his patients, and what he found in the documents and artifacts of the past that echoed or anticipated those experiences. He thought he saw an unmistakable archetypal pattern in the history of humankind, a drama of the collective unconscious emerging in countless ways to be transcribed by the consciousness which emerged with and from it. Thus far he was willing to go, and that is far indeed. It makes for an arresting thesis that does have theological and philosophical significance. It does not go as far as Tomlin would have him go, to see and to say that "All action, in the true sense, involves final causality," which would posit in Jung's psychic cosmology a kind of Aristotelian First Mover, first cousin to the Judeo-Christian God. But this does not support the conclusion that "Jung's values, then, are wrongly or inadequately located."[6]

The breadth of Jung's interests and accomplishments is such that it is easy to look for more, and thus to conclude that there is less in his work than there is. His is not a psychologism, although the center of his work is the psyche. Neither is it a theologism, although his transcriptions of the history and inner life of the collective unconscious are replete with the values that critics like Tomlin feel that Jung has not sufficiently articulated or embraced. The point is that the values are there, not because Jung or anyone else wants to put them there but because, as those who read human history and the life of the psyche in archetypal terms would insist, they are instinct in that life and history. Jung does have a system of values, but it is not one that he often

[6]E. W. F. Tomlin, *Psyche, Culture and the New Science* (London: Routledge, 1985), pp. 163-164.

courts or pleads for openly. His axiology, his approach to value judgments, comes before rather than after he makes his observations. It is the basis upon which he chooses material for observation rather than a means for making judgments once the observations have been made. The judgments themselves are as much ours as his to make, and they are more often implicit than explicit. If final causality – a First Mover or any other metaphysical structure – can be found in the world Jung confronts, narrates, analyzes, and records, so be it.

It can be argued that at one crucial stage in the development of his approach to the materials of depth psychology, Jung did in fact err on the side of the all-embracing value judgment. In the chapter of *Psychological Types* on modern philosophers' typologies, Jung examines William James's terms at length, with particular attention to James's distinction between the rationalist, the man of feeling James calls tender-minded, and the empiricist, the skeptical temperament James calls tough-minded. Jung's bias was clearly toward his own distinction between introvert and extrovert. It can be argued, as Jacques Barzun does, that "Jung honestly misunderstood James's terms. He did not even see that they do not amount to a through-and-through division of mankind, but only indicate tendencies." The irony here is that Jung's usage of his own typology, after fierce metaphysical beginnings, departed from such "through-and-through" categories, whatever his devoted followers might make of them. A further irony is that what Barzun as a historian finds uncomfortable in Jung's autobiography, his "lumping of dreams, legends, and hearsay with recorded fact as if they were equal in evidential strength," is in fact a significant indication that Jung had moved to a position not unlike James's, which Barzun approvingly quotes and summarizes: " 'We should not treat our classifications with too much respect'; the reason being that individuals are not standard units." Amen.[7]

Jung is, of course, as often criticized for egregiously spiritualizing the materials of the psyche as for neglecting the religious implications of his data. Peter Gay's sarcastic description of the response of the insufficiently equipped Germans of the 1920s trying "to distinguish among Freud, Adler, and Jung" is typical. These sadly ignorant, although educated, people "often preferred Jung, with his supposed spirituality, to Freud, with his rejection of religion. . . ."[8]

Sarcasm, reductions, and ardent espousals will not work. In the religious arena, Jung is not a direct combatant; it is those who use him

---

[7]Jacques Barzun, *A Stroll with William James* (New York: Harper and Row, 1983), p. 235.

[8]Peter Gay, *Weimar Culture: The Outsider as Insider* (New York: Harper and Row, 1968), pp. 36-37.

for religious or semireligious or antireligious positions who are the combatants. The Jesuit Robert M. Doran, in the first of three provocative pieces on "Jungian Psychology and Christian Spirituality," surveys the controversial terrain.

> John A. Sanford and Morton Kelsey are two well-known authors who have drawn on Jung to promote and understand Christian self-discovery. On the other hand, James Hillman has maintained that Jung's guidelines to "soul-making" are of a completely different order from the well-known paths to spiritual transformation in Christ and from the insights of the other major religious traditions of the world. Martin Buber entered into direct conflict with Jung, claiming that the psychology of individuation and Yahwistic faith are diametrically opposed orientations of the human spirit. Jung himself, as we shall see, gives some indications of his own that the process of individuation will lead the *cognescentes* to the position of being able to dispense with all forms of traditional religious involvement; but he also attempted to offer his psychology as an aid to the pastoral care of souls.

Father Doran's survey is fair enough. There are clergymen who have found Jung inspiring, or at least a major support, as they have joined analytical work to their religious vocation; Sanford and Kelsey are strong examples. There are those, like Hillman, who have begun to remap the Jungian territory more or less from within, trained as Jungians but with differences that begin to assume the resonances of a new metaphysic. Buber's disagreements with Jung say more about his own faith than about Jung's psychology, but they should not be simply shrugged aside. Father Doran's variations on Jungian themes, like Buber's assertions, lead to serious theological speculation, more sympathetic to and guided by Jung than Buber's but still directed primarily to a religious claim.

Doran's thinking about Jung and religion concludes that the "ground of the individuation process . . . must be the gift of God's love, and the eye of that love which is faith." Using Jung's central symbol of wholeness, the mandala, Doran insists that "the goal of the process is not properly symbolized in the utterly closed mandala with no opening onto the absolutely transcendent." But this once again, it seems to me, asks more of Jung than Jung would ask of himself. For Jung, the life of the symbol was self-enclosed and its meaning, in a sense, self-proclaiming. It is certainly not wrong to associate Jung's reticence to open the mandala onto the "absolutely transcendent" with events in his personal life, with his relationship with his clergyman-father, with what he reveals about his religious attitudes in *Memories, Dreams, Reflections*. Doran seems to be on more secure ground in recognizing that while Jung does not reduce spirituality to psychology, he is of value to spirituality and spiritual theology in "the negative way" of "helping us to recognize inordinate projections and disoriented affections" rather than by "orienting us positively to the God of the Christian faith and to Christ."[9]

Almost all who are caught by Jung, whether to end up a votary, a defector, a revisionist, or less strongly in or out of the Jungian world, seem drawn to find the exact terms of their affection or disaffection set forth in Jung. Their very act of finding, somewhere in his work, the failure or success, the line of argument or misapplied metaphor or reluctance to come straight through to their conclusion, supports the reading of Jung as transcriber of the collective unconscious, as historian of the archetypes. However incomplete his achievement, it is large enough to provide, for a remarkable range of people and attitudes, a series of charts and commentaries that make human interiority accessible and magnetic in its accessibility. Jung's charts and commentaries offer inspection and guidance of a collective unconscious that resembles nothing so much as the "Mind" that the seventeenth-century poet Andrew Marvell described in "The Garden":

> The Mind, that ocean where each kind
> Does streight its own resemblance find. . . .

The compelling power of the oceanic unconscious is constantly revealed in the responses of those either sympathetic or antipathetic to Jung's treatment of it. Reductionist simplification is the great temptation. Frithjof Schuon, a notably sane comparative religionist, says fairly enough that, according to Jung "the figurative emergence of certain contents of the 'collective unconscious' is accompanied empirically, as its psychic complement, by a noumenal sensation of eternity and infinitude." He then concludes, alarmingly, that such thinking "is

---

[9]Robert M. Doran, "Jungian Psychology and Christian Spirituality, I, II, III," in *Carl Jung and Christian Spirituality*, ed. Robert L. Moore (New York: Paulist Press, 1988), pp. 67, 107, 99. Father Doran is also the author of *Subject and Psyche: Ricoeur, Jung, and the Search for Foundations* (Washington: University Press of America, 1979), which rests heavily on the "analysis of human intentionality" in the work of the Jesuit theologian Bernard Lonergan. It is not in any way an attempt to show "Jung's relevance to theology or . . . the theological pertinence of Jungian analysis." It does offer some provocative comments on Jung and Hegel, on the "therapeutic dialectic of the psyche," on individuation and the Self, on what Jung called the "*a priori* factor" in the structure of the psyche, and an extensive examination of psyche and intentionality, in which Doran says he finds Jung's "notion of individuation . . . extraordinarily accurate and fruitful," but is left uneasy with Jung's handling of the problem of evil (See especially pp. 27, 126, 167–170, 174–182, 191, 210–252). There is more of the same sort of examination of Jung in the context of Lonergan's ideas in Doran's *Jungian Psychology and Lonergan's Foundations: A Methodological Proposal* (University Press of America, 1980).

the way to ruin insidiously all transcendence and all intellection for, according to this theory, it is the collective unconscious, or subconscious, which is at the origin of 'individuated' consciousness, human intelligence having two components, namely the reflexions of the subconscious on the one hand and the experience of the eternal world on the other. . . ." Schuon then argues from this awkwardly paraphrased presentation of Jung that "since experience is not in itself intelligence, on this showing intelligence will have the sub-conscious [sic] for its substance, so that one has to try and define the sub-conscious on the basis of its own ramifications. This is the classical contradiction of all subjectivist and relativist philosophy."[10] Schuon is clear that there are what he calls "secondary modalities of a psychic, and even of a corporeal order" in anything that is truly spiritual. He does not see that Jung is not proposing a "psychology of the spiritual" and might find in such narrow terms all the contradiction, all the falsification and negating of the spirit, that Schuon does. Nor does he understand that Jung's association of the noumenal – using the Kantian vocabulary with which Jung was comfortable – with the psyche was not made to locate sensations of eternity and infinitude in fixed psychic boundaries. Far from ruining "insidiously all transcendence and all intellection," Jung's understanding of the symbolic character of the revelations of the collective unconscious invites us to extended contemplation of the world of the unconscious, with a deepened and more assured intellection and an encouragement to find in it adumbrations and presentiments of the transcendent.

In his examination of the present-day "crisis in religious studies and theology," Joseph Cahill uses the Jung of *The Undivided Self* to deal with the problem Schuon offers. "Rational argument," says Jung, "can be conducted with some prospect of success only so long as the emotionality of a given situation does not exceed a critical degree." Not exactly a breakthrough, the statement is significant here "not only," as Cahill points out, "because of the transparent and instantaneous historicity, hermeneutic, and understanding that the emotions imperiously dictate, but also because the emotions themselves" have a history of definite and historical causes.[11]

A vivid sense of what it means to find the definite and historical cause of an emotion, or, more particularly, of the constitution of a given psyche at a pivotal point in its development, can be gathered from the lengthy comparison British philosopher of religion Bernard

---

[10] Frithjof Schuon, *In the Tracks of Buddhism* (London: Allen and Unwin, 1968), pp. 71–72.

[11] P. Joseph Cahill, *Mended Speech: The Crisis of Religious Studies and Theology* (New York: Crossroad, 1982), pp. 24–25.

Towers makes of Jung and Teilhard de Chardin. Both saw themselves as "empirical scientists, devoted to purely objective observation, in so far as any observation is ever purely objective – except it be trivial." Both have been accused of betraying science and have sometimes been "contemptuously dismissed as unreliable, outside the scientific pale." Both have been in trouble with scientists, especially those for whom science is a religious faith, for introducing "the concept of purpose into their accounts of the phenomena they have studied."

The purpose Jung sees at work in the psyche, says Towers, is "like that perceived by Teilhard, to be operating at the core of the cosmos, intrinsic in character and essentially immanent. . . ." That is to say, purpose is unmistakably present; it can be observed in each person's development – in "the ontogenetic evolution of the psyche." With the emphasis Jung places on the collective unconscious, "some consideration of phylogeny" – the history of the human race – is also necessary. For Jung, this individual evolution and its corollary collective associations always imply and sometimes make explicit a goal for all of us, "the realization one might say, of what he has called the Self." It is a stunning prospect, this potentiality in all of us for the birth and development of the Self, parallel to Teilhard's vision of a birth and development, "the realization again, in mankind as a whole, of what he has called the Omega." For one, the emphasis is upon community; for the other, upon the individual. "For Jung . . . the whole aim of psychic existence is precisely to extricate oneself from the power of the collective," not, Towers hastens to assure us, from a "collective *super*conscious, but . . . from that collective *un*conscious in which our psychic life is rooted." Everything in Jung's language moves "towards the uniqueness of the personality, towards the elevation, salvation almost of the individual. Islands of consciousness, representing the psyches of individuals, are visualised as rising out of the sea of the unconscious." We are moved in the Jungian universe to discover more and more about our individual selves. "In the process the island will grow in area, and will rise higher out of the water. It will achieve greater form and significance . . . the person concerned will certainly develop more control over his own emotions and reactions, and more understanding of those of others."

It is a heady mixture of prescription, proscription, and vision. For some Jungians, it approaches the majestic proportions of a faith message. It promises an understanding of self and other which can make even the utmost isolation in the island-psyches bearable. For Towers, it is the inexorable companion piece to Teilhard's paradisal speculation. He asks us to contemplate "Teilhard's concept of *enroulement* in phylogenetic development" – the great opening up of human resources, moral, intellectual, spiritual – "with Jung's *individuation* as the proper end of ontogeny." Thus do we find purpose in our lives, what Kant preferred to call purposiveness, a harmony of aim if not of accomplishment.

Individuation must come before "the final state of mankind, that of the collective superconscious," as Towers reads the two men. When individuation becomes "the norm for many generations of men and women," the Jungian (along with "other schools of depth-psychology") will have served its purpose, "having demonstrated the hazards to which the developing psyche is exposed and having taught us how to avoid disaster. . . ."[12]

Somewhere in our assessment of Jung's usefulness to religious thought and his considerable influence upon some religious thinkers, we must join the visionary reading of a Teilhardian like Towers to a more narrow understanding of Jung as a historian of the collective unconscious and its archetypal divisions, or, in a language some distance from Jung's terms, as a chronicler of human emotions and a tracer of their roots. Here the words of a scholar far from sympathetic to Jung, the biblical archaeologist W. F. Albright, are valuable. In the concluding section of a long essay, "Toward a Theistic Humanism," Albright speaks of the vital role of religion in Western literatures. "It is in ancient religious literatures"—his immediate references are to the literatures of Egypt and Mesopotamia, of Greece and the Jews of the Hellenistic and Roman periods—"that we find the profoundest statements of human aspirations and the most poignant expressions of human needs. These literatures are of more interest to the student of psychology than anything else handed down from antiquity; in this respect we may agree with C. G. Jung, even though we may differ radically with him on interpretation."[13]

What must be stressed here is not the precise interpretation of the religious literatures of the ancients, in small part or in large. That surely will always be open in some measure to vigorous contention, in spite of the ardors of Albright and others to make biblical archaeology into a science. What is important is the content to which Albright points—statements of aspiration and expressions of need—and his recognition of its appropriateness for psychological study. Here is the history of the emotions and its significance, and here is the uncertainty principle in the midst of religious certitude. It is what the psychiatrist Mortimer Ostow and the philosopher Ben-Ami Scharfstein emphasize in their intelligent and sympathetic treatment of Jung in their attempt

[12]Bernard Towers, *Concerning Teilhard and Other Writings on Science and Religion* (London: Collins, 1969), pp. 56–58, 62–63, 125, 64.

[13]See William Foxwell Albright, *History, Archaeology and Christian Humanism* (New York: McGraw-Hill, 1964), pp. 50–51.

at a psychology of religion, *The Need to Believe*. Reviewing the arguments in Jung's *Modern Man in Search of a Soul*, they remind us that, for Jung, "since we have no idea of the manner in which the psychic may arise from the physical, it is just as well to assume that the psyche arises from a spiritual principle our understanding cannot penetrate." We cannot conceptualize our inner life, but the "unconscious has an instinctive wisdom of its own, and unless we come to terms with it and draw on the reserves of its wisdom and strength, we can never be whole, happy, or truly productive."

Ostow and Scharfstein recognize the importance for Jung of "the continuity of the psychic processes," which may not be broken even by death. This does not result in a structured metaphysic, the product either of revelation or a reasoned natural theology. It does lead Jung to conclude, in effect, as these writers say, that "to be a conscious unbeliever – a state of mind also motivated by irrational forces – is to invite psychic disaster." Finally, in this discussion, they make the crucial distinction: "To Freud, the religious person manifests the continued illusions of the child, to Jung the cumulated wisdom of mankind."[14]

We are talking in terms of metaphors here, "root metaphors" as Gibson Winter calls them, interpretations of "founding symbols," those of "family and kin, work and play, neighborhood and governance, moral order and religious world – these are the shared meanings that hold a people together over time, preserving its identity and sustaining its hope in the future." As symbols, they "tend to coherence," but "lived interpretations in these various spheres of dwelling tend to lose coherence, at least this is the case in a modern complex society." Jung's tracing of "the connections between personal symbolizations and the archetypes which they disclose" amounts, for Winter, to "a testimony to the creative powers of the person which existentialism asserted" and as well to "the symbolic mediation of the human world."

For Winter, as Jung's work lays one foundation for a hermeneutic of symbols, so his Swiss contemporary, the painter Paul Klee, puts down another. In Klee's "hermeneutical circle," a way is opened to "the genesis of form," in which "the form is free, nothing natural, yet thoroughly nature." It is a "synthesis" in which the painter "discloses the human as image of God, liberating the symbol of creation that has been reduced to the analytic and geometric." It is a persistent but not deterministic reading of history as something alive and enlarging to the human, whom it constantly attends to and instructs. The creative

---

[14]See Mortimer Ostow and Ben-Ami Scharfstein, *The Need to Believe: The Psychology of Religion* (New York: International Universities Press, 1954), pp. 150–152.

is a transforming process, moving, as Klee puts it in his *Notebooks*, "from prototype to archetype," unwilling simply to imitate tradition, as Winter paraphrases Klee, "yet learning from tradition to penetrate more deeply into the way things are."[15]

This is the world of the Jungian "self," where symptoms of mental stress and realms of fantasy are often signs of breakdown and disaster but are also invitations to transcendence, where the structures of the self, however dimly perceived and poorly understood, do indeed provide access to the symbolic world. Here is where the insights of religion and the procedures of depth psychology come together, not to reduce the life of the spirit to a psychological enactment, but to allow us to see how much can be gathered of the nature of the self from close attention to a psychology of symbol and metaphor. For the social scientist M. Brewster Smith, "Jung gave a sensitive meta-metaphorical formulation to metaphorical persons that a science of persons must eventually come to terms with." This is not to read Jung as a scientist but "in the interpretive humanistic vein." Doing so, Smith finds himself "reformulating one set of his 'archetypes of the collective unconscious' as proposals for relatively pan-human metaphors of recurrent experiences and relationships in the human condition, including metaphors provided by the seasonal cycle of the natural and agricultural world and by the life cycle inherent in the lives of individual persons and families." Smith recognizes in the archetypes the themes that recur in world folklore and the constituents of personhood. The abiding question remains, is the archetype of the Self, that "metaphoric ideal that supposedly provides a template for 'individuation,'" a universal truth? With it, Smith asks also, "What indeed are the cultural limits to his formulations?"[16]

In the same book in which Smith addresses his questions under the heading of "The Metaphorical Basis of Selfhood," an Indian anthropologist, Agehananda Bharati, suggests that Jung has somehow transcended cultural boundaries. Bharati insists that Hindu values — "*all* Hindu values" — have been infused with the "seemingly recondite" metaphysical concepts of Eastern thought, just as notions of the self in the West emerged from "the empirical epistemologies" of ancient Greece and the Judeo-Christian and Islamic "doctrines of the soul as an ontological, self conscious entity." In ecumenical meetings, Hindus work to absorb into their system the empirical ideas of the West. The

[15]Gibson Winter, *Liberating Creation: Foundations of Religious Social Ethics* (New York: Crossroad, 1981), pp. 26, 63, 70, 108–109.

[16]M. Brewster Smith, "The Metaphysical Basis of Selfhood," in *Culture and Self: Asian and Western Perspectives*, ed. A. J. Marsella, George DeVos, F. L. K. Hsu (New York: Tavistock, 1985), pp. 80–81.

compliment is not returned. Western thinkers do not attempt to assimilate Hindu concepts of the self in the vocabulary of empiricism, except for those who "underwrite a Jungian paradigm or who have converted to Asian modes of thinking. Jung himself can well be seen as a prime convert to Eastern modes of thinking about the self."[17]

It is too much, I think, to claim Jung as a convert to Eastern ways of thinking, but surely not wrong to see here again, in the domain of the self, the openness of his sensibility. He is eager to discover the footprints of the archetypes, wherever they may be found. That inevitably requires some assimilation of the kind Bharati describes, without necessarily ending in conversion. A moving example is reported in a survey of "Zen in the Contemporary World," offered by Jikai Fujiyoshi at the 1985 Kyoto Zen Symposium. Fujiyoshi reports on Professor Hisamatsu Shinichi's meetings with Western thinkers in the late 1950s, such men as Paul Tillich, Martin Heidegger, Rudolf Bultmann, Gabriel Marcel, and Jung. The talk with Jung, in Switzerland, left many questions unanswered. Fujiyoshi's impression was that Jung wanted to know more about the Buddhist concept of the *alaya-vijñana*, the all-containing or ever-enduring Mind. Some compare this to the Platonic realm of ideas. While the concept "somewhat resembles Jung's idea of the collective unconscious," what Fujiyoshi stresses is Jung's "particularly keen interest in the point when the alaya-vijñana turns into perfect, all-reflecting Buddha-wisdom."[18]

Jung was a collector. Because, as the historian Alan Bullock puts it in his lectures on *The Humanist Tradition in the West*, the "psychological function of religion, whatever its content, seemed as important to Jung as its social function had to Emile Durkheim, and he devoted much of his time to collecting diverse and arcane material, ranging from the Gnostics and the alchemists to the Chinese classic of meditation, *The Secret of the Golden Flower*, all of which are concerned with different versions of the same spiritual quest, the search for something greater than oneself, which he saw as the dominant feature and need of human beings once they had reached maturity."

The spiritual quest in Jung is the result, to use Lord Bullock's words, of "recognizing and accepting some higher authority or purpose than the Ego." Only "by finding his or her own myth, could men and women overcome the conflicts in themselves and achieve what he called 'individuation,' realizing their own selfhood." What gives the search substance and takes it beyond the "Who is the real me?" lucu-

---

[17]Agehananda Bharati, "The Self in Hindu Thought and Action," in *Culture and Self*, pp. 189–190.
[18]Jikai Fujiyoshi, "Zen in the Contemporary World," in *Zen Buddhism Today* (Kyoto: Institute for Zen Studies, 1985), pp. 11–12.

brations of late-night bull sessions and dying cocktail parties is its attachment to an undying reality, the objective psyche, the collective unconscious. It is Being itself one looks to find and to bring into some heightened degree of consciousness, Being that seeks us as insistently as those who, following injunctions like Jung's or some inner compulsion or other pressing line of inquiry, seek it. It is that omnipresent reality to which the words of the Delphic oracle, carved in Latin over the door of Jung's house, give testimony: *Vocatus atque non vocatus, deus aderit,* "Invoked or not invoked, the god will be present." That, as Bullock emphasizes, is the source of Jung's view "that the inner world and its images, which Freudians saw as derived from infantile experience and as a hindrance to accepting reality, could actually be the source on which men and women draw for the means of adapting to the external world, whether this takes the form of religion, culture, art or science."[19]

The move in Jung toward a heightening of consciousness is not a stage in a systematic assault on Being. Jung is not a system-thinker but a problem-thinker, to follow the "elaborate contrast" between the two kinds of thinking of the philosopher Nicolai Hartmann with which Walter Kaufmann associates Jung in his study of Nietzsche. Nietzsche, like Plato and others identifiable by their use of "dialectical" thinking, uses premises but not to deduce "a system from a set of unquestioned assumptions." What stands out in such thinking is its "search for hidden presuppositions rather than a quest for solutions." The departure point for such inquiry "is not a set of premises but a problem situation – and Plato, of course, excelled at giving a concrete and dramatic setting to this." In the development of the inquiry, premises may be evinced, but the end-product is "less a solution of the initial problem than a realization of its limitations: typically, the problem is not solved but 'outgrown.' "

It is here that Kaufmann points to Jung, who "has developed a strikingly similar notion on the basis of his psychoanalytical practice. He claims that the normal and healthy way of dealing with psychical problems is 'overgrowing' them (*überwachsen*) and thus achieving an elevation of the level of consciousness (*Niveauerhöhung des Bewusstseins*)." It is the approach Plato "suggests when he contrasts mathematical deduction, which takes for granted its assumptions, with philosophic 'dialectic' which questions these assumptions, and thus moves backward, 'reductively,' to a first principle." In Hegel, we see this

---

[19]See Alan Bullock, *The Humanist Tradition in the West* (New York: W. W. Norton, 1985), p. 148. The passage on Jung should be read in context; it establishes the large sources of the Delphic utterance in Jung's life as well its significance for the outside world.

approach in the *Phenomenology of Mind*: "no premises are explicit to start with; no problems are solved, but each problem is outgrown in turn while—to use C. G. Jung's phrase—the level of consciousness rises."[20]

    The theologian David L. Edwards, in his survey of the challenges to religion in "the *secular* century," as he defines our time, speaks of "the undiscriminating gusto" of Jung's "religious enthusiasm" and wonders if that does not "raise the question whether, by the standards of the rational tradition of the West, he was interested in religious truth." Edwards's reading of Jung so emphasizes the irrational and the symbolic that he sees those who follow such thinking as being led into a kind of suicidal secularism in the name of religion. He recognizes the strength of Jung's argument that Western Europe had become "excessively masculine in the toughness of its industrial, commercial and political life" and its corollary conclusion that "masculinity was not enough even for a man, since every man had a feminine side to him." But he does not share Jung's defense of the Catholic dogma of the bodily assumption of the Virgin Mary into heaven "on the ground that it was a symbol for the glory of womanhood."[21]

    Jung is elusive here in his reach across religious phenomena, now too accommodating, now not accommodating enough; threatening, in his openness to religious past and present, to attenuate the substance of religion and leave it exposed in the resulting thinness to secularist reductions, or, at the opposite extreme, reducing it to an altogether irrational mystagogy. But Jung, in his role as observer and collator of myths and archetypes, went on looking, gathering, making such order as his equipment and experience permitted, and not being unduly disturbed by the contradictions and confusions of the archetypal world of religion. He would be bound to agree with Alex Comfort's description of the "authentic archetypes," even though Comfort dissociates himself from the idea of the collective unconscious and sees the content of what he calls our "inner fauna" as "manifestly programmed, like other content-features of our sense of identity, by social pattern." Comfort understands, with Jung, that these authentic archetypes are "contentless, or capable of receiving almost any content—they are preferred ways of objectifying structure."

    Comfort says with a fine bluntness of phrase that these archetypes "have clearly a hardnosed psychobiology of their own. To regard them as arbitrary products of human fancy is to neglect a source of

---

[20]Walter Kaufmann, *Nietzsche: Philosopher, Psychologist, Antichrist* (New York: Vintage, 1968), pp. 82–83.

[21]David L. Edwards, *Religion and Change* (New York: Harper and Row, 1969), p. 128.

information, and is as naive as to take them seriously as comments on real cosmology." It is precisely their "archetypal character" which makes them right, "however much their objectification offends our rationalism," and we know that they are right because they are "products of our self-experience." They fit us the way "a waffle fits a waffle-iron." There may be awkwardnesses as a result, dubious beliefs, support for questionable and irrational cosmologies, but, Comfort pronounces, "it is notable that sophisticated observers and users of the fauna of numina, as opposed to naive believers, have in all traditions recognized their true significance." None of which is to be offered as support for the "uncritical use of archetypes," a resurgence of which we are now seeing, "fueled to a large extent by a long tradition of religious literalism and monotheism — the archetypes fill needs and have uses; but one of those uses is certainly not to supersede rational cosmology."

Comfort's pronouncements about Jung's use of archetypes come in the course of his presentation of an arresting thesis about religion. As he sees religion, it springs from an arousing human experience, the "homuncular vision" of an objective "I" caught up in dialogue with a "not-I," which Comfort calls "That." From the relationship of I and That, he constructs what he calls a biology of religion. The usefulness of psychoanalysis in the biology of religion is the attention it brings to the leading place in human experience, from the time of infancy, of the self, of "standards," and of "real or imaginary parental figures . . . father, mother and child being the figures of a family trinity which pattern all these manifestations." In Freud's system, religion is "an aberration, natural to man but displaceable by insight"; in Jung's, it is "a paradigm of a number of important mental structures common to humans (which Jung himself was inclined to mysticize rather than to regard as evolved adaptations, but no matter) and to this extent [is] functional." Jung gets higher marks than Freud because his "field of cultural investigation was wider" and he is, as a result, "closer to recognizing religion as an adaptive behavior in spite of his disabling unwillingness to look for the biology of the experiences he catalogs."[22]

Comfort has been picking at Jungian ideas and texts for a long time, discovering contributions he can support alongside procedures that leave him uneasy. His most considered examination of Jung before *I and That* was in *Reality and Empathy: Physics, Mind, and Science in the 21st Century*. There, this physician, biochemist, poet, variously psychiatrist and specialist in geriatrics, author of books on sexual "joy" in almost all possible combinations, declares Jung a man

---

[22]Alex Comfort, *I and That: Notes on the Biology of Religion* (New York: Crown, 1979), pp. 104–106, 86.

of "exceptional perceptivity with the style of a charlatan," in effect, a sixteenth-century thinker, capable of "voluminous scholarship without rigour," producer of " 'charismatic' theatricals," but also one who offers a fullness of documentation. He finds Jung incapable of linear thinking and yet "an able, sympathetic, and intuitive psychotherapist." In spite of "the illicit introduction of religiosa by smuggling rather than by statement, Jungian analytical psychology is a valuable resource in dealing with troubled people whose troubles are likely to be improved by introspective education. While the use of Freudian models is clinically rather limited, we use Jung even when we are shocked by him." He is, Comfort acknowledges, "attuned to the way the non-discursive human mind works and to the uncanniness characteristic of processes orthogonal to normal logical reality." Although he is not able to find evidence in Jung's "voluminous writings" that the psychologist had discovered recursion, the operating of something upon itself, he does seem to understand the appositeness of the ourobouros as an emblem for Jungian observation and judgment – and thus, of the place of recursion (a highly honorific term for Comfort) in Jung: "By having its tail in its mouth the archetypal alchemical snake is not prevented from also having the last word. The pursuit of world models has not ceased to be a journey in the Jungian sense – it is like the magical journeys of legend, which, for reasons not fully clear to us, it behoves us to take."[23] All of which is another way around to religious experience translated into language that is simultaneously literary, psychological, and philosophical.

Jung's understanding of religion and his methods of arriving at that understanding are defended by Christopher Bryant, an English Cowley Father, in several volumes but most particularly in *Jung and*

---

[23]See Alex Comfort, *Reality and Empathy: Physics, Mind, and Science in the 21st Century* (Albany, N. Y.: State University of New York Press, 1984), pp. 233–235, 238–239. The Jesuit philosopher J. F. Donceel deals effectively with Comfort's kind of speculation in his *Philosophical Psychology* (New York: Sheed and Ward, 1955). Donceel sees what Comfort calls recursion in Jung's view of the psyche as "a self-regulating system, that is a system which tends unconsciously to counteract any one-sided development which circumstances may have forced upon the individual." It is a system of checks and balances in which a scientist's excessive brain development will be counteracted by eruptions from the unconscious and faced with an "infantile archaic emotionality." Neurosis is not only a breakdown but "an opportunity for mental growth and development if it is well treated." Facts are what we get this way, observations, not simply Jung's bias. And thus it is with Jung's use of theology. He does not reduce "supernatural realities to mere psychological symbols," and in Jung's later work, Donceel thinks, he makes it "increasingly clear . . . that his intention is not to evaluate the reality of supernatural facts (that is the work of the theologian), but only to show as a psychologist that, deep in his Unconscious, every human being shows a yearning towards them and a readiness to accept them" (pp. 314–316).

the Christian Way. The book is brief and full of the author's admiration for the "set of valuable tools for exploring the mystery which confronts us in every man and woman" that he found in Jung's ideas but does not make extravagant claims for analytical psychology as a guide to religious experience. If anything, Father Bryant's bias is in the direction of enlarging and enriching Jungian insights by application to Christian worship and prayer. The "self-awareness" that the study of Jung intensified for him is clearly an extension of an established regimen in the spiritual life, and it is in that self-centered area that his book finds its identity and its conviction. It is, by the same token, most persuasive where it rests directly upon the writer's own experience and his attempts to understand and deepen that experience. Thus it is that the empiricism he defends in Jung becomes most convincing when it moves into what Jung would have called Father Bryant's own myth, when he looks to find in himself the truth of what he is, to paraphrase the title of his epilogue.

Does one need Jung to push on beyond the humdrum and the commonplace in the life of the spirit? Must one have his kind of psychological insight to overcome the aridity, the boredom, the frustration, the sense of neither being seen nor heard nor in any other way received, that so often afflict those who seek to sound the depths of mental prayer? The questions are rhetorical. The life of the spirit does not require the intervention of Jung. But as Father Bryant's earnest pleading makes clear, Jung provides some significant aids to deepening and refreshing the religious imagination, and some substantial strengthenings of one's inner resolve come with the trust and faith in human interiority that close acquaintance with Jung so often breeds. In the best of Bryant's book, the concluding chapter, "Individuation and the Spiritual Life," he has useful things to say about meditation and "a contemplative waiting on God," on the acceptance of one's "psychic reality" — neurosis, guilt, and all — as a significant means to the glowing ends of a transformation of the person, whether one sees this as a psychologically charged event, a spiritual one, or some mysterious compounding of the elements of both.[24]

It is not hard to see why David Edwards, notwithstanding his own reservations about Jung's religious thinking, should have reviewed Bryant's book so warmly. "Jung without tears," he called it. The tears are altogether present in Wallace Clift's *Jung and Christianity*, the work of a religious scholar who is also a pastoral counselor and a well trained Jungian. Although he carries the cards of Jungian identity and speaks authoritatively and plausibly for Jungian language,

---

[24]See Christopher Bryant, *Jung and the Christian Way* (London: Darton, Longman and Todd, 1983), *passim.*

process, vision, and hope, he is not hesitant to express reservations about what he calls Jung's "theologizing." His treatment of "Jung's challenge to Christianity with his teaching on 'the dark side of God' " is itself challenging, and his suggestion that "a closer look at the symbols and implications of the Christian story reveals more serious and saving answers than many Jungians realize" is followed by a splendid chapter on "Evil and the Resurrection Symbol," which should be read closely by both Jungians and Christians, whether they are one and the same or not.

The crucial issue is Jung's imputation of a Manichaean evenness of power to good and evil in his affirmation of a *complexio oppositorum* in the Godhead. Jung's hopes rest on people choosing good rather than evil in the supernatural pairing of the two at the center of being that his "theology" posits. But, as Professor Clift reminds us, Jung's "symbolic expression for that force which seeks to overcome evil is largely missing." Jung depends, in effect, on the "assumption" that "still lingers on, even in our post-Christian world," that we can choose the good, that it is real and that it "works." But that assumption on Jung's part, lacking an adequate symbolic expression for evil and, some of us might say, an adequate confrontation with the forces of evil, does not reflect a faith or trust in a redemptive supernature. "Along with the alchemists, Jung tended to make the individual the Redeemer, rather than God's Christ. It is to that extent, 'work' (something earned) rather than a 'free gift.' It is no longer the 'good news' that so excited the many slaves in the Christian community."

For all the inadequacy in Jung's dealing with the mystery of evil, as Christians at any rate might judge it, Jung did know "the experience of *grace* (a gift with power) in his therapeutic work," as Professor Clift freely admits. The difficulty is that he did not make use of that experience in his reflections on the nature of evil and its apparent reigning strength in the *complexio oppositorum* of the Godhead. The limitation here is perhaps Jung's failure to examine more fully, if only as symbols, the Cross and the Resurrection as they move from their grounding in personal experience into "the Christian answer to the problem of evil." Clift sees the need for larger psychological examination of these symbols "in relation to the vast human experience of evil" and sees far more hope in such an investigation than in "further pursuit of Jung's theory of evil in the Godhead—certainly for Christians, and quite possibly for others as well."

Hope is the final note of Clift's book. It is grounded in that movement toward consciousness which is, one can say, positively creedal in Jung's reading of our age and its potentialities. "Life entails choice. There is both dark and light. The 'Fall' into consciousness (as Jung interpreted the old story of a Garden of Eden) was a tremendous leap forward in the story of life. Is there another leap ahead?" While Professor Clift is too much both a Christian and a Jungian to answer with a rhetoric of optimism, he does suggest in his final pages the solid basis for hope that emerges from a Christian reading of Jung.

In the "cosmic process" in which we all take part, we move all but inexorably toward increasing awareness of "the whole." Jung looked to make this clear in his "myth of God's need of us," drawing upon the Western mystics as well as his own experience. Clift quotes a nicely turned sentence from a late letter of Jung's, "We are still looking back to the pentecostal events in a dazed way instead of looking forward to the goal the Spirit is leading us to." This is the enlarging significance of the encounter with the self in Jung's terms. Far from being a retreat into psychologism, as some might say, it is an opportunity for those of religious conviction to draw from "the framework of symbolic meaning" the conclusion that meeting the self brings an increased awareness, another way of describing an enlarged and enriched consciousness, and a response with heightened energies to the movements of the Spirit. "It was Jung's (almost despairing) hope," Professor Clift concludes, "that the Christian community would take up this challenge."[25]

Jung's insistence on maintaining the sharp distinction between symbol and sign is essential for any understanding of what he makes of human interiority and thus of religion. A sign points. What it points to is knowable. If it were not, the pointing would be pointless or at best a vague gesture. A symbol speaks in its own terms, has its own life, reveals, but in its revelation does not exhaust meaning or truth. The theologian Gerald H. Slusser, in his book *From Jung to Jesus*, in a searching examination of the "creation and dynamics" of the symbol, makes much of the distinction between sign and symbol. He quotes Jung's compact statement: "A symbol always presupposes that the chosen expression is the best possible description or formulation of a relatively unknown fact, which is nonetheless known to exist or is postulated as existing." So it is that Jung followed symbols where they led, and Slusser, following the trail of "Myth and Consciousness in the New Testament," finds a dynamism in Jungian thought which brings him to the proclamation of a Jesus-Hero story, to the Father-Spirit as "the procreative aspect of the Divine Center, the God archetype of the psyche," and to a definition of the ego's destiny which can be said to be consonant with Jungian readings of the psyche and Christian doctrine. The destiny of the ego "is to be a center of consciousness on behalf of the Divine Center."

---

[25]See Wallace B. Clift, *Jung and Christianity: The Challenge of Reconciliation* (New York: Crossroad, 1982), pp. 143-145, 149, 156-157.

Slusser's appropriation of Jungian terms and procedure is not simply facile; it is skillful and fitting. It is based on his own firm conviction that "the world is created by consciousness through myth." This world, however, although very much "our creation," can only reflect upon, and yet not really know about, the "Ultimate Reality," the universe that lies beyond it. We must understand, as do the mystics, the impossibility of speaking about this, "the final state of consciousness," or even thinking about it. "The Tao that can be spoken is not the Tao. Christ-consciousness is direct, immediate, and nonverbal. In principle, no description, names, forms, words, or thoughts can be applied to this realm of consciousness. It is quite literally boundless."

We may come in time to the ineffable, where words cease and understanding, although reached within the boundaries of time and space, transcends them. But we do move through this time, this space, using language, gestures, and images; even abandoning words and pictures and body movements as attempts at communication and comprehension, we manage somehow to stay at the edge of consciousness of this defining apparatus of the human. That is what Slusser's use of Jung to explicate and comment upon Ignatius Loyola seems to indicate. The founder of the Jesuits says, in a kind of catechetical simplicity, "The human was created to praise, do reverence to, and serve God our Lord, and thereby to save the soul." Jung's summation and explanation move through language at once religious and psychological: "Man's consciousness was created to the end that it may (1) recognize (*laudet*) its descent from a higher unity (*Deum*); (2) pay due and careful regard to this source (*reverentiam exhibeat*); (3) execute its commands intelligently and responsibly (*serviat*); and (4) thereby afford the psyche as a whole the optimum degree of life and development (*salvet animam suam*)."

The great strength of Slusser's book is what is made in it of the hero myth and its association with the figure of Jesus. It is in these terms that one should understand that last quotation from Jung and see how its divisions correspond, now exactly, now inexactly, to central moments in a given human life. The application to the hero figure, the Son of God, as he "pioneers the way of the ego back to its proper connection with God," is clear enough. Whether it is appropriate to associate this with what Slusser summarizes as "Jung's conviction that there was no way for psychology to differentiate between the God archetype and God" is, perhaps, more questionable. If it can be said, as Slusser does at the beginning of this discussion, "The Hero as archetypal figure represents the destiny of the psyche, of the soul," then one need not introduce the personification of psychology standing firm, refusing to make the distinction between the archetype of the Supreme Being and the Being itself. Furthermore, as critics of Jung have not been slow to point out, Jung himself is far from consistent in preserving that stubborn conviction. Psychology, no matter how much one personifies it and gives it the powers of choice or refusal to choose, remains an abstraction. Jung was a person and notably inconsistent in serving or observing his abstract pieties, and especially those enunciated in tones of absolute finality. Thus it is that he is mocked as unscientific by some, prone to follow the inclinations of belief, of wavering and uncertain consciousness, of a commanding but notoriously fickle spirit.

It is precisely because of such inconsistency on Jung's part, of his wavering but unmistakably commanding spirit, of what may be an unscientific procedure but one that remains scrupulous in reporting what wells up from the archetypal world of the collective unconscious, that it is not useful to psychologize here about the sameness of the God archetype and the Godhead. Slusser's demonstration through the course of his book of the applicability to Jesus and the Gospels of hero symbolism and mythology, of the hero's birth story, initiation, battle with inner and outer tempters, with shadow and dragon, and sacred marriage, is argument enough. It all fits together—*alter Christus* of medieval fable and legend and Jesus himself, archetypal Hero and the ego as center of consciousness for the Divine Center. It is neither necessary nor useful to assert the inseparability of archetype and deity to make the Christian point, or indeed to draw away from or toward any specific creed in terms of analytical psychology.

Slusser's own summation, early in his book, arguing to support the transformative power each of us possesses to make our own images out of our own symbol systems and our own myths, is terse and persuasive. "Jung was laying a foundation for theology, an empirical foundation as firm as that of biology. Jung was doing the work of the theologian, but he did not push on to draw the obvious conclusions. Nonetheless, he prepared the way for a new approach to theology by creating a metasymbol system founded on the natural symbols of the human psyche. This sort of system is *the* requirement for any hermeneutic of human experience."[26] Thus it is that Jung makes his extraordinary contribution to what can be called either a science or an art of the most obscure reaches of the life of the psyche. That those mysterious depths should also be the province of religion neither psychologizes religion nor sanctifies psychology. All that we can conclude is that psyche and soul live their lives bound together and that any method of interpretation of the dual experience must make sense of the

---

[26]See Gerald H. Slusser, *From Jung to Jesus: Myth and Consciousness in the New Testament* (Atlanta: John Knox, 1986), pp. 136-137, 15, 147, 100, 34. The Jung quotation is from *Aion, CW* 9ii, p. 165, par. 253.

movement across the boundaries of the two great divisions of human interiority.

In a book closely related to Slusser's, by a scholar with similar training and interests, Wayne Rollins's *Jung and the Bible*, the obligations of psychotherapist and Scripture scholar are shown to be very much alike. "Understanding the special perspective of a patient places a great demand on the therapist, Jung tells us. It is not enough to be an observer; one must be a 'fellow participant' in a process encompassing both." And so it is with the biblical scholar as well. Objectivity is not enough. "One must cultivate an approach of *empathy* to understand what the authors have to tell us. 'Understanding' means standing 'with' and 'under' those whose word we wish to comprehend." It means, according to Rollins, following Jung, a kind of identification with the writers of Scripture, with their questions, their dreams, their issues. When we can accomplish that sort of coming together with the transmitters of the word, we see ourselves as "part of a story being told by the divine."

We move, in Rollins's adaptation of Jung to biblical interpretation, from listening thoughtfully and empathetically to listening broadly, going beyond the limits of the rational, entering the precincts of prayer with the aid of "active imagination." To understand this last, Rollins offers Jung's elucidating words: we "dream the myth onwards and give it a modern dress." With active imagination, we stir the subliminal and raise deeply buried contents up to the light. We make contact of a much more than peripheral kind with the collective unconscious and with our own personal conscious. It is, one might say, an audacious linking together of the primordial and the prosaic, of an almost impossibly distant past and an all-too-present contemporaneity. It has for Rollins what perhaps should be called unction, anointing the scriptural interpreter, "who, from Jung's perspective, must dare to dream the Word onward and so hopefully advance its work of bringing souls into God-consciousness." That is the way Rollins understands Jung's own definition of the "function of Scripture . . . to tutor the soul in God-consciousness and to bring its readers into the presence of the holy."

The presence of the holy, Rollins suggests, is where Jung's life and work have directed him. He quotes once again the Delphic inscription over Jung's doorway, which as he reminds us is also on Jung's bookplate and gravestone, here translated as "Summoned or not summoned God will be present," and cites a late letter from Jung in explanation of the words: "I have put the inscription there to remind my patients and myself: *timor dei initium sapientiae* (the fear of God is the beginning of wisdom). Here another not less important road begins, not the approach to Christianity, but to God himself and this seems to be the ultimate question." This in turn leads Rollins to a brief epilogue in which he sums up the value of applying the insights of depth psychology to the analysis of scriptural texts, with particular emphasis on the usefulness of Jung's work in the development of what he calls psychological criticism of Scripture.

There are seven functions as Rollins defines the discipline of psychological criticism, all in a sense in support and extension of the purpose succinctly inflected in the brief quotation from Jung's autobiography which Rollins uses as the epigraph to these last pages: "Man's task . . . is to create more and more consciousness." The first of the seven is a sharp underscoring of "the reality of the psyche and of the unconscious as a function, not only of the biblical authors, but of biblical readers as well." The methods for achieving this understanding may not yet be clear, but the territory is. Psychic process must be added to the traditional areas of examination of the biblical fraternity. The second of the seven points is a reinforcement of the first, a recognition that Scripture may express latent meanings that must be found, as a New Testament scholar puts it, at "levels below the historical, actual, verbal statement or narrative." This in itself is hardly news, but using psychological criticism to rouse scholar's and reader's consciousness is to add a fresh note. So would be the third recommendation, to become aware of the archetypal character of biblical motifs and symbols, which is so much a part of "widely scattered mythic traditions."

In the fourth function of psychological criticism, a hermeneutic is sought that reclaims and reevaluates "the ancient Hebrew midrashic, patristic, and medieval Christian insight that the intention of the biblical text is not only to convey a literal meaning but to evoke a moral, spiritual, and transformative meaning in the life of the reader." Again, something less than a revolutionary suggestion, but one that reaches well beyond the obvious if, in addition to making use of the long established apparatus and procedures of biblical exegesis, the reading and interpreting of texts is conducted with some respect for the insights of depth psychology. This would bring biblical scholars—the fifth of the seven points—to some significant awareness of the "psychological dynamics operative within biblical stories," not, Rollins stresses, "to import Freudian or Jungian structures haphazardly into the text," as some have done. No psychologizing allegory, no submission of a text to "the template of a model foreign" to it, but simply a larger opening to meanings, an extending of our understanding of symbol and metaphor in Scripture.

It is toward that widening of opportunity in interpretation that the last two functions ask us to look. We must make more of "certain psychological and spiritual realities fundamental to biblical consciousness, e.g., the experience of sin and grace, of forgiveness and spiritual

enthousiasmos, the phenomena of conversion and prophetic inspiration." If we understand that biblical presentation of the experience of
salvation "means changes . . . in how we think, in how we feel, in how
we act," then it can be concluded that "psychological intuitions and,
perhaps, even explicitly psychological models and terminology can
give us insight into what these changes are in ourselves and others."
And so it is that the final injunction is to note the effect of Scripture on
its readers, "individually and corporately, religiously and theologically,
socially and institutionally."[27] This is very much a late twentieth-
century emphasis. It sits well beside all the "reader response" analysis
and criticism with which the examination of literary texts has been
endowed in recent years, especially if accompanied with caveats
against the accommodation of Scripture to psychoanalytical theory
and the teasing of biblical tale and character into the orthodoxies and
pieties of psychotherapy.

   A useful caution here is the one with which the philosopher David
L. Norton opens his book, *Personal Destinies: A Philosophy of Ethical
Individualism*. Using a passage from *Memories, Dreams, Reflections*
in which Jung speaks of the *daimon* in him which at times made him
"ruthless" in his hastening on "to catch up with [his] vision," Norton
asks us to pay attention to the two things which Jung's words signify.
One is a "deep human dilemma in the present," and the other, which
really explains the nature of that dilemma, is our great discomfort
"that that about which we instinctively believe we can be most
certain – ourselves – is in fact our sorest bewilderment." We worry that
if we turn toward our inward lives, what we will discover will be "at
most only meaningless murmurings, that a resort to the inner self will
be a dizzying tumble into a bottomless pit." And so instead we turn
from the inner to the outer, "secretly treasure the atmosphere of world
crises, for the mental ambulance-chasing it affords." We do not
respond to experiences with our own resources, with our own innermost thoughts and feelings. We depersonalize the experience even of a
film or a painting, borrowing the words from somebody's published
review, or we "desperately scrape the walls of memory for some fragment of a course" taken in college.

   The issue is the issue of inner voices not heeded, of self-awareness
not merely left undeveloped, but deliberately turned away from. "In
short," Norton sums up, "what Jung seems most confident of, his oracle within, is just that about which most of us altogether lack assurance. We do not know what Jung was talking about, and we rather
wish to believe that neither does he."

----

[27]See Wayne G. Rollins, *Jung and the Bible* (Atlanta: John Knox, 1983), pp. 106,
103, 111, 127-129.

Some readers may translate *inner voice* into *conscience*. That will not do for Norton. In our culture, "the idea of conscience carries either a Judeo-Christian or a predominantly Freudian meaning." He is not talking of anything that has the authority of the superego, of parents or community or the deity, of anything that might serve "to deflect inquiry away from the individual. . . ." This is not "a voice of prohibition" that Norton so earnestly seeks to make commendable with his invocation of Jung: "what Jung speaks of and what current life most urgently requires is a voice of constructive determination."

Norton's book, which uses Jung as its departure point, is a handsome elaboration of a classical philosophical doctrine, that of eudaimonism. The conventional understanding of the doctrine is of a system of ethics that bases moral responsibility on the possibility of our actions producing happiness. But happiness will not do in Norton's ethics of *eudaimonia*, nor will the usual reduction of its doctrines to the gratification of desire: "Eudaimonia is both a feeling and a condition. As a feeling it distinguishes right from wrong desire. Moreover it attends right desire, not only upon its gratification, but from its first appearance."

Norton's use of Jung moves far into the inner reality of his thought. He recognizes the significance of Jung's choice of *daimon* for the inner voice, "its meaning constituting the nucleus of the Hellenic sensibility to which critical exposition was ultimately given by Socrates, Plato, and Aristotle." It is our identifying mark to ourselves, both as our inner voice and as the root and stem of the ethics based upon it. When eudaimonia is "fully present to right living at every stage of development," what it signals to an individual is that a given activity "is in harmony with the daimon that is his true self."

Norton makes felicitous use of Jung on the stages of life: "We cannot live the afternoon of life according to the programme of life's morning; for what was great in the morning will be little at evening, and what in the morning was true will at evening have become a lie." This is to give voice, according to Norton, to all those many attempts in history to develop "a workable doctrine of stages," something for which ethical philosophy has had too little time or interest, looking instead "to subsume the whole of life under a single set of normative principles."

Norton is caught by Jung's "supposition that nothing exists without good reason." If this may be understood as questionable metaphysics, nonetheless "it remains invaluable methodologically." Jung is not daunted by those who see no special meaning in old age except age itself, which is to say "mere deterioration." To those who bring "fresh eyes" to their contemplation of old age, "it displays evidence of a rebirth under novel criteria."

We neglect childhood in our turning away from inner voices, that period, as Jung defines it, when one is "a problem strictly for others." Heedless of the daimon within, we may then fail to recognize the beginning of adolescence, that "moment at which the individual, having been exclusively a problem for others, becomes a problem to himself." These failures to pay attention are not minor lapses from grace, for the "intrinsic requirements of each stage relinquish their hold only when they are fulfilled, hence neglect or the attempt to bypass a stage produces developmental arrest." Arrested at adolescence, an individual can only pretend to maturity; "his adolescent behavior is ever likely to outcrop disastrously." In the same way, old age is burdened with left-over materials from earlier stages and the corollary refusal of both those who live it and the culture of which they are a part to "affirm its exclusive virtues and responsibilities." Again, Jung offers a succinct summary. "So for many people all too much unlived life remains over – sometimes potentialities which they could never have lived with the best of wills, so that they approach the threshold of old age with unsatisfied demands which inevitably turn their glances backward."

The force of Norton's use of Jung is to concentrate our attention on our inner voice. The *daimon* at the center of the philosopher's *eudaimonism* is that inner awareness which moved the psychologist so far into the precincts of religion and made his appropriations from the collective unconscious to the life of the spirit so captivating to so many, even, I think it can be said, to many of those who set themselves so strongly against what they called his psychologizing of religion or his mystagogy. He was, as he confesses in the epigraph that opens Norton's book, ruthless in his determination to follow where his vision led because he was "in the grip of the daimon." But that apparently pitiless drive to gather all he could from his personal unconscious and from the objective psyche was in fact not very far from Norton's "ethical individualism," for which a more honorific term would be *eudaimonism.*

In the end, Norton says, in what he calls the "Unscholarly Epilogue" of his book, "the only philosophy that profits a person is his own; and in the beginning he does well to adhere to his own intuition until (if such be the case) it proves untenable, and to furnish its replacement himself." All of this comes from the "bud for which this study is meant to provide branch and trunk," namely, "the reader's intimation of his own unique, irreplaceable, potential worth."[28] That surely is what Jung's forays into religion amount to as well. There is, then, compas-

---

[28]See David L. Norton: *Personal Destinies: A Philosophy of Ethical Individualism* (Princeton, N. J.: Princeton University Press, 1976), pp. 4–5, 160–161, 164–165, 180, 170–171.

sion in his ruthlessness, a reaching out to his readers as to his patients, not in an effort to convert them to a body of doctrines, but rather to expose them to the workings of the collective unconscious into human consciousness. The exposing becomes, often enough, a disclosure not only of a massive, sometimes self-contradictory or at least paradoxical content, but of a method as well. The method, too, presents its own paradoxes and self-contradictions, with so little chagrin or apology on Jung's part that devotees of scientific method, looking for something like the elegant proofs of mathematics or the higher physics, find themselves put off by what seem to them to be wild flights into a rambling metaphysics. They may be that. They also contain their share of revelation, although without any claim to be theologically firm in source or structure or conviction. They are the gatherings with commentary of a historian of the collective unconscious who has found in his observations endless promptings of the Spirit, or what he prefers to call the Self, with a strongly underlined capital 'S'. That is, finally, neither a theology nor a psychologism but really a philosophy of religion, one that, as many have seen, is to be taken seriously.

Jung plays a curious role in the theology of Paul Tillich, not unlike that of Martin Heidegger. He is, like the philosopher, a shadowy presence in Tillich's work, not often referred to by name but unmistakably there for those who know the thinking of the two men. He is a definer of terms, a maker of distinctions, a contributor of psychological and metapsychological ideas. Even when he has doubts about a term carried over from Jung, Tillich can appropriate its meaning easily enough. In a brisk discussion in the first volume of his *Systematic Theology*, for example, in support of the thesis that "Christianity must reject the idealistic separation of an innocent nature from guilty man," he makes good use of the "questionable term 'collective unconscious,' " for it "points to the reality" of the "social dimension of unconscious strivings." What he says then is pure Jung, handsomely paraphrased:

> The centered self is dependent not only on the influences of its social surroundings which are consciously given and received but also on those which are effective in a society without being apprehended and formulated. All this shows that the independence within an individual decision is only half the truth.

Once again in the same volume he uses the "questionable term," though this time without any expressed reservations. "The theologian," he says, "cannot give a judgment concerning the life or death of the symbols he interprets. This judgment occurs in the consciousness of the living church and has deep roots in the collective unconscious." Questionable or unquestionable, the concept is clear to Tillich and useful, as is the whole realm of the unconscious, as, for example, it operates to fix the effect "of a sacrament on the conscious . . . without the consent of the will."

Everywhere, anywhere, there may be a deepening of our understanding of the workings of the Spirit. Contrary to what many Christians believe, "the fact that secular psychology of the unconscious has rediscovered the reality of the demonic in everyone must be interpreted as an impact of the Spiritual Presence." For "secular psychology" here, read "Jung"; the "reality of the demonic" is his contribution, his emphasis. As with his demurrer about the "collective unconscious," Tillich had some difficulty in giving full credit to Jung, at least while Jung was still alive. In his *Theology of Culture*, he salutes Jung as one who "knows so much about the depths of the human soul and about religious symbols," but still must add that in many "representatives of contemporary depth psychology (including Jung) we miss the feeling for the irrational element that we have in Freud and in much of the existentialist literature." That is, to say the least, an odd reservation about Jung, whose "feeling for the irrational" is surely the most developed of any of the founding figures of depth psychology. It is, I suspect, part of Tillich's clearly expressed uneasiness about the use of any part of psychology "to interfere with knowledge of revelation." A "revealed psychology" is no more acceptable than "a revealed historiography or revealed physics." And thus he does not see it as "the task of theology to protect the truth of revelation by attacking Freudian doctrines of libido, repression, and sublimation on religious grounds or by defending a Jungian doctrine of man in the name of revelatory knowledge." The fact is, however, that Jung's doctrine of man and even to some extent his doctrine of God are "defended" in Tillich, not as Jung's but as his own, where they fit into his theology, which is constantly alert to the psychological textures of being.

Where Tillich draws most close to Jung is in his treatment of symbols, in his *Systematic Theology*, in his *Theology of Culture*, in his *Dynamics of Faith*, in *The Courage to Be*. "The knowledge of revelation, directly or indirectly, is knowledge of God, and therefore it is analogous or symbolic," he says in a kind of addendum to Thomas Aquinas on the *analogia entis*. The analogy of being, "like 'religious symbol,' points to the necessity of using material taken from finite reality in order to give content to the cognitive function in revelation." Working with analogy and symbol is not a way of "discovering truth about God"; it is simply the shape that revelation takes and in which we must find it. Thus the dismissive phrase "only a symbol" is to be discouraged, "because nonanalogous or nonsymbolic knowledge of God has *less* truth than analogous or symbolic knowledge."

That confidence in the power of the symbol, so much like Jung and perhaps tutored by him, is the sustaining power of Tillich's Terry lectures, *The Courage to Be*. It is the "power of being" as Tillich defines it in a volume dedicated to and filled with that power. "Since the relation of man to the ground of his being must be expressed in symbols taken from the structure of being," he reasons, "the polarity of participation and individualization determines the special character of this relation as it determines the special character of the courage to be." The distinctions that follow bring the personal and the collective into a mysterious balance that touches upon the mystical. Self-surrender and self-affirmation go together. The courage to be grows out of the encounter of the human and the divine and something like a course of Jungian individuation, in which the strength to claim the shadow is translated into "the courage to accept acceptance in spite of the consciousness of guilt." Succinctly, Tillich sums up: "In the communion of healing, for example the psychoanalytic situation, the patient participates in the healing power of the helper by whom he is accepted although he feels himself unacceptable." This is the world of the objective psyche. There is no disguising of reality, no smudging of guilts – or feelings of guilt – in an efflorescence of good intentions. The guilt must be claimed, taken into one's self-affirmation. The healer "accepts the patient into his communion without condemning anything and without covering up anything."

These pages of *The Courage to Be* are as strong as they are, as realistic and consoling as they are, because they are so firmly rooted in psychological understanding. They offer no false comfort. They recognize, with a certainty and force that everywhere echoes Jung, that the traditional symbols of Christianity have lost their meaning in the modern world. But the life of the symbol is still unmistakable and its power still with us. Tillich here, in the last paragraphs of his book, is as stubborn and as satisfying as Jung in his Terry lectures, *Psychology and Religion*, proclaiming the majesty and integrity of the symbol. Yes, says Tillich, even now, in this world, where " 'providence' has become a superstition and 'immortality' something imaginary that which once was the power in these symbols can still be present and create the courage to be in spite of the experience of a chaotic world and a finite existence." Even the reductions of a too simplistic depth psychology, say those of *The Future of an Illusion* or *Totem and Taboo*, need not hinder us. Tillich does not name Freud or these volumes, but it is their nagging negativity he is answering in saying, "When 'divine judgment' is interpreted as a psychological complex and forgiveness as a remnant of the 'father-image,' what once was the power in those symbols can still be present and create the courage to be in spite of the experience of an infinite gap between what we are and what we ought to be."

What Tillich is mooting is something very close to Jung's conception of a psychic totality. This is not a series of nostrums and panaceas, although there is much hope in these barely prescriptive speculations. It is a hope founded upon faith. And it is a "faith which says Yes although there is no special power that conquers guilt." We go as far as an affirmation of being permits, finding in a kind of psyche-centered asceticism the "courage to take the anxiety of meaninglessness" upon ourselves, discovering at the "boundary line" which separates us from non-being the "courage to be . . . rooted in the God who appears when God has disappeared in the anxiety of doubt."

One can dismiss this, as some have, call Tillich "a modern gnostic," summarize his defects by saying that "Tillich has grafted C. G. Jung on Schelling's pantheism . . . and produced a theological system which resembles traditional Christianity only in superficial aspects," as William F. Albright does. Or, in a more responsible summary, one can say as the Jesuit Gustave Weigel does, "The symbolist insists that he does not take the affirmations [of Scripture and dogma] literally; but he equally insists that he takes them seriously. In his position he avoids the unseriousness of absurd literalism and the equally unserious treason of those who will not take the scriptural affirmations as statements of truth." What Weigel offers, less in defense of Tillich than in explanation, is the great resource of analogy or proportionality. It makes sense of Tillich's position and, at least by implication, of all that is in it of the Jungian *complexio oppositorum.* We cannot turn away from the complexity. "With the symbolists we can consider as unserious and rather puerile the assumption that the biblical writers were writing history with the purpose a modern historian pursues in his work. This is fundamentalism, which always runs the risk of becoming ridiculous." But that does not mean we can reject out of hand scriptural historiography; that to Weigel "seems willful and unfaithful to the books before our eyes." We must not "change a record of flux into static Platonic didacticism."

Tillich's tribute to Jung at the New York memorial meeting in the year of Jung's death addresses the issue directly and defines the terms precisely, not only for Jung but for himself and all others who understand the nature of the symbol.

Jung wants to understand the symbols; he cannot accept them in believing subjection; he wants to demythologize them, although he knows that this contradicts their very nature. He is in the same dilemma in which critical theology finds itself: It lives in a world of symbols, which is its concrete foundation, and tries to understand the symbols, with the risk every anti-literalistic criticism runs of losing the power of the symbols. To avoid just this was one of the main concerns of Jung's life work.

Tillich's discussion of Jung in this warm and generous address is in the present tense. The ideas and the man behind them are very much alive. They are at the center of any serious discussion of religious symbols, of the transcendent, of the nature of being. A quick summary of Jung in this central area yields "the basic elements of a meaningful doctrine of symbols":

> ... the distinction of symbol from sign as well as from allegory ... the necessity of using symbols in order to grasp dimensions which cannot be grasped in any other way ... the mediating, opening-up, healing power of symbols . . . their arising from a union of the collective unconscious with the individual consciousness. . . .

There are differences between Catholic and Protestant attitudes here. The Catholic stresses the *analogia entis*, as we saw with Weigel. The Protestant, "existential and dynamic" where it is effective, sees symbols as emerging from "revelatory experience." The symbols die if such experience "can no longer be revived. . . ." There are real threats on both sides. The Catholic understanding of analogy is rationalistic, deals with symbols as "known" things, is "essentially static." The Protestant, as Jung constantly warned, was without life, its symbolic experience inert.

Tillich saw the two attitudes as useful when combined – analogy plus "particular revelation" – and best brought together and given new life and understanding in "Jung's doctrine of archetypes." Jung's understanding of the archetypes as "potentialities" sets them off against symbols, which are "actualizations conditioned by the individual and social situations." We can see in their preformation in the unconscious the odd strengths of archetypes, greatly variable and yet limited in variation by their "definite structure."

Tillich recognizes a metaphysical ground here, in spite of Jung's "anxiety about what he calls metaphysics," a fear he "shares with Freud and other nineteenth-century conquerors of the spirit. . . ." But there is no missing "the ontological dimension" of the archetypes. Jung calls them "primordial," a term as he applies it that "oscillates between early past and eternal past . . . a transtemporal structure, belonging to being universally. . . ." Jung sees the archetypes as revelatory and "to be revelatory one must express what needs revelation, namely, the mystery of being." And so the archetypes "represent" what is "lasting, the symbols the variable element in the development of religion." We cannot separate "the lasting element in the growth and development of religious symbols . . . from the variable element." We are left with the constant tension that comes from the urge to demythologize in order to understand better and the contradictory knowledge that we must lose everything that is in religious symbols in the demythologization process. It is a tension we can live with. It is, as both Jung and Tillich understand, potentially a healing tension. That is the center of these cogitations and what brings the psychologist and the theologian together. Tillich's little homily on potentiality near the end of his spritely essay on "The Relation of Religion and Health" speaks to the point eloquently as, in effect, it stresses what is healing in the work of Jung directly and as he is adapted by Tillich.

The unconscious becomes actually what it potentially is, and for which it strives, by reaching the state of consciousness; and the consciousness includes the potentialities driving within the unconscious as its vital reservoir. Potentiality is not actuality, but neither is it nothing; it is *potentia*, power: the most destructive power, if it conquers the mental unity of consciousness after having been repressed; the most creative power, if it enters and widens the consciousness through union with the integration (or disintegration) of the personality; it decides between disease and health, and between destruction and salvation.[29]

[29]See Paul Tillich, *Systematic Theology, I* (Chicago: University of Chicago Press, 1951), pp. 41-42, 165; *Systematic Theology, III* (Chicago: University of Chicago Press, 1963), p. 122; *Theology of Culture*, ed. Robert Kimball (New York: Oxford University Press, 1959), p. 122; *Systematic Theology, I*, pp. 130-131; *The Courage to Be* (New Haven, Conn.: Yale University Press, 1952), pp. 156, 163-166, 189-190; 196, *The Meaning of Health*, ed. Paul Lee (Richmond: North Atlantic Books, 1981), p. 49. The remarks by Tillich at the memorial meeting for Jung on December 1, 1961, were published in a small volume by the Analytical Psychology Club of New York, where they appear in pages 29 to 32. The quotations from Albright and Weigel appear in *Paul Tillich in Catholic Thought*, ed. T. A. O'Meara and C. D. Weiser (Dubuque, Iowa: Priory Press, 1964), pp. 190-191, 196. An interesting book-length excursus, in effect, on Tillich's little homily on potentiality as it touches on the unconscious is the work of a woman religious, Mary Wolff-Salin, *No Other Light: Points Of Convergence in Psychology and Spirituality* (New York: Crossroad, 1986). Jung and a number of Jungians sit very well here alongside John of the Cross, Teresa of Avila, and others of like authority in the life of the spirit. The informing conviction that animates the book, well supported by example, is that "Psychology does not replace spirituality – any more than spirituality can replace psychology. But if the two speak of a common experience, however much their understandings of it differ, then what each can learn from the other can only be of benefit to both" (p. 120). A similarly welcoming response to Jungian psychology is to be found in the work of the controversial Brazilian Franciscan priest Leonardo Boff, *The Maternal Face of God: The Feminine and its Religious Expressions* (London: Collins, 1989), especially in the chapters devoted to "Mary in the Language of Myth" and "The Marian Dogmas" (pp. 217-252).

CHAPTER 4

EASTERN RELIGION

Jung's explorations of Eastern thought and religion, strong, unquenchable, alternately sober and gleeful, have stirred responses almost as far-ranging and full of feeling as his psychological investigations. The philosopher of religion Ninian Smart, making the point that psychologists and psychoanalysts are not well grounded in religion, cautions that even Jung, clearly well informed in religious areas, ranging "widely in Asian and other traditions, was harvesting a crop of symbolism determined greatly by his own metaphysics."[1] The anthropologist Mary Douglas reminds us of Jung's own caution in approaching Eastern religion. It may be valuable to Christians to free themselves of symbols that have become meaningless to them in their attempt to reach an enduring interiority, but, in Douglas's words, "what a falling off he sees in the embracing of alien religious forms." She quotes Jung on the Protestant, stripped bare of meaningless symbolic forms, going East: "If he should now go and cover his nakedness with the gorgeous dress of the Orient, like the theosophists, he would be untrue to his own history. A man does not work his way down to beggarhood and then pose as an Indian king on the stage."[2]

Jung followed his own injunctions. Whatever the appeal of the East for him, it never led him to deny his roots nor to become a starry-eyed comparative religionist, for all the correspondences to Western

---

[1]Ninian Smart, *The Phenomenon of Religion* (New York: Herder and Herder, 1973), p. 140. Smart is a philosopher who has taught in India as well as his native England and the United States and speaks persuasively in his books for "an international forum of philosophical argument" (*The Yogi and the Devotee*, 1968, p. 169), and it is his conviction, so much like Jung's, that "It is an inevitable consequence of the logic both of theology and of descriptive religious studies that our gaze should not be confined to one tradition. Voyages can, happily, be both stimulating and refreshing" (*Secular Education and the Logic of Religion*, 1969, p. 89). Gaze yes, conviction not necessarily; no more than Jung is Smart a boundary-smashing syncretist.

[2]See Mary Douglas, *Natural Symbols: Explorations in Cosmology* (New York: Pantheon, 1970), pp. 164–165.

symbols and symbol systems he found in the East and the deepening of understanding of religious experience it brought him. Besides, his own experience here was sharply divided. Richard Payne puts it well:

> What does need to be clarified about the man and his work is that his understanding of Western (European) life came largely from his patients, while his understanding of Eastern (Asiatic) life came primarily, if not exclusively, from the lives of Eastern saints and from their scriptures. To the best of my knowledge, he never interviewed a Jewish or Christian saint, nor did he ever treat any wide number of psychological disorders of Asiatics.

Having made clear in this way what he calls "the experiential limitations of Carl Jung," Payne feels free to use him as his guide in his own explorations "into the psychology of personal and collective unconscious," with materials drawn from both East and West. Jung is helpful in Payne's discussion of the mandala, and its function to "bring persons to beatitude," and of the Tantric Buddhist's goal, "to unite the two contrary principles, male with female, wisdom with compassion." In dealing with this last, Jung's anima/animus vocabulary is clarifying as is his understanding of the "individuated or whole person" as the "contrasexual" one "in whom the male and female polarities circulate and complement each other rather than fight and extinguish each other." Finally, in his instructive recourse to Jungian insight and procedure, Payne takes up the subject of sublimation of sexual energies, "intelligent instruction" in which is so sadly lacking in seminaries and monasteries: "Jung called this process 'canalization of the libido,' with symbols being used to effect the transformation, a process which was known three thousand years ago in India in Patañjali's time as pratyahara."[3]

There is little question that those familiar with both Eastern and Western religion and Jung's work find his definitions and speculations clarifying, to use a word which, for Buddhists, possesses unction. The vocabularies and insights go together, Eastern and Western, religious and psychological, as an American Benedictine, Pascaline Coff, shows

---

[3]Richard Payne, "Circles of Love: In Search of a Spirituality of Sexuality and Marriage," in *Sexual Archetypes East and West*, ed. Bina Gupta (New York: Paragon House, 1987), pp. 51, 56, 61, 66. The resources provided by religion and the metaphysical are probed by a fine-spirited intelligence in the opening chapter of Elémire Zolla's *Archetypes: The Persistence of Unifying Patterns* (New York: Harcourt Brace Jovanovich, 1982), as for example, "Metaphysical experience transcends opposites and whoever pursues it will place health and morbidity in a metaphysical perspective, adopting or rejecting either—or rather, the conditions that go under their name—according to expediency, in view of the goal. Jung stressed that Buddhists favor hallucination and make elaborate works of art of them, with the aim of breaking the crust of aimless social sanity. Even dissociation and schizophrenia proper, he noted, are used in meditation" (pp. 24–25).

in two paragraphs which conclude felicitously with a quotation from Ann Ulanov's *The Feminine in Jungian Psychology and in Christian Theology.*

> To achieve quality behavior, integration and wholeness, we must understand the influence of the *anima* and *animus*, and through whatever praxis, *sadhana, tapas,* or asceticism that is necessary, allow the "marriage within" to happen. In religious terms, this is called redemption.
>
> As the *yin* and *yang* are the gates of change, so the *anima* and *animus* are considered to be "gateways" to the self, and only through the fullest relationship and expression of the feminine and masculine polarity can this "inner wedding" take place: "These archetypal aspects of the psyche . . . can never be known directly in themselves, but only as we encounter them in images, patterns of behavior and emotional response."[4]

It is the possibility of the "inner wedding" that leads so many to interpret Eastern religion with Jungian instruments. So it is that a Jungian, Mokusen Miyuki, interprets the *Ten Oxherding Pictures* of Zen Buddhist iconography. These medieval pictures present, step by step, the whitening of a wild black ox as an allegory of the way one achieves *satori* or enlightenment in Zen. In Buddhist terms, one moves from the darkness to the reality of the self, to one's Buddha-nature. In Jungian terms, Miyuki suggests that "the *Oxherding Pictures* can be understood as depicting the attempt of the oxherd, or the ego, to creatively relate itself to the inexhaustible treasure of the 'mind-ox,' or the unconscious." In a few pages, he makes a persuasive case for a psychological reading of the pictures as a tracing of the individuation process, ending with the ego "freed from 'egocentric' ways of functioning, which are conditioned by the darkness of ignorance and passion," and enabled as a result to "function in an 'ex-centric' manner in perfect unison with, and in the service of, the Self." One reaches a state that can be called, says Miyuki, "Self-centric," the equivalent of what the Zen master Lin-chi Hui-chao calls "the total action of the total being" or, says the Jungian, "the Self realizing itself in totality."

In Miyuki's collaboration with J. Marvin Spiegelman, *Buddhism and Jungian Psychology,* the *Oxherding Pictures* are reproduced in two versions. A commentary and an attempt at "A Fictional Portrayal" of the pictures are offered by Spiegelman, and in a half-dozen short pieces Buddhism is looked at under the rubrics of Jungian psychology by Miyuki. It is a bracing experience and a good one, I think, if we can accept what we read with something like a meditative attitude.

[4]Pascaline Coff, "Eve, Where Are You?" in *Sexual Archetypes, East and West,* p. 19.

It moves, all of it, the Buddhist and the Jungian materials, to a conclusion in the dreams of a Japanese Buddhist scholar in analysis with Miyuki. Here we have a phenomenology of the Buddhist-Jungian connection in brief. It is something less than a scientific demonstration, but it has its own unmistakable logic, in which form and content move inexorably together. The scholar himself was looking to achieve what he called "a simultaneous nod between Eastern subjectivity and Western objectivity," a synthesis of Eastern and Western spiritual traditions. We are presented, in Jungian language, with one who has achieved his goal in "repeated experiences of the archetype of the Self." The dreams show the 52-year-old scholar reaching the "Great *Nirvana*," that point "into which his whole being, body and mind, ultimately converges." He has accomplished his "ego-oriented academic goal of synthesizing Eastern subjectivity and Western objectivity" in an individuation process which, dream by dream, dramatizes what Jung calls "becoming one's own Self" or "the Self realizing itself."[5]

It is often suggested that those who undergo Jungian analysis tend to dream Jungian dreams. It is at least as clear that if one prepares oneself in one or another scheme of meditation, and especially one so carefully laid out in iconographic and terminological ways as the Buddhist schemes, one is bound to end up with experiences that look like textbook illustrations of the method employed. Conditioned reflexes? A kind of psyche-washing? Perhaps so, but only if one has bracketed out, in a kind of caricature of the phenomenological *epoché*, all sense of who one is, of one's culture and tradition and ordinary language and image-systems. One must "remain rooted in one's own culture," as Radmila Moacanin says just before a brief recital of the dangers involved in the coming together of "Western and Eastern Paths to the Heart," the subtitle of her book *Jung's Psychology and Tantric Buddhism.* This, as she notes, is something in which Jung and Tantric Buddhists would concur – "And most of all, every Buddhist would be in perfect agreement with Jung's statement that 'We must get at the Eastern values from within and not from without, seeking them in ourselves. . .'."

We are in a realm here of explosive potentialities, where the release of "unconscious contents without proper safeguards and precautions . . . may overwhelm consciousness and cause its collapse, resulting in serious consequences, even psychosis." We must be prepared on the inside for what comes at us from the outside that is directed to our interior depths. Jung and the Tantric masters stress the need to be well grounded in the ordinary procedures of one's life,

[5]See J. Marvin Spiegelman and Mokusen Miyuki, *Buddhism and Jungian Psychology* (Phoenix: Falcon Press, 1985), pp. 30–31, 39, 174–183.

work, family, all the ways one usually fills one's days. And so it is, Moacanin reminds us, that "Tibetan Buddhists urge Westerners not to abandon the values of their own culture." One must be firmly rooted in one's own earth before moving off into practices so far removed from one's culture and traditions, where there is the constant danger of "grasping the literal rather than the intrinsic meaning of symbols and rituals. . . ." Archetypes greet us from their dark as well as their light sides. Moacanin cites Erich Neumann with the example of the Great Mother archetype, "nurturing and creative . . . devouring and destructive." If one is "fragile," and without a "well developed" consciousness, one may find the confounding contraries in such an archetype shattering.

It is a world we are in, both that of Jung and of Tantric Buddhism, in which the identifying textures and images may seem to be those of paradox and opposition. But these are all in aid, says Moacanin, "of portraying the fullness and richness of life and different ways of perceiving it, which conventional language with its limitations is unable to express." The Tantric way is not one "of asceticism but of fully experiencing life in all its joy, spontaneity and creativity." It could be argued here, I think, that this is a form of asceticism, too, in which the abstinences and the exultant practices may be very different from what one normally associates with religious convention, but the spiritual transformation sought and the inner vision obtained are very much the familiar ones. As Moacanin says, simply enough, "the work of redemption, whether in alchemy, in Tantra or Jung, cannot be left to nature; it requires conscious effort." It does not matter where one is, for as the alchemists proclaimed, "the divine secret is everywhere . . . even in the most loathsome filth." Everything that happens to one, as Tantric Buddhists see human experience, good or evil, can be a means of spiritual transformation. And for Jung as well, nothing in the psyche is to be thrown away or looked at askance; all of it, all of what it encounters, is valuable. "In Tantra and in Jung's model the mundane and spiritual dimensions of life are closely connected; in fact they are two sides of the same reality that need to be reconciled."[6] For the modern world this may well be the most stern and demanding ascesis of all.

[6]See Radmila Moacanin, *Jung's Psychology and Tibetan Buddhism: Western and Eastern Paths to the Heart* (London: Wisdom Publications, 1986), pp. 96–98, 104, 66. There is a large and growing bibliography of articles and books relating Jung and Eastern traditions. John Borelli's annotated listing in Harold G. Coward's *Jung and Eastern Thought* (Albany, N. Y.: State University of New York Press, 1985) covers 112 items. The Coward volume, in which Borelli, like Coward a professor of religious studies, J. F. T. Jordens, dean of the faculty of Asian studies at the Australian National University, and the Jungian analyst Joseph

L. Henderson are collaborators, is rich in its exploration of the encounters of Jung with Yoga, Kundalini, and related asceticisms. The conclusion of Jordens's chapter on the Indian concept of *prana* and libido is very much to the point:
"Jung sees the fulfillment of the basic drive for individuation as realizable only by exceptional individuals; the *Kausitaki*, more than other early *Upanishads*, heralds the esotericism of medieval Tantric sadhana; and for both the realization of the supreme goal means the recovery of the original psychic identity of macro and microcosmos, and the reconciliation or transcendence of all opposites. Most of these basic characteristics call up the epithet 'Gnostic,' and in the final instance that epithet may well be one of the most appropriate with which to describe the overall trend of Jung's thought, however repugnant it may have been to him" (p. 184).

CHAPTER 5
MYTH

Jung's understanding of myth is greatly instructed by his study of religions, and especially the religions of the East. In this he both follows and sets patterns which by now have become firmly established in the scholarship of myth. Some of the inflections of Jung in his examination of myth are anthropological, some theological, some psychological. What gives his readings their strong individual flavor is not their psychological bias, which was clearly to be expected, but what some might call their moral tone or, more appropriately I believe, their inclination to the ascetical. Implicit in Jung's treatment of myth, and sometimes quite open, is the strong attraction he seems to feel to the exercises in self-discipline to which the tales, the legends, the fables, the figurative language of myth so often seem to be directed.

I would prefer to call what Jung finds so attractive in the configurations of myth discipline of the self rather than self-discipline. Individuation is the goal and the process, whether named or not, and it draws many in the field to Jung, from scholars like Mircea Eliade to popularizers like Joseph Campbell. It also puts off some serious readers of Jung, philosophers or theologians, who find a yielding to "pagan" values in his delvings in what the poet Philip Larkin called "the myth-kitty." What they miss, perhaps, is Jung's participation in the ascesis of modernity, a set of exercises of mind and spirit that insists upon drawing from all sources, myth high among them, whatever continues to be valuable, hoping as St. Augustine did a millenium and a half ago to preserve the gold and silver from distant times and cultures and to leave the dross behind.

What is so difficult about the ascesis of modernity is its constant opening to what the philosopher Thomas Molnar calls "the pagan temptation." In a "weakened" or "residual" Christian civilization, it is only too easy to surrender to what Molnar summarizes as "the nostalgic cultural diagnoses made by Lévi-Strauss, Gilbert Durand, Eliade, Jung, Paul Tillich, and others. . . ." He himself has "explained the inrush of the Asian creeds and of the occult by the incredible desiccation of our civilization under the aegis of the industrial-technological formula, the culmination of rationalism." But so has Jung, and, as we have seen, Jung is very uneasy about replacing Western symbol systems that have lost their appeal with a refulgent Eastern dress, and is precise about getting at Eastern values "from within . . . seeking them in ourselves."

It is a double temptation we are talking about, first to be drawn to the rich colors and narrative power of pagan myth which, in Molnar's words, "seems to withstand the erosion of time better than the Christian religion, for all its truth," and then to find oneself arraigned with those for whom "God is a human product" and to come to believe that that is a fair description of one's position. That is to say, one will either agree with Molnar that Jung "regarded religious belief as a potent means of therapy but as hardly privileged over other means such as sexual fantasy, ideology, or the recollection of childhood events," and simply accept that as a fair description of Jung's thinking, of the truth, and of one's own convictions, or be appalled to think that that is what one has come to with all that meddling in the East.

What, on the other hand, if the quest archetype, as Jung has called it, is an irrepressible one in the human makeup? Does it merely produce neutral findings, rather like first-amendment religion, untouched by the contamination of belief? For Molnar, it is questionable to credit "or burden" Jung, Eliade, René Girard, Paul Ricoeur, and others like them in their study of myth "with partiality to monotheism in general and to the Christian religion in particular." The assertion that religious attitudes have a primordial origin "does not necessarily lead one closer to the area of faith; it merely induces a more sympathetic approach to the hypothesis that there is a place in one's inner structure for religious beliefs and related manifestations."[1]

That would be enough for scholars to do, of course, if that is what their study determined, at least as long as they confined themselves to the practice of their scholarship in the "area of faith," to the examination of the structure of religious myths and their history, of the participation of the psyche in religious rite and doctrinal formation, and the general effect of religion in the shaping of civilizations from antiquity to the present. But in fact none of these men, for all their moments of positivist protestation, attempts to offer a neutral scientific statement. They are greatly involved in a personal way in their pursuit of knowledge about religion and religious experience. They do not write confessional volumes, but the textures of belief in Jung, Eliade, and

---

[1]Thomas Molnar, *The Pagan Temptation* (Grand Rapids, Mich.: Eerdmans, 1987), pp. 181, 43, 172, 128.

Ricoeur, for example, are unmistakable. To see Jung as reducing religion to a therapeutic aid of no greater consequence than a sexual fantasy or a childhood memory is to have missed that bias toward the future which remains the identifying factor in his understanding of the individuation process and makes him such a formidable witness of the evolution of the structures of consciousness toward what Jean Gebser calls the aperspectival.[2]

It is fair, I think, to say as J. T. Fraser does that "Jungian archetypes, if taken seriously, must then be regarded as products of organic evolution as are toes or facial expressions. They are primordial images which evolved as potential forms of mental constructs and survive in the collective unconscious." That is why if we look to discover more of their history and sources, we must examine "experiences that have been common to all men, such as life and death, the transitional stages of growth, the daily journey of the sun, darkness and fear, hunger, or the forces of reproduction." It would not necessarily follow, as Fraser indicates, that they would be "largely independent" of epoch, geography, culture, nor have they been for Jung and Jungians in spite of an emphasis upon the commonalty of primordial materials in fable and fairy tale, in dream and fantasy imagery, even, as Fraser says, "in the delusions of the insane."[3]

Wendy O'Flaherty uses two metaphors to explain this commonalty as it is expressed in myths. "Myths may function as the bridges between foreign cultures." A Christian, for example, may be at ease with the Krishna story because of "superficial resemblance to the myth of Jesus." There are bridges that figure in Chinese and Jewish story. As a network, the bridges suggest a railroad roundhouse, a metaphor for the coming together of the world's myths, a "common ground" and yet an "infinity where . . . all parallel variants meet." O'Flaherty defines the roundhouse for Jungians as the collective unconscious, as it is culture or kinship for anthropologists, or the world of ideal forms for Platonists, or God for theologians.

God as roundhouse may not seem much of an addition to the rhetoric of religion, but the metaphor works well enough as filled out in terms of myth and the archetype and the way we think about both, using the imagination.

> The roundhouse is the home of the invisible man that we call the archetype, the disembodied ghost of the living myth. The myth is a real thing, that one can hear or read, a thing that leaves tracks on

---

[2]See the discussion of Jean Gebser's *Ever-Present World* in Chapter Ten.

[3]J. T. Fraser, *Of Time, Passion, and Knowledge* (New York: Braziller, 1975), pp. 295-296.

the human mind; these are the tracks that run into the round-house. But the roundhouse is not real. It is a thing that *we construct* in order to get to the tracks of the myths.

Invisible but real, a construction that we make—those are the defining elements both of myth and the way we make whatever sense we can make of myth. Earlier O'Flaherty quotes Jung's observation in *Answer to Job* that "myth is not fiction" but rather sets of facts many times repeated and as often observed: "It is something that happens to man, and men have mythical fates just as much as the Greek heroes do." But though this insists strongly on experiences that can perhaps be described as being held in common, a set of universals that transcends the boundaries of history, geography, and culture, it does not say that such boundaries do not exist. Nor does Jung say that the boundaries simply disappear in the world of the unconscious, that archetypal myths are altogether without the colors of epoch or ethnic background or physical place.

O'Flaherty speaks with good cause of dreams in myths in which two different people dream of exactly the same things and, what is more startling, of things that they have never met when awake. It is fair enough to say that such myths "describe an intense heightening of the basic bond that joins all humans." Certainly that is consistent with Jung's reading of archetypal myth. What is not is the attribution to Jungians that follows, that "everybody's unconscious perfectly understands everybody else's unconscious," which is drawn from a piece on "Telepathy in Analysis" by Nandar Fodor, in which Fodor cites J. N. Rosen as authority for the statement. Neither Jung nor any representative group of Jungians would make such a statement. There is much sharing of symbol and fantasy in the realm of archetypes, a realm in which we all move with greater or lesser frequency in Jung's reading of the collective unconscious. Its universality is for him beyond argument; hence its alternate name, the objective psyche. But in it, unconscious does not speak to unconscious with that assurance of understanding that the quotation from Fodor and Rosen suggests, in a kind of jolly party line of the collectivity. It is not unreasonable to describe the collective unconscious as "the shared mental matrix of the human race," as O'Flaherty does to characterize the Jungian term, as a way of deepening our understanding of that "human substratum" where universal dreams are linked, "a kind of dream ether, an all-pervading substance in which we move like fish through water."

The constant recourse to metaphor and simile in this discussion of myth and archetype is an indication of just how elusive the material is. Indeed, it is often enough a struggle even to remain within a given figure of speech, as O'Flaherty demonstrates in the roundhouse appropriation for the collective unconscious, which has emerged from a network of bridges and soon becomes still another figure, "a kind of cave where all the myths in the world come together, the common ground. . . ." We can call this the common ground, but its produce, its symbolic vegetation, falls into no common vocabulary or rhetoric. It is, as Jung never tired of saying, a world of mystery, palpable only in the way that the materials of dream seem to be accessible to touch or taste or other sensory exploration. If unconscious speaks to unconscious, it is so far removed in its transmissions from the ordinary lines of communication that we can only depend upon the operations of the imagination to assure us that we are somehow in touch in this way. This is where myth plays its part and especially, I think, Eastern myth. Even with myth, however, we must balance expectation with caution to avoid extreme disappointment, to find some point of contact with that common ground we have been talking about, which, to shift metaphor once again, is better configured as the bottom of the sea, ground barely reachable even with the most sensitive instruments and perhaps most elusive when it is apparently within grasp. It is not *like* the world of dream; it *is* that world, and most particularly that world when it floats tantalizingly close to consciousness and translation into word and nameable image and then, just as we are about to name it and transcribe its words, slips away.[4]

Wendy O'Flaherty's book is dedicated to the late Mircea Eliade and his wife. This historian and philosopher of religions is a master of myth, trained in Italian Renaissance philosophy in his native Bucharest, in Indian philosophy and in Sanskrit in Calcutta. He was, in his time, a teacher in Bucharest, in Paris, in Chicago, a cultural attaché for Romanian legations in London and Lisbon during World War II, a novelist, an essayist, an indefatigable student of religion. In almost everything, including his novels, there is a feeling—one is tempted to call it natural—for that " 'universal' perspective," as he himself calls it in his journals, which links him to Jung.[5] His cultural hermeneutic seems to have been shaped early on by the Romanian philosopher Lucian Blaga, himself greatly influenced by Jung.[6] Whether from Blaga or from Jung directly or from his own grasp of the archetypal world, Eliade is drawn everywhere into the mysterious tracings of the

---

[4]See Wendy O'Flaherty, *Other People's Myths: The Cave of Echoes* (New York: Macmillan, 1988), pp. 162-163, 156, 163-164.

[5]See Mircea Eliade, *No Souvenirs: Journal, 1957-1969*, trans. F. H. Johnson, Jr. (New York: Harper & Row, 1977), p. 189.

[6]See Ivan Strenski, *Four Theories of Myth in Twentieth-century History: Cassirer, Eliade, Lévi-Strauss and Malinowski* (Iowa City: University of Iowa Press, 1987), pp. 122-123.

collective unconscious. Eliade himself describes his interest in Babylonian cosmology in terms that make this central thrust of his life very clear. He is speaking of a book published in Romanian in 1937, *Babylonian Cosmology and Alchemy*: "In this little book are found, *in nuce*, all my interpretations relative to the symbolism of the center of the world; the archetypal models of temples, cities, and dwellings; the Platonic structure of archaic and Oriental thought – interpretations developed later in *The Myth of the Eternal Return (Cosmos and History)*, *Patterns in Comparative Religion*, and *Images and Symbols*."[7]

Jung is mentioned by name only in the last of those books, but there is no mistaking the common interests, the shared convictions, the redemptive power of what Jung calls the Self archetype, in all of Eliade's work. Perhaps it is appropriate to describe his system of interpretation of religion as a "neo-Jungian hermeneutics."[8] It is more important, I think, in noting what he shares with Jung and where he finds his own individuality, to recognize the profound psychological textures of his work of collation and interpretation, which are similar to other historians of religion he mentions as being stimulated by Jung's "careful study of archaic and oriental religions" – Heinrich Zimmer, Carl Kerényi, Joseph Campbell, Henry Corbin.[9]

Of all of these, he is surely the most determinedly philosophical. He is also, with his novelist's gifts and his understanding of the rhetoric and the poetic of the essay form, a constant joy to read. Although he was a familiar contributor to the Eranos conferences, those largely though not exclusively Jungian gatherings, he was never a collaborator with Jung as Kerényi was, nor so directly connected with the making of a Jungian scholarship in the history of myth and religion as Campbell or Zimmer or Corbin. What one finds instead where Jung turns up in Eliade's work is, apart from his scrupulously fair description or adaptation of Jung's ideas, a provocative set of insights. One knows not only Eliade and Jung better because of these darting illuminations, but the psyche caught up in religious experience. A splendid example is to be found in the foreword to his *Mephistopheles and Androgyne: Studies in Religious Myth and Symbol*, invoking the scientific study of caves as a way of understanding the great descents into darkness of archetypal exploration:

---

[7]See Mircea Eliade, *Autobiography Volume II: 1937–1960*, trans. M. L. Ricketts (Chicago: University of Chicago Press, 1988), p. 8n.

[8]Strenski, p. 125.

[9]See Mircea Eliade, *The Quest: History and Meaning in Religion* (Chicago: University of Chicago Press, 1969), p. 22n.

The psychoanalytical technique has inaugurated a new type of *descensus ad inferos*. When Jung revealed the existence of the collective unconscious, the exploration of these immemorial treasures – the myths, symbols and images of archaic humanity – began to approximate its techniques to those of the oceanographers and speleologists. Just as the deep sea diving and cave exploration revealed elementary organisms that had long disappeared from the earth's surface, so analysis discovered forms of deep psychic life hitherto inaccessible to study. Speleology placed at the biologist's disposal tertiary and even secondary organisms, zoomorphic forms *that are not fossilizable*, that is to say forms that had disappeared without a trace from the surface of the earth. By the discovery of "living fossils," speleology has considerably advanced our knowledge of archaic forms of life. In the same way, archaic forms of psychical life, the "living fossils" buried in the darkness of the unconscious, now became accessible to study, thanks to techniques developed by the depth psychologists.

In that same book, there is a fascinating account of a businessman, "satisfied with his occupation and seemingly in no way prepared for a semi-mystical illumination," who moves from dream experience of embrace in a kind of mystic light, to some conscious sense of the presence of Christ in his life, to an intense experience of being altogether suffused in a supernatural light. The story is a familiar one, taken from R. M. Bucke's 1901 *The Cosmic Consciousness*. What makes it attractive to Eliade as a historian of religion is what it demonstrates of the effect of suppressing "the religious feeling for existence," so that it must find "refuge" in the unconscious. "Nowadays," Eliade comments, "as Professor C. G. Jung says, the unconscious is always religious." The long discussion that follows, including some splendid pages on *The Secret of the Golden Flower* (that Taoist classic on the circulation of the inner light for which Jung provided a commentary when it was translated into German), concludes in a paradox. The light is inevitably a "personal discovery," a real discovery, and yet it is equally clear that what we discover is what we are "spiritually and culturally prepared to discover." Still something remains which for Eliade is a fact: whatever the ideology of a person, "a meeting with the Light" marks a "break" in one's life and a revelation of "the world of the Spirit, of holiness and of freedom; in brief, existence as a divine creation, or the world sanctified by the presence of God."

This is not special pleading for Jung's ideas on Eliade's part, nor is his recollection of the high place of the concept of psychic totality in the work of Jung as a way of making sense of "the union of opposites in God. . . ." "It is sufficient," as he says, "to recall that the expressions, *coincidentia oppositorum, complexio oppositorum*, union of opposites, *mysterium coniunctionis*, etc., are frequently used by Jung to describe the totality of the Self and the mystery of the dual nature of Christ." It

is a bright, clear statement of the defining role of the meeting of opposites in the process of individuation, for "the Self comprises both the
whole consciousness and the contents of the unconscious" and in Jungian theory the *coincidentia oppositorum* is to be seen "as the ultimate
aim of the whole psychic activity."

Eliade shies clear of reliance "on the Jungian conception of the
'psychic totality,' " he tells us in a footnote that accompanies the last
series of statements. "Jung's views on the reality of evil have aroused
passionate discussion," he adds by way of toneless explanation, citing
H. L. Philp's *Jung and the Problem of Evil* and Victor White's *Soul and
Psyche*, for further elaboration. With or without such reliance, however, there are Jungian colors in the ensuing pages, forty-two of them,
on "the mystery of the whole." They touch on Goethe's *Faust*, Balzac's
Seraphita, Indian thought, and "myths of divine androgyny and primal
bisexual man" in such ways that Jung's anima and animus material
and reading of the *coincidentia oppositorum* as an impetus to recover a
lost integration are inescapable associations for those who know
Jung.[10] It is a sparkling discussion, very much Eliade's in structure
and emphasis and supporting detail, that cannot help but remind us,
as he puts it in another, much earlier book, of how well the psychologists, "C. G. Jung among others of the first rank, have shown us [that]
the dramas of the modern world proceed from a profound disequilib-
rium of the psyche, individual as well as collective, brought about
largely by a progressive sterilisation of the imagination." Imagination,
he says, offers "a richness of interior life, an uninterrupted and spontaneous flow of images." To have it is "to be able to see the world in its
totality," for images reveal everything "that remains refractory to the
concept. . . ." That explains the difficulty, the incompleteness, of those
who lack imagination. That is the essential Jungian point. Those without imagination are "cut off from the deeper reality of life" and their
own souls. Psychic totality is not possible for them as long as they do
not "have imagination."[11]

Eliade asks us to consider "what has become of myths" in our
world, what has taken "the *essential* place" myth held in older societies.
He cites Jung's thesis in *Modern Man in Search of a Soul* that the
modern world is at a critical turn because of its "break with Christianity" and points to the recrudescence of Golden Age mythology in
Marxist communism, with its version of "the Judaeo-Christian eschat-

[10]See Mircea Eliade, *Mephistopheles and the Androgyne: Studies in Religious
Myth and Symbol*, trans. J. M. Cohen (New York: Sheed and Ward, 1965), pp.
10, 20–21, 77, 81, 82–124.

[11]See Mircea Eliade, *Images and Symbols: Studies in Religious Symbolism*,
trans. Philip Mairet (New York: Sheed & Ward, 1961), p. 20.

ological hope of an *absolute goal of History. . . .*" These quotations are from a book that looks at myths, dreams, and mysteries in a contemporary setting, to see how they reflect the encounter in our time between "contemporary faiths and archaic realities." The book ends with a quotation from Heinrich Zimmer, that Indologist so important to Jung, which suggests that the answer to "our poverty and all our trials" is not far off, but rather in ourselves, "behind the stove, the centre of the life and warmth that rule our existence, the heart of our heart, if only we knew how to unearth it." Still, Zimmer muses, we seem to need a journey into distant places and the voice of a stranger, "of another belief and another race," to make sense of our own inner voice, what Jung calls our daimon. And this, says Eliade in his terse coda, "is the profound meaning of any genuine encounter; it might well constitute the point of departure for a new humanism, upon a world scale."[12]

Eliade everywhere supplements and complements Jung. To miss what he does with mythology is for a Jungian to hear Jung's notes without many of their necessary resonances. At the very least, Jungians should not deny themselves Eliade's elegant little book on alchemy, *The Forge and the Crucible,* and especially the penultimate chapter on the "Arcana Artis" and the six-page note on Jung and alchemy with which the book concludes. It is a book packed with insights, familiar and unfamiliar detail, and a depth of understanding of the nature of the psyche, especially those far reaches of the unconscious where religious experience seems to have its roots and to color almost everything, whether one welcomes it or not, wants to call it that or not. What Jung "established," Eliade says, is that "the unconscious undergoes processes which express themselves in alchemical symbolism tending towards psychic results corresponding to the *results of hermetic operations.*" This for Eliade is a discovery of inestimable importance, not only for psychology but for religion. What it

---

[12]See Mircea Eliade, *Myths, Dreams and Mysteries: The Encounter Between Contemporary Faiths and Archaic Realities,* trans. Philip Mairet (New York: Harper, 1960), pp. 25–26, 245. Zimmer is a constant resource for Eliade; he cites him in his *Yoga: Immortality and Freedom* and *Shamanism: Archaic Techniques of Ecstasy,* volumes which share pride of place in the Bollingen Series with Zimmer's works. The Indologist is one of the "savants" Eliade felt so pleased to join when he was invited to lecture at the 1950 Eranos Conference—this type of "multidisciplinary symposium" so long associated with Jungian ideas (see *Autobiography Volume II,* p. 139). The papers from Eranos meetings gathered by Joseph Campbell in six Bollingen volumes—*Spirit and Nature, The Mysteries, Man and Time, Spiritual Disciplines, Man and Transfiguration, The Mystic Vision*—are rich in representation of Jung's inside and outside worlds, with contributions by Jung himself, Erich Neumann, Kerényi, Eliade, and John Layard, Adolph Portmann, Hugo Rahner, Erwin Schrödinger, Henry Corbin, Gilles Quispel, Friederich Heiler, Paul Tillich, Jean Danielou, and Heinrich Zimmer, among others.

amounts to is this: "in the very depths of the unconscious, processes
occur which bear an astonishing resemblance to the stages in a spiritual operation – gnosis, mysticism, alchemy *which does not occur in
the world of profane experience*, and which, on the contrary, makes a
clean break with the profane world." Individuation – psychic integration, psychic totality – is the goal. The famous Philosopher's Stone or
Elixir of Life of the alchemist represents not simply a transmutation of
base metals into gold, but the transformation of the morally or psychologically low into a spiritual elite. The initiation process is compact in
imagination and dream, even hallucinatory experience, in the way that
it is in the *opus alchymicum*. As Eliade, in his own compact way,
summarizes discoveries in the alchemical world, the *"elixir vitae"* would
be the attainment of the Self. . . ." What is promised by alchemy, which
joins Christianity in its emphasis upon "the freeing of the human soul
and the healing of the cosmos," is the chance to go beyond human
salvation to the redemption of nature. "It is the alchemist's dream to
heal the world in its totality; the Philosopher's Stone is conceived as
the *Filius Macrocosmi* who heals the world, whereas, according to the
alchemists, Christ is the Saviour of the Microcosm, that is, of man
only."

For Jung, Eliade reminds us, what the alchemists identified as
Matter was in fact the Self. The *anima mundi*, the soul of the world,
which in alchemy is the *spiritus mercurius*, is imprisoned in Matter,
and must be saved, freed, transfigured into the *corpus glorificationis*,
the glorious body. Alchemical experiment, the operations of the psyche, and sacred mystery come together. As Eliade stresses, the *"opus
alchymicum* had profound analogies with the mystic life." He quotes
an alchemist, Georg von Welling, to make this point: "our intention is
not directed towards teaching anyone how to make gold but towards
something much higher, namely how Nature may be seen and recognized as coming from God, and God in Nature."

We are, in alchemy and in the experiences it reflects and refracts,
in a world of "secret language," where communication does not come
through ordinary language. Communication comes through cryptic
symbols. The oblique is the defining angle of vision. "The hierophanies,
owing to the very fact that they manifest the sacred, change the ontological regime of things: base or insignificant, a stone, a tree, a stream,
as soon as they incorporate the element of the sacred, become prized
by those who take part in this religious experience." For Jung, all of
this transforming use of language and experiment in alchemy is, as
Eliade sums up, "a projection on to Matter, of archetypes and processes, of the collective unconscious." It is in those terms that Eliade
ends his examination of alchemy and its significance for the modern
world. He sees ours as "a completely new type of civilization" in the

making. The "only revolution comparable to it in the past" is the introduction – he calls it "discovery" – of agriculture, which brought with it changes of a size and a violence we cannot really understand today. Everything that went with "the world of nomadic hunters . . . its religions, its myths, its moral conceptions, was ebbing away." The effects of "man's decision *to call a halt and bind himself to the soil*" were to be felt for millennia. What then of the modern world, its technologies, its "conquest of Time and Space. . . . [its] secularization of work," which Eliade characterizes as "like an open wound in the body of modern society." He holds out the possibility of "resanctification" and "a reconciliation with temporality." But those hopes, although so often implicit in Eliade as in Jung, are not to be generalized here. What he aimed to do "was simply to show that the spiritual crisis of the modern world includes among its remote origins the demiurgic dreams of the metallurgists, smiths and alchemists." The somewhat sorrowful accompanying meditation is that our sense of history and "the deeds and ideals" of our ancient progenitors reflected in the myths and dreams to which we are heir seem to be tolerable to us only when we break them "loose from their original significance."[13]

In a discussion of a late novel of Eliade's, *Fôret Interdite*, Vintila Horia speaks of modern man, whether "postcartesian," positivist, or caught up in "Hegelian or Marxist ritual," as able "to destroy the possibility of returning to a mythic conception of history as well as the hope of an eternal life. . . ." Horia's piece is called "The Forest as Mandala" and finds its thesis in a distinctly Jungian reading of Eliade's book. For he sees Eliade's novel as having "mythic significance" in its lengthy perambulation through "a total Romanian universe . . . set in motion in the period which began around 1935 and ended in 1945 with the victory of the communists." The novel's Jungian psychology is one whose "roots are not, so to speak, existential but essential." Its drama reflects an understanding of human behavior as shaped by "a psychic inheritance that precedes the individual and that is related directly to his lineage and race." In a word, the collective unconscious.

The people and the events in Eliade's novel support this reading, and more than that. Through personifications of ideas and political positions and historic divisions in Romanian history, an obscure corner of Western civilization is illuminated, the enduring power of mythology is illustrated, and the fearful difficulties involved in the individuation journey are dramatized. The issue is to find life at its center, in the *fôret interdite*, the prohibited forest, where time is cosmic time and integration is not only attractive but feasible. Horia puts it simply:

[13]See Mircea Eliade, *The Forge and the Crucible*, trans. Stephen Corrin (New York: Harper, 1962), pp. 201, 203–204, 165–166, 177–178.

MYTH 63

"our civilization kills time, it is a daily assassin of our personal time. It carries us at fantastic velocity outside life. But how shall it be avoided?" Horia suggests an answer through Jung: "I find it logical to relate this 'prohibited forest,' the symbol of a definitive realization in the beyond, to what Eliade himself called in another novel 'the celestial marriage,' to the Jungian 'Mandala.' " If we see the human struggle as a quest for "equilibrium," a journey toward individuation, "it is evident that 'to dream in the forest' means that one has arrived at interior equilibrium, at a final phase in a process of psychological healing."[14]

Horia's piece is one of a large number of "studies in honor of Mircea Eliade" published under the title of *Myths and Symbols*. Focusing on a narrative and characters and situations immensely Romanian, it makes us see Eliade in his own mythology, in the setting and with the materials from which he crafted the myth of himself. In the last piece of the volume, that master of the gnomic utterance, old friend and fellow Romanian, E. M. Cioran, finds a larger place for Eliade. In a brief personal memoir, of times, attitudes, and experience in which Eliade figures alongside Cioran, the writer turns to Eliade as religious thinker, as religious being: "I believe that if he has perfect understanding of sin, he lacks a sense of it: He is too feverish for that, too intoxicated with the possible." Those who do have this sense "are the kind who chew over their past endlessly, who take root in it and cannot tear themselves free. . . . Ever since Pascal and Kierkegaard, we can no longer conceive of 'salvation' without a retinue of infirmities, without the secret delights of the inner drama." Can someone of Eliade's learning make the descent into hell which the present-day fashion for "accursedness" demands? Cioran thinks not. Eliade's place is on the periphery of this sort of religion, of "*every* religion, by profession as well as by conviction." Having refused to organize religions into a "hierarchy" of the better and the best, how can he make a choice, "sponsor" a particular belief, "invoke" a particular divinity? The last sentences are a brilliant arraignment of Eliade and of Cioran himself. Acerbic, pained, painful, they tell us much about the Romanians, about others like them, gifted, trained, driven to spend a lifetime looking at the center of religion but perched on the periphery.

It is impossible to imagine a specialist in the history of religions *praying*. Or, if indeed he does pray, he thus betrays his teaching, he contradicts himself, he damages his *Treatises* in which no *true* god figures, all the gods being viewed as equivalent. It is futile to

[14]See Vintila Horia, "The Forest as Mandala: Notes Concerning a Novel by Mircea Eliade," in *Myths and Symbols: Studies in Honor of Mircea Eliade*, ed. J. M. Kitagawa and C. H. Long (Chicago: University of Chicago Press, 1969), pp. 388, 391, 389, 394–395.

describe them and comment upon them with insight; he cannot blow life into them, having tapped them of their sap, compared them with one another, and, to complete their misery, frayed them with rubbing until they are reduced to bloodless symbols useless to the believer, assuming that at this state of erudition, disillusion, and irony there is someone around who still truly believes. We are all of us, and Eliade in the fore, *would-have-been* believers; we are all religious minds without religion.[15]

Is Jung one of these *would-have-been* believers? Is the fate of such people a kind of twentieth-century limbo, an annex to Dante's limbo at the gates of hell, where one lives forever in desire without hope? The company there, in Dante's prescription, is a handsome one, tenants of a Noble Castle, built to accommodate Plato, Aristotle, Socrates, Virgil, Sophocles, and others of that majestic society who came to their wisdom in the wrong place and at the wrong time to benefit from the Messianic redemption. As Eliade sees Jung at the end of his life, he carefully, consciously prepared himself for death. He seemed to be recovering from liver and gallbladder attacks. "The doctor had assured him that he would recover," Eliade notes in his journal some weeks after Jung's death, "but Jung didn't want to. He didn't want to begin a 'new life' again." There were signs: "A few days before his death, he dreamed that he found a stone at the top of a mountain. The next morning he was happy. It was, he said, the exemplary sign that his life had attained its end. He had found the *lapis philosophorum*." He died, says Eliade in his *Autobiography*, "serene and reconciled."[16]

Was Jung a *would-have-been* believer or someone always in search of the Philosopher's Stone who did finally possess it? Or was he, as some have called him, a mystic, whether to praise him or stand in awe or uneasiness before the mystical traces in his psychology? A useful addendum to the discussion of Eliade and Jung, which is an answer of sorts to these questions about Jung, is in the place and discussion Ben-Ami Scharfstein finds for him in his book, *Mystical Experience*. Scharfstein makes clear that he himself has no use for "the metaphysical claims of mysticism. . . ." As he sees it, "mysticism is a name for our infinite appetites," and in less generalized terms, he has the conviction that such appetites can be "satisfied" and that "some particular attitude towards 'reality' " can be supported by "perfect contact" with that reality. Jung qualifies for this definition in a gathering

[15]See E. M. Cioran, "Beginnings of a Friendship," in *Myths and Symbols*, pp. 413–414.

[16]See Eliade, *No Souvenirs: Journal, 1957–1969*, trans. F. H. Johnson, Jr. (New York: Harper and Row, 1977), pp. 132–133.

of creators – scientists, artists, mystics – who have in common a "like-ness" which Scharfstein defines as "Buddha's smile." Jung would be pleased, I think, because that smile is seen here as a balance between "opposite passions." Suffering, a "constructive answer" to suffering, and the ability to transform it, perhaps by atonement, "into a certain pleasure," and through distance "into a certain intimacy," are involved. But what matters above all in this group of masters is their creative effort.

Scharfstein links Jung with two physicists, Erwin Schrödinger and Albert Einstein, as a transitional figure, on the borderline where scientist turns into artist. Scharfstein's portrait depends chiefly on *Memories, Dreams, Reflections*, and reduces much that is rich in detail in the autobiography to quick strokes, a few quotations, a somewhat reductive summary. But the picture is arresting, and in its concentration, however lacking in detail, revealing. Its last sentence, which leads Scharfstein to an examination of two "artist-intellectuals," moves Jung where he belongs, I think, away from the *would-have-been* believers to the believers, not true believers but believers in the true. "Not only is Jung always in search of deeply-felt images, focal points of his own and everyone's life, but his writing constantly expresses the poetic, mystic strain between separation – within his mind, between his mind and body, between himself and others, between himself and everything – and unity."[17]

As a result of his collaboration with Jung in a volume called *Essays on a Science of Mythology*, his teaching at the Jung Institute in Zurich, and other appearances in a Jungian habitat, Carl Kerényi has often been classified as a card-carrying Jungian. He himself was very careful to disclaim the classification. In a number of places, in almost exactly the same words, he explains that before he knew Jung, he "managed quite well without the term 'archetypal.'" The word he used at first was "primordial." What made the terms *archetype* and *archetypal* attractive to Kerényi were their familiarity in Western culture; they were long used "in the languages of the Western nations to designate a phenomenon with which any empirical investigation of mythology has to deal." But let us be clear about this: he speaks of "'archetypal' images not on the basis of any explanatory theory but *phenomenologically*, describing mythology and tracing it back to its foundations in Greek existence." And again, he is meticulous about his distinctions: his use of the word *existence* is not as it is employed in existentialist philosophy – "I do not use it in a strictly 'existentialist' sense – but as it is familiar to us in Western civilization." His work, he

---

[17]See Ben-Ami Scharfstein, *Mystical Experience* (Indianapolis: Bobbs-Merrill, 1973), pp. 3, 1, 71–72.

stresses, "is not 'existentialist' any more than [his] *Gods of the Greeks*
and *Heroes of the Greeks* are 'Jungian mythology.' " His work is "limited by no psychological theory, nor, for that matter, is it one-sidedly
influenced by the ideas on ancient religion of Sir James Frazer and
most classical scholars." Furthermore, while we are getting things
straight, the source of his association with Jung "was not that I took
any of his theses as a foundation but, rather, that he believed he could
take my investigations as a foundation."

What was pleasing to this historian of religions and classical
philologist turned mythographer, was that what he had learned in a
"purely historical field" could be applied to "the suffering human
beings with whom physicians and psychotherapists deal." He was helping Jung, for example, by providing him with the phenomenology of
the child archetype. He does not underestimate the value of psychological insights, but he sees their limitations and is particularly troubled
by sexual distinctions in descriptions of the Self. If as Jung "insists,"
the Self is the total person, that is the person as he or she really is, a
wholeness involving the unconscious psyche as well as the conscious,
then it "cannot be one thing in the man and something else in the
woman." The "archetype of feminine destiny," which in Jung's appropriation of the Kore or Primordial Maiden to the Self and the anima is
not confined to women, is for Kerényi "only a step on the way to the
Self." Jung himself recognized that a "purely psychological explanation" was insufficient in the case of the Demeter-Kore myth. Kerényi is
only too happy to support this and to say that psychology has not
yielded "thus far" the secrets of the Eleusinian mysteries. Jung gets
good marks, however, for having "prudently confined himself" to commentary of a psychological kind on the Kore figure.

Kerényi speaks of himself as a post-Jungian, but says that at
least as far as Eleusis is concerned his post-Jungian view of the Primordial Child and the Primordial Maiden is not notably different from
his pre-Jungian one. For him, there are no exclusive claims that can be
made, say by Jungians or existentialists, for words like *archetype* or
existence. When he speaks of the archetypal facts of human existence
he is not confining himself to "mere realities of the psyche" nor existence in an individual human being. "An archetypal element of *bios*,
the individual human existence, is first of all human existence itself;
another is life, *zoë*, which in the Greek language is distinguished from
bios and which is proper not to man alone but to all species."

Thus speaks the classical philologist. He does not do so to reject
all that we might associate with the sexual archetypes. At the very
least, in the archetypal imprint of the beginning, "the *arche* in every
bios," we must deal with archetypal images of both the masculine and
feminine sources of life. Here he can point to his own study of the

masculine in his *Hermes der Seelenführer* (Hermes, Guide of the Spirit) and Erich Neumann's *The Great Mother*, but not as a final explanation of the Eleusinian Mysteries.[18] The task is one of reconstruction of the "content," which Kerényi identifies in his book *The Religion of the Greeks and Romans* as the substance of myth.

What Kerényi offers is a very careful sifting through of the contents of myths, not unlike the *carefulness* and *regard*—the italics are his—which in both their negative and positive "aspects" he attributes to Roman piety. Again a word captures his interest, the Latin *religio*. "A human attitude like *religio* can never be understood from the external causes which may occasion it," he says, as a Jungian might say too, "but only from the human being who is capable of it." But the psyche alone or in combination with other aspects of an individual will not provide the understanding. The "richness of content in *religio*, the *attention* and *carefulness* exercised by the Romans in all circumstances, did not necessarily mean a personal richness of religious feelings proceeding out of a man's own self." It is not "a theory of the gods" but rather "the 'being' of the gods, which presupposes them and uninterruptedly affirms them in a natural, unemphatic way, just as *pietas* does." One could say perhaps that *religio* meant, then, " 'to be open' to the 'being' of the gods, not just physically, but also mentally. . . ." But that is not good enough. In fact, it is "just what we cannot say of the Romans. Their *religio* was more than merely being open, it was the complete opposite of deafness." In *religio*, as Kerényi sums up this illuminating discussion, there are two assumptions, "first that something divine was being realised in what was happening all the time and secondly that this divine something was audible to anyone who 'listened' well."

It is an instructive discussion, somewhat more generalized than what Kerényi offers in his volumes on Prometheus and Eleusis, Asklepios, Zeus and Hera, and Dionysos. Here, in what becomes in effect a statement of the informing principles in Kerényi's scholarship, he rejects "anything which could be implied by a negative word like 'demythologisation' " to describe the work of "priestly Romans" in *religio* activities that "made divine images out of the stuff of life, as the Greek sculptors made them from marble. . . ." What these Romans achieved was "a relationship between the archetypal world of mythology and the ectypal world of life and history." Myth literally comes alive here as *mythos* and *bios* come together, "the myth as prototype,

[18]See Carl Kerényi, *Prometheus: Archetypal Image of Human Experience*, trans. Ralph Manheim (New York: Pantheon, 1963), pp. xxiii–xxix, and *Eleusis: Archetypal Image of Mother and Daughter*, trans. Ralph Manheim (New York: Pantheon, 1967), pp. xxvii–xxxiv.

the life as imitation. . . ."[19] The realization may never have been more than approximate, but it had many forms, a flow from a mythical past into a living history, a translation into conception, abstraction, and schematization of what the Greeks made into images. This is a mythography that is essential to our understanding of the Greek and Roman worlds.

Kerényi may be well described by his own term, as a post-Jungian, whatever he may have meant by it. Clearly, he was an important collaborator of the psychologist's, and he remains one still, offering his investigations as a foundation for analytical psychology just as he did at the beginning. In isolating and defining by example the central elements of Greek and Roman religion, what he calls their *style*, he provides Jungian speculation with an enduring phenomenology. If it is not a remythologization, it is because there never was in fact anything so destructive to civilization as a completed demythologization. To that, Kerényi's stirrings of the content of Greek and Roman myths and Jung's demonstration of their survival in the collective unconscious are sufficient witness.

The seminal effects of Jung's thought in the history and philosophy of religion can be seen dramatically in the work of Henry Corbin, the French scholar of Islam. More precisely, perhaps, I should talk of the cross-fertilization of disciplines here. As analytic psychology extends, deepens, and provides useful language and procedure for the research and speculations of scholar-thinkers such as Eliade, Kerényi, and Corbin, so do they add abundant example and understanding to Jungian thought. In his magisterial work, *Avicenna and the Visionary Recital*, which suitably appeared in English in the Bollingen Series so closely associated with Jung, Corbin cites what we have come to expect in this setting from those who make use of Jungian ideas. In dealing with the initiatory cycle of the eleventh-century Persian mystic's "recitals," he several times refers to *Psychology and Alchemy*, makes use of Jung on the *Puer aeternus*, the child archetype, and employs where fitting the concepts of individuation, synchronicity, and "the elucidation of *quaternity* as symbol of the totality of the Self" in *Aion*. Whether Jung is cited by name and concept or not, the footnotes that accompany the translation of a Persian commentary by a disciple of Avicenna's are threaded through with psychological insights. These, in effect, add another level to "the valorization of the symbols," to use Corbin's phrase. The recurrence of the symbols of Darkness, the Water of Life, the boundless sea, the sacred mountain in

---

[19]See Carl Kerényi, *The Religion of the Greeks and Romans*, trans. Christopher Holm (New York: E. F. Dutton, 1962), pp. 16, 159–161, 237–238.

a section of the commentary on "The Spring of Life," for example, is shown by psychological research "each time that the soul, confronting the obscure abysses of the Unconscious . . . emerges from it into the progressive light of consciousness of self. . . ."

Corbin is very clear about his purpose, "in sum to inquire what *Avicenna's lesson* could be for us *in the present*." As his use of italics suggests, he is certain that he is not merely performing a scholarly exercise, however satisfying that might be. His vigorous language speaks to an *interiorization* through the life of the symbol, in which the soul is enabled, "instead of *subordinating itself* to an external and foreign world, to *integrate* that world with itself." We become "spectators," through the offices of Avicenna and Corbin, of "a supreme effort for liberation that conditions 'emergence' from this world, and performs as it were a *transmutation* of the physical cosmos that rehabilitates it as a universe of symbols. . . ." We are brought to a "*full* and autonomous reality" which is presented to us "by the intermediate world of the symbolic Imagination," just as it is to the Islamic mystic, if not with the same "spontaneity" or lasting effect.

We are, in this reality, confronted with "the *objectivity* of the world of symbols," if we can understand that objectivity is not "posed here as exterior to natural consciousness of the sensible and physical world." We have something here quite contrary "to naturalistic interpretations and those inspired by Freudian psychoanalysis, which tend to 'explain' myths and symbols by reducing them to sublimations of biological contents. . . ." Rather, "the spontaneous flowering of symbols should appear to us as corresponding to a fundamental psychic structure, and *eo ipso* as revealing to us not arbitrary and 'fanciful' forms but well-founded and permanent contents corresponding to this permanent structure."

Corbin's grasp of his materials at both ends of their operation is bracing. He is meticulous in presenting in large detail a phenomenology of Avicennan symbols. He is equally responsible in declaring the nature of the "full and autonomous reality" of those symbols as they come to the psyche: "They are not mere projections performed at the 'subjective' pleasure of the mind; they reveal to the mind a region no less 'objective' than the sensible world. Their spontaneity is so far from being arbitrary that it exhibits striking recurrences in cultures far apart in time or space, recurrences that no filiation through historical causality could explain to us." It is those recurrences that have led him to refer, he says, to the research of Jung.

It is not, he cautions us, simply a matter of trying "to 'disengage' the intelligible meaning hidden 'behind' each purely sensible reality." Such a reduction of symbolic understanding to scheme and formula "would inevitably miss what constitutes the peculiar reality and the autonomy of the universe of symbols: the symbol is mediator because it is silence, it speaks and it does not speak; and, precisely thus, it states what it alone can speak." He will have no part of attempts to declare final meanings, "to take one's stand on the intelligible signification that one substitutes" for the reality of the symbol and our experience of it. If we do so, "the whole mental dramaturgy" of the recitals disappears; "nothing is left but pallid 'allegories,' and our whole effort . . . has been directed toward a fidelity to Avicenna's intentions that should keep our recitals from falling into such a vapidity, which makes any mental creation vain and sterile."

Corbin is discussing the transmutation of the soul and "the configuration and the vision of its most personal symbol, the central symbol of the Self, which is not knowable in any other way. . . ." That vision — that archetypal symbolization — "can be perceived neither by the senses nor by pure intellect, but only by the Imagination that is its place of epiphany. . . ." Again, a few pages on, he stresses that he is not dealing with an engaging historical relic: his aim is not to explain Avicenna as a "man of his time." That time, "*his own time*, has not here been put in the past tense; it has presented itself to us as an immediacy." It does not originate "in the chronology of a history of philosophy, but in the threefold ecstasy by which the archangelic Intelligences each give origin to a world and to consciousness of a world, which is the consciousness of a desire, and this desire is hypostatized in the Soul that is the motive energy of that world."

What gives unction to this discussion is that it does present itself to us — and Corbin makes sure that it does — as an immediacy. Whether or not we understand it as "hypostatized," that is, linked to our essential nature, present in our souls, we must understand that it does deepen our reach into our psyches, into the motive energies of our conscious and unconscious worlds. Thus as he moves, in the last two pages of his text, before going on to the translation of the Persian commentary, to a brief examination of "the connection between angelology and the process of individuation," he must evoke for many of his readers a Jungian presence. Certainly the question he poses in his last paragraph, about the mystics, poets, and philosophers he calls "the Faithful in Love," and the comment that follows as a kind of answer are what Jung proposes one way or another in his sorties into myth and symbol, philosophy and religion. Corbin is talking about members of a "community of cult and destiny" that includes Avicenna and others from the East and West. "Shall we ask if the course of their way still has other than a historical meaning, a meaning for our historical *present*? There is no general answer or theoretical program for this type of question. It is for *each* of us to decide it, by deciphering . . . the document of his own destiny, the private document of his soul." We do not accomplish this by reduction. There is no precise schema that can induce for us "the encounter that befell Avicenna on the outskirts of the inner city of his soul – that is, on the threshold of subliminal consciousness." But if we ever do have such a meeting we must each decide if we "will reply as Avicenna replied to the invitation of his own Hayy ibin Yaqzan" – his inner voice, his daimon, his *spiritus rector*, personified as a "Sage-youth" – if we "will do what will enable us to reply and to testify with Avicenna: *'Lo, we are on the road, we are journeying in company with the King's Messenger.'* "[20]

Jung's predisposition to take seriously anything that might lead to a deeper penetration of the unconscious is probably what stands behind Martin Buber's characterization of him as a Gnostic in *Eclipse of God.*[21] Perhaps "accusation" would be a better word, for as the scholar of early Christianity Gilles Quispel points out in a spirited essay, "The Birth of the Child: Some Gnostic and Jewish Aspects," for Buber "Gnosticism and not atheism is the true enemy and opponent of faith in the Jewish or Christian sense of the word." It is not an easy label to bear if one thinks of Gnosticism as that heretical set of doctrines attacked in the second and third centuries by Irenaeus, Tertullian, and Hippolytus. For in those teachings, distinctions are drawn between the spirit and matter that seem to make this world evil and reduce the figure of Jesus to a kind of divine messenger who found temporary embodiment as a human being or may even have been a kind of wraith. On the other hand, the exaltation of knowledge, which the name of the movement proclaims, and the determination to pierce the veils which separate the human from the divine are, as Eliade suggests, the almost inevitable first motions of the mind and soul

[20]See Henry Corbin, *Avicenna and the Visionary Recital*, trans. Willard K. Trask (New York: Pantheon, 1960), pp. 360n., 322n., 257-262, 266, 270. Corbin is another of the distinguished Bollingen company, almost all of whose volumes show a commonality of purpose with Jungian ideas and procedures, but nothing like a lock step reproduction of them.

[21]See Martin Buber, *Eclipse of God: Studies in the Relation Between Religion and Philosophy*, trans. Maurice S. Friedman and others (New York: Harper Torchbooks, 1957), pp. 78-92, 133-137. The first of these two discussions is the larger part of a lecture, "Religion and Modern Thinking," in which Buber identifies the concept of Self in Jung as "no longer a genuinely mystical concept," as it was "originally," but, as "transformed" by Jung, into "a Gnostic one" (p. 84). The second is a "Reply" to Jung's reply to his lecture, in which Buber insists all the more upon his diagnosis, associating Jung with "The psychological doctrine which deals with mysteries without knowing the attitude of faith towards mystery ... the modern manifestation of Gnosis ... mystically deifying the instincts instead of hallowing them in faith." He sees Jung as having "proclaimed in all clarity the ambivalent Gnostic 'God' who balances good and evil in Himself" (pp. 136-137). See on this conflagration issue, in addition to the Quispel essay noted below and discussed in the body of my text, the quotation from J. F. T. Jordens in footnote 6 of Chapter Four.

seeking spiritual understanding. Furthermore, as Quispel and many others have recognized, the extraordinary collection of Coptic texts found at Nag Hammadi in Upper Egypt in 1945 and 1946 reveal a large Jewish or Jewish Christian influence in the development of Gnosticism.

The invidious distinctions drawn by Buber, and others as well, between Judaism and Gnosticism assume a pagan ethos in Gnosticism or a severely distorted appropriation of Jewish beliefs. The Nag Hammadi texts suggest something different, an evolution of Gnosis, as Quispel puts it, "out of Judaism, or Jewish Christianity, as a result of dialectical process." The emanations that over a sequence of stages bring the knowledge-seeker from the god who creates, a kind of demiurge, to some awareness of an ultimately unknowable Supreme Being, have clear parallels to the system of emanations in the *Kabbalah*, the Jewish theosophical doctrine. Whether or not the Gnostics influenced the development of Kabbalistic thought, the impulse to Gnostic formulation is an unmistakable part of Jewish and Jewish Christian thinking and experience, and indeed is intrinsic to all religious experience which looks to go beyond ephemera to some permanent wisdom, however insecure one's grasp of it may be.

Quispel's definitions indicate what makes the association of Jung and Gnosis inevitable, whether as a simple characterization or a corrosive judgment: "Gnosis is based on the idea that there is something in man, his unconscious spirit, which is related to the ground of being. In order to restore the wholeness it has lost, the deity has an interest in redeeming this spiritual principle in man."[22] That is the animating principle in what might be called Jungian Gnosis, to find the lost wholeness, to discover those elements that make a psychic totality possible, not as a Utopian dream, but as a psychological process characterized by the redemptive structure that he called the integration of the personality or individuation.

Quispel makes much of a psychological approach to a difficult scriptural text in his work on the Apocalypse, *The Secret Book of Revelation: The Last Book of the Bible.* He explains that his book is essentially an attempt "to demonstrate how fruitful it can be to examine the Johannine Apocalypse on the basis of what we know about Jewish Christianity." The demonstration is by way of verbal and pictorial commentary on the chapters and verses of the Book of Revelation. It is almost everywhere a delight, to eye, to mind, to spirit. Because Quispel is so much at ease with Jungian ideas and language, he can turn comfortably to Jung's reading of the Apocalypse in terms of the

[22]See Gilles Quispel, "The Birth of the Child: Some Gnostic and Jewish Aspects," in *Jewish and Gnostic Man* (Dallas: Spring Publications, 1986), pp. 3–5.

chthonic symbols the psychologist finds there. What this provides is a demonstration in small of the psychological approach to the text and its special values, as for example in a brief passage summarizing what Quispel finds "quite new and of the utmost importance" in Jung. It speaks to our understanding of John and in particular of the figure that incarnates wisdom in the book, the Lady who might be called the "world-soul . . . she who adds darkness to light . . . who signifies the sacred marriage of opposites . . . who reconciles nature and spirit."

> John is not only confessing with his lips his faith in the thousand-year realm here on earth; for even the symbols which welled up from the profoundest depths of his soul bear witness to his faithfulness towards the earth too. The unconscious never lies. To formulate this in a slightly different way from Jung: to the consciousness of the seer, the Lady is the Holy Spirit, as it used to be for all Jewish Christians.

Some pages on, Quispel treats the Apocalypse "as a process of individuation." He passes quickly, but with simple and clear explication, over basic Jungian terms and concepts to make the point, first in general and then with particular application to the Apocalypse, that "Visions resemble dreams." He promises no easy understanding: "Neither dreams nor visions are coherent." But he does support his assertion that "Psychologists study dreams, visions, and myths because they possess healing power" with a vigorous examination in Jungian terms of the enigmatic symbols of the Book of Revelation. Individuation process is the key. Examining Shadow, Lady, Mother, Whore, and associated archetypal elements, Quispel comes to his (and other Jungians') provocative identification of the Christ figure as "a type of the Self which embraces both the positive as well as the negative sides of man's being." It is not a reductive identification. We see Christ also as the Son of Man, "the god Man (14:14) who is surrounded by the *quaternio* consisting of the four living creatures." And we see the figure fitted out with "a feminine element, because he is also Venus the bright and shining morning star (22:16)."

Much is crammed into these pages of symbolic analysis, which for Quispel "show that John, the intuitive introvert, has at the end of his visions finally been reconciled with reality." It represents a triumph of the concrete imagination over abstract concepts, a kind of thinking, which for this commentator the Apocalypse represents, one which "bestows upon man's wounded soul a profound feeling of liberation; but it also embraces eternal truth." We are to "remain faithful to the earth," but not as a way of turning aside from the Kingdom of heaven, "because the Kingdom of God is indeed coming into *this world*."[23]

In *The Road to Daulis: Psychoanalysis, Psychology, and Classical Mythology*, Robert Eisner argues intelligently for the selective use of myth in the therapeutic disciplines, whether for theoretical or practical application. His title takes us to the drama of the crossroads, where Oedipus fighting with a stranger over the right of way kills the man, who is ultimately revealed to be his father, Laius. Oedipus is en route from Delphi, where the oracle would tell him only that he was destined to kill his father and marry his mother when he asked about his true parentage. He has vowed not to return to Corinth and his adoptive parents, the king and queen, Polybus and Merope. He chooses instead to proceed to Thebes, besieged by the Sphinx, the monster of the riddles who slays those unable to unravel them. Oedipus is the exception; he solves his riddle and marries the widowed queen of Thebes, Jocasta, his mother. Eisner's shrewd alternative for Oedipus, and the center of this thesis, is that there were, in fact, three roads to choose from: Oedipus could have taken the third, the road to Daulis. Furthermore, if Oedipus really "had had an Oedipus complex he would have killed Polybus and married Merope, the only parents he ever knew."

Eisner's case is not only for a selective use of myth but of analysis. What is involved in the analytic process may indeed occupy us for a lifetime, for what it offers is "a chance at freedom and at writing our own roles in life." But that does not mean it should "occupy us fully for more than a few of our middle years, unless we are a Freud or Jung; for the constant reference of our lives to styleless myth, Greek or Viennese, ceases after a while to be useful unless it is made the substratum of a sportive, inventive something else that takes up where the myths end." That is our third road, the one Oedipus failed to choose.

Jung figures at some length, in a chapter on "Daimon and Archetype," in this strategy of the third road, as well as more briefly where Eisner deals with incest, the Electra complex, the interpretation of Dionysus, Attis (in the Cybele and Attis story) in "the numinous service of the archetypes," the figure of the hero, and the Will to Power as the shadow side of Eros. Jung is not dismissed, but he is seen as an obstacle to the freedom of choice which the third road represents. Jungians have an appropriate respect, for example, for an artist's access to the unconscious, but not for his or her powers of control over the elusive materials of art. "Without such skill Picasso would be no

---

[23]See Gilles Quispel, *The Secret Book of Revelation: The Last Book of the Bible* (New York: McGraw-Hill, 1979), pp. 5, 125, 129, 131, 134.

better a painter than one of Jung's patients." Jung's response to symbols is to invite their "mystical emanations to wash over us." He ends
up confusing life with literature, finding "as many symbols in daily life
as he does in literary or mythological texts." Eisner sees in all of this a
kind of surrender to the collective unconscious, a retreat from the
style-centering discriminations of the ego, and an avoidance of "clarity
of expression." The indictment is strong: "Jung actually preaches the
virtues of the imitative fallacy as an investigative and stylistic principle. But the ineffable cannot be made more intelligible by opaque language; and although the numinous may impose its presence on us in a
compelling but also an obscure manner, it cannot serve as a model for
good, expository prose. Jung took it as such."

Of course, Jung's primary concern was never "good, expository
prose," although it can be argued, I think, that he often achieves it. Nor
can it be said, as Eisner does immediately afterward, that "Jung's anti-
intellectual tendency must be blamed for depth psychology's refusal to
look closely at any myth and respect its historical, social, and artistic
context and content." His collaborations with Kerényi suggest just the
opposite conclusion and the works of such scholars as Eliade and Corbin, so strongly influenced by Jung, also indicate a very different and
far from anti-intellectual inclination on Jung's part. For these questionable assertions and others, such as the flat statement that "Jung
was basically a polytheist born into a rigorously monotheistic (or
dytheistic—money and Christ) Switzerland," Jungians may not want
to bother with Eisner. They would miss, then, some thoughtful associations of Jung with Plato and Lévi-Strauss, and summations of Jungian thinking, whether in Eisner's words or someone else's, that deserve
serious examination, even when offered with something less than
approval. Thus, for example, the quotation from Philip Rieff: "the
object of therapy, in the Jungian sense, is, therefore, to reconcile the
individual to whatever authority he carries within himself. Such an
authority is inescapable; the wise man adapts himself to it." Similarly,
when Eisner tells us that he is "arguing that the archetypes, or their
manifestations, are evolving as consciousness evolves," as if Jung were
somehow at odds with this, he may be reading Jung loosely; but his
argument is irreproachable in a Jungian perspective when he fits it out
with examples that show "a prototype of the anima in Athena and
occasionally in other goddesses" developing into "Socrates' daimon or
voice . . . into Platonic eros . . . and eventually into the Jungian anima,"
and the evolution of eudaimonism ("how to lead a happy life") from the
simple idea of glory in the *Iliad*, through the more complex concept of a
"spiritual integral man" of the *Odyssey* and the "obligation to lead the
virtuous life" which is in Socrates and Plato, to the idea of individuation in Kierkegaard, Nietzsche, Jung, and Freud. The pages that fol-

low, on the "rise of consciousness," to get us from Athena to Socrates's "famous daimon," and on the Roman poet Ovid's understanding of self-awareness and its agonies, will make particular sense to those well read in Jung. An example is this parallel: "Jung has instructed us about the real dragons a too-careless probing into the cave-dark unconscious can release. Ovid performed a similar admonitory service for turn-of-the-millennium Romans and he can do as much for us. No more subversive a poem than the *Metamorphoses* was ever written."[24] Almost in spite of himself, and certainly against some of his own arguments, Eisner has made a case for Jung flitting from myth to myth, as he at one point characterizes his method, "flipping through the pages of his notebooks with one hand and composing with the other." Eisner's own method is remarkably like Jung's. full of flits and flips, and with nothing quite so original to show for it. What he should recognize in this method, which mixes rather than confuses literature with life, is its instinctive aversion to the fateful first and second roads, to Corinth and Thebes, and its almost certain choice of the third, to Daulis and freedom.

Mythology assumes the dimensions of a religious faith in the work of Joseph Campbell. Myths are his guide to the human imagination and its treasurable outpouring, "the symbolic forms in which wisdom-lore has been everywhere embodied. . . ." What keeps him close to Jung, as he moves systematically or speculatively through the myths of history and pre-history in all parts of the world, is the conviction that when those forms

> are interpreted not as referring primarily to any supposed or even actual historical personages or events, but psychologically, properly "spiritually," as referring to the inward potentials of our species, there then appears through all something that can be properly termed a *philosophia perennis* of the human race, which, however, is lost to view when the texts are interpreted literally, as history, in the usual ways of harshly orthodox thought.

Campbell serves no orthodoxy except perhaps the Jungian, if one can reduce the psychology to such terms. He is also devoted to Joyce's *Finnegans Wake*, which he and his collaborator Henry Morton Robinson were among the first to decipher for general appreciation. He is not only stunned that "this greatest literary genius of our century was never awarded the Nobel Prize," but by the associated "fact" that "at

---

[24]See Robert Eisner, *The Road to Daulis: Psychoanalysis, Psychology, and Classical Mythology* (Syracuse, N. Y.: Syracuse University Press, 1987), pp. 11, 249, 82–84, 87, 95–105.

the present moment we have no known creative work at all to match the requirements and possibilities of this fabulous period of ours – post World War II – of perhaps the greatest spiritual metamorphosis in the history of the human race."[25]

Campbell's indefatigable labors to penetrate "the masks of God," his generic name for the mythologies, the archetypes, the symbolic "wisdom-lore" of the world, are his creative work, his attempt to deal with the inattention to the spiritual changes that seem to him to have marked our time so significantly. As with Ovid in his *Metamorphoses*, he likes to tell tales, gathered from many sources, and then, somewhat less poetically than the great Roman, to ruminate upon them. His ruminations are supported wherever possible by quotations or paraphrases of Jung and, although less frequently, by reference to the work so dear to him, *Finnegans Wake*. He found a large audience for his tale-telling and insistent underscoring of the place of myth in the television series he did with Bill Moyers, where his years as a teacher and editor were reflected engagingly.[26] He served a smaller audience particularly well in his six-volume gathering of papers from the Eranos Yearbooks and another set of volumes of the work of the philosopher and collator of Indian myth, religion, and art Heinrich Zimmer. For some of us, his most compelling study is the early one of *The Hero with a Thousand Faces*. There he uses Eastern and Western materials with great skill, makes guarded but highly effective use of Jung among other analysts and anthropological theorists, and stands firm against reductionist simplification.

The best of Campbell is in that standing firm. He uses words from Homer's *Odyssey* to support his point: "There is no final system for the interpretation of myths, and there never will be any such thing. Mythology is like the god Proteus, 'the ancient one of the sea, whose speech is sooth.' The god 'will make assay, and take all manner of shapes of things that creep upon the earth, or water likewise, and of fierce fire burning.' " He provides us, even while commending the great mythological products of the archetypal and symbolic imagination, with strong balancing cautions very much like Jung's: "The unconscious sends all sorts of vapors, odd beings, terrors, and deluding images up into the mind – whether in dream, broad daylight, or insan-

---

[25]See Joseph Campbell, *Myths to Live By* (New York: Viking, 1972), pp. 255, 50.

[26]*The Masks of God* volumes appeared with subtitles which explain their concentration, *Primitive Mythology, Oriental Mythology, Occidental Mythology, Creative Mythology* (Viking, 1959, 1962, 1964, 1968). The television series with Bill Moyers appears in book form under the title of *Joseph Campbell and the Power of Myth* (New York: Doubleday, 1988). A complementary work is the five-volume *Historical Atlas of World Mythology* (Harper & Row, 1988), large, sumptuous, coffee-table fodder.

ity. . . ." When we go down into our "unsuspected Aladdin caves," we find "not only jewels but also dangerous jinn. . . ." The hero makes the best possible use of these resources, overcoming the limitations of personal history and the collective, of his time and of his place, the better to live with and live out the "visions, ideas, and inspirations" that come to such a person "pristine from the primary springs of human life and thought." The hero may die as our contemporary; he returns "as eternal man – perfected, unspecific, universal man – he has been reborn." His task is to give back to us, transfigured, the visions, ideas, and inspirations which may renew even our "disintegrating society and psyche."

Campbell knows how distant his views are from the conventional wisdom of this century. But that is less cause for retreat or apology than for a studied sadness, "for the democratic ideal of the self-determining individual, the invention of the power-driven machine, and the development of the scientific method of research, have so transformed human life that the long-inherited, timeless universe of symbols has collapsed." The modern hero will not be dismayed. Man can still "be the measure of the inexhaustible and multifariously wonderful divine existence that is the life in all of us." The tocsin call from Nietzsche is not "Dead are all the gods" but "Live as though the day were here."

In 1948, when he finished his study of the hero, Campbell's final appeal was an uncomfortable matching of that Nietzschean blazon, with its ugly political associations, and the ultimate textures of defeat: "And so every one of us shares the supreme ordeal – carries the cross of the redeemer – not in the bright moments of his tribe's great victories, but in the silences of his personal despair."[27] A quarter of a century later, answering the opening question of his book, *Myths to Live By*, "What is – or what is to be – the new mythology?" he offered a more consoling prospect. It is right out of Jung, with whom he had been spending so much of his time as writer and teacher and editor, and from the resources of the objective psyche or collective unconscious to which they had both given so much of their attention:

> It is – and will forever be, as long as our human race exists – the old, everlasting, perennial mythology, in its "subjective sense," poetically renewed in terms neither of a remembered past nor of a projected future, but of now: addressed, that is to say, not to the flattery of "peoples," but to the waking of individuals in the knowledge of themselves, not simply as egos fighting for place on the surface of this beautiful planet, but equally as centers of Mind at

[27] Joseph Campbell, *The Hero with a Thousand Faces* (New York: Meridian, 1956), pp. 381, 8, 19–20, 387, 391.

Large—each in his own way at one with all, and with no
horizons.[28]

The metaphysical implications of myth looked at through the
Jungian prism are large. They lead to a deeper understanding of self, in
Jung's use of the word, both with a small "s" and a capital one. They
ground us in the body; they tie us to earth; they extend the ontological
meaning for us of what the philosopher David Michael Levin calls *our
own* culture of experience." For Levin, engaged in bold combat against
nihilism, "cancer of the spirit . . . the challenge of the modern epoch,"
depth psychology is a major agency to be added to his principal
sources of modern wisdom, the phenomenological writings of Heidegger and Merleau-Ponty. "I believe," he says, "that the work of Carl
Jung and Erich Neumann can supplement in essentially required ways
Heidegger's formal analytic of the *Dasein*'s potential for becoming an
authentic Self." That is to say, everything that is latent in our being
human to reach to wholeness can in fact be made explicit: *we* can
achieve wholeness. To continue with Levin's words, "Since the pre-
conceptual, pre-reflective experience of our primordial relatedness-to-
Being-as-a-whole would seem to be articulated first, and perhaps also
most satisfactorily, in terms of the archetypal symbols of our body's
'collective unconscious,' a Jungian interpretation of cultural symbols,
myths, and rituals of self-transformation can significantly clarify
Heidegger's discourse concerning our deepest self-understanding and
our existential possibilities-for-becoming.' "

[28]*Myths to Live By*, p. 266. Consolations in Campbell have an uncomfortable
tendency to turn into rude awakenings, as one might gather from Brendan Gill's
bitter piece on "The Faces of Joseph Campbell" (*The New York Review of Books*,
September 28, 1989), in which he conveys, in some detail, the shock of discovering that what he had thought was "mere eccentricity" in Century Club conversation was in fact, no matter how muted, part of Campbell's "continued champion-
ing of a right-wing anti-humanitarianism that he and Ayn Rand had first
proposed back in the Forties" (p. 19). The discovery leads Gill to conclude, "with
sadness, that my friend had become my enemy." I have no desire to defend
Campbell here, but I think in this context—Campbell as part of Jung's outside
world—it is important to say that the task Campbell appointed himself was
anything but "anti-humanitarian." He was a mythographer with strong, if sometimes simplistic and reductionist, Jungian convictions. He saw himself as a
humanist, really, as the aftermath of an exchange with Martin Buber reported
in *Myths to Live By* suggests. He doesn't understand what Buber means by his
talk of a God who "today has hidden his face and no longer shows himself to
man." He has just returned from India where he "found that people are experiencing God all the time." For Campbell, "The ultimate divine mystery is there
found immanent within each." In terms redolent of both Jung and Tillich, his
"divine mystery" is not " 'out there' somewhere." He sees as "the final sense of all
adult teaching . . . the point that the mystery transcendent of categories, names
and forms, sentiments and thought, is to be realized as the ground of one's own
very being" (pp. 91–93).

With Heidegger and anyone making good use of him, the hyphen is all. We are a body of connections. If they remain latent, the connections are hyphenated to possibility. If they disclose themselves, they are all the more yoked together with hyphens, grounded now in a visible earth. "Earth, in its deepest truth, is the Being of beings, presencing *in our world* as its elemental ground: the ground which underlies the 'worlding of the world.'" And, says Levin, "Jung recognizes this hermeneutical disclosure of the ground, and even perceives the mediation of the body, when, in discussing 'The Role of the Unconscious,' he reflects on the fact that, 'The soil of every country holds some . . . mystery. We have an unconscious reflection of this in the psyche: just as there is a relationship of mind to body, so there is a relationship of body to earth.'"

Levin is uncomfortable with Jung not making "the relationship of body to earth explicit . . . except insofar as it is refracted through the symbols of the psyche." But that, of course, *is* an explicitation, as much as is possible for Jung, of the relationship. For Heidegger, the history of Being, which is in human recollection, is "the repetition of a possibility of existence that has come down to us." For Jung, the history of Being, which is in the primordium recorded in the psyche, is inscribed in such forms as myths and mandalas. They become our "instruments of meditation, concentration, and self-immersion, for the purpose of realizing inner experience." They may bring us "an inner order. . . . They express the idea of a safe refuge, of inner reconciliation and wholeness."[29]

---

[29]See David Michael Levin, *The Body's Recollection of Being: Phenomenological Psychology and the Deconstruction of Nihilism* (London: Routledge and Kegan Paul, 1985), pp. 18–19, 1, 284, 287, 72, 335–336. Jung is a major resource in dealing with that "sickness unto death" which is nihilism in our time, "a sickness in comparison with which even death itself may seem like a blessing" (p. 1). Levin insists on this, with an intensity that he thinks requires italics: "*Heidegger's formal analytic of the three dimensions in the Dasein's unfolding self-understanding is very much in need of a corresponding developmental psychology of the Self—a psychology such as Jung's, with the appropriate depth and orientation*" (p. 18).

CHAPTER 6

LITERARY THEORY

I n literary theory, literary history, and literary criticism, Jung
often appears in serial listings as a major figure in the modernist
epoch, or in more discriminating accounts as a significant influence in
the work of a poet, a theorist, or a novelist. In the history of ideas,
there is no escaping the association of Jung with adumbrations of the
collective unconscious, archetypal categories, extrovert and introvert,
and related or unrelated theories of psychological types. When René
Wellek takes up Sainte-Beuve early in volume four of his *History of
Modern Criticism: 1750–1950*, he quotes the mid-nineteenth-century
French critic in an expansive visionary mode in which he looks toward
a future in which Sainte-Beuve "can see links and connections; and a
broader, more luminous, and yet refined spirit may someday discover
the great natural divisions which correspond to the families of the
mind." Wellek sees Sainte-Beuve here as envisaging the characterology
of a modern such as René Le Senne or the "types of world-view defined
by Dilthey, Jaspers, Spranger, and even Jung, as a dim ideal of the
future to which literary study would supply empirical evidence."[1]

Jung's place in such a roll call is an indication of how far he has
come from doing simple duty as Freud's partner in citations or definitions of the place of depth psychology as a major influence in shaping
modern culture. Here he is a Summist of sorts, a maker of a "world-
view" in the German philosophical manner. So it is that Wellek associates him in the following volumes with major figures in the history of
literary ideas, either in his own words, or theirs, or those of other
commentators. He is either the aforementioned significant influence,
or, *mirabile dictu*, no influence at all. D. H. Lawrence is seen by John
Middleton Murry, for example, as producing in his *Fantasia of the
Unconscious* "a criticism of our civilization independent of either

[1]See René Wellek, *A History of Modern Criticism: 1750–1950, Vol. 4: The Later
Nineteenth Century* (New Haven, Conn.: Yale University Press, 1965), pp.
35–36.

Freud or Jung," a view with which not all of us would agree. Herbert Read, who worked with Jung, moves from tentative applications of psychoanalysis in his criticism to more certain use of the understanding of archetypes and the collective unconscious he gathered from his reading of Jung and his direct work with him.

Yeats's early assertion of art, in principle, as "not a 'criticism of life' but a 'revelation of a hidden life'" may seem to "anticipate the collective unconscious of Carl Gustav Jung but could be suggested also by Emerson's Oversoul or the Neoplatonist Anima Mundi." But the fact is that in these words or the emphasis, which Wellek properly sounds, on the "great mind and the great memory," Yeats is speaking in terms inescapably associated with Jung. It is not a matter of influence but rather of a territory so boldly staked out by one man, Jung, that those who move into it, with or without consciousness of his work, can best be understood with precise reference to it. When Wellek takes up T. S. Eliot's dictum that there is no such thing as "nonsense poetry," reminding us of Eliot's insistence that a poem which is "gibberish and has not meaning is no poem . . . merely an imitation of instrumental *music*," he invokes Jung: "Thus the term music suggests the frontiers of poetry and consciousness: the contact of the poet with what we call, since Jung, 'the collective unconscious.'"

Eliot is not, of course, now to be counted a supporter of Jungian interventions in literature. Although he may have approved the reading of some connection between the symbolist movement and the primitive psyche, Wellek is quick to add that "it is inconceivable that Eliot could really accept an irrationalistic mysticism." He will have no part of "the fashionable primitivism of our time and doubts the main assumptions of Jungian symbolism." In support of this last, Wellek cites Eliot, asking what Herbert Read means "by unconscious symbols? If we are unconscious that a symbol is a symbol, then is it a symbol at all? And the moment we become conscious that it is a symbol, is it any longer a symbol?" The Eliot of the 1920s sees the symbol, in Wellek's summation, as "simply the rightly charged word and not a pointing to the supernatural." And although he does make constant use of myth, it is only, says Eliot discussing Joyce's *Ulysses*, as a "way of controlling, ordering, of giving shape and a significance to the immense panorama of futility and anarchy which is contemporary history. . . ." Still, Wellek is bound to add that, for Eliot, "the artist is both old and new. . . . He contains all history which is the essence of his universality."[2] Not a great distance, this, from Yeats's great mind and

[2]See Wellek, *A History of Modern Criticism: 1750–1950*, Vol. 5: *English Criticism, 1900–1950* (New Haven, Conn.: Yale University Press, 1986), pp. 112, 139, 3, 197–198.

great memory – and thus Jung's collective unconscious – filtered through the poet, "the unified sensibility," in Eliot's language.

The historian and philosophical critic Erich Kahler makes sense out of this curious coincidence of meanings in opposing treatments of the symbol, treatments in which Jung's understanding of symbolization figures importantly. "Only consciously formed images are real symbols," Kahler says. But the lines separating unconscious and conscious, "sheer expression and intentional representation," are not sharply defined. And "as Jung has amply demonstrated," Kahler goes on, "archetypal patterns, which operate in the unconscious, pass over into the conscious work of artists, poets, thinkers, who create cultic images." The conclusion is strong, and important for the debate about symbols: "These images, as far as they are *made* and intended as means of communication with divine powers and their worshipers, are actual symbols, capable even of embodying complex doctrines."

Kahler distinguishes between symbols in art and the signifying purpose of images in the natural sciences, where we go well beyond the "imaginable" in diagrams and geometrical figures which abstract rather than represent reality, "to clarify phenomenal or rational complexities through exemplary visual reduction; they are a sort of pictorial metaphor." Only in art does representation "prevail over the signifying act." There the act is embodied in the finished form, so that the image does not stand for or lead to reality; it is "the very figuration of reality," and more, "is in itself a new, independent reality."

Jung, I suspect, would not make such a strong structural distinction between signifying image in science and embodied image in art. He would find the life of the symbol in the pictorial abstractions of science, at least some of the time, for the psyche and its unconscious depths cannot ever be fully suppressed, even by the most austere methodologies or circumscribed forms of image-making. Kahler, for his part, concedes to Jung – and human reality – the existence of "a realm beyond the individually based unconscious," the realm of the collective unconscious. But he finds the term itself "misleading," for "what Jung presents is not a collective but a *generic unconscious* – primal images, primal attitudes, which became established in primordial, mythic ages and repeatedly arise in the psyches of generation after generation." He instances in support of his reading the "graphic picture" to be found in Thomas Mann's *Joseph* novel and the associated lecture of Mann's on Freud where he speaks "of the pre-temporal, time-foreshortening life-in-myth, in which the whole of life is *imitatio*."

Kahler reserves the use of the term *collective unconscious* for what "our collectivized, organizational society" has produced. It is for him a frightening collectivity, "made up of residues of certain clichés, slogans, elements of standardized modes of thinking and acting, which sink in from outside, from modern collective life below the threshold of consciousness, and imperceptibly affect men's characters." In it a power is developing that fights against the generic unconscious "or at any rate weakens it." Jung thought that the unconscious set free would bring healing powers into the world. Kahler sees instead in the "superpressure of the collective upon consciousness, and its forcing of material from consciousness into the unconscious . . . a serious threat to these healing powers."

A further level of the unconscious remains to exert its pressures, what Kahler calls the *existential unconscious*, where we find our "transcendental security." But in a world notable for "the shattering of all faiths" and a "panic-stricken confusion of mind and emotions," the existential has become "the most repressed of all parts of the unconscious" and yet it is still very much with us. We find it "in the stubborn, irrational clinging to discredited doctrines and ersatz ideologies, in the mania of proving oneself by acts of brutality." We have reached the most distant, dark layers of the unconscious only to find ourselves "shattered by the contact." In a world of such violent penetration of the unconscious, a collectivized and "depersonalized" world, we are "more and more . . . astonished that there is such a thing as consciousness at all." The problem is consciousness: "Starting from the vast reaches of the unconscious, we must explore consciousness, must seek to attain and to cling to a consciousness of our present situation."[3]

What Kahler is proposing is something like Eliot's unified sensibility, not for the singular artist now, but as a means of survival for a battered modern collectivity. The terms in both cases – Kahler's employed in an attempt to wrest consciousness out of its punishing sojourn in the limbo of the unconscious; Eliot's, in the service of an answering control and order to a prevailing futility and anarchy – are remarkably close to Jung's. Kahler, with suitable emendation, draws directly from Jung to make his argument. Eliot wants no part of the language of analytical psychology, and expressly banishes the supernatural from his symbolic combat. But as he reminded us, as he made his way to open embrace of the supernatural, between the idea and the reality falls the shadow.

The work of Herbert Read, as poet, critic, and art theorist, cannot be reduced to one set of principles, aesthetic, psychological, philosophi-

---

[3]See Erich Kahler, *Out of the Labyrinth: Essays in Clarification* (New York: Braziller, 1967), pp. 76–77, 158–160. See also Kahler's *The Inward Turn of Narrative*, trans. Richard and Clara Winston, on the expansion of consciousness in the modern into something of ever-increasing complexity, in the Bollingen Series (Princeton, N. J.: Princeton University Press, 1973).

cal, political, whatever. He was, in his later years, an ardent Jungian, one of the editors of the *Collected Works* and perhaps the principal mover in getting the great project under way. But he was also moved by the sense of the individual that he found in Freud and other depth psychologists and was early caught by the reach beyond conscious levels of experience to the unconscious plane that he found in surrealism, what he called superrealism. He was a special pleader for that movement, but at one time or another, he made special and persuasive pleas for all sorts of painters, sculptors, designers, architects, poets, philosophers. He could in 1940 honestly describe himself as "anarchist, romanticist, and agnostic," in contradistinction to the terms of self-identification of his good friend and constant opponent T. S. Eliot — royalist, classicist, and Anglo-Catholic. Yet he edited and greatly admired T. E. Hulme's *Speculations*, as much a classicist statement as is to be found in the annals of early twentieth-century modernism, and anarchist or not, he accepted the honor of knighthood from the British crown, which, it must be added, he fully deserved.

Read is many things. His tastes have a becoming catholicity. Where he does come down sharply is on the side of the modern, eloquently and persuasively, it seems to me, in an exchange of letters with Jung. The psychologist was responding to an essay of Read's published as a pamphlet to celebrate Jung's eighty-fifth birthday. Jung said, in the course of a warm appreciation of Read's essay, speaking of Joyce and Picasso, "Both are masters of the fragmentation of aesthetic contents and accumulators of ingenious shards." Read respectfully turned aside the characterization of these "two great initiators," as Jung called them: "The whole process of fragmentation, as you rightly call it, is not, in my opinion, wilfully destructive: the motive has always been (since the beginning of the century) to destroy the conscious image of perfection (the classical ideal of objectivity) in order to release new forces from the unconscious." The move into interior depths was their attempt to "be put in touch with the Dream, that is to say (as you say) the future." The artist has "dark urges" that he cannot identify. They overwhelm him. "He clutches at fragments, in driftwood and floating rubbish of all kinds. But he has to release the flood in order to get nearer to the Dream." Clearly, whatever Jung's personal tastes, this was an argument he could understand, as he could Read's summation of his strong support for modern art: "that art must die in order to live, that new sources of life must be tapped under the crust of tradition."[4]

It was an old theme with Read that made him a natural ally of

---

[4]See C. G. Jung, *Letters, 2: 1951–1961*, ed. Gerhard Adler and Aniela Jaffé (Princeton, N. J.: Princeton University Press, 1975), pp. 586–592.

Jung's. In his "Mutations of the Phoenix," he appeals to the bird of myth to follow its predestined awakening from its own ashes,

> And soaring in the golden light
> survey the world;
> hover against the highest sky;
> menace men with your strange phenomena.

This was creedal to Read, for whom everything he did as critic, editor, theorist had its source in his work as a poet. Gather the shadow world is his constant injunction; revel in the contrarieties:

> Utter shrill warnings in the cold dawn sky;
> let them descend
> into the shutter'd minds below you.
> Inhabit our wither'd nerves.[5]

He is not often shrill; his is a softer voice. It is also a cautionary one. Fail to heed the promptings of the unconscious, he warns, turn away from the crystallizations of self that come to us in dreams, fragments though they may be, and we lose a major sense of purposiveness in our lives. This is the burden of much in his Norton Lectures at Harvard, *Icon and Idea: The Function of Art in the Development of Human Consciousness*, and especially of the sixth, "Frontiers of the Self." What he asks his listener – and reader – to do is to accept the "existence" of the unconscious, "a level of the psyche that is dynamic and purposive, and that even in a fragmentary presentation, possesses significance as a making conscious of hitherto unknown features of the artist's self. It seems to be an inexhaustible mine of images." As a case in point, he offers the example of Paul Klee, "the artist who has gone farthest in this exploration of the self. . . ." Here in works that are "not necessarily beautiful" we find what is dream and purposiveness and what "we might almost call . . . a cognitive activity. . . ."

Read speaks for the knowledge that is compact in dream and for the wresting of such knowledge into consciousness. "In our time we have had great painters and sculptors, great poets and musicians, and they are precious witnesses to the continued development of human consciousness. I believe that such artists have been representative, and that a Wordsworth, a Proust, a Cézanne, a Klee, a Mondrian, a Schoenberg, and a Stravinsky do make conquests of consciousness that are afterwards occupied by the mind in the widest commonalty." Education must speak to this understanding, should "be conceived as primarily a cultivation of these sensuous activities, as *aesthetic* educa-

[5]See "Mutations of the Phoenix," in Herbert Read, *Collected Poems* (New York: Horizon Press, 1966), pp. 55-60. The quotation is from part 7, p. 59.

tion." Art cannot be reduced to a mere "ornament of civilization," for it "is really a vital activity, an energy of the senses that must continually convert the dead rain of matter into the radiant images of life." If we reach beyond mere animal existence, "if our minds are transfused by a sense of glory and can therefore lift themselves above a brutal sense of nullity, it is because we possess this gift of establishing images, the bright counters of our poetic and philosophic discourse."[6]

The forces arrayed against such education are large and powerful. The more deeply the "vision of the creative mind" searches, the more "strange" it becomes "to mankind in the mass" and the more it "provokes an ever greater resistance in all those who occupy conspicuous positions in the eyes of the mass." There are no short cuts, no easy ways of restoring the poet, the artist, to a position of honor, the special and necessary honor of being heeded in his or her transcriptions and transformations of the old myths. "A deep rift divides the poetic consciousness from the collective instincts of mankind. The poet is an outcast, isolated." The poet turns inward "and analytically self-destructive." The mass responds by ignoring him and, with him, whatever mythology with which he might be working.

Can new myths and symbols appear? "No doubt the new myths will be archetypes of the collective unconscious and therefore of similar structure to the old myths, but they must appear spontaneously in our midst. . . . There can be no new mythology until there is a new iconography, a ritual precipitating new symbols." The crucial question is "whether modern subjectivisim is a state of mind compatible with the mythopoeic process, with the creation of the impersonal and collective myth. . . . Have we carried self-awareness to a stage where symbols no longer have any collective force?"

The answer, if answer there can be, must come where culture normally makes itself known, "in images that move the heart rather than the mind, symbols of sensuous appeal. . . ." Read instances the *Iliad*, the Vedas, the Bible to make his point, but not to hold out hope for a resuscitation of "the most prevalent archetype of Western civilization – the passion of Jesus of Nazareth." For him, the Church has stripped the Passion "of its tragic significance." He offers instead, at least for contemplation, the Homeric image of "the uroboric snake, the primordial ocean ringing the world, the source of creation and of wisdom. . . . It is the Great Round whose significance Erich Neumann has elucidated for us: The Archetypal Feminine, 'which is and contains the universe.' "

The great symbols, that "for the moment lie scattered and con-

---

[6]See Herbert Read, *Icon and Idea: The Function of Art in the Development of Human Consciousness* (New York: Schocken, 1965), pp. 119, 138-140.

fused . . . can be unified and harmonized only by the silent operation of a collective will such as does not exist in the Western world today." Against that disorder, he posits some sense of self that can understand and make some connection to that "archetypal foundation" within it "that is common to Man. . . ." Therein lies "the possible justification of a new concept of humanism."[7]

Read was calling for, hoping for, pleading for some opening to the symbols of reconciliation, the symbols of transformation, upon which his psyche was all but fixated. He was, in effect, linking the symbolic presences of his own life and works—Coleridge, Bergson, Hulme, the poets of romanticism, the painters and sculptors and designers of modernism, Jung. It was an evolving like the creative one that Bergson contemplated, out of an organic rooting in nature of the sort that Read gathered from Coleridge, that he could speak to as possessing the necessary archetypal order which the heart, if not the mind, could understand and accept. It was the power of art he was commending: "Art is the name that we give to the only human activity that can establish a universal order in all we do and make, in thought and in imagination." But this is not, even in its most hopeful moments, to make an idol of art or artist. In his splendidly polemical *To Hell with Culture*, he proposes "that the artist should be abolished: art is not a separate 'profession,' but a quality inherent in all work well done."

Read's proposal springs from a carefully mixed sociology and psychology of art in which a Jungian understanding of consciousness and the unconscious is the shaping force. In the conflict between the will to live and the will to die which defines "the curve of life" of a civilization, "the highest expression of its will to live is a free and original art." But that art, like its practitioners, should not be a thing apart: "in a healthy society the citizens are not too conscious of their 'culture': they create works of art automatically, instinctively." Neither forms nor contents would be dictated. Schools, types, movements, techniques would mix, come together or fall off according to the interests and aptitudes of the individual artists. "Constructivists and superrealists [i.e. surrealists], realists and expressionists, could live and work side by side in perfect amity."

How then do we find value in art? Is there any appropriate measurement? Read finds four measures in general use, either one at a time or in combination: (1) an accepted "canon" such as geometrical proportion or ways of combining color or of organizing bodily relations or architectural orders; (2) human sensibility, the quantity and inten-

[7]See "The Reconciling Image," in Herbert Read, *The Forms of Things Unknown: Essays Towards an Aesthetic Philosophy* (New York: Horizon Press, 1960), pp. 188–205.

sity of "vibrations" elicited by color, texture, composition; (3) "our intuitive apprehension of space and time, and our expression of their relations in rhythm and harmony: our intuition of the absolute values of form"; and (4) our response to the drama and symbolic meaning of a picture, the feelings evoked by an artist's images.

And how do we choose among these measures? We "tend to select the critical approach appropriate to the psychological type to which we belong." It will come as no surprise to learn that the types are Jung's. Read's way of using them is anything but clumsily deterministic: "Whether the wholly harmonious mind exists – the mind equally balanced between thought and feeling, between intuition and sensation – is perhaps doubtful, but surely that is the ideal towards which we ought to strive." If society makes it impossible for such a "complete and harmonious being" to exist, then we should be working to change society to encourage and support that kind of being.

Read's ardent partisanship in support of modern art may be open to criticism – "Perhaps some of us have been guilty of believing blindly in certain phases of modern art, and we may have been emotionally deceived" – but not his understanding of its aim, its "search for reality, for the 'most high truth.'" For him, a particular group of painters, sculptors, poets, musicians, and architects "have been and still are engaged in a spiritual enterprise which may one day be reckoned as a decisive phase in the history of human culture." This is not only the mark of the best of our time, it is "the nature of the creative or mediative activity we call art," something testified to by Plato, Aristotle, Goethe, Coleridge, Buber, and Lawrence among others. They "have agreed that spontaneity, unconsciousness, is the essential condition. 'The most superb mystery we have hardly recognized,' Lawrence called it: 'The immediate, instant self.' 'The fruitful zero,' Buber calls it; 'the headlong powers of utter newness' – an instinct of origination that is autonomous and not derivatory."

That understanding of the unconscious is a necessary prelude to dealing with such a manifestation of our "sick, disgustingly sick" modern society as pornography: "The trouble with sex, Lawrence used to say, is that it has gone to the head. It has become an affair of instruction and understanding: it must be restored to the unconscious." And yet we need understanding to get beyond understanding. Yes, Read says, quoting Lawrence, "we *must* know, if only in order to learn not to know. The supreme lesson of human consciousness is to learn how *not to know*. That is, how not to *interfere*. . . ."

For the artist this means "a conscious effort, an assertion of the self, often an angry protest" against the isolation he feels, the alienation "from his fellow-men and from nature." It is essential for us all that we gather into communal understanding, in some mixture of individual consciousness and the collective unconscious, what Read calls "the aesthetic sense . . . the faculty that enables man to modify the quality of his environment."⁸ It is this that gives a work of art significance, he says in his splendid essay on the sculpture of Henry Moore: the "privileged access" of an artist of the "visionary type" to the collective psyche. His summation here is a gathering in small of almost everything that Read's work, and that of the artists, and the psychology he spoke for, represents, complete with quotation from Jung.

> All people have access to such a realm in their dreams, and a work of art is like a dream in that it presents an image from the artist's unconscious mind and allows us to draw our own conclusions as to its meaning. An artist is a man who can represent his subjective visions in tangible and perceptible form. "He has plunged into the healing and redeeming depths of the collective psyche where man is not lost in the isolation of consciousness and its errors and sufferings, but where all men are caught in a common rhythm which allows the individual to communicate his feelings and strivings to mankind as a whole."⁹

The literary theory of Northrop Frye is for many people associated with Jung because of the high place accorded the archetype in it. But Frye's archetype is not Jung's, as the definition he offers in the glossary of his most systematic presentation of his ideas, *Anatomy of Criticism*, makes clear: "A symbol, usually an image, which recurs often enough in literature to be recognizable as an element of one's literary experience as a whole." Recurrence is the point. Archetypes do not determine; they just keep coming back. They have their own grandeur, but it is not that of causation: "The archetypal view of literature shows us literature as a total form and literary experience as a part of the continuum of life, in which one of the poet's functions is to visualize the goals of human work." There are major duties assigned archetypes in Frye's reading of the literary imagination, for they are "communicable symbols" and at the center of their existence there are "universal symbols." But that is not to say that there is any "archetypal code book which has been memorized by all human societies without exception."

Frye is attempting to present "a comprehensive view" of what literature "actually is doing." He looks toward the happy moment when the student of literature will be able to say that he is learning his

---

⁸See Herbert Read, *To Hell with Culture and Other Essays on Art and Society* (New York: Schocken, 1964), pp. 92–93, 97, 117, 123–125, 150, 167, 165, 193, 175.

⁹See Herbert Read, *Art and Alienation: The Role of the Artist in Society* (New York: Viking, 1969), p. 124.

science, with the important distinction that literature is an "object of study" rather than a subject. Criticism is its special resource, related to it as to all art, as "history is to action and philosophy to wisdom. . . . And just as there is nothing which the philosopher cannot consider philosophically, and nothing which the historian cannot consider historically, so the critic should be able to construct and dwell in a conceptual universe of his own."

One should not construct one's dwelling out of the materials of the determinisms which, in "the absence of systematic criticism" in literature, have "moved in" to fill the "power vacuum" thus created. "It would be easy to compile a long list of such determinisms in criticism, all of them, whether Marxist, Thomist, liberal-humanist, neo-Classical, Freudian, Jungian, or existentialist, substituting a critical attitude for criticism, all proposing, not to find a conceptual framework for criticism within literature, but to attach criticism to one of a miscellany of frameworks outside it." In the study of literature, we have the choice of accepting "the principle of polysemous meaning," what we might call a judicious pluralism, or of electing one of the competing determinisms or "neighboring disciplines" and then trying "to prove that all the others are less legitimate." Anthropology and psychology have their uses in the work of archetypal critics as they face "ritual and dream": in particular, "the work done on the ritual basis of naive drama in Frazer's *Golden Bough*, and the work done on the dream basis of naive romance by Jung and the Jungians. . . ." But one must be on guard against "the danger of determinism." And as for explaining "the communicability of archetypes . . . by a theory of a collective unconscious," that, says Frye, is "an unnecessary hypothesis in literary criticism, so far as I can judge."

Jung does have his uses for Frye. He can offer, with others, "reference tables" for alchemical symbols, but not much more—"the atmosphere of oracular harrumph" about typologies and paradigms, "which recurs in some forms of archetypal criticism, is not much to the point." Jung has a place, too, along with Joseph Campbell and Lord Raglan, as backing of a sort for Frye's postulation of "a central unifying myth" of which the "four *mythoi* . . . comedy, romance, tragedy, and irony, may now be seen as four aspects. . . ." Freud is "most suggestive" for the literary critic in the theory of comedy, Jung in the theory of romance. Jung really comes into his own, in Frye's gingerly treading of psychoanalytical paths, in his discussion of what he calls the archetypal masque. He means by the masque, following an old tradition, "A species of drama in which music and spectacle play an important role and in which the characters tend to be or become aspects of human personality rather than independent characters." Time and space are not localized in the archetypal masque. We are "in a world of human types, which at its most concentrated becomes the interior of the human mind." Frye's instances are old morality plays, *Everyman*, and, at least by implication, the modern theater of Maeterlinck, Pirandello, Andreyev, and Strindberg.

Because in "such a setting, characterization has to break down into elements and fragments of personality," his use of the word *archetype* here is "in Jung's sense of an aspect of the personality capable of dramatic projection." And so for him, "Jung's persona and anima and counsellor and shadow throw a great deal of light on the characterization of modern allegorical, psychic, and expressionist dramas, with their circus barkers and wraith-like females and inscrutable sages and obsessed demons." By the same reasoning, it seems to me, Jung's constructions are helpful to our understanding of the drama that followed what Frye is describing, in small or large detail and in theatrical spirit, the theater of the absurd, the work of Ionesco, Beckett, Pinter, Stoppard, Genet, and their followers and imitators. The pages that follow, in which Frye examines the epiphanic drama in and out of Scripture and then treats the "thematic forms" of lyric and epos, show how skillfully Frye can move among "neighboring disciplines" without falling into the dreaded determinist trap.

The "poem of community" leads to that "cardinal point of the lyric" which he has already defined "as the charm or response to some kind of physical or quasi-physical compulsion," from nursery rhymes "through college yells, sing-songs, and similar forms of participation mystique." A parallel line of development is the genre of "commandment or exhortation," with its high point in the sermon and panegyric. In the celebration through "elegy or threnody on the death of a hero, friend, leader or mistress" of poets following ancient oratorical ritual, there often is "a strong tendency to mythological expansion: the subject is not only idealized but often exalted into a nature-spirit or dying god."

These are not simply felicitous readings or good passing insights. They are parts—impressive ones, I think—of a systematic attempt to recapture the past, or at least significant elements in it, for a working critical present. In his "Tentative Conclusion," Frye likens himself to the reader of *Finnegans Wake* who must fill out the "metaphorical identifications" that the dreamer of that great nightwork has failed to make or has forgotten, becoming in relation to the *Wake* and all such undertakings what Joyce prescribed, the "ideal reader suffering from an ideal insomnia," that is to say, the critic. Frye then allows himself a splendid claim, which approaches and without noticeable embarrassment even echoes the grandiose conclusion of *A Portrait of the Artist as a Young Man*: "Some such activity as this of reforging the broken links between creation and knowledge, art and science, myth and concept, is what I envisage for criticism." Lest this bring him too close to that shelter which, in a manner of speaking, Jung would only too easily offer him, even though he remains so uneasy about offering it to Jung, he softens the claim, without altogether withdrawing it: "Once more, I am not speaking of a change of direction or activity in criticism: I mean only that if critics go on with their own business, this will appear to be, with increasing obviousness, the social and practical result of their labors."[10]

The ardors of Jungian extremists in the literary jungles, exactly of the kind Frye feared, are elegantly satirized in Douglas Bush's "Mrs. Bennet and the Dark Gods: The Key to Jane Austen." So skillfully does that doughty old Harvard scholar perform his task that professionals in the field have been known, when not warned by their own inner voices or the louder cautions of friends, to be taken in. "The revolutionary exponents of archetypal myth," Bush informs us, "who have revealed unsuspected depths in many familiar works of literature, have quite failed to see Jane Austen's essential affinity with Melville and Kafka." The Gurney Professor of English at Harvard proposes to remedy the failure, for he is persuaded that even a "brief examination of the occult structuring of *Pride and Prejudice* will establish Jane Austen's claim to be the first great exemplar of the modern mythic consciousness." Not clear on the surface? Why, that's just as it should be: "it is of the essence of the mythic technique that it should be at least half unconscious. . . . In mythic criticism the great thing is to find some semi-submerged rocks to stand on." And how Bush does find them!

We start with Mr. Bingley, the "highly eligible bachelor" who offers the five marriageable daughters of the Bennets such tempting prospects. He plays Dionysus to Mr. Bennet's Pentheus, the Theban king "who resisted the newcomer and was torn to pieces by the Maenads, led by his own mother." But Mr. B is protean in the Austen archetypal world: "as an intellectual and the parent of five daughters,"

---

[10]See Northrop Frye, *Anatomy of Criticism: Four Essays* (Princeton, N. J.: Princeton University Press, 1957), pp. 365, 115, 118, 11–12, 6, 12, 72, 193, 108, 111–112, 359–361, 192, 214, 366, 291, 295–296, 354. See also Frye's review of *Man and Time: Papers from the Eranos Yearbooks* and five books by Eliade, "World Enough Without Time," in *Northrop Frye on Culture and Literature*, ed. R. D. Denham (Chicago: University of Chicago Press, 1978), and especially "Forming Fours," on Jung's *Two Essays on Analytical Psychology* and *Psychology and Alchemy*, where, after making a connection to Goethe and Blake, he concludes, "With this additional connecting link, we can see that Jung's book [*Psychology and Alchemy*] is not a mere specious paralleling of a defunct science and one of several Viennese schools of psychology, but a grammar of literary symbolism which for all serious students of literature is as important as it is endlessly fascinating" (p. 129).

he is Adonis as Edmund Spenser described him, "the father of all Forms," and his wife, in this persona-relationship, is Spenser's Venus, "simply unformed Matter." However that is not all for Bennet mère: "she is Dionysiac in her devotion to Bingley." The crucial characters, Elizabeth and Darcy, are a younger Venus and Adonis, threatened by a variety of Boar-Bores. The book when read in Jungo-Bungo fullness offers many splendors, such as a possible association of Elizabeth's uncle, Mr. Gardiner, to Adam and to the Fisher King—"and what," Bush asks temptingly, "of the veiled phallicism in the allusion to fishing tackle?" Although there are no deaths of central characters here or elsewhere in Austen, there is "a dark mythic background of death," a plentiful "stress on physical frailty," enough of seasonal coming and going to support a pattern of death and rebirth if one looks hard enough, and a plausible casting of Darcy in the role of a "saving Hercules" who rescues one daughter and marries another, if anything in this sort of reading can ever be called plausible. Bush concludes, "The subject of archetypal myth in Jane Austen needs a book, and will doubtless get one."

The wild lengths to which archetypalists will go are surely no greater than those of maddened structuralists or deconstructionists. To say that is not to excuse them but only to indicate how attractive the gaudy extravagances of fixed systems and set vocabularies are to those who should know better. It is particularly sad to see this sort of possession by flashy jargon and method in archetypal and myth criticism. For archetypes and myths offer only models of approach to understanding, not a fixed content, as Jung's own practice shows. His psychological types and functions are modal and generously suggestive but not commanding categories. If this is true in the analytical encounter, how much more so must it be in the half-conscious and semi-submerged world of literary character and event.

Bush entertainingly suggests Jane Austen's "essential affinity with Kafka and Melville." There are endless examples of hunts for submerged meanings in Kafka and Melville with Jungian guide in hand.[11] Anthony Storr, a British analyst and academic, quickly sets limits for himself in a paper on "Kafka's Sense of Identity," explaining that he approaches "the study of Kafka from the point of view of a psychiatrist rather than that of a literary scholar." Nevertheless, what he gives us, in an essay of exemplary economy, is altogether acceptable as literary scholarship, as he draws the fugitive childhood of the writer into the threatening worlds of *The Trial* and *The Castle*. The world of archetype and myth that Storr finds here is the one created by the

---

[11]See Douglas Bush, *Engaged and Disengaged* (Cambridge, Mass.: Harvard University Press, 1966), pp. 20–26.

writer to affirm himself, to ward off the threat of "psychotic phantasy," and in the act of writing to find his "means of communication" and retain "contact with others, albeit at a distance."

Storr brings together Jung, William James, and Erik Erikson in the opening paragraphs of his paper, all of them in support of "the experience of being positively, fully oneself, without equivocation or pretence, and they are affirming that this experience is fulfilling and life-enhancing." Erikson and James are logical, tidy, and altogether relevant in the citations Storr makes, the one speaking of "a suggestive sense of invigorating sameness and continuity," the other of the way in which a man's character becomes apparent to him "in the mental and moral attitude" in which he feels himself "most deeply and intensely active and alive. . . . moments [when] there is a voice inside which speaks and says: 'This is the real me.' " Jung speaks to the same point, Storr says, when he writes, "Personality is the supreme realization of the innate idiosyncrasy of a living being. It is an act of high courage flung in the face of life, the absolute affirmation of all that constitutes the individual, the most successful adaptation to the universal conditions of existence, coupled with the greatest possible freedom for self-determination."

Jung here speaks of the human personality as he does of the living symbol. Each one has his or her or its own individual life. Each one, personality or symbol, can be found and described at some point in its existence as sui generis. At that point, it is self-determined, self-affirmed. That is the answer to the nonsense of the archetypalists and myth collectors parodied by Douglas Bush in his transformation of Jane Austen's light-centered world into dark undersea maunderings.

Whether from critic or novelist, archetypalist or myth collector, literature is neither made nor found except where it discovers "the innate idiosyncrasy of a living being." That is what Storr does, speaking both as critic and analyst, seeing Kafka "driven to affirm his identity through writing," and then becoming more confident "through recognition of his talent by others, and their acceptance of the self which manifested itself in his stories." One learns much about Kafka and his characters this way, about the extent to which his writing is "bound up with the more pathological parts of his personality."[12] None of them becomes a predetermined fixture in an archetypal scene, a counterpart to figures imprisoned in an inflexible understanding of

[12]Anthony Storr, "Kafka's Sense of Identity," in *Paths and Labyrinths: Nine Papers from a Kafka Symposium*, ed. J. P. Stern and J. J. White (London: Institute of Germanic Studies, University of London, 1985), pp. 1, 21, 23. The Jung quotation is from *CW*, vol. 17, p. 171, par. 289.

myth. None of them, writer or character, becomes any less idiosyncratic, any less his or her own set of colors.

Anton Ehrenzweig coined the term *poemagogic* to stand in some
fashion for the various ways of "inducing and symbolizing the ego's
creativity." His extended exhibit for this understanding is drawn in his
book *The Hidden Order of Art* from the work of Marion Milner, but he
sees a high place for Jung as perhaps the only one before her who
"grasped the poemagogic quality" of Sir James Frazer's reconstruc-
tions of the primordial world in his *Golden Bough.* In Jung's theory,
Ehrenzweig says, "the images become 'archetypes' watching over creative processes of integration." It is only a passing mention in a long,
thoughtful, detailed attempt at a psychology of the work of art. But it
is germane here, in its author's need to find a special word, if one
uncomfortably redolent of jargon, and it is fair-minded in its indication
of Jung's early understanding of the psychology of art of the poemagogic. It is not fully satisfying to Ehrenzweig himself, however, any more
than is Jung's anticipation of Melanie Klein's "findings about the pre-
oedipal mother." He tells us that "the ordered progress of a complex
science like psycho-analysis is not helped by boldly anticipating leaps.
I myself was not really helped by Rank, Graves or Jung. The stratifica-
tion of poemagogic imagery is too complex for that."[13]

In fact, I would suggest that anticipations of this sort, whatever
their limitations, are central to the development of psychoanalysis,
whether it is to be described as "a complex science" or art or some
remarkable amalgam of art, philosophy, anthropology, medicine, and
whatever else may have come floating up through the half-conscious
and semi-submerged worlds of its founders and developers. It does not
matter that it took so long to recognize and chart the large roles played
in the drama of psychoanalysis by Goethe and Nietzsche, Carus,
Eduard von Hartmann, Bachhofen, and so many others in the generations before Freud and Jung. Their "boldly anticipating leaps" left
footprints in the psychoanalytical soil and in the development of the
arts. When the time came, they were found; the footprints were walked
in; they were greatly useful, whether as indicators of the right paths or
to show how not to go.

---

[13]See Anton Ehrenzweig, *The Hidden Order: A Study in the Psychology of Artistic Imagination* (Berkeley, Calif.: University of California Press, 1971), pp. 176,
181.

In 1900, Yeats addressed the way Shelley "allowed the subconscious life to lay its hands so firmly upon the rudder of his imagination" and associated himself with the experience:

> Any one who has any experience of any mystical state of the soul knows how there float up in the mind profound symbols, whose meaning, if indeed they do not delude one into the dream that they are meaningless, one does not perhaps understand for years. Nor I think has any one, who has known that experience with any constancy, failed to find some day in some old book or on some old monument, a strange or intricate image, that had floated up before him, and to grow perhaps dizzy with the sudden conviction that our little memories are but part of some great memory that renews the world and men's thoughts age after age, and that our thoughts are not, as we suppose, the deep but a little foam upon the deep.[14]

Graham Hough, in the moving essay on Yeats which concludes his book on *The Last Romantics*, calls this "a surprising anticipation" of Jung and the collective unconscious, which Yeats seemed "to know about" when he "came to write the preface to *The Words upon the Window-pane*." But that was thirty-four years later. He had made his footprints in that great path long before he could connect the path itself to a name and a theory. He knew, too, of the long line of anticipations of his experience which were compact in what he was to call the Anima Mundi or Spiritus Mundi. In the great gathering of images, phrases, organized writings, disorganized fragments, which is The Soul or Spirit of the World, "One must allow the words and pictures to pass before you linked by certain associations." Yeats cites Goethe in support of this assertion when the German poet explains to a friend something of basic poetic process: "If one is critical too soon," Goethe wrote, images "will not form at all." Thus Yeats quotes Shelley in that 1900 essay: "Those who are subject to the state called reverie, feel as if their nature were resolved into their being," and comments that Shelley "must have expected to receive thoughts and images from beyond his own mind."

In this bold anticipation of Yeats's, as Hough describes it, "he derives the power of symbolism from its ability to cut through all modern experience and chatter about contemporary interests to the emotions and experiences that are eternally recurrent and are primitive in human life." The parallels "are sufficiently obvious. Yeats's Anima Mundi from which the images of the poet are derived is Jung's collective unconscious, from which come the archetypes of myth and legend. Yeats's mask is the unconscious, in Jung's sense, not in

---

[14]See William Butler Yeats, "The Philosophy of Shelley's Poetry," in his *Essays* (New York: Macmillan, 1924), p. 96.

Freud's—not the waste-paper basket for discarded experiences and desires, but the vehicle of the buried faculties, those which are unused in the conscious life." The power of the mask corresponds, Hough asserts, to the "psychic rebirth" which for Jung comes with the freeing of the buried faculties.

The peroration that follows says a good deal about Yeats and even more about Jung. It contains the answer to the fatuities of those literalists of archetype and myth who are properly taken to task in Bush's satire and at the same time counters Ehrenzweig's dissatisfaction with "boldly anticipating leaps." Those leaps, after all, keep us in touch with the Anima Mundi or collective unconscious, not allowing its rich provender to fall away from us for want of a language of clear identification. Anticipators in the world of the unconscious or the poemagogic or the Anima Mundi bring us connection, for they are easily recognized and understood by others of the same species who come after them. What they must also find then are just the right others to put what they have found in the right places. So Hough says it very well:

> So great a mythologist as Yeats needs another mythologist to interpret him, and Jung's mythopoeic faculty is very much of the same kind. Like Yeats he is unsatisfied by the established religious formulas, yet is profoundly concerned with religion; like Yeats he uses sub-rational or supra-rational intuitions to complete the thin and abstract picture of the world given by logic and the senses. We find in both the same fertility and the same obscurity about the exact status of the myth. When Jung explains ecstatic and mystical experience in terms of the unconscious we feel the same uncertainty as we do when Yeats talks about "the condition of fire." Into what country are we being led? Are Byzantium and the collective unconscious psychological or metaphysical entities? All remains obscure, but involved with the obscurity is a sense of richness and adequacy, the antithesis of the cheap desire to explain away what cannot be immediately understood; and it is perhaps not an accident that the closest analogy to Yeats's thought is to be found in the work of the psychologist who has done most justice to the depth and variety of human experience.[15]

Hough salutes here what Alex Comfort mocked, the apparent replacement of one mystique by another, "Yeats instead of Aquinas." Of course this is not a replacement but a continuation. Whether one accepts Yeats's language or finds more ease in Jung's or looks to discover another rhetoric or poetic or depth psychology, if one has any

---

[15]See Graham Hough, *The Last Romantics* (London: Duckworth, 1949), pp. 229, 261–262.

sense of how far down the roots of the modern go, one must ultimately come to some such formulation as this one.

For all those reasons and many more, Yeats and Jung are natural companions, but in life they were "strangers" to each other, as James Olney says in the introduction to his book *The Rhizome and the Flower: The Perennial Philosophy—Yeats and Jung*. There are fly-specks in the papers of the two men that suggest something like a meeting, but in fact they never met, probably never read each other or even much about the other. Still, the closeness of idea, conviction, understanding, inflection of thought and feeling are unmistakable. Both were fixated upon the conflicts, coincidences, and mergings of opposites, on archetypes and archetypal symbols, on the inner voice that each called the *daimon*, on typologies of persons and stages in history that seemed to possess a cyclical character. Olney sets these forth in a useful list that begins with the parallels between Jung's collective unconscious and Yeats's *anima mundi*, and between the personal unconscious and *anima hominis*.

These resemblances and equivalences, engaging or provocative as they may be, are not what draw them together for Olney, however. Wisely, he does not offer a comparative study, reading each through the work of the other. As he says, "Yeats had no great love for psychology; Jung had even less for what he called 'modern art,' and modern poetry he found especially offensive." And so he chooses the precise methods neither of psychology nor of literary criticism, although he uses the resources of both at various times. His procedure is to look for the common root system, the mass of rhizomes below ground from which the great Yeatsian and Jungian flowerings spring. It is not a metaphor invented by Olney. Both men speak in just these terms in describing what is perennial in their worlds, as the book's epigraphs show. From Yeats, "symbols, blossoms, as it were, growing from invisible immortal roots, hands, as it were, pointing the way into some divine labyrinth." From Jung, "What we see is the blossom, which passes. The rhizome remains."

We start in the tracing of the roots with the pre-Socratic philosophers who were so important for Plato, Pythagoras, Heracleitus, Parmenides; then we find the great weaving round of their stems in the Platonic rootstock. All remain important throughout the book, but the commanding figure is Plato: "The philosophic-poetic system for which Yeats speaks and the philosophic-psychic system for which Jung speaks are to the comprehensive historic-philosophic, psychic-poetic system for which Plato, his predecessors, and his successors speak as flowers to a perennial rhizome." In spite of a row of hyphenated adjectives that seem like a burlesque in imitation of Polonius, there is good sense here, as there is in the use of the last sentences of Plato's

Timaeus to conclude the book. We have been in a world of real and of would-be mystery, of would-be and of real wisdom. Olney's paraphrase of Yeats says it: "The poet descends continually into the world of becoming that he may rescue therefrom that sad bundle of accidents that does sit down to breakfast, transform the bundle into the essence of his own personality, and with it reascend to the world of being." It is the Platonic posture, rooting in the shadows to find substance, discovering the eternal through ephemera, pushing endlessly at the gates that are never fully open, the gates of the unconscious, to bring being into consciousness and consciousness into being. "So it remained for Jung to redo in our century what his alchemical and Gnostic predecessors had done four, eight, and sixteen centuries earlier—i.e., mine the depths and draw those contents back up from beneath the surface where history and individual prudence had forced them."

Yeats found his adumbrations of permanence often enough sitting in his square tower. Jung found his, as often as not, in his round tower. Some of what this means Olney gathers under the nicely turned rubric of "The Poetics of Mummy Wheat," speaking of "chthonic and forgotten truths, long-buried and long-neglected in the tomb" in terms of a figure drawn from a poem Yeats wrote about his son, "Conjunctions":

> If Jupiter and Saturn meet,
> What a crop of mummy wheat!

The ancient truths are found again, processed, made into the bread of life. It is a mode of transformation, as Olney describes another poem by Yeats—"Among School Children"—one of Jungian dimension, or more precisely of that metamorphosis which all votaries of the perennial philosophy look to achieve: "Through an intensity of memory, reverie, and mythifying imagination in the central stanzas, Yeats transforms the commonplace 'real world' of the first stanza into the Platonic 'really real' world of the final stanza."

Olney follows the metaphor where it leads in Jung, for Jung also "harvested a great crop of old mummy wheat, which he first formed into the visionary loaves of *Septem Sermones ad Mortuos* and then baked into the bread that he called 'analytical psychology.' " Under the heading of "Psychology of the Pleroma," Jung's pursuit of a fullness of understanding of the spiritual universe, of its root and its flower, is shown as both drawing him close to Yeats and pulling him apart. There are commanding descriptions: "Hear, then, the ancient unconscious becoming conscious in the person of Jung, posing as the long-deceased but now resurrected Basilides of Alexandria ('where the East toucheth the West'), preaching to his unruly, even rather disrespectful, collection of the dead." There are cautions: "as Basilides tells his audience or as Jung told his patients, the unconscious, when undirected by consciousness, spells destruction." There is the large question—metaphysical, poetic, psychological—which we all come to in these precincts: "How does the vital but mad swarm of the Pleroma, where everything is everything else, ever sort itself out to become that unique, separated, and individual self that Jungian psychology holds to be the ideal end (and paradoxically also the beginning) of all psychic process?" And there are the many oblique answers, which tell us something about how to live with the question, even if they do not come close to discharging it, such as Yeats's: "Our imaginations are but fragments of the universal imagination, portions of the universal body of God, and as we enlarge our imagination by imaginative sympathy, and transform with the beauty and peace of art the sorrows and joys of the world, we put off the limited mortal man more and more and put on the unlimited 'immortal man.'" The parallel in Jung is equally oblique, as Olney describes it, but more of an answer to the question:

> This old phylogenetic being, whose psychic development is recapitulated in each of us individually, stands, in Jung's eyes, very close to God; and when we dream the Jungian Big Dream, it is not easy to say whether it is a dream of God or of the Great Man, since, for Jung, God is a psychic experience, present to us as an *imago Dei*, an archetype, and when the dream is an affair of two-million-year-old psyche, then the *imago* will be so infinitely expanded that it will be nearly indistinguishable from *Deus*.

The somewhat ironic tone Olney adopts here—"the Jungian Big Dream"—is not a dismissal of the Jungian metaphysic, nor in the brisk discussion that follows is he making small the "kind of hopefulness" with which Jung proposes "a psychic nullification of time" or, in an even more curious phrase, the idea of a "relative eternality." Jung's understanding of "the other world" is founded on his "experience of *this* world" and both are for him "psychologically determined . . . and so his eternity inevitably bears the coloring of time." Jung's shrewd distinction here is between the religious attitude, which "puts the accent on the imprinter" of archetypes, and the psychological one, which "emphasizes the *typos*, the imprint—the only thing it can understand." There is, I must say, something disingenuous about the final disclaimer—the psychologist, even the scientific one that Jung is telling us he represents, is not limited, either by professional obligation or imagination, to positivist procedure, to so-called scientific method, as Jung himself demonstrates again and again. The distinction remains, however, and it does point to a significant difference in strategy, separating those commanded by a poetic or philosophical urge from those, however much their imaginations may incline them toward the religious and the metaphysical, who feel impelled to confine themselves to what they have observed.

Olney's concluding sentences in this, his penultimate chapter, remind us that both strategies serve the same purpose. They also sum up the value of his book and support the proposition that to understand what these figures, Yeats and Jung, represent, neither literary criticism nor psychological analysis will do, that a third language must be found that in its "syntax and grammar" is sufficiently like the grammar and syntax of the poetics of the first and the psychology of the second.

> Perhaps we would do well to leave this tangled question with the observation that there is a hen (or a swan?) and there is an egg; there is a rhizome and there are multifold blossoms; there is eternity (at least "relative eternity") and there is time; there are Forms that provide the paradigm on which the cosmos was created and on which its continued existence depends, and there are archetypes that have been precipitated out of human existence for aeons, and continue to be so precipitated out, and yet these archetypes are coextensive with our psychic existence and determine that existence. The Pleroma, whose service we all must do in these matters, forbids us to make any statements that would be harder, more purely sensible, and less tinged with the nonsensical than this.[16]

The psychological and metaphysical constantly run into each other. The fact that those strongly addicted to the one often shudder at the other is of little consequence to those who follow a Yeats, a Jung, or an Aquinas into the worlds of interiority. What comes this way, as Hough says, is "a sense of richness and adequacy, the antithesis of the cheap desire to explain away what cannot be immediately understood." It is not wrong to call it a mystique, or better still, a *participation mystique*. It leads to knowledge by the deepest sort of association, "participatory knowledge" as Stephen R. L. Clark calls it in his *From*

---

[16]See James Olney, *The Rhizome and the Flower: The Perennial Philosophy — Yeats and Jung* (Berkeley, Calif.: University of California Press, 1980), pp. 6–8, 370, 129, 245, 285, 288, 297, 303–304, 340, 343–344, 8, 345. The rhizome turns up a number of times in Jung. His attachment to it as signifying symbol is succinctly presented in the opening pages of the autobiography: "Life has always seemed to me like a plant that lives on its rhizome. The true life is invisible, hidden in the rhizome. The part that appears above ground lasts only a single summer. Then it withers away — an ephemeral apparition . . . I have never lost a sense of something that lives and endures underneath the eternal flux. What we see is the blossom, which passes. The rhizome remains." (*Memories, Dreams, Reflections*, p. 4) See also Jung, *Alchemical Studies, CW*, vol. 13, pp. 194–196, pars. 241–243.

Athens to Jerusalem: The Love of Wisdom and the Love of God, a book based on his Gifford lectures.

Clark defines such knowing as "the process of living with the same life as those we would know," which "enables us to know from within what we could not otherwise know at all." One reaches to a reality here that "cannot be known merely externally." For Clark, following directions set by theists and semi-theists, "the principles and powers of the world are not merely 'out there,' but here within." It is a falsification to see these knowings as "psychological constructions." Rather, he says, "we, as we normally conceive ourselves to be, are the psychological constructions." Jung understood this, Clark suggests, "though he does not seem entirely to have understood it." The example of Jung's understanding of this "truth" is his 1958 dream of unidentified flying objects shaped like lenses that were transformed into magic lanterns pointed at him, as reported in his autobiography. Not quite emerged from his dream, Jung speculates: "We always think that the UFOs are projections of ours. Now it turns out that we are their projections. I am projected by the magic lantern as C. G. Jung. But who manipulates the apparatus?"

Poor Jung, doomed to have partial understanding, even when he sees the truth! Clark does not specify where Jung has gone off. Perhaps it is that he would not be able to follow Clark "entirely" when the latter says, speaking of that Best which it is beyond us fully to take in: "We 'know' by participating in the one straight way, by turning from the distractions of the demon-world." Jung's demon-world, if not always to be welcomed with open hand and heart, was never altogether to be turned from. The demon's voice must be heard. The shadow must be claimed. He would agree with Clark that "to love is to be wise," and perhaps would go along with the accompanying conclusion that those who find their own centers also discover the center of "all other life, the source from which all things get such strength as they have," and in so doing are in themselves "the ones who are the voice of the divine." But theirs is not, a Jung or a Yeats or even an Aquinas would say, the only voice. Participatory knowledge which acknowledges as worthy of contemplative examination even lens-shaped UFOs will find a better way than simply "turning from the distractions of the demon-world."[17] It will not stand beaming with jolly expectations in the face of all the madnesses that inhabit our fantasy lives, but neither will it see as a threat to its psychology the impoverished imaginings that have been thrown up by comic books and television and films shrunk to the same level. If our demons are such poor things, then that must be duly

---

[17]See Stephen R. L. Clark, *From Athens to Jerusalem: The Love of Wisdom and the Love of God* (Oxford: Clarendon Press, 1984), p. 194.

noted. If they are somehow satisfying to millions, as manifestly the two-dimensional figures of filmdom's galactic wars and extraterrestrial melted-rubber dolls such as E.T. have been, then that too must be dealt with. In Jung's terms, it means holding open to speculation the possibility that we may be their projections at least as much as they are ours. That is the way of the poet and all other artists according to Jung, even those of the pop-film and comic-book variety.

What is particularly difficult for many in Jung's recursive thinking is that the ambivalences and ambiguities of some events seem to make these events, in which apparently unrelated or even contradictory occurrences come together, into self-created conjunctions. Causes seem to disappear, or rather to be a part of their effects, not something separate and anterior to them. Alan Gould, dealing with "Attempts to Explain ESP," puts it succinctly: "Jung holds that ESP [extra-sensory perception] and kindred phenomena demonstrate the existence in the universe of a form of order not hitherto explicitly recognized, a form of order which is totally different from the causal order in which scientists and philosophers of science have commonly traded." In spite of the difficulties he has with Jung's "doctrine" of archetypes and the diffidence he feels in attempting to interpret Jung, Gould finds very interesting Jung's notion of the way we achieve rather than "acquire" certain knowledge, take into us or discover in ourselves information which cannot even be said to "arrive." He quotes Jung: "However incomprehensible it may appear, we are finally compelled to assume that there is in the unconscious something like an a priori knowledge or immediate presence of events which lacks any causal basis." This Gould calls anomalous knowledge. It has fascinating possibilities for theories and theorists of the paranormal, psychokinesis, precognition, and all the rest of that world of odd experiences or fantasized phenomena, dubious to so many, and just as intriguing to so many others, to philosophers of the quality of William James and C. D. Broad, and not merely for those whose crackpot language or personalities would seem to put them off-limits for any serious discussion and to ally them only with comic-book and science fiction. Gould rises above such dismissive groupings in his generous conclusion: "It is perhaps possible that in the end synchronistic a priori knowledge will prove as interesting, and every bit as perplexing, to philosophers as synthetic a priori knowledge."[18]

---

[18]See Alan Gould, "Attempts to Explain ESP," in *Readings in the Philosophical Problems of Parapsychology*, ed. Anthony Flew (Buffalo, N. Y.: Prometheus Books, 1987), pp. 79, 83–84. This area of exploration of what Gould says might be called "aberrant beliefs" is a mine field for Jungians but one that must be entered when questions of a Jungian approach to the literary or aesthetic imagination are broached. There is Jung's celebrated – and sometimes derided – essay

What he is telling us is that Jung has strayed into Kantian fields
and found a new category of being, perhaps, where paradoxes, antitheses, antinomies, and apparent contradictions-in-terms live happily side
by side. The identifying tone is reconciliation, if not out and out resolution in which the active ingredient is the imagination. Albert Rothenberg, a clinical professor of psychiatry at the Yale Medical School and
director of research at the Austen Riggs Center, gives the name of
"janusian thinking" to this sort of thinking, where conscious process is
related to synchronicity. In his book *The Emerging Goddess: The Creative Process in Art, Science and Other Fields*, he defines such thinking procedure as a matter of "actively conceiving two or more opposite
antithetical ideas, images, or concepts simultaneously." These opposites exist "side by side" and are "equally operative and equally true."
Inherent in creativity, this sort of thinking is not to be confused with
"dialectical thinking, ambivalence, and the thought processes of children or of schizophrenics." Rather, "it is the mirror image of a dream
quality and of primary process thought."

What Rothenberg is describing is not to be understood, for all its
primary-process and dream characteristics, as simply working from or

on "Flying Saucers: A Modern Myth of Things Seen in the Skies" (*CW*, vol. 10).
There is his belief in reincarnation, attested to by the Jungian analyst Erlo van
Waveren, himself a believer in "rebirth": "I once spoke to Professor Jung about
this subject, and later his wife came to me and said, 'Don't talk to anyone about
this, the time isn't right for it.' That was in 1950, and I also had a warning dream
that told me not to speak openly about this." See Jonathan Cott, *The Search for
Omm Sety: Reincarnation and Eternal Love* (New York: Doubleday, 1987), p. 204.
What is involved in Jung's unwillingness to reject out of hand the world of "aberrant beliefs," in UFO's, reincarnation, and the like, is less a literal-minded acceptance of them than that response to history and archetypal continuity that Eliade
deals with in *The Myth of the Eternal Return*, trans. Willard Trask, published in
the Bollingen Series (New York: Pantheon, 1954). Eliade speaks of the simultaneous discovery by "modern man and historical man" of both "personal freedom and
continuous time (in place of cyclical time)." The crucial discovery is that "In the
horizon of archetypes and repetition, the terror of history, when it appeared, could
be supported" (p. 161). A similar understanding, though with the bias of a physicist, is to be found in the writings of Jean E. Charon, who says that "Jung's ideas
of the 'archetype' and the 'collective unconscious' come to us along the path of
genetics and space-time." He stresses what is a fact for him, that we can know the
archetype "through its translation into symbols." For him, "It is supremely important that man should be able to 'give birth to' his own unconscious archetypes by
giving them conscious symbolic expression." See Charon's *Man in Search of Himself*, trans. J. E. Anderson (New York: Walker, 1967), pp. 88, 99, 203. See also, for
a prolonged speculation on the possibility of including "the Spirit . . . in the range
of scientific phenomena," Charon's *The Unknown Spirit* (London: Coventure,
1983). There, elaborating on his conviction that "a part of the unconscious memory can, under certain conditions, gradually become conscious memory," he
asserts the belief "that our 'conscious I' not only communicates with the 'unconscious I' but also with the data memorised by the electrons exterior to the body,
those which are enclosed in the bodies of others, and in all that constitutes our
'outer' world" (pp. 14, 109).

participating in the life of the unconscious. Janusian thinking is, in fact, "a special type of secondary process operation." While its materials "resemble the reversals and multiple opposites found in dreams," Rothenberg tells us, "its psychological characteristics and functions are the obverse of dreaming." The creator has a clear end in view. He may unearth quantities of unconscious stuff, but his is secondary-process cognition "which obeys the rules of ordinary logic," for "janusian thinking occurs during full consciousness and with full rationality. . . ."

Janusian thinking "does not involve a synthesis"; it involves "simultaneity of opposites or antitheses rather than sequence." What is clear, in the almost impossibly shrouded world of art and artist and all related creators and creations, is that opposites coinhere in significant ways in the creative process. Rothenberg confines his understanding of the creative to the "great individual achievements" that seem to spring from the heads of their creators full grown, as in Greek myth Athena does from the head of Zeus. She, "the emerging goddess," stands for the "grand works" that "do not seem to traverse the ordinary pathways of gestation and delivery."[19] Jung, in contradistinction, with a less sharply marked borderline between the conscious and the unconscious and a perhaps more open understanding of the incidence of creativity in small as well as grand works, offers us, in his speculations about synchronicity, a meditation on human potentiality.

Morris Philipson's *Outline of a Jungian Aesthetics* (1963) remains the indispensable inquiry "into the accessibility of C. G. Jung's psychology for the problems of aesthetics," as the author defined the purpose of his book. It is perhaps even more than that. Himself an accomplished editor, teacher, and novelist, trained in philosophy, Philipson writes with the authority of a theorist who is also a practitioner. The result in this book is a compact survey of Jung's understanding of symbol and of the development of a hermeneutic from that understanding, an examination of Jung's criticism of Freud's aesthetic and his separation of his thinking from its reductive definitions and exercises, and a measuring of the special meaning of Jung's conception of archetypes and the collective unconscious for the understanding of

---

[19]See Albert Rothenberg, *The Emerging Goddess: The Creative Process in Art, Science and Other Fields* (Chicago: University of Chicago Press, 1979), pp. 55-56, 256, 1. Buffie Johnson's *Lady of the Beasts: Ancient Images of the Goddess and Her Sacred Animals* (San Francisco: Harper and Row, 1988) is an invaluable companion to works like Rothenberg's. It offers another example of what André Malraux called a museum without walls—an exhibition of art in print reproduction. Here we have art joined to idea in what is at its best a splendid gallery of goddess images, gathered together by a woman moved by Jungian theory and her own experiences as a painter to urge upon others, in this fashion, the case for the recovery of the sacred.

works of art, especially the literary. The book concludes with a thoughtful criticism of Jung's arguments in these areas. We are made to confront the inadequacy of Jung's development of his thinking about "the creative process in art" and the ambiguity of his presentation of his reading of "form" and "matter" in works of art, and to face the question of the value of his theory of knowledge in art and of its limitations. Philipson cannot be accused, then, of special pleading, although even in the midst of his sharpest arraignment of Jung as aesthetic philosopher and psychologist his sympathy and respect for Jung's thinking are unmistakable. What takes the book beyond the author's presentation of his own warm affection and esteem for his subject is the scrupulous care with which he has drawn a literary and philosophical theory from psychological texts where it does indeed appear, but in something less than systematic form. That is what makes this tidy compendium so trustworthy.

Philipson clearly means to remedy the imbalance in attention of those who have made some attempt to apply psychoanalytic concepts to the arts. Freud is to be found everywhere, and after Freud, his disciples and reformers. Jung is ranged somewhere at the distant edge of the meeting of art and psyche, Philipson says, although it should be added that that has changed a good deal since the time of Philipson's book. What his book accomplishes is a fine clarity of distinction, following Jung, between sign and symbol, between Jung's "prospective" view of the work of art, of its psyche, so to speak, and the Freudian "retrospective reductive" analysis of the artist. The complexity of the life of the symbol is here given its due, in testimony to the possibility of the renewal of the life of the spirit, which for Jung was the symbolic value of the work of art, and especially that one encompassed in what he calls the Visionary Mode, as against the Psychological Mode, which more straightforwardly says exactly what it means.

The refusal of Jung to reduce art to the "insufficiencies and conflicts" of the artist's personal life, "to disclose the material and efficient causes of the product in the same terms by which a neurosis is explained," is the negative foundation for the positive heuristic Jung draws from the experience of art. It is a future-directed, visionary bias that moves Jung, but one that also takes good notice of the most distant past, the world of the primordial, where artists find so many of their images and their archetypal structures, "the psychic residua of numberless experiences of the same type." Jung, as Philipson shows, is willing to generalize about art: it "is a kind of innate drive that seizes a human being and makes him its instrument." He will not do the same about the artist: "As a human being he may have moods and a will and personal aims, but as an artist he is 'man' in a higher sense—he is 'collective man'—one who carries and shapes the unconscious, psychic life of mankind." And so, as Philipson summarizes the position, "the term 'artist' does not designate a specific type or class of psychological nature, such as the term 'psychotic' or 'neurotic' does; rather it is the name of a class of people determined a posteriori, on the basis of their creative accomplishments." Thus artists are to be compared, as a group, with "such class designations as 'English gentleman' or 'Prussian officer.'" Jung is stressing, and Philipson with him, the "impersonal role" of the artist, the very opposite of the "official capacity" of the gentleman and officer classes cited, but one that nonetheless shares with them "a peculiar objectivity."

Jung's is not the final penetration of the mystery of art, but as Philipson has reconstructed his reasoning, it remains a seminal set of perceptions. Jung sees the difficulties of the lives of artists, unsatisfactory often enough, even tragic, and recognizes that a "special ability means a heavy expenditure of energy in a particular direction, with a consequent drain from some other side of life." But he also sees the power of art and its hold on all of us as a result of its "return to the state of *participation mystique* – to that level of experience at which it is man who lives, and not the individual, and at which the weal and woe of the single human being does not count, but only human existence." So it is that the artist emerges from the work of art and that the artist's psyche is shaped by it rather than the other way around.

In the concluding section of his book, Philipson shows that this understanding of the shaping force of the work of art in the life of the artist is not a simplistic one. Whatever the limitations of Jung's thinking about the arts or the aesthetic that might be drawn from his psychology, his is not a rigid determinism in which all can be explained by the operation of the collective unconscious. He understands the importance of the technical equipment an artist must have. He has a strong sense of the life of the symbol in art, which leaves the critic and the audience in art with functions analogous to but not precisely the same as those of the analyst. There are clear associations, as others besides Philipson have noted, to be made between Jung's readings of symbolic art and those of the Romantics of their defenders and explicators. But beyond such distinctions and associations, what matters here as everywhere in Jung is the move toward "wholeness," the prospective value to be found in the systematic uncovering of symbols. "This is the structure of an epistemological analysis of Jung's conception of symbolism. His greatest concern is with the usefulness of such means for the on-going understanding of 'psychic reality.'" It is future-directed but it does offer "practical knowledge" of that reality. For in the modern world, as Ernst Cassirer says in a memorable passage that Philipson quotes, "Man lives in a symbolic universe." Direct confrontation of physical reality is less and less likely in this universe whose "symbolic net" is composed of language, myth, art, and religion. Unable to deal "with the things themselves, man is in a sense *conversing with himself.*"[20] That conversation, which for Jung is an exchange between consciousness and the collective unconscious, contains foreshadowings of human development. It is not an easy exchange; there are almost always elements of struggle in it. But its conflicts are hopeful and positive ones, promising as art does the prospect of wholeness, if not necessarily its fulfillment.

James Baird retraces much of the same terrain that Philipson maps in his *Outline* in an examination of the theoretical problems posed by "Jungian Psychology in Criticism," but he is a scholar-critic in literature rather than a philosopher, with solid volumes on Melville and Wallace Stevens behind him at the time of the writing of this piece and accents of understanding and concern that are very much his own. Like Philipson, he backs into the material from Jung's response to Freud's aesthetic. He stresses Jung's disinclination to account for the artist's vision as "a problem in pathology," where "the curious images of the vision" are identified as no more than "an attempted concealment of the basic experience." The critic, says Baird, can in fact go many places for light on the basic experience, can see it as part of our "common inheritance," or as emerging from the "mysterious depths of the unconscious," or may look for guidance to Freud or Frazer. "But the problem of the anagogic in the genesis of art will continue to disturb him. He cannot totally escape Jung's insistence on the unnamable vision."

Jung's pursuit of the basic experience elicits some engaging speculations from Baird. He turns to architecture, for example, looks at the ruins of Delphi in the light of the cosmology of the Acropolis and at the domes of Isphahan through the symbol system of Persepolis and its reflection of Darius, "master and cosmic king." What ones finds in "these monumental evidences of *vision*" leaves one inarticulate in Baird's accounting, except for the reach through Jung for an understanding of architecture as "an art of manifesting the basic experience, the vision, through symbols, varying from culture to culture, of the human impulse to reflect, or to rival, a suprahuman cosmic order." Jung's large contribution here is not as critic but as "expositor of the basic experience." It is a function that permits him to examine Longfellow's *Hiawatha* and the Gilgamesh epic side by side without looking like an absolute idiot, searching for and finding archetypal images, sequences, and successions of imprints which Jung calls "engrams."

---

[20]See Morris Philipson, *Outline of a Jungian Aesthetics* (Evanston, Ill.: Northwestern University Press, 1963), pp. vii, 91, 99, 123, 126-127, 133-135, 177, 174-175, 190-191, 197.

These highly charged reflections of "the most frequently and intensely used functions of the human soul" convey mythologies, religious experiences, literary understanding. They bring all together in such a way that Baird suggests that "it may be argued that Wallace Stevens, among poets in the twentieth century, most closely approximates Jung's concept of 'a split-off sum of the libido, which has activated the God-*imago.*'" He instances two works of Stevens, "Chocorua to Its Neighbor" and "The Auroras of Autumn," in support of his suggestion, which may startle some readers of Stevens who look to the poet for aid and comfort for their philosophical materialism and please others, Jungians or not, who realize how far beyond the bounds of materialism Stevens's metaphysical speculations took him.

Baird has some other equally interesting couplings with Jung to propose. There is the Wordsworth of the immortality ode and some portions of *The Prelude*: "To possess the soul in Jung's terms and, I think, in Wordsworth's sense is to experience the unobstructed thrust of the libido in its power of intuition, God in man, and to know joy." Similarly, he touches on "archetypal material scrambled in the irrationality of sleep" that may be found in Lautréamont and Rimbaud, upon the mythic depths of *Moby Dick*, upon Jung's "predilection for Romantic art," and on "manifestations of the anagogic" in Whitman and Mallarmé. "The question must be asked," he says, "whether it is possible for the anti-Jungian fully to criticize Romantic literature."

One should not conclude from such statements that Baird is constructing a litmus test for critics or literary theorists which involves Jungian certification. He is saying that some set of related interests, concerns, or perceptions of the content of the unconscious, some grasp of archetypal materials and of primordial survivals in mythic forms and others, whether tutored directly by Jung or not, may be necessary to make sense of this large tradition and the body of work created within it. Toward our understanding this, he finishes with some thoughtful pages on people influenced by but by no means caught up in Jungian approaches. Maud Bodkin, for example, is an archetypal critic but not fully committed to Jungian procedure. Northrop Frye is a scholar and critic skillful in crafting his own vocabulary for the discussion of archetypal materials, one that specifically spurns Jung's, as does Philip Wheelwright's similar examination of archetypal symbols. In related contradistinction, Mircea Eliade is cited for his dissociation from "the problems of depth psychology" and "the concept of the collective unconscious" in his *Cosmos and History* and his use of " 'archetype' . . . as a synonym for 'exemplary model' or 'paradigm,' that is, in the last analysis, in the Augustinian sense."

What these figures, all of whom modify or reject Jungian theory, have in common with each other and with Jung is their inclination to "perceive, and sense, on 'the anagogic level,'" their assumption, in words drawn from Frye, of "humankind to be ... containers of nature." Baird is arguing, not for a "purely Jungian literary criticism," but for our recognition of "the perseverance of questions of the anagogic, of the visionary in the sense of Jung" as central to the critical imagination.[21]

Earlier, Baird had dealt with the meeting of religious and literary feelings and capacities in his *Ishmael: A Study of the Symbolic Mode in Primitivism*. Calling his book *Ishmael* was a way of pointing to the center of his ruminations, Herman Melville. His subtitle suggests the high place of Jungian ideas and procedures in his study, although it does not necessarily invoke Jung himself. Baird does that only once at great length in the volume, but the archetypalist mode is never far from the surface and the Jungian terms of the inquiry are defined in the epigraph from Jung: "We have let the house that our fathers built fall to pieces, and now we try to break into Oriental palaces that our fathers never knew."

His exhibits are many. The obvious figures and the not-so-obvious mix well – Conrad and Stevenson alongside Melville, Lafcadio Hearn, Arthur Rimbaud, Leconte de Lisle, Pierre Loti, Paul Gauguin, Ernest Fenollosa, the Imagist poets, Hesse, D. H. Lawrence, Eugene O'Neill. There are countless illustrations of archetypes, brief, persuasive, unforced. The archetype of the wise man, for example, "apparent in Queequeg," the Polynesian prince who is Ishmael's roommate on the whale boat in *Moby Dick*, draws a parallel in a passage from a letter of Henry Adams on some Samoans – "Grave, courteous, with quiet voices and a sort of benevolence beyond the utmost expressiveness of Benjamin Franklin. . . ."

Baird makes good use of Jung's *The Integration of the Personality*, in his demonstration of "the impoverishment of Protestant symbolism," his characterization of the history of Protestantism as one of "chronic iconoclasm," and his assertion of the possibility, now in the

---

[21]See James Baird, "Jungian Psychology in Criticism: Theoretical Problems," in *Literary Criticism and Psychology*, Yearbook of Comparative Criticism, Vol. VII (University Park, Pa.: Pennsylvania State University Press, 1976), pp. 3-6, 10, 12-16, 22-28. Other treatments of Jung's usefulness, or appositeness, at the very least, in discussions of literary theory are to be found in William Troy, *Selected Essays* (New Brunswick, N. J.: Rutgers University Press, 1967); F. A. C. Wilson, *W. B. Yeats and Tradition* (London: Methuen, 1968); J. A. Mazzeo, *Varieties of Interpretation* (South Bend, Ind.: University of Notre Dame Press, 1978); A. E. Dyson, *Yeats, Eliot and R. S. Thomas: Riding the Echo* (Atlantic Highlands, N. J.: Humanities Press, 1981); Kathryn Hume, *Fantasy and Mimesis: Responses to Reality in Western Literature* (London: Methuen, 1984); Ewa Kuryluk, *Salome and Judas in the Cave of Sex* (Evanston, Ill.: Northwestern University Press, 1987); Vincent B. Leitch, *American Literary Criticism from the 30s to the 80s* (New York: Columbia University Press, 1988).

"decadence of Protestantism," of rediscovering "the gods as psychic factors." The same book provides him with an opening to discuss the *puer aeternus* in Melville, working from Jung's categories to Melville's people, ending with that prime example of the Eternal Youth, Billy Budd, defined "as the full symbol containing both Polynesian innocence and the original innocence of Christ in the world as man," as the young sailor "hangs from the main-yard-arm in a new crucifixion."

The apocalyptic ending of Baird's book suggests that the life of symbols, to which so much of the best of Jung testifies, is an affirmation of human life and its all but certain guarantor. Melville, he says, "stands in our time as the heroic Christian." His faith rests upon the Christ of the Christian past and upon symbols that "restore in art" a lost oneness. The special repository of "his symbolistic ideal" is the Orient, "the dominant realm of an imagination which sought the meaning of humanity in the meaning of all time."

What he leaves us with is a Jungian vision, "the power of man as the symbol-maker," which has its source in "the same progenitor who made the beginnings of time in its mighty redness of burning stars." It is that power which "orders the continuity of our earthly life of spirit" and as long as man is upon earth "will wrest meaning from chaos in the abstractions of its art. . . ." The abstractions may transcend anything we have ever known before in our art or thought, but, he says in a fine fateful last sentence, "So far as civilized man's necessity for describing the meaning of his existence through symbols is concerned, this is the future."[22]

Baird's work is a fair indication of what can be done with Jungian attitudes and ideas in examining works of the literary imagination and their implications without turning them into psychoanalytical case histories. Five other examples support the point very well, I think, with a becoming range, good humor, and probity.

Few figures attract psychoanalytic interpretation the way the Victorian sage John Ruskin does. His stern morality and blighted sexuality seem to model all that attaches itself to the folklore image of the censorious repressed Victorian. His unconsummated marriage to Effie Gray, his lingering attachment to Rose La Touche, thirty years younger than he, his carolling address to the goddess Athena, "Queen of the Air," the magnetism he felt in the figure of Ursula in Carpaccio's painting of *St. Ursula's Dream* — all this and much more add up to a neurotic splendor to delight anyone bent on psychoanalyzing the past. And so the psychoanalytically minded have gone at Ruskin with a

---

[22]See James Baird, *Ishmael: A Study of the Symbolic Mode in Primitivism* (New York: Harper Torchbooks, 1960), pp. 247, 55–62, 427–428.

vengeance, most of the time, it is good to be able to add, with sympathy. For this art critic and social thinker, allegorist and philosopher is, whatever his problems, a giant in his age. He looked at works of art with a fullness of vision that matches the penetrating examination of the German art historians who were beginning to come into their rich years at the end of his life and administered theory in his writing with far less pomp and ceremony than they did and with at least as much breadth of understanding. He looked at the world around him – the land, the air, the waters – and saw everywhere a terrible reflection of human failure in a dying earth. All this is gathered up, one way or another, in Raymond E. Fitch's *The Poison Sky: Myth and Apocalypse in Ruskin*, a work of analysis in which Jungian ideas and procedures are used, often ingeniously, to fill out our understanding of the sage with almost no concessions to the neurotic of folklore.

In Fitch's many-sided portrait, we can see the wisdom of Ruskin as a social philosopher, as a prophet of ecological doom, as an observer of ancient and modern worlds drawn to the Middle Ages, uncomfortable in the Renaissance, but never in the fullness of his observations a falsifying reporter or critic. We recognize, in this intelligent employment of Jungian insights, the archetypal eye which was Ruskin's. The result is that we neither have to turn away in repugnance from Ruskin's sexual "homelessness" nor embrace it with stoic determination to give it its place in his life and thought. Fitch's simple point is that a sensitivity to myth as a critical element makes it possible to locate symbols "at and beneath the level of conscious intention," and that Jung's writings are particularly useful here "because they seem to shed light on the relation between archetypal symbol and individual psychic development."[23] He does not abuse the method. He does not reduce Ruskin to a figure in a Jungian landscape. He gives us instead the anima-haunted world of a man of genius, with explanations of a sort for the sexual incompleteness of his life and for his mythopoeic gifts that help us to see that both the disordered and the ordered in Ruskin work together to produce not only a gifted analyst of myths but a maker of them as well. We do not lose any of Ruskin this way; rather, with the shadow claimed, with the anima-archetype more openly exposed, we have restored for us a figure of greater stature and of infinitely larger dignity. We can, with Fitch's and, in effect, Jung's intervention, think more intelligently about what it is in past times and in present that poisons the sky.

[23]See Raymond E. Fitch, *The Poison Sky: Myth and Apocalypse in Ruskin* (Athens, Ohio: Ohio University Press, 1982), pp. 451, 14.

A thoughtful and original use of Jungian material marks Allegra Stewart's treatment of Gertrude Stein. Her emphasis is upon an "underlying experience of contemplation and creative dissociation" which she finds in the writer's "metaphysical outlook," discovering in her work a phenomenology of mind. Her originality lies in drawing this texture in Stein closer to Jung than to Hegel. Her use of the Jungian vocabulary is unforced. Her vision of the place in Stein of individuation, the mandala, temenos, persona, the law of enantiodromia, shadow, anima, *puer eternus*, and the whole world of the archetypes never imposes any direct consciousness of the material upon Stein. What we have instead, especially in the long examination of the 1938 opera libretto *Doctor Faustus Lights the Lights* (for which no music was ever written), is a striking reading of the predicament of modern man in the first third of this century, with particular and peculiar emphasis upon the "mass American . . . psychically undeveloped and lacking in true individuality." Here she has Jung's acknowledged indebtedness to Goethe's *Faust* to go upon as well as her own intelligent reading of the psychologist-philosopher-theologian (which is what Jung becomes here) and the librettist-philosopher-poet (as Stewart sees Stein). What is most moving about the book, as much a reading and application of Jung as it is of Stein, is her subject's "preoccupation with the achievement of true selfhood," and the possibility of the reconciliation through the right images of "unconscious depths and conscious purpose," uniting the world of the primordial with the seeds of worlds still to come. This is salubrious in Stein's 1914 collection of prose poems, *Tender Buttons*, "where cubistic dislocations unite to suggest archetypes of natural growth." Those who know Jung, or Bachelard's application of him, will recognize the strength of the image Stewart uses to support her conclusion, that "of a lived-in house . . . symbolic . . . of the self at home in its body," and, as she finishes her description of the image, the force of its employment of a celebrated similitude for the deepening of the life of the spirit of a saint both Stein and Jung knew well, Teresa of Avila: "and here is a green, watered garden — again symbolic of a woman's body, of a life well ordered, of a mind in harmony with its natural surroundings and its work."[24]

Shakespeare and Jung — that would be a stirring encounter, if it could be brought off. Alex Aronson, an Israeli academic, shows that it can be done in his *Psyche and Symbol in Shakespeare*. What Aronson manages is less a meeting between Jung and Shakespeare than between man and his unconscious as Shakespeare's plays illuminate

---

[24]See Allegra Stewart, *Gertrude Stein and the Present* (Cambridge, Mass.: Harvard University Press, 1967), pp. vii, 25, 185, 211, 205-206.

and dramatize it. He locates Shakespeare's dramatic imagination in a complex movement between "psychological" and "visionary" modes: "somewhere in between these extremes of self-knowledge and negation of self Shakespeare's universe can be found."

Questions are raised in this book, happily without dispositions that dissolve the mysterious textures of the psyche in a sea of jargon. The symbolic presentation of archetypes cannot be reduced to "oracular proof." If the invisible becomes visible, it is to the inner rather than the outer eye. Still the archetypes are alive for us in Shakespeare's symbols: "consciousness, that of the figure on the stage and spectator in the theatre, claims them for its own."

Aronson's appropriation of Jungian insight leads him to a three-stage division of his inquiry: "The first, THE EGO, defines the Shakespearean hero in terms of his conscious mind only. . . . ANIMA, the name given to the second part, indicates the shift from the personal to the transpersonal, from the prevalence of the conscious mind to the gradual domination of the ego by unconscious forces over which it has only partial control. . . . The third and last part, THE SELF, leads from conflict to resolution." The integration of ego and self is what is pointed to here, although in Shakespeare "the process of individuation . . . is never more than a remote possibility."

There are some arresting judgments of character and event in the book, some delicate employment of Jungian concept and procedure, some that is more brusque. But none of it is terminative; the use of depth psychology is never pressed to an intrusive finality. We are given good evidence for seeing Edgar in *King Lear*, for example, as "Shakespeare's most accomplished portrayal of a man who, having taken upon himself

> the basest and most poorest shape
> That ever penury, in contempt of man
> Brought near to beast. . . . (II, 3, 7)

is raised to the highest level of individuation." We see Prince Hal in *Henry IV, Part II* deliberately choosing his mask and in the choice making "his unchanging persona the sole criterion by which he is to be judged." Macbeth, in contrast, "becomes increasingly entangled in the dualism of face and mask," a division that "is finally dissolved in the darkness that reflects nothing but its own ambiguity."

Troilus in *Troilus and Cressida* is "inexorably placed between his anima and shadow" and in a "last heroic attempt at strengthening his disintegrating ego" is doomed to choose "a senseless death in the defense of a nonexistent honor." Parolles, that epitome of unction in the service of dishonor in *All's Well That Ends Well*, "is clearly not a *character* in the conventional naturalistic meaning of the term. He stands for Bertram's unconscious, his 'old Adam'. . . ." He is, in a word, Bertram's shadow, and when he is recognized as such, we can make some sense of the complexities, the contradictions, the movement toward consciousness in Bertram which involves the acknowledgment and repudiation of Parolles and leads the play to its problematic conclusion. The pervasive point remains: "Shakespeare's villains frequently are embodiments of the tragic hero's unconscious. As the shadow side of the psyche they justify their existence by constant rationalization."

Aronson posits no " 'development' of archetypes in Shakespeare's dramatic vision. As they are psychic contents, they elude historical analysis. They have no duration in time . . . . they can only be understood in terms of those universal assumptions that have, from time immemorial, guided human destiny." With that understanding, he follows the anima/animus paths through Shakespeare's plays, the father-daughter-lover entanglements under the rubric of logos, the son-mother-lover imbroglios under the heading of eros. Finally, here, he considerably enlarges our understanding of *Hamlet, Macbeth*, and *The Tempest* in his delineation of Shakespeare's use of the Hecate figure – witch, goddess, Great Mother, guiding force in the transformation from myth to Shakespearean drama in "Man's tortuous pilgrimage from the unconscious, its instinctual drives and orgiastic frenzies of self-abandonment, to self-hood . . . deepening of consciousness and self-realization."

In the last section of the book, the presiding deities are Prometheus, Orpheus, and Asklepios, the special concern the self-archetype, glimpsed through such figures as Theseus in *Midsummer Night's Dream*, Vicentio and Friar Francis in *Measure for Measure*, Prospero in *The Tempest*, and Camillo in *The Winter's Tale*. There are seminal passages on the "mana-personality," nonconformist, magical, integrated, on the spiritually restorative powers of music, on the archetypal healer. We end, with these configurations of "spiritual excellence . . . in their awareness of being human and not divine, yet existing on a transpersonal level of intuition and prescience, quite beyond the confines of limited time and space as represented on the stage."[25] It is a fitting conclusion, which is no termination, for an encounter between

---

[25]See Alex Aronson, *Psyche and Symbol in Shakespeare* (Bloomington, Ind.: Indiana University Press, 1972), pp. 17, 26, 39–40, 35, 56–57, 61, 93, 107–109, 155, 255, 271, 282–287, 308. Another work in which Jung is used to salutary effect is the study of *Marvell and Alchemy* by the Australian scholar Lyndy Abraham (Aldershot, England: Scholar Press, 1990). It is alive with insights into the

Shakespeare and Jung, a complexity of resonances rather than a resolution.

One of the most skillful employments of Jung in critical analysis is the use Kathleen Raine makes of his *Answer to Job* as the final piece of evidence in her examination of William Blake's "twenty-two pictorial emblems in which he . . . sought to communicate Job's inner experience of God. . . ." She finds so much of Jungian insight in Blake's reading of the Book of Job that she thinks "one might say that paradoxically Blake's view is more 'Jungian' than that of Jung himself."

The trail is clear: individuation process, a full facing of the *complexio oppositorum*, Blake's understanding "that disaster was bound to strike at Job from what Jung has called his shadow-side, the neglected, disregarded, all but extinguished 'contrary' of his righteousness." Raine makes the appropriate apologies—hers is "not primarily a work of scholarship," she is "not qualified to write on Jung with authority," she is not an "analytical psychologist," has not in fact "undergone analysis" and may misuse technical words. The trail remains, nevertheless, brilliantly staked out, movingly contemplated by a distinguished poet and critic. In Kathleen Raine's *The Human Face of God: William Blake and the Book of Job*, we learn much about "the inner worlds of human consciousness" through Job, Blake, and Jung.

Everywhere in this reading of Blake, we follow a "view of the unconscious" like Jung's, "as a source of wisdom and enlightenment," but nowhere does that view become simply a doctrinaire spelling out of Blake's ideas, insights, or concerns in Jungian terms. She uses Jung's distinction between archetypal or "big" dreams and those that come from the personal unconscious. She finds an anima figure in the apparatus Blake uses to describe "communications which come from the transpersonal mind by 'inspiration'. . . ."

There is a clear religious separation of Blake from Jung. When the analytical psychologist "writes 'God' he is writing from a lifetime's experience of the anguish of poor mortals at the mercy of the transpersonal Self." He takes the side of a Job looking to God as a superior being, "better, higher, nobler." Blake's God is not the Mosaic crafter of the moral law: "who, Blake would say, knows what in God's eyes is good or evil?" Still, although Jung may emphasize again and again the dark side of God, his deity remains like Blake's "at once the supreme

alchemical textures to be found in late Renaissance literature, in England especially, a book as Frank Kermode says in his introduction that is "the result of much pertinacious research [and] will have henceforth to be taken into account by serious students of Marvell"—and also, I would add, by serious students of alchemy.

reality and unknowable otherwise than in human terms, as 'the Human Imagination'. . . ."

Where the divergence becomes most marked is in the appropriations of Satan. Blake's Satan is "the Selfhood, the empirical ego, the mind of the natural frame, and as such the rebel against God in every man"; Jung's "is not the human ego, not an aspect of Job but of God, of the transpersonal Self." Job, for Jung, is God's moral superior; self-doubt rises in God from the encounter, producing in God an awareness "of his own duality" from which he immediately retreats—"God is reluctant to become conscious of himself. . . ."

Jung's is an evolving God, his Jesus "an imperfect or one-sided symbol." The not entirely parallel reading of Blake's is "the Swedenborgian view that Jesus took on the fallen nature of man with all its evil potentiality . . . was not conceived and born without sin . . . was in his nature fully human in all ways." Both see the Second Coming not in one person but in multitudes; in Jung's words, "the divine child . . . in accordance with the divine trend towards incarnation, will choose as his birthplace the empirical man." But first for Jung there must be "an enantiodromia in the grand style," the great drama of reversal, "a coming of Antichrist manifesting the dark side of God."

The moving point of agreement between poet and psychologist is that "God is born in man, not only once in the historical Jesus, but in the eternal Christ in every man, sinners as we are." Both Blake's sense of a Divine Humanity, to which he gives the name of Saviour, and Jung's idea of a collective redemption are really other ways of contemplating what St. Paul calls the mystical body of Christ. Perhaps with something like that in mind, Raine ends her own work of contemplation—literary, psychological, metaphysical—with a quotation from the last of Jung's recorded interviews: "What I have tried to do is to show the Christian what the Redeemer really is, and what the resurrection is. Nobody today seems to know, or to remember, but the idea still exists in dreams."[26]

Just how far one can explore the domain of the literary imagination with Jungian concept and precept is entertainingly demonstrated

---

[26]See Kathleen Raine, *The Human Face of God: William Blake and the Book of Job* (London: Thames and Hudson, 1982), pp. 10, 24, 57, 267, 90, 88, 276, 270, 280, 282, 285, 287, 293, 295-298. Jean H. Hagstrom, in the thoughtful chapter on Blake which concludes his *Eros and Vision: The Restoration to Romanticism* (Evanston, Ill.: Northwestern University Press, 1989) is less enthusiastic about Jung's closeness to Blake. He sees "Jung's archetypal structure" as "essentially bland compared to Blake's." It misses "the terror Blake finds in omnipotent Urizenic authority and also lacks the intense love the poet bestows upon the Jehovah of the Covenant, the Jesus of mercy, or the redeemed Heavenly Father. Nor is there in Jung the fierce antitheses of cruel patriarch and

by Timothy O'Neill in *The Individuated Hobbit*, an ardent pursuit of analytical psychology in Middle-earth, with volumes five to sixteen of the Collected Works to guide him. "Attempting to reconcile Jung and Tolkien is much like fondling the tail of a tiger in each hand," says O'Neill, an assistant professor of behavioral sciences and leadership at West Point when he wrote this book. But he is game. He offers justification out of the general field of psychology for a reading of "Tolkien's vast map of Middle-earth and its dizzying array of strange beasts, rich history, enchanting landscape, and the rhythmic prose and poetry of the quest itself [as] no more or less than an intricate map of the human psyche" and of Jung's theories in particular as applicable to *The Lord of the Rings*, *The Hobbit*, *The Silmarillion* and all the rest of the saga.

There are pictures to help us, not only of the geography of Middle-earth, but of the topography of the psyche, of the Self, of inflation, of individuation, of a balanced psyche, and of a resolution of conflict in Tolkien's world as a *coincidentia oppositorum*. There is a reasonably concise presentation, "Theory and Construct in Analytical Psychology," and an intelligent bare-bones glossary at the end of the book. The applications of Jungian theory to person, place, and event in Middle-earth are similarly restrained, with notably successful associations of Jungian one-sidedness – the loss of the bridge to the unconscious – and quaternity to materials in Tolkien.

O'Neill has been true to both Tolkien and Jung. Tolkien is resolute against those who "confuse 'applicability' with 'allegory' . . . the one resides in the freedom of the reader . . . the other in the purposed domination of the author." O'Neill applies Jung; he does not allegorize Tolkien. Equally, in making his applications, he does not stretch Jungian theory to turn it into an all-purpose instrument of interpretation. He does what he set out to do, to show that "the framework of Tolkien's world is truly in harmony with 'real' myth and fairy tale . . . woven of the same strand of human psychology." And while he works through speculation and conjecture, with no pretensions to "scientific inquiry," he makes a good case for his conviction that the "common denominator" of the translation of human psychology into myth and fairy tale "is to be found in the theoretical framework of analytical psychology – in

embracing father, nor the everlasting tension of warring contrarieties engaged in the mental battle that Blake called the 'War & Hunting' of Great Eternity (*Milton* 34:50; 35:2 [E., pp. 134, 135]). Blake believed that redemptive force fully existed only in a devine being who is 'The God *of fire* and Lord *of love*' (Jerusalem, pl. 3, 'To the public' [E., p. 145])." Curious to find Jung censured for lacking what is in fact the central tension, the pronounced judgment, the abiding religious position of his *Answer to Job*, which have often earned him just the opposite criticism, for too much of the fierce antitheses, the warring contrarieties, the mental battle that Hagstrom finds missing in him (Hagstrom, pp. 241–242).

the concepts of the collective unconscious and in the search for Self-realization."[27]

It is difficult to know whom to credit for what is persuasive in *The Individuated Hobbit*, Jung, Tolkien, or O'Neill. It held me as it moved through the cycles and transformations of hobbitry, and I am by no means an aficionado of Middle-earth. Perhaps it did so because, as with all effective applications of Jung to the world of the literary imagination, it deepens and extends symbolic meanings; it does not reduce them to an unfruitful finality.

---

[27]See Timothy R. O'Neill, *The Individuated Hobbit: Jung, Tolkien and the Archetypes of Middle-earth* (London: Thames and Hudson, 1979), p. xi, 154, 3, 165.

CHAPTER 7

THE NOVEL

The psychoanalytical novel has become almost a commonplace genre, whether conceived as such by the novelist or so identified by critics. The identifications sometimes are as awkward as those which bring Hamlet to the Berggasse couch for sessions with the Founding Father. The novels conceived under direct Freudian inspiration sometimes seem little more than case histories and often less inventive than the real thing. But then there are the masters of the fiction of the psyche, with or without benefit of acquaintance with depth psychology. The works of Dostoevsky, Joyce, Kafka, Lawrence, Mann, Conrad have become major outposts of the psychological terrain, necessary reconnoitering places for those who look to deepen their knowledge of the psyche.

As with literary theory and criticism, pride of place here has been given to the Freudians. And as with the theorists and the critics, there is a large body of distinguished work in the novel influenced, guided, shaped, or just touched, but touched with distinction, by Jung and Jungian ideas. Sometimes it is a darting into bits and pieces of the collective unconscious or a sense of the archetypal world of anima and animus, sometimes a feeling for Jungian characterology, based on type or function. The more considerable achievement of what might be called the Jungian novelist is a psychological alertness, a discerning judgment, which while caught by this or that Jungian insight never falls into simplistic reductions of character or psychological event. Complexity – the *complexio oppositorum* – remains the identifying mark.

When Edwin Muir, that discerning, psychologically alert poet and critic, reviewed *Happy Valley*, Patrick White's first published novel, he made note of its movement on two planes, "one of genuine powerful imagination, and the other of impromptu fancy." He recognized the Australian novelist's lengthy involvement with thought-association and the originality of his "crystallisations of misery." That was in 1939. Two years later, he said of White's second novel, *The Living and the Dead*, that reading it was like one's first confrontation with the work of James Joyce and D. H. Lawrence: "it has the same unexpectedness and one feels that it may turn out to be even more significant." What so moved Muir this time was the writer's "imaginative region," his closeness to the feelings and thoughts of his characters, a style which at its best revealed "the closeness and the imaginative venturesomeness of poetry." Everything seemed alive, immediate, without any loss of the "relation between the present and the past, the moving sequence, which makes it possible for us to read experience." Muir's summary judgment was very strong: "Compared with what he does in this book with the raw material of experience, most novels seem to do nothing at all."[1]

Many years, many novels later, Patrick White was awarded the Nobel Prize for literature, which made good sense to those who had come to know his movings about the objective and subjective psyche, the personal and the collective unconscious. It was not simply to give Australia its share in the prize-giving, as often the Nobels seem to be meted out, continent by continent, world by world. But in his abundant fancy, White did not see himself accepting the prize; he asked a good friend, the painter Sidney Nolan, to receive it for him.

White is an idiosyncratic man writing idiosyncratic novels. He has been compared with Thomas Mann in his intellectual reach, his odd, often fussy philosophizing. He has Faulkner's daring in his willingness to go where obsessions of the flesh or the spirit lead, where not only the center does not hold but almost nothing else around it. The motion in White's books is circular. Things, people, events go round and round, or at least in something that comes close to an unending circulation and recirculation as they look for something, try to achieve something approaching completeness in their lives, even in a few remarkable cases see the possibility of self-unity. The title of one of White's most considerable narratives, *The Solid Mandala*, describes the nature of his world, and does so more than symbolically, for the probings of the psyche and the spirit which his characters do, which he does, really seem to move urgently, desperately, in orbit, toward the closing of a mandala figure in the life.

The first of White's major characters, Theodora Goodman, the spinster aunt of *The Aunt's Story*, is mad at the end of the tale, but her madness is not to make an entirely pessimistic point nor is her progress to the "hot car" which will take her off to the asylum a wholly

---

[1]See Edwin Muir, *The Truth of Imagination: Some Uncollected Reviews and Essays*, ed. P. H. Butter (Aberdeen, Scotland: Aberdeen University Press, 1988), pp. 78–79, 87–88.

bleak one. She has reached the point suggested in the epigraph of the third and last part of her book, from Olive Schreiner: "When your life is most real, to me you are mad." In this concluding section of the book, much the briefest of the three that make it up, she talks to her most intimate companion, Holstius, one she has created in her imagination to accompany her. "I am an intruder in your house," she says, and she is, but she is more easily accommodated in the reality of the imagination than in the outside world which most people take for the only reality.

Theodora, whose name is allegorical, who is a Goodman, a good woman, journeys to Europe from Australia and to the United States. She moves through scenes of dispossession and default, where people pretend to titles that are not theirs, to lives that are not theirs, through a destructive fire at a hotel in France, a kind of halfway house for professional pretenders, the Hotel du Midi. She introjects the madness of a pastry cook with the whimsical name of Jack Frost, who "one Sunday . . . cut the throats of his wife and three little girls. Just like that." It was his way of keeping his family with him in a happy, smiling moment. Theodora finds it difficult to talk about: "I have thought about it. And it is still so close. Like something one has done oneself." She will indeed have thoughts about killing her mother, which gives a fine ironic cast to the opening line of the novel—"But old Mrs. Goodman did die at last."—when one finally fits it into place. It is the appropriate beginning, in medias res, of a small epic packed with parallels in its journeyings to The Odyssey.[2]

Patrick White is no Homer, although he is fixated on things Greek. His life's companion was a Greek, Manoly Lascaris, and his interior landscapes are often fitted out with the land itself, with experiences of people there, with its inescapable associations with the primordial. "Greece," he says in his self-portrait, Flaws in the Glass, "is the greatest love-hate for anybody genuinely hooked." It is "mindless enough"; it is also a land where one asks what there is to eat and can be told, at least in some places, O ti thelete (whatever you want) and discover that "miraculously, there was indeed every dish we had ever dreamt of." It is one answer to such a despairing thought as that which arrests Theodora Goodman in a world where she cannot seem "to take for granted the logic of growth and continuity" as others do: "Why then," she asks herself, "is this world which is so tangible in appearance so difficult to hold?"

White defines his sexuality as equivocal and ambivalent, but he finds little that is appealing in homosexual society: "Those who discuss

[2]See Patrick White, The Aunt's Story (New York: Viking, 1948), pp. 247, 270, 90–92.

the homosexual condition with endless hysterical delight as though it had not existed, except in theory, before they discovered their own, have always struck me as colossal bores. So I avoid them." No simple category for him. Rather, he sees himself "as a mind possessed by the spirit of man or woman according to actual situations or the characters I become in my writing." Again, no fixed categories: "I don't set myself up as an intellectual. What drives me is sensual, emotional, instinctive. At the same time I like to think creative reason reins me in as I reach the edge of disaster."[3]

Knowledge comes from disaster much pondered on in *The Tree of Man*, one of the novels of combat with "the Great Australian emptiness" which followed White's return to his native land in 1948. When it comes, it comes in elemental terms, to people stripped to nakedness, physical, spiritual, psychical. It comes in descents of pentecostal fire in a scene in which the Adamic figure rescues a kind of Magdalen and finds Godlike, manlike, Godmanlike passion unleashed in him. The tones, the characterizations, the mandala openings and closings are those of fable and dream. The book is noisy with myth.[4] It also begins to make the point which so many of the books that follow insist upon, that "sexuality refreshes and strengthens through its ambivalence, if unconsciously – even in Australia – and defines a nation's temperament." For White, "the little that is subtle in the Australian character comes from the masculine principle in its women, the feminine in its men. Hence the reason Australian women generally appear stronger than their men. Alas, the feminine element in the men is not strong enough to make them more interesting."

White is able to turn the myth of himself and its noisy enactments of sexual ambivalence and spiritual equivocation into any fable that lies near to hand – or dream. Wartime isolation as an RAF censor, in the Egyptian desert, sounds of life that others were leading in radio broadcasts, an intense asthma attack many years later, and ramblings in a "half-drugged state" all came together. "I could hear snatches of conversation, I became in turn Voss and his anima Laura Trevelyan."[5]

It is that transformation of White, now into Johann Ulrich Voss, now into Laura Trevelyan, that gives their troublesome book, *Voss*, its quiet strength. The feminine side of Voss is more than merely embodied; it becomes the nineteenth-century frontier which the German is trying to cross in Australia as well as the means of crossing it.

[3]See Patrick White, *Flaws in the Glass: A Self-Portrait* (London: Jonathan Cape, 1981), pp. 201-202, 5-6, 80-81; *The Aunt's Story*, p. 266.
[4]See Patrick White, *The Tree of Man* (New York; Viking, 1955), pp. 10, 109, 116, 230, 36, 495, 499.
[5]*Flaws in the Glass*, pp. 154-155, 103.

It has all the qualities of a sacrament, both the end in sight and the symbols which point to it. *Voss* is a violent novel, filled with open hatred and truncated love and killings and suicide, but it is also a meditative work. The expedition, commissioned by Laura's uncle, led by Voss, and equipped with a full range of persons, including a poet, moves against the new and the old unknown and unknowables. In the struggle to understand what the self amounts to and where power resides in the world, Voss wills himself to be God, wills himself to defy God, wills enough strength into himself to become a man at last, a man with a womanly side, even a man before God.

Voss the character, *Voss* the book are crawling with symbolism, confusing sometimes, even irritating, but always in the service of the circle of understanding. Man and book remind us of that other "arch megalomaniac," as White calls Hitler. Woman and book tell us of the resource of contrasexuality, the great well of otherness in us, of the intercessory strength that resides in anima (or animus), which may be where power really rests in the world. It is enough to make Laura think that Voss did indeed have "a little of Christ in him," but that this simply made him, in fact, like other men.[6]

We are told these things through symbol and allegorical enactment. We are artfully reminded of many things. We are not instructed, except as art and dreams instruct, as we teach ourselves to make sense of the alchemy of the personal and collective unconscious, as the oddments of understanding which those shadowy worlds can provide come floating to the surface. In *Voss* and the next even more heavily symbolic work, *Riders in the Chariot*, the reader's art, like the writer's, is nothing less than an alchemical work. One can have little of the assurance of a modern scientist here. The terms are ancient and even when the names point like signs at a crossroad, we are not absolutely sure of where to go. In *Riders*, we have an epigraph from William Blake with pointers from Isaiah ("my senses discovered the infinite in everything") and Ezekiel ("The desire of raising other men into a perception of the infinite") and a title that takes us right into the Bible, but awkwardly, joltingly, in a chariot, something less than a speedy or governable conveyance. The movement of the chariot is ungovernable in this book, mysterious, as uncertain and intractable as the four riders who make up the brilliant, stubborn, awkward allegorical tale.

White's hands shape his surrealist allegory in odd ways, bring us Mary Hare, as mad as a March hare, shy and jumpy as the animal is in its rutting season; Mordecai Himmelfarb, whose first name in the Bible is the name of exiles, appropriate to this refugee from the Nazis,

---

[6]Patrick White, *Voss* (New York: Viking, 1957), p. 438.

and whose second tells us he wears the color of heaven; Alf Dubbo, an Aborigine painter of saintly intuitions, and Mrs. Godbold, the rider who survives. The shaping is as bold as the God of the Old Testament, but its lingering form in our minds, and dreams, too, perhaps is the crucifixion of Himmelfarb, an almost trivial Good Friday in this book, its new testament to the sacrifices we make whether we like it or not. It is said of Himmelfarb, "It was in the same reluctant frame of mind that he entered, or returned, to Jerusalem – as if he alone must refuse the freedom of that golden city. . . ." He is reluctant to enter Jerusalem; we are reluctant to enter the holy city, and it almost seems at times as if White were equally reluctant in the way he constructs his tableaus in the Australian twilight. All are unwilling victims. All are disinclined to accept the holiness that seems to be thrust at them.

We are told about Himmelfarb's life in Germany, as a learned academic, that he would spend time alone, reading, drawing "idly," listening to "the sound of silence," that he "was sometimes, it seemed, transported in divers directions." Transported by such a chariot as he "was scribbling" on paper, that his wife asks him about, which he cannot quite identify, for her or for himself, the Chariot of Redemption, perhaps, "shadowy, poignant, personal." Such transport cannot carry him far enough away from the home, the land, where, when he is away for a short time, his wife is almost inadvertently picked up by the Nazis, leaving him to go "whimpering, directionless, somewhere down, into the pit of creaking darkness."[7]

This is the world of White's riders in the chariot, who are our intercessors as they emerge from their clotted collectivity. White found some such intercession in Jung's *Psychology and Alchemy*, given to him by a painter friend. "It projected me," he says, into "my *Solid Mandala*." It did more: "Jung's teaching also bolstered me up during a wavering of faith on realising I could not accept the sterility, the vulgarity, in many cases the bigotry of the Christian churches in Australia." Against the empty religion of his "upbringing," he "evolved" what his closest friend calls his "non-religious or mystic circus."

That is what White thinks "rubbed off on the *Solid Mandala*. It is a book full of ambivalence and unease – transitoriness." Its protagonists, the twins Arthur and Waldo Brown, White sees as his own "two halves." Arthur could be understood as a portrait of a cousin of White's, if that cousin's "childish wisdom had matured; instead he was

---

[7]See Patrick White, *Riders in the Chariot* (New York: Viking, 1961), pp. 199, 141–142, 160.

admitted to an asylum in his teens, and remains in one to this day."
Waldo is identified by the writer as himself at his "coldest and worst."[8]

The color which fixes the twins in their Jungian allegory is just
right: a prosaic brown, without individuality, safely drab, emptied of
almost all presence, T. S. Eliot's color of universal sterility, of the
wasteland. But White's Browns are too much alive in this beautifully
realized novel to stay reduced, even in their most frustrated and frus-
trating moments, to the colorless color that so accurately describes the
surfaces of their lives. Waldo is a librarian, a failed intellectual, a
pseudo-stoic who tries to suppress the femininity he feels somewhere
inside himself, that at least he can make a stab at by working at a
novel, called with a kind of semi-conscious cunning, *Tiresias as a
Young Man*, or by his thrusts at the twin with whom he spends his
whole life but would rather not be associated with. Arthur is the perfect fool, the perfect foil for Waldo.

Arthur, the wise fool, writes a primitive poetry, badly spelled, in
which wisdom, when it comes, is not childish but primordial:

> my heart is bleeding for the Viviseckshunist
> Cordelia is bleeding for her father's life
> all Marys in the end bleed
> but do not complane because they know
> they cannot have it any other way

Arthur is a visionary who treasures the mandalas in the glass marbles
he carries with him, who can instantly spot the mandala at the center
of a Turkish rug ("That! That! That is it!"), who unlike his brother is at
ease with the feminine both in himself and in women. He even dances a
mandala for one of the two women of special importance to him, for
however awkwardly, however much beyond translation into words or
graceful actions, he is connected to that great symbol of completion.
He understands and in his own clumsy touching way lives the mandala's rhythms. He reaches out in love to his brother and descries something like love in his brother's movements toward him, whether rejecting or in some frightened, furtive way accepting. Arthur finally sees in
Waldo the hatred he "was directing, had always directed at all living
things," and cries out in the terrible agony of discovering – he thinks –
that "he, not Waldo, was to blame. Arthur Brown, the getter of pain."
Waldo dies of his hatred and of "their joint discovery," the brothers
both understanding at last the pain and the ugliness in Waldo, Waldo
dying of it, attacking Arthur with it, grabbing him by the wrist in his

---

[8]*Flaws in the Glass*, pp. 146–147.

last moments, Arthur blaming himself for it, thinking he has killed his brother.[9]

We are once more in Eden, with Cain and Abel as figures in a Jungian landscape. One is dead, the other is making ready for the life of the asylum, the place of refuge of goodness in White's bedeviled collectivity. This will be the burden of the remarkable flow of fables that come afterward, mandalas effected or mandalas contemplated, stories of a world of harsh twinnings, of soft couplings, a world where the alchemy of grace still exists, but is more often refused than corresponded with.

If there is grace in the world of the artist, Patrick White seems to be saying in *The Vivisector*, it comes only through the dissection of living beings. Hurtle Duffield, whose violences as painter and person make up the material of this long, painful, profound work, sets himself up early against his mother's "particular interest . . . the prevention of vivisection." When he paints, he works on a battleground where bodies are "interlocked on a compost of leaves under a glittering rain of blood." He works abrasively, out of half-darknesses and out of dreams, to make people go "weak at the knees," as seeing a familiar painting makes him do. He strains not to be caught in "that state of half-cocked reality, neither life nor art, which is perhaps the no-man's land of human failure." It is not merely a piece of furniture that he paints but "the archetype of a table." In his convulsive meetings with himself, with others, with paint, he is always looking to cut through, to be the thing in itself, to "reach the last inch. . . ." In his last moments, lying on a pavement, he thinks himself to have reached the color that has been haunting him all his life, a kind of indigo, a "vertiginous blue" he has never really been able to visualize. But now he finds himself "dazzled not so much by a colour as a longstanding secret relationship." In a style that owes something to Joyce, but finds its own distinct accents, the painter ceases to paint, becomes a maker of words, finally ceases, "Too tired too end-less obvi indi-ggodd."[10]

"What do I believe?" White asks himself in his self-portrait. "I am accused of not making it explicit. How to be explicit about a grandeur too overwhelming to express, a daily wrestling match with an opponent whose limbs never become material. . . ."[11] White, like Hurtle, is a "Viviseckshunist," and like Arthur Brown, his heart bleeds for that

---

[9]See Patrick White, *The Solid Mandala* (New York: Viking, 1966), pp. 202, 241–242, 284.

[10]See Patrick White, *The Vivisector* (Harmondsworth: Penguin, 1973), pp. 102, 158, 279, 364, 616–617.

[11]*Flaws in the Glass*, p. 70.

archetypal figure, the artist who creates as he destroys and destroys as he creates.

How much Elizabeth Hunter, the predatory Great Mother in *The Eye of the Storm*, destroys is clear enough. The abiding question is how much she creates. She produces two children who are worldly successes, one of them a French princess by marriage, the other a beknighted actor on the English stage. They achieve their greatest feeling, as children, as lovers, as persons, in a night of incestuous coupling, the cruel and the delivering moment in their period of attendance on their dying mother. But feeling frightens; in retreat the sister calls the brother "absurd" and "such a shit" and can only moan "O, fuck – fuck everybody!" The brother's response is suitably terse: " 'Yes,' he agreed."

There is a creative power in Elizabeth which the rituals of decay bring out. She has felt it in her own attendance on the dying, as she watched her husband fall away, moving to give him the necessary hypodermic, "pulling down the pyjama pants over the wasted buttock," only trembling when she catches "sight of the slender testicles, the blue head of the shrivelled penis." She allows the reader to feel it in her own death as her corpse is picked up from the chamber pot where she has died, her personal depths joining the larger, deeper ones of the collectivity – "Till I am no longer filling the void with mock substance: myself is this endlessness."[12]

White's pursuit of the archetypes is saved from an oracular pretentiousness in his unblushing manipulation of his characters, of their language and his own, by a sense of humor that enters comfortably, roguishly in Elizabeth's book, moving unsteadily on stage with graceful randy postures like the porter in *Macbeth*. In *A Fringe of Leaves*, the sexuality is at least as boisterous, but there is not much to make the reader laugh. How can there be when the cannibalism that is in the Christian Eucharist is dramatized by an actual eating of a young woman's flesh by the book's central figure, Ellen Roxburgh, who finds it easy enough to doff civilization's fringe in the Australia of the 1830s. Questioned later on about the terrible event, she will admit only to playing a woman's part, to witnessing the "secret ceremony." She cannot or will not describe it. "It was too private. For me too, I realized later. A kind of communion." A little later, in a related conversation, she says to an insistent evangelizing chaplain, "I do not know . . . whether I am true, leave alone Christian."

She is true in spite of all. She has lost her husband in a battle with the Aborigines. She has been made to suckle a sick black child –

---

[12]See Patrick White, *The Eye of the Storm* (New York: Viking, 1973), pp. 509, 197, 551.

unsuccessfully. She has had her body hacked at and smeared and then brought back to life in an odd-and-even pairing with Jack Chance, an escaped convict who has murdered the last of his women for her infidelity. But she, out of the Cornish soil and an uneven marriage and a too brief escape from it, and he, a bird catcher, a stump-toothed oversized criminal, fit by chance. He will not stay with her when they come to the edges of civilization. She must make her way now alone and yet not alone. For what remains of the green life in her that he nourished cannot be killed. In her frenzied joinings with Jack Chance she has, in the words of the book's last sentence, come "through thoughtscape and dream"; she has found in her "grasp," even if only for a brief moment, that "circumstantial straw which may indicate an ordered universe."[13]

There is a frenzied clutching at circumstantial straws in *The Twyborn Affair*, which followed the *Fringe* three years later. The title suggests the spy stories and sex-and-suspense extravaganzas that top the best-seller lists and become films in the way that bad books so often can. The sexuality of this *Affair* is hardly suspenseful, but it is mysterious. Sexual identity is the charge of this adventure story that stretches from one World War to another, that moves, not simply as the title indicates, in doubles, but more decisively still, in threes. The book has three parts. In the France of Part I, Eddie Twyborn, an Australian lieutenant in the First War, hides beneath the clothing and the ambiguous femininity of Eudoxia, wife of a sportive Greek more than forty years older than she. In Part II, Eddie is a jackeroo, an apprentice at an Australian sheep farm and is caught up in the bosomy charms of the owner's wife, Marcia Lushington, whose name tells all. He is also the victim or victimizer of the ranch foreman, Don Prowse. In the last part, Eddie has become Mrs. Eadith Twist, master and mistress of a splendid London bordello, a sexual ascetic presiding like a Madame of the Sacred Heart over his community.

Eddie is man, Eddie is woman, Eddie is man-woman and woman-man. As he makes his way from the ranch, from his male and his female entanglements, he thinks, "Men are frailer than women. Don Prowse, for all his meaty male authority, was not much more than a ping-pong ball knocked back and forth in a sinewy female set. Most sinewy of all, an aggressive anima walled up inside her tower of flesh." Such animadversions fill the last pages of Part II, self-censurings by a hopelessly epicene figure who cannot accept how pleasing he is to both sexes.

Finally, just before a bomb gets him in the "brick no-man's land" of wartime London, Eddie makes his peace with his mother. Her sexual

---

[13]See Patrick White, *A Fringe of Leaves* (New York: Viking, 1976), pp. 364, 385, 405.

identity is as equivocal as her son's, but considerably less interesting, which may be the reason, in the final irony of the Twyborns, why she outlives him.[14] The lasting strength of the woman, of the book, of White's archetypal world, is the inexorable collectivity. When we allow its sometimes tragic, always capricious humors to emerge from their captivity in the unconscious, we stand a chance, as Ellen Roxburgh does unfringed, as Eudoxia/Eddie/Twist does refringed, when he/she becomes master and mistress of ceremonies at the brothel, forgoing the discomfort of direct participation in the sexual rites for the love of a man he cannot in the ordinary way possess. "You reach a point where you have had everything, and everything amounts to nothing," White says in his own persona. "Only love redeems." He is quick to add that he does not mean an undifferentiated Christian love: "To lavish what is seen as Christian love, indiscriminately on all mankind, is in the end as ineffectual and destructive as violence and hatred. Love in homeopathic doses can be more effective than indiscriminate slugs of the other doled out to a sick society." The strength of White's conviction is clear. What he means by a redeeming love is one "shared with an individual, not necessarily sexual, seductive though sexuality may be." And he is not worried if he, as one who does not really understand Christian love, is thought to be an old man, past the possibilities of passion, clutching at straws. "If it is making do, let us make do, whatever our age, in a world falling apart."[15]

That last statement provides the program for the alternately comic and anguished opera buffa which is his last book, *Memories of Many in One*. In it he affects to be the editor of a manuscript left behind by the flamboyant Alex Xenophon Demirjian Gray, relict of an old school friend, Australian-Greek, the maddest of merry widows. He plays some several roles in the tale, putting it in order, appearing as the lady's trusted confidante, subject at the end to the unwanted filial attentions of her daughter. What he is doing in all of this is putting his own house of fantasies in order.

We are held in an archetypal grip in White's land, where those who look to read the signs that confront them, hoping to find simple easy understanding, are astonished to discover that the signs are not in fact signs but symbols of transformation and far from easy to read. The picture Alex offers of herself working on her *Memoirs* fits the only begetter of her book only too well—it is Patrick White describing himself: "I was sitting writing in what I am vain enough to call my study, though I have studied practically nothing beyond my own intuition—

[14]See Patrick White, *The Twyborn Affair* (London: Jonathan Cape, 1979), pp. 294, 423–432.

[15]*Flaws in the Glass*, pp. 251–252.

and oh, and by fits and starts, the Bible, the Talmud, the Jewish mystics, the Bhagavad Gita, various Zen masters, and dear old Father Jung who, I am told, I misinterpret." Does he misinterpret Jung? Is Jung's so clearly demarcated a set of texts or so precisely defined a set of orthodoxies that we can hold an imagination as rich as White's to precise rules of interpretation? What White has accomplished in his novels, and in some of his stories and plays as well, is at least in one way of seeing his work a tour of Jungian territory. He too is a historian of the collective unconscious. He has added very much both to our confusion about and understanding of the ambivalences and equivocations of sexual identity, and for all the bleakness of the world he describes, he has made a strong case for the redemptive powers of love when it is not so generalized in its application that it can be called indiscriminate or so overdetermined in its sexual acting-out that it has no object except self-gratification. He is an alchemist in one of the late great guises of the esoteric practice, a homeopath of the imagination who has taken comfort and understanding from Jung in his intensive application in his stories of the diseases of the modern world as a means of curing them. He is well represented in one of her last moments by Alex Gray who, instead of the line she is supposed to speak—"I am the spirit of the land, past, present, and future"—shrieks "I am the Resurrection and the Life." At which moment, she is picked up by an "archetype Aborigine" and whirled around his shoulders.[16] Australia has served White well, almost as well as he has served it.

How much was that most intelligent of modern novelists, Robert Musil, influenced by Jung? To judge from the scorn he directs at psychoanalysis in his brilliant little piece, "Oedipus Threatened," and his linking of Jung with Freud and Klages as a pseudo-poet, one would have to conclude that the only effect was negative. On the other hand, this greatly gifted novelist, playwright, essayist, and journal-keeper, in spite of his misgivings about the claims of psychoanalysis to total explication, saw much in it to be grateful for. Sexuality could be dis-

---

[16]See Patrick White, *Memoirs of Many in One* (New York: Viking, 1986), pp. 9, 54, 151. For an unsympathetic view of this book and others "in the later phase" of White, see David J. Tacey, *Patrick White: Fiction and the Unconscious* (Melbourne: Oxford University Press, 1988), a book which makes good use of Jungian materials but fails, I think, to see the simple strengths of the late volumes and their extraordinary reach into the complexities and contradictions of sexual identity. John Colmer, another Australian, provides a brief, informative survey of White's work in Methuen's Contemporary Writers series (London, 1984). Peter Wolfe's *Leaden Choirs: Fiction of Patrick White* (Lexington, Ky.: University Press of Kentucky, 1983) is, I think, the best of the books on White, in spite of its only perfunctory acknowledgment of Jung.

cussed publicly. And even if the world of the unconscious was not yet sufficiently respected, Freud, Jung, and the others had brought it to some serious attention. Musil deeply valued the wanderings of the imagination between the rational and the irrational, the conscious and the unconscious, the dependent and the independent, its movements urged by the fact that none of these areas of human experience was a fixed territory with precisely definable boundaries. So it is that he moves into Jungian regions in his masterpiece, *The Man Without Qualities.*

In that long, unfinished and probably unfinishable novel, Musil brings his protagonist, Ulrich, into a relationship with his sister Agathe that in psychological detail, dramatic expression, and spiritual reach makes one think again and again of Jung's exploration of the anima and animus archetypes. We know from jottings in his unpublished papers that he was reading Jung's prefatory essay to *The Secret of the Golden Flower* (published in 1929) when he was in the later stages of his novel, where the Agathe-Ulrich relationship dominates, and that although he was not entirely at ease with the Jungian vocabulary he recognized in the elaborations of mode and meaning in the male and female archetypes something close to what he was doing with the brother and sister. Was this simply in the air? Had Jung put it there? Was it inevitable that Musil, trained in psychology and philosophy as well as mathematics and engineering, would come to it? Musil's parable of anima and animus, almost a third of his multivolume work, either reflects or supports Jung here. One way or the other, it is a document essential to our understanding of the terrain, as instructive in its ambiguities as in its clarifications.

If it were not for the psychological and spiritual fullness of Musil's double-portrait, this would simply be a narrative of incest. It never is. One long sentence, as sister makes her way toward brother, as anima lines are drawn, shows Musil's understanding: "Agathe's relationship to him, which floated undefined, with something about it of 'sister' and something of 'woman,' something of 'stranger' and something of 'friend,' yet without her being exactly what any of these things meant for him, did not – as he had already quite often mused – consist in any particularly far-reaching agreement of thought or feeling between them." When Ulrich reflects on central issues, such as the Good and the Bad, "the rising arc" of his reflections inevitably leads him back to Agathe. They live in "disarray" together and find "in everything a pretext for the sort of excessive high spirits generated by a picnic when one has a meal on the grass more uncomfortably than one would need to at a table." With his sister's presence and seeing her effect upon men, he can understand and feel at ease with what a woman and her clothing can bring of "a consummately curtained theatre of the erotic, its breath-taking darkness illumined only by the dim torches of imagination." When Agathe asks him, "Wouldn't strangers, if they could see and hear us, think there was something perverse about our feelings?" Ulrich's answer is out of a Jung copybook: "Nonsense!" says the brother. "What each of us feels is the shadowy doubling of his or her self in a complementary nature. Here am I a man, you a woman. It's widely believed that every human being has within him the shadowy or repressed counter-quality to each of his qualities: certainly he feels the yearning for them whenever he isn't damnably satisfied with himself." Ulrich/Musil goes on, after further exchanges over several days, to provide an anima etiology: "it's what I've always wished for. When I was a boy I resolved to marry only a woman I'd have adopted when she was a little girl and brought up myself."

The textures are almost all positive, the meetings of mind and soul often ecstatic, but the negative anima and animus have their outings too in this archetypal drama which exposes its characters and viewers so courageously to the tensions of the moral imagination. Musil is willing to dig as far as necessary to expose what Ulrich calls the "psychic entrails." Musil's bitter comic-opera name for the Austro-Hungarian Empire points to entrails. It is crafted of the two K's that begin the Emperor's two titles – Kaiser (Emperor) and König (king). Thus we have Kakania, which in Viennese or almost any other German slang means the Kingdom of Shit.

What is amiss in Kakania is the failure to see the difference between "the way in which the various epochs have developed the rational mind," Ulrich muses, "and the way in which they have kept the moral imagination closed and static." Again, the tone is Jungian, for "the consequence is a line that runs, despite all scepticism, more or less straight through history, a rising line of rational intellect and intellectual patterns, and, contrasting with it, a mound of broken shards, which are feelings, ideas, and life's potentialities, heaped up in strata just as they came into existence – always no more than side-issues – and subsequently discarded." In sum, Musil tells us, "what Ulrich called moral imagination, or, more simply, feeling, has for hundreds of years been in a perpetual state of fermentation without ever, as it were, maturing into wine."[17]

[17]See Robert Musil, *The Man Without Qualities, III: Into the Millennium (The Criminals)*, trans. Eithne Wilkins and Ernst Kaiser (London: Secker and Warburg, 1960), pp. 98, 185, 319, 321–322, 325–327, 431, 440, 442–443. There is nothing of Jung in the finely speculative chapter on Musil in John McCormick's

To analyze the work of James Joyce in Jungian terms is a tempting proposition to which a number of critics and scholars have responded warmly but with varying degrees of success. Some have lost either Joyce or Jung in the process. Others have given us greater access to Joyce's darker corners by their temperate use of Jung (as of Freud). William Tindall is one of the best, perhaps because his application of Jungian insight is so often proffered tentatively, as for example in his reading of Joyce's substitution of Leopold Bloom "for God and earthly father" in the life of Stephen Dedalus in *Ulysses*, and Bloom's wife Molly "for the Virgin and his earthly mother." Stephen finds "humanity in Bloom," Joyce "life itself in Mrs. Bloom. The realization of Mrs. Bloom must have had the effect of what Jung calls the reconciling symbol." But, Tindall reminds us, "Jung's place in *Ulysses* is more problematical than that of Freud," even allowing for the reading of Stephen as "the typical introvert, trying to come to terms with the world around him," and of "Bloom, with his interest in externals, as the typical extrovert." There is simply "no proof that Joyce had Jung in mind while creating these standard types." But equally, Molly "could be the *anima* or archetypal woman, and Bloom could be the archetypal wise man or wandering hero."[18]

Jung's own reading of *Ulysses*, first presented as an introduction to the third Swiss edition of the book, is remarkably un-Jungian and unsympathetic, although it does recognize a persuasive transcription of reality in the work, even if it is, as Jung first saw it, the reflection of a schizophrenic mind. Joyce himself was struck by the humorlessness of Jung's preface and suggested that "the only thing to do in such a case is to change one's drink." Meeting the publisher, Joyce said, "Why

Fiction as Knowledge: The Modern Post-Romantic Novel (New Brunswick, N. J.: Rutgers University Press, 1975), and he insists that Musil's work is "not psychoanalytical" and only psychological "in the sense that all fiction is psychological in a certain measure. . . ." He does make the important point, however, not at all at variance with anima/animus theory, that "Musil's use of incest is less a parallel to Byronic egotism and eroticism than it is evidence of Musil's post-Romantic fascination with the chameleon-like changeableness of historical reality, his doubts about various philosophies of history, and his search through the single, incestuous Ulrich-Agathe figure – and they are one, not two – for a satisfactory philosophy of history and of nature" (pp. 82–84). A much more psychoanalytical understanding of Musil, and of Jungian associations in particular, is to be found in Frederick G. Peters, *Robert Musil: Master of the Hovering Life* (New York: Columbia University Press, 1978). See also David S. Luft, *Robert Musil and the Crisis of European Culture* (Berkeley, Calif.: University of California Press, 1980); Hannah Hickman, *Robert Musil and the Culture of Vienna* (La Salle, Ill.: Open Court, 1984); and for the special concern the title indicates, Lisa Appignanesi, *Femininity and the Creative Imagination: A Study of Henry James, Robert Musil and Marcel Proust* (London: Vision, 1973).

[18]See W. Y. Tindall's *James Joyce: His Way of Interpreting the Modern World* (New York: Scribner, 1950), pp. 37, 48.

is Jung so rude to me? He doesn't even know me. People want to put me out of the church to which I don't belong. I have nothing to do with psychoanalysis." Jung revised his piece and sent it off to Joyce with a letter which confesses his trouble in trying to make sense of *Ulysses* and his gratitude in learning so much from it. By turns bored, grumbling, cursing, admiring, he came to the forty-page unbroken soliloquy of Molly Bloom at the end to discover "a string of veritable psychological peaches. I suppose the devil's grandmother knows so much about the real psychology of a woman. I didn't." And so he commends his "little essay" to Joyce as "an amusing attempt of a perfect stranger that went astray in the labyrinth of your Ulysses and happened to get out of it again by sheer good luck."

Joyce was pleased, but that did not, understandably, make him eager to acknowledge his indebtedness to Jung or Freud or psychoanalysis, as Mary Colum urged him to do, nor did it persuade him to send his greatly troubled daughter Lucia to Jung for treatment. He had refused the invitation to work with Jung made by his patron Edith McCormick, when he was living in Zurich in 1919, and blamed Jung and their mutual friend Ottocaro Weiss for the loss of her patronage that followed. When other doctors and other treatments had failed, he did send Lucia to a sanatorium in Küsnacht where Jung was available. There were some early successes; Lucia seemed to feel at ease with Jung, although later, Jung reported, she exclaimed, "To think that such a big fat materialistic Swiss man should try to get hold of my soul!"

Jung's success with Lucia was short-lived. Joyce was not pleased by Jung's diagnosis of his daughter as schizoid, with evidence from her poems to support it. Joyce saw her as clairvoyant and her writing as innovative, just simply not yet understood. He would have been even less pleased by Jung's reading of her as Joyce's anima, his "unconscious psyche . . . so solidly identified with her, that to have her certified would have been as much as an admission that he himself had a latent psychosis." He saw Joyce's " 'psychological' style" as schizophrenic, but "willed" by the writer and "developed with all his creative forces" which, for Jung, explained why Joyce "did not go over the border." Lucia, lacking her father's genius, simply fell ill.[19]

Joyce has fun with Jung a number of times in *Finnegans Wake.* He cannot resist the obvious play on the name which many less accomplished punsters have allowed themselves, though what follows from it is something more than playful in its sharp comment on talk therapy: "we grisly old Sykos who have done our unsmiling bit on 'alices, when

[19]See Richard Ellmann, *James Joyce* (New York: Oxford University Press, 1959), pp. 641–642, 691–693.

they were yung and easily freudened, in the penumbra of the procuring room and what oracular comepression we have had apply to them!" He footnotes the phrase "the business each was bred to breed by" with "The law of the jungerl." Twice he has his happy way with contrasexuality, first providing the paradigm "Anama anamaba anamabapa," and then, following "When is a Pun not a Pun?" as the title and subject matter of a school exercise with "Is the Co-Education of Animus and Anima Wholly Desirable?" The last is accompanied with a footnote that makes its own wry comment: "Jests and the Beastalk with a little rude hiding rod."

Happy with Jung or not, ironic or straightforward, Joyce says enough in *Finnegans Wake*, his great polyglot dream book, to indicate that Jung is a major source. Joyce prided himself on his conscious control of materials, especially of the unconscious, his prime subject matter in the *Wake*, and so we must take seriously his reference to his sources in the statement "Everyday, precious, while m'm'ry's leaves are falling deeply on my Jungfraud's Messongebook I will dream. . . ." The puns are clear: Jung, Freud, Jungfrau – meaning the young lady, Issy or Isabel, the daughter in the five-person holy family of the book, which is not simply a message book but one of dream (*songe*, in French) messages. Furthermore, Joyce, a master of the method of *coincidentia oppositorum*, is often most serious when most ironic, which is to say when he is pointing to the condition contrary to fact, which could be called fancy or fantasy, where dream-truth resides. Thus in the latencies of dream, which is where everything in the *Wake* is to be found, we find simple truths in oneiric complexes. Then Jung as "the joke that bilked the hoax" – remember the house that Jack built? – has it all wrapped up, and "the jest of him who goes for the jungular" is the solemn truth that is to be traced back to the primordial jungle, Jung's homeland. Ergo –

> – So this was the dope that woolied the cad that kinked the ruck that noised the rape that tried the sap that hugged the mort?
> – That legged in the hoax that joke bilked.
> – The jest of junk the jungular?
> – Jacked up in a jock the wrapper.[20]

Even the association of Jung, the jungular, the joke that bilked the hoax, with Jack the Ripper is both something less – and something more – than an insult. Tindall's words are right to the point here: "Reappearing in art, the horrors of life have become elements in a joyous, impersonal structure. The dominant tone of Joyce's great har-

[20]See James Joyce, *Finnegans Wake* (New York: Viking, 1939), pp. 115, 68, 460, 511.

monies of sound and rhythm is one of brightness and gaiety." He reminds us, in this concluding passage of his fine little book on Joyce, that in his Paris notebook "Joyce called comedy the greatest of arts because the joy of comedy is freest from desire or loathing" and could never understand why people did not see the humor in his work.[21]

One might just as well ask why people do not see the humor in their dreams, where displacement through punning makes great comics of the most solemn among us. But see it for its comedy or see it for its multilevel, multilingual presentation of a cyclical theory of history, *Finnegans Wake* is an incomparable repository of myth, fable, allegory, and parable as they are presented to us in the eruptions of the collective unconscious that reach consciousness, if only dream consciousness. They come to us in an astonishing repertory of disguise plays. On some rare occasions they even identify themselves for those who have the wit, the training, and the conviction necessary to meet them cheerfully and accept them for what they are. Joyce was one such person in his *Wake*, which is just what the word means, a joyous last rite of a kind he knew very well as an Irish Catholic, a translation into daytime terms of nighttime experiences, following "the immense and embracing concept of the universe as a dream, the legacy of Hindu philosophy that recurs in Carl Jung," as one of the better books about Joyce puts it.[22]

Joyce's sensitivity to dream is very clear from his writings, even in some of the first stories and poems, and in the dream notebook that he kept. We know that before 1915, he possessed pamphlets by Freud ("A Childhood Memory of Leonardo da Vinci") and Ernest Jones ("The Problem of *Hamlet* and the Oedipus Complex") and Jung ("The Significance of the Father in the Destiny of the Individual"). We know how much the plot to make him Jung's patient rankled and how raspingly and wittily he mocked the offer of Mrs. McCormick to effect the connection and the partnership of Ottocaro Weiss, her co-conspirator, as he saw it. In 1919, he wrote his friend Frank Budgen about Weiss: "He forgets only what he dislikes to remember, viz., that he promised me as a gift Doktor JUNG'S (prolonged universal applause) Wandlungen der Libido (shouts *Hear! Hear!* from a raughty tinker and an Irishman in the gallery)." Two years later, he recalled the event for his faithful patron, Harriet Weaver: "A batch of people in Zurich persuaded themselves that I was gradually going mad and actually endeavoured to induce me to enter a sanatorium where a certain Doctor Jung (the Swiss Tweedledum who is not to be confused with the Viennese Twee-

[21]Tindall, pp. 125–126.
[22]Marvin Magalaner and Richard M. Kain, *Joyce: The Man, the Work, the Reputation* (New York: Collier Books, 1962), p. 226.

dledee, Dr. Freud) amuses himself at the expense (in every sense of the word) of ladies and gentlemen who are troubled with bees in their bonnet."[23] In his final statement about the dastardly attempt to have him analyzed, Joyce's mockery is unmistakable, but so is his good humor. It occurs in the middle of the fifteenth chapter of the *Wake*, in a trial scene, where a pallid second-generation version of the book's central figure defends his father-son-self. "Are you to have all the pleasure quizzing on me?" he asks. "I have something inside of me talking to myself."

The tone is of aggrieved patient to analyst. The analyst is quick to respond: "You're a nice third degree witness, faith! But this is no laughing matter." Whereupon, in typical Joycean manner, the comedy begins. "Can you not distinguish the sense, prain, from the sound, bray?" Can't you tell the difference between the pain in the brain and the hee-haw noises, pray tell? This, then, is the diagnosis: "You have homosexual catheis of empathy between narcissism of the expert and steatopygic invertedness. Get yourself psychoanolised!" Everything suggests a fixation on the rear end, the buttocks, and anality, with a nice pun on "cathexis," an analytical jargon-word for concentration of energy on one channel, and "katheis," Greek for one-by-one delineation.

The patient's repudiation of diagnosis and prescription is rich in allusion to Jung and to Freud. "O begor, I want no expert nursis symaphy from your broons quadroons and I can psoakoonaloose myself any time I want (the fog follow you all!) without your interferences or any other pigeonstealer." No specialized nurse's sympathy (or symbol system) for him, from this dark mixed-blood analyst. He can psychoanalyze himself – as, of course, Freud did, as founder of the race – whenever he likes (a cloud of obscurity on the whole profession!), without any mediation from you (take that, Doktor Jung!) or any other thief of messages from the pigeons whose appointed task is to carry them.[24]

What Joyce is telling us in his good-humored oblique way is that he will play both parts, not so much analyst and analysand as dream and dreamer. He is his own expert. He will craft the symbols and tell us how to read them – or how not to. And that is exactly what he does in *Finnegans Wake*, with craftiness, pointing to this, not pointing to

---

[23]See *Selected Letters of James Joyce*, ed. Richard Ellmann (New York: Viking, 1976), pp. 244, 282.

[24]*Finnegans Wake*, p. 522. A constantly good-humored use of Jung is made by Anthony Powell through the character of General Aylmer Conyers in his multi-volume Proustian survey of British life from the First World War to the 1960s, *A Dance to the Music of Time*. General Conyers, who appears in eight of the twelve volumes, finds "interesting stuff" in Jung, is insistently aware of the

that, giving and taking away like the Dreamer-Deity he affects to be in that book, insisting that there can never be any final summary or reduction of its contents or even of its method and form. The same can be said, of course, about any really successful work of art and especially one so rich in the artifacts of the literary imagination. But here, as one of the more discerning and well equipped of writers about the *Wake*, Clive Hart, puts it, "Joyce is clearly allowing his Dreamers, whoever they may be, to draw on the whole quasi-Jungian collective unconscious for the substance of their fantasies."[25]

The process is elusive. The aim is to describe a world—*the* world—of mystery, mystery of gender and sexual identity, mystery of generation, mystery of purpose. It is an archetypal world, "quasi-Jungian" at the very least. That is not to say that the words of Jung about archetypal models can be applied literally to Leopold and Molly Bloom or the whole cast of *Finnegans Wake* as one commentator tries to do—"There is nothing in their behavior to suggest that they have an ego-consciousness. . . . They show, on the contrary, all the marks of fragmentary personalities. They are masklike, wraithlike, without problems, lacking self-reflection with no conflicts, no doubts, no sufferings; like gods, perhaps, who have no philosophy."[26] The Blooms and all of the *Wake* family, father, mother, sons, and daughter, are an *omnium gatherum* of conflicts, doubts, sufferings, problems. They wear masks but their substance is much too large to call it wraithlike. They may be fragmentary personalities; but they also have philosophies, and not simply as symbolic enactments of Joyce's thought. To speak of them as archetypal figures should not be to reduce them to robot-like personifications.

It is an equal mistake, I think, to separate Joycean archetype entirely from the Jungian as another commentator tries to do. To say that "the Joycean archetype is lexical, and hence to be relegated to linguistics and language studies," while the Jungian is "primarily conceptual and by its very genesis is relegated to psychology and psycho-

---

"personal myth" in people, identifies the central figure of folly of the books, Widmerpool, as a "typical intuitive extrovert" and diagnoses an egregious narcissism in him. See Anthony Powell, *At Lady Molly's* (Boston: Little, Brown, 1957), pp. 81, 226; *The Valley of Bones* (Boston: Little, Brown, 1964), p. 70; *The Military Philosophers* (Boston: Little, Brown, 1968), p. 231; *Books Do Furnish a Room* (Boston: Little, Brown, 1971), p. 147; *Temporary Kings* (Boston: Little, Brown, 1973), p. 17; *Hearing Secret Harmonies* (Boston: Little, Brown, 1975), pp. 31, 119.

[25]See Clive Hart, *Structure and Motif in Finnegans Wake* (Evanston, Ill.: Northwestern University Press, 1962), p. 80.

[26]See Sheldon Brivic, *Joyce Between Freud and Jung* (Port Washington, N. Y.: Kennikat, 1980), p. 198.

analysis," is simplistic in the extreme, both about Joyce and Jung.[27] We need everything – the resources of language and linguistic analysis and all that the work of analysts and analytical theorists can teach us – and we need to remember how incomplete, how clumsy, how tentative the conclusions we reach in this area must be. Hart's description of Joyce's task in the *Wake* suggests the limits perfectly; they come from a judicious reading of both Joyce and Jung. The task is "that of creating for the reader's contemplation a complete working-model of a collective unconscious in which his symbols could function. All the characters and even the inert symbolic objects are steeped in a fluid medium of generalised dream-consciousness; the motifs and motif-symbols, recurring again and again in this compendium of all minds, are subtly shaped and defined by their environment so that they finally come to have a significance, relative to the frames of reference of the book, analogous to that which is alleged for the Yeatsian or Jungian symbols."[28]

In late 1933, Samuel Beckett moved from Dublin to London to see if he could do something about his bodily miseries – persistent flu symptoms, boils and cysts that would not go away – and his troubled psyche – depression and its twin, anxiety. A good friend and physician strongly recommended psychoanalysis and led him to the Tavistock Clinic, where he worked with Wilfred Bion, a redoubtable original, but at least in part a Kleinian in his understanding of persecutory anxiety and movements through acceptance of negative "positions" to positive "reparation." It was a good and useful relationship, but not productive in any direct way. Beckett saw no results he could clearly point to. He was glad to accompany Bion, then, in the fall of 1935 to the third of five lectures Jung was giving at the Tavistock. Maybe the Swiss psychologist would have something of value to offer.

According to Beckett's biographer Deirdre Bair, the lecture had "a powerful impact on him." In the course of a very full lecture, Jung emphasized the capacity of complexes to speak for themselves, with identifiable voices "like the voices of definite people," with personalities of their own, however fragmentary, which reflect aspects of the psyche in which they appear. When the psyche is that of a writer, his characters inevitably reflect the complexes. Jung went on to describe the fascination of a patient with the world of the unconscious, to the degree where he becomes the "victim of a new autonomous activity that does not start from his ego but starts from the dark sphere." For

---

[27]See C. George Sandulescu, *The Language of the Devil: Texture and Archetypes in Finnegans Wake* (Chester Springs, Pa.: Dufour, 1988), p. 370.

[28]Hart, p. 147.

Beckett, says Bair, this was crucial. It brought Jung in tandem with Descartes, the Belgian Calvinist Arnold Geulincx, and André Malraux, thinkers who were providing Beckett "with necessary stimuli to shape the novel" he was writing, *Murphy*. Jung was persuasive to Beckett, in spite of his discomfort with the idea that a writer's work reflected the state of his psyche, or perhaps because of his own unmistakable experience of the autonomous activity Jung had described. Beckett knew about Jung; his poem "For Future Reference" had appeared in the same issue of *transition* in 1929 that featured Jung's "Psychology and Poetry."

The most important of Jung's statements in the lecture was in answer to a question about children's dreams. Jung instanced a ten-year-old girl with startling mythological dreams, which he felt he could not explain to the child's father because they seemed to foretell an early death. A year later, she was dead. "She had never been born entirely," Jung commented. For Beckett this was revelation. He found in Jung's words, according to Bair, the impetus to identify his own "womb fixation" and behavior that related to it, "from the simple inclination to stay in bed to his deep-seated need to pay frequent visits to his mother . . . all aspects of an improper birth." His analysis made sense at last. His own strong distrust of an ego-centered art or philosophy was supported. He had found confirmation and explication of at least some of the shadows he was to spend his writing life looking to penetrate.[29]

There is no missing Beckett's fixation upon the dark sphere of the unconscious, nor his genius in dramatizing its textures, its rhythms, its habitues, in novel, play, even film scenario just barely verbalized to give direction to Buster Keaton's acting, not to forget gloomy poetry of the utmost compression. Nor is there any difficulty finding rumination on Jungian themes and topics, openly in his radio play *All That Fall*, written in 1956, more covertly in other works, although never so hidden that the material can be dismissed as the wishful imposition of dogged psychologizers.

In the radio drama, Mrs. Maddy Rooney, a woman in her seventies, remembers "attending a lecturing by one of those new mind doctors." She cannot remember what they call them. "A lunatic specialist?" her blind husband suggests. "No, no, just the troubled mind, I was hoping he might shed a little light on my lifelong preoccupation

---

[29]See Deirdre Bair, *Samuel Beckett* (New York: Harcourt Brace Jovanovich, 1978), pp. 178-179, 207-211. The Jungian encounter is also described in Mary A. Doll, *Beckett and Myth: An Archetypal Approach* (Syracuse, N. Y.: Syracuse University Press, 1988), which promises more than its brevity (82 pages) permits it to deliver.

with horses' buttocks." (Beckett, it is not often enough remembered, is a funny man.) Mr. Rooney is more serious. He offers "neurologist." No, no, Maddy insists, "just mental distress, the name will come back to me in the night." The name is Jung. The occasion has stayed with her because of the story of the strange little girl whom the "mind doctor" had treated for some years and had finally to "give up." All that was wrong was that she was dying. "And she did in fact die, shortly after he washed his hands of her." Is there something wonderful about that, asks Mr. Rooney. No, it was something the doctor said and the way he said it which has "haunted" her ever since.

The description that follows shows how strongly Jung's words and manner haunted Beckett. When the lecturer had finished talking about the girl, Mrs. Rooney reports, "he stood there motionless for some time, quite two minutes I should say, looking down at his table. Then he suddenly raised his head and exclaimed, as if he had had a revelation, The trouble with her was she had never really been born!" She is struck by the fact that he spoke "throughout without notes," a remark that calls for a pause. So does her final observation about the evening: "I left before the end." Mr. Rooney, in good form, offers his laconic comment: "Nothing about your buttocks?" Mrs. R. responds by weeping and an all-purpose conclusion: "There is nothing to be done for those people!"

The finality of those words, half-funny, half-serious, is quickly dramatized. We are within a half-dozen pages of the end of the 58-page radio play. In the last moments a little boy, who has earlier appeared supporting Mr. Rooney in the blind man's advance onto the railway-station platform which is the location of the play, explains why a train is late. Its lateness has caused much talk. "It was a little child," the boy explains. "It was a little child fell out of a carriage. On to the line, Ma'am." He pauses. "Under the wheels, Ma'am." The play ends in a series of sound effects, picking up from silence and the boy's running off. A wind-and rainstorm begins, abates as the Rooneys move on, and then, after slow steps and a halt, begins again.[30] That is very much the rhythm of Beckett's work – a windstorm, a rainstorm; some mitigation, some blunting of the misery; then, increasingly slow, even dragging steps, many halts, back to the wretched state of things, into the barrel, up to the neck in sand. Krapp, memorialized in *Krapp's Last Tape*, when the last of his reels of recording runs out of content, stands motionless, staring ahead, while the tape runs on in silence. In the

[30]See Samuel Beckett, *All That Fall: A Play for Radio*, in *Krapp's Last Tape and Other Dramatic Pieces* (New York: Grove Press, 1958), pp. 31–91, with particular attention to pp. 82–84, where the Jung-Tavistock incident is brought vividly into play.

Buster Keaton *Film*, Keaton "sits, bowed forward, his head in his hands, gently rocking" and holds the disconsolate pose "as the rocking dies down." In the brilliant anti-theater ending of *Endgame*, which brings all the endings of this drama of terminus to a close, the filial servant Clov says, "This is what we call making an exit" as prelude to a brief exchange of statements of mutual obligation with his wheelchair-enthroned, paternal master Hamm. Then follow some pauses and halts, an exit, a return, a play at the covering of Hamm with a sheet, and more of the same sort of stage business to accompany Hamm's long concluding monologue of soft staccato comments. Clov's eyes remain fixed on Hamm as the father-master figure speaks of darkness, from the darkness, which he assures himself will surround him at the very end, after injunctions to "speak no more," by covering his face with a handkerchief.[31]

The most considerable, perhaps, of modern vaudevilles, and Beckett's most celebrated work, *Waiting for Godot*, ends both its acts with the simple stage direction for its actionless central characters, Estragon and Vladimir: "They do not move." The second dramatic motionlessness, at the end of the play, is made more poignant by Estragon's not realizing that his trousers have fallen down, adding to an atmosphere of mixed perplexity, tragedy, and delight. Estragon and Vladimir do not go. Godot does not come. The message that does always come for those who are waiting for Godot is that he won't come now, say this evening, but he will come sometime, say tomorrow. Without fail? Yes, Sir. In the last moments of the drama, just before the fall of the trousers and the last "They do not move," we learn that Godot has a beard, probably a white beard, and that he does nothing. All of which information extracts an exclamatory *Christe eleison* – Christ have mercy on us! – from Vladimir and an injunction to the messenger to make sure that Mr. Godot knows that the messenger-boy saw Vladimir.[32]

In many ways, Beckett's characters spend their time waiting, waiting for what or whom they cannot really say – perhaps a train, just to see whether it will be on time or late, or for speech to stop or to start, or for some motivation to let their trousers down or cover their faces, a reason to move, or to pause, or to halt forever. They are archetypal enactments of fragments out of the dark sphere, reflections of a psyche in and out of control of its unconscious contents. The surehandedness of the writer's control can be seen in the characterizations that have

---

[31]See Samuel Beckett, *Film* (New York: Grove Press, 1969), p. 52; *Krapp's Last Tape*, p. 28; *Endgame* (New York: Grove Press, 1958), pp. 81–84.

[32]See Samuel Beckett, *Waiting for Godot* (New York: Grove Press, 1954), pp. 35b, 58b-60b.

been so well represented by the great icons of comedy, Bert Lahr, Buster Keaton, and their like. The power of the bubblings from below can be felt in the constant reiteration of the theme of a despairing incompleteness, dramatized in the lives of figures, like the little girl in Jung's Tavistock lecture who "had never been born entirely," both in their actions and actionlessness, in their words and in their silences.

Beckett's is a vision and iconography of the dark unconscious, punctuated by glimmerings of light, shards of dim understanding that permit him, or allow those fragments of his person that are his characters, to speak. His is very much the world unveiled to Beckett in that epochal Tavistock lecture of Jung's, with echoes here and there, it may be, of the Jung piece that appeared alongside his own in *transition* and the essay on Ulysses, which Beckett, as Joyce's amanuensis and friend, must surely have known. The iconography is nowhere so archetypally pure, so plunged into the deep dyes of the unconscious, as in *The Unnameable*, third of the trilogy of novels which begins with *Molloy* and *Malone Dies*, written and published in French, then translated into English by the author.

The problem for most readers of *The Unnameable* is to translate it from any language into understanding. It is a work rooted so deeply in the unconscious and yet tied so firmly to its speaking image, in precisely the terms with which Beckett has limned that image and granted it speech, that it often defies conscious intellection. But if we bring to the process of understanding some sense of what Jung was saying at the Tavistock Clinic and what is reflected of it in Beckett's other work, we must find some ease in this, the most artful distillation of the "never been born entirely" material. It is worth the effort, whatever that may be, for here is a greatly gifted writer at his best, turning over and over and over again the procedures and contents of the conscious-unconscious and unconscious-conscious world in which we live so much of our life, or do not live it or only approximate a life, never having been born entirely.

What is the idea? The idea is that the Unnameable has been alone, and "here," that is, in the place of those who are alone, "ever since I began to be. . . ." He is alone in a silence, a torso who speaks from a jar, as he tells us, the trunk of a person endowed with just enough physicality, education, and the sands of existence, to speak and to have something to speak about. He has no reason to be anxious, nothing to be afraid of; he is alone, speaking from "a great smooth ball" of a head, "featureless, but for the eyes, of which only the sockets remain." But he is no horror movie, he is not a repulsive fantasm; nothing in Beckett can be reduced to that. He is simply the epitome of the never entirely born, a compulsive speaker ("I have to speak. . . . Nothing can ever exempt me from it. . . ."), to his own astonishment "confoundedly well informed," though for all that, "a mine of useless knowledge."

Can a talking torso with a ball-joint head command our feeling? Are our feelings stirred to the point of empathy or even sympathy to learn that he–it–the Unnameable–has "lost" all his members "with the exception of the onetime virile?" He himself thinks not. Even those who are appalled by what they see, and incapacitated for work or happiness, have only to look again to be made easy, he tells us: "For my face reflects nothing but the satisfaction of one savouring a well-earned rest." He would like to turn away from everything. He enjoys having his face shrouded, mourns his loss of arms for a moment, then muses that "to start masturbating again" at his age "would be indecent." There is life in him, after all, whatever its percentage, a half-life, a quarter-life, some life, enough life to contemplate death as proof of life. If he dies, he will know that he has lived.

He takes comfort in opposing conditions, in reflecting that the "impossible . . . cannot be prolonged, unduly." It is a fact that he has "endured," although he should not have, that he has remained with a voice he should have fled from, finding hope in suffering, a solace of sorts in thinking, in a parody of Descartes, that his "existence is only a matter of time." He wonders if he has had blackouts, missed whole sentences, or "Perhaps . . . missed the keyword to the whole business." Well, maybe one day he will know what he is "guilty of."

As the extraordinary soliloquy mounts to the inevitable combined climax and anti-climax, the Unnameable speaks the crucial words: "Be born, dear friends, be born, enter my arse, you'll just love my colic pains, it won't take long, I've got the bloody flux." It's not "so easy as it looks . . . you must have the taste for it . . . you must be born alive . . . it's not something you can acquire. . . ." Finally he comes to doubt that he is really there. He knows that he is there where he has always been, to the extent that he has ever been: "I haven't stirred, that's all I know, no, I know something else, it's not I. . . ."

The rejection of the ego for the silence is the endgame, the last turn of the plot, the shutting-up that will bring peace. This is Beckett. This is the world of the never entirely born, this collectivity of fragmentary, conscious unconsciousnesses, never at a loss for words, and never more verbal than when silence is promised and itself promises an end to all things. And so the last words really are the first words, the words the unconscious insists on speaking even in such a truncated life as this one, where the never entirely born is visible in its limblessness: "you must go on, I can't go on, you must go on, I'll go on, you must say words, as long as there are any, until they find me, until they say me . . . in the silence you don't know, you must go on, I can't go on, I'll go on." Limbless, yes; wordless, no.[33] Trousers fall, faces are covered, figures stand motionless, the rocking dies down, no more words from an unnameable talking torso in a specimen jar. We see how much life Beckett has been able to give to those "who had never been born entirely," those in whose incompleteness he found his fulfillment.

"Every symbol has a hundred interpretations, each of which may be right," says Hermann Hesse, writing about *The Brothers Karamazov.* "In this book," he continues, "during a period of great upheavals, mankind has fashioned for itself a symbol, set up a picture in the way an individual in his dreams produces a copy of the instincts and forces battling and reaching an adjustment within him." In those words, written in 1919, the same year that *Demian* appeared, Hesse might just as well be describing his own novel, of all his works the one that most unmistakably shows Jungian influence.

There is no question that *Demian* was largely shaped by the analytic hours he spent with the Jungian therapist Joseph B. Lang in Lucerne in 1916 and 1917, when Hesse was 29 and 30. Lang appears in the book as Pistorius, a master of mythology, and all the struggles of the book's central character, Emil Sinclair, from the age of ten to twenty, could well be interpreted as the rich reflections of the battles and forces that emerged in something more than seventy analytic sessions. Demian's name may indeed be a way of telling the reader that he is a *daimon*, Sinclair's inner voice. That he is also one way or another Hesse's interior tutor becomes quite clear as the novel moves through its Jungian drama. There are all the requisite struggles to claim an ego, to deal with rough forces, dark forces, forces bursting from the unconscious, to find a self. There is an encounter with a Gnostic deity, Abraxas, whose shadowy mixture of good and evil, light and dark, is interpreted for Sinclair by Lang in the persona of Pistorius. Much is made of the symbolism of a bird emerging from a great egg and sexual identity is cunningly worked into the story, first with a chance encounter with a girl in a park, then with a full-fledged anima figure. The girl, whom Sinclair never addresses, he names Beatrice and weaves a worshipful fantasy around her like a Germanic version of Stephen Dedalus pursuing his blessed damozel in *A Portrait of the Artist as a Young Man.* The anima incarnation is Demian's mother, Frau Eva, who might just as well be the Great Mother for Sinclair, as Theodore Ziolkowski suggests in his fine long treatment of the novel in his book on Hesse.

Symbols pop up on every page of *Demian.* Interpretations are

[33]See Samuel Beckett, *The Unnameable,* in *Three Novels* (New York: Grove Press, 1965), pp. 291, 293, 301–303, 305, 314, 316–317, 327–328, 331–332, 361–364, 366–368, 380, 412, 414.

bound to follow, hundreds as Hesse has said of the Dostoevsky novels, each of which may indeed be right – unless, as may also be true, Hesse has so boxed in his character's movement toward individuation with his own experiences of analytic psychology and his musings on it that we must look everywhere for signs of the apparatus gathered meticulously by the writer from Lang and Jung and Bachofen and the Gnostics. Lang was not only his analyst; he was a close friend. Jung was not simply the provider of materials for analytic discussion; he was the compelling interpreter of *Wandlungen und Symbole der Libido – Transformations and Symbols of the Libido*, which we know now in English as *Symbols of Transformation* – a book that Hesse read with great care in 1916. And so we can move in *Demian* as through a doctrinal exposition and find every argument to support such a reading – and quite miss the book. For it is indeed a kind of Jungian soul drama, but it is also a work with its own wryness, a texture which should produce smiles, even grimaces in the reader as the writer offers himself to our view, like Joyce's author-bird, Stephen Dedalus, bursting from his shell. It would not be wrong, I think, to see in the unmistakable ironies that are in *Demian* the fashioning of a portrait of this young artist, Hermann Hesse, as a young man, a rather fussy, somewhat pompous, but not altogether humorless young man, sitting in exaggerated pose for a photographer of similar character.[34]

In a shrewd statement, "Artists and Psychoanalysis," contemporary with the writing of *Demian*, Hesse acknowledged the value of the material turned up by the theorists and therapists, Freud, Jung, Stekel, Rank. Here was "another key – not an infallible magic key, but nevertheless a valuable new conception, a splendid new tool. . . ." The artist would be wrong to bring psychoanalytic techniques into his work directly and equally mistaken not to take it seriously. In the world of analysis, the artist will find "confirmation of the value of fantasy," will find that "what he at times is inclined to regard as 'only' a fiction is actually of the highest value. . . ." Hesse looks with pleasure on the experience of "a warmer, more fruitful and passionate exchange between conscious and unconscious" and the bringing into the light of what otherwise would be discarded, left "below the threshold," wasted in disregarded dreams. But the artist must be on guard, and here

---

[34]See Hermann Hesse, *Demian*, trans. Michael Boloff and Michael Lebeck (New York: Harper and Row, 1965). In the 1948 introduction that Thomas Mann wrote for *Demian*, he underscores Hesse's analytic method: "even as a poet he likes the role of editor and archivist, the game of masquerade behind the guise of one who 'brings to light' other people's papers," and points to *Magister Ludi* (*Glasperlenspiel* in German) as the finest example of Hesse's gamesmanship, that "sublime work of his old age . . . drawn from all sources of human culture . . ." (p. viii).

Hesse quotes a passage from Schiller "discovered" by Otto Rank, which warns against that relaxation before the impulses of the intellect which will allow ideas to stand unexamined, paradoxically enough, isolated, without that testing by association with other ideas which makes judgment possible. On the other hand, to extend the paradoxical tension for the creative mind, Schiller insists, the guard must be withdrawn and ideas allowed to "rush in pell-mell . . . only then does the intellect survey and criticize the whole assembly."[35]

In *Siddhartha*, ideas do rush in pell-mell, the intellect does look over and judge the quality of the ideas and those to whom they have come. But more important, a serene and gentle, perhaps even saintly, peace arrives to define the Buddhist achievement. One face becomes many faces; one man becomes hundreds, thousands. Then all disappear in an extraordinary translation of Nirvana into what looks like the Jungian Self.[36]

Jung thought that *Siddhartha* and the book that followed it, *Steppenwolf*, were, as he wrote an American professor of German who was writing a dissertation on the relationship of Jungian psychology and Hesse, "the direct or indirect results of certain talks" he had had with the writer. Jung could not say "how much he was conscious of the hints and implications I let him have. I'm not in a position to give you full information, since my knowledge is strictly professional."[37] Hesse did have a few sessions with Jung in 1921, at the time that he was working on *Siddhartha*, and did speak at some meetings of Jungian groups in Zurich. Writer and psychologist stayed in touch, disagreed about the value and meaning of "sublimation," the one publicly, the other privately, and whether by systematic appropriation of ideas or doctrines or analysis or for some other reason, were important each for the other.

The sense of value one finds for oneself through analysis was certainly something Hesse took with him from his two-year work with Lang and his encounters with Jung, both on the printed page and in person. The path from the low irresponsibility of childhood to the high irresponsibility of the realm of spirit surely owes something, as Hesse developed it in *Demian* and afterward, to the Jungian understanding of growth from ego to Self. But most clearly, Hesse's life was given

---

[35]See Hermann Hesse, *My Belief: Essays on Life and Art*, ed. Theodore Ziolkowski, trans. Denver Lindley (New York: Farrar, Straus and Giroux, 1974), pp. 47–48, 50–51, 189–190.

[36]See Hermann Hesse, *Siddhartha*, trans. Hilda Rosner (New York: New Directions, 1951), pp. 120–122.

[37]See C. G. Jung, *Letters*, ed. Gerhard Adler and Aniela Jaffé, trans. R. F. C. Hull (Princeton, N. Y.: Princeton University Press, 1973), vol. I, p. 52.

direction and his novels sure footing in the thickets and brambles where conscious and unconscious meet. He was able, as Theodore Ziolkowski emphasizes, to acknowledge his place in suffering humanity; he is "an almost archetypal model" for it. Through analysis, he was able "to understand himself more fully than ever before, to look deep into his heart and acknowledge his own guilt in the evil that had befallen him and the world."[38] Thus it is that he participates in his novels after *Demian*. As Sinclair, he makes clear his sinful failings. As Demian he attends to his daimon. He retraces in hopeful vision the journey of the Buddha in *Siddhartha*, one that even at a third or fourth remove he can attempt to emulate. He marks his own presence by the names he gives the central figures of *Steppenwolf* and *The Journey to the East*, Harry Haller in the first, simply his own initials, H. H., no more, in the second. Even in the would-be medieval allegory, *Narcissus and Goldmund*, and the intellectual rituals of *The Glass Bead Game* (*Magister Ludi*), he is omnipresent, as prototype, antitype, cautionary example, motivating figure. He had learned, and learned well, to play with the fragments of the objective psyche and the guises of the personal unconscious, as analysis had revealed them to him, and his own peregrinations in the thickets and brambles of the collective unconscious brought him increased ease in that territory.

Hesse's labors are intense to the point of exhaustion in *Steppenwolf*, the tale of a figure who seems to step out of a silent film of the 1920s at least as much as to emerge from Middle European intellectual debate, as the title suggests. Harry Haller, the lone wolf of the steppes, wears the masks of a suicidal intellectual and of a wanderer through pop culture. He is tutored by a prostitute and a jazz musician, both well extended by Hesse beyond the limits of cliché characterization, and also by himself, as keeper of the records of his own life. He becomes a contemplative of the symbols of personal transformation; he grasps, first tentatively, then with some security, the multiplicity of selves within him, looking at them in a magic glass offered by Pablo the jazzman. Finally, in this high end of the book, he can see himself and discuss himself in the third person, unpretentiously, almost with a sense of humor. He has moved from a simple-minded adolescent typology to the point where contradictions and opposing types are more interesting to him than fixed ones.[39]

The opposition of types is dramatized in *Narcissus and Goldmund*, a lengthy parable in medieval clothing. The first, a cloistered

---

[38]Theodore Ziolkowski, *The Novels of Hermann Hesse* (Princeton, N. Y.: Princeton University Press, 1965), p. 10.

[39]See Herman Hesse, *Steppenwolf*, trans. Basil Creighton, Joseph Mileck, Horst Frenz (New York: Holt, Rinehart and Winston, 1963), pp. 214–217.

monk who becomes abbot of his community, aids and abets the second, a woodcarver who begins his journey of self-understanding with him as a cloister boy at Mariabronn. The names are suitably allegorical: Narcissus, a prodigy in all the intellectual and spiritual disciplines of the all-purpose medieval setting of the book, is enraptured like his mythological precursor by an image of himself, or rather an image of Self. Goldmund (Goldenmouth) speaks through his "violent, exclusive friendship" with Narcissus, through the images that come to him in dreams, through an eloquence stirred by nature and by beautiful things, by women, by what he can draw, by what he can carve into wood. When he leaves the cloister, he becomes a mixture of artist and wastrel, a candidate for the gallows from which Abbot Narcissus ultimately rescues him. Each in his own way has made the ascent and descent. Each, with or without clear consciousness, has reconciled the opposing pieties of reason, spirit, flesh, art, nature.[40]

There is nothing adolescent about the way *Narcissus and Goldmund* winds its way through its mixture of asceticism and aestheticism to its conclusion, nor about where Hesse's ruminations about art and the unconscious and the threefold and twofold paths took him. In a very short novel, *The Journey to the East*, and a very long one, *The Glass Bead Game*, Hesse describes the voyages to the homeland, to the motherland. Each journey involves trial and error, much from the world of asceticism, much from the aesthetic. Each is a teasing game, with some of the mock-seriousness of *The Magic Flute*, and some at least by aim of the Mozart opera's profundity. Each finds some resolution in what looks like the practice of active imagination. How much Hesse drew upon Jung in fashioning these dramas of what Eugene Stelzig calls the "confessional imagination" is not easy to describe or to define. As Stelzig says, "In the case of Jung and Hesse, there is a shared literary and cultural heritage that can be readily invoked without getting into the quagmire (or infinite regress) of particular and demonstrable 'influences.' "[41]

The activity of the imagination is central. With falling and rising consciousness, the pivotal figures in the two journeys move past guilt and disillusionment into a higher irresponsibility, where as artist, dreamer, analysand, and devotee of the realm of spirit they can accept the inevitably disordered mixing of opposites. It is not simply a *coinci-*

---

[40]See Hermann Hesse, *Narcissus and Goldmund*, trans. Ursule Molinaro (New York: Bantam, 1971), *passim*.

[41]See Eugene L. Stelzig, *Hermann Hesse's Fictions of the Self* (Princeton, N. Y.: Princeton University Press, 1988), p. 142. There are excellent pages on Jung and Hesse in this book and in Ralph Freedman's *Herman Hesse: Pilgrim of Crisis* (New York: Pantheon, 1978), as well as Ziolkowski's pioneering work (see footnote 38).

dentia but a *complexio oppositorum* here, a complicated bringing together and connecting of opposites. The wax figure which the musician H. H. contemplates at the end of *Journey* looks like a piece of sculpture "which could be called 'Transitoriness' or 'Decay,' or something similar."[42] Unity need not be made visible – assuming, for a moment, that that is even possible. To make the transitory eternal, it must be accepted as somehow a significant part of the eternal. That is one way in which the artist can claim his shadow. It is not an easy claim to make, as the epigraph with which *The Glass Bead Game* opens reminds us. It is easier, we are told in the words of Albertus Secundus, to represent nonexisting things than existing ones, in the ordinary course of events. If one is a "serious and conscientious historian," it is just the opposite. Or more precisely, what must be done, for all its difficulty, is to describe those things "whose existence is neither demonstrable nor probable." The improbability of dealing with these refractory things and bringing them into life is further suggested, with that glint of irony which turns up in all the best of Hesse's work, by the ascription of the epigraph, quoted first in Latin and then in translation, to Albertus Secundus, an ancient master invented by Hesse. Furthermore, the translation is exactly the opposite of what seems to be presented. Hesse wrote the epigraph in the vernacular, and then had it made over into Latin by two friends whose German names, rendered in Latin, appear as editors of the nonexistent work of Albert the Second, a treatise on the spirit, like *The Glass Bead Game* itself, like all the late works of Hesse.

What is simple acceptance of the *complexio oppositorum* in *The Journey to the East* becomes a highly complex undertaking in the dialectical interplay of *The Glass Bead Game*, requiring for its completion nothing less than the fullest living through of a reasonably long life. More than that, it requires all the graces of the imagination, which come and go, as Hesse knew from his own experience and as his protagonist in the *Game*, Joseph Knecht, must learn again and again, with an infuriating uncertainty their only trustworthy element. But even if the ability to conceive images, or at least something substantial, of "what is neither demonstrable nor probable," is not dependable, there is a way of invoking their presence, of stimulating the imagination, of moving within the orbit of its graces. It is what Jung called active imagination. It is a moving with all deliberateness into the experience of the fictive. One becomes the imagined thing, the would-be person. One forms an image or a concept, not simply by intellectual process, but by such fullnesses of transformation – extravagances,

---

[42]See Hermann Hesse, *The Journey to the East*, trans. Hilda Rosner (New York: Bantam, 172), p. 122.

even – that one becomes a thing, person, event. That, it seems to me, is what Hesse is doing in his *Game*; that is what the game is about. It is a moving through one central life, Knecht's and an intellectual and cultural kingdom, Castalia, which is both a utopia and a dystopia, to identify, replicate, and become one with the realm of spirit, Hesse's deeply, insistently, provocatively imagined highest realm of the imagination.

The clue everywhere is in the processes of active imagination. "The artistically inclined delight in the Game," one of the wisest of the teachers, the Music Master, explains to Knecht, "because it provides opportunities for improvisation and fantasy." It is despised by scholars and scientists because it lacks the strictures of their disciplines. Good enough, the Master says, but one must get away from "violent inclinations and disinclinations. . . . Each of us is merely one human being, merely an experiment, a way station. But each of us should be on the way to perfection, should be striving to reach the center, not the periphery." But perfection, as the journeys of Knecht and his contemporaries and their teachers demonstrate, is more a matter of verbal and dream image, of manipulation of the beads of the game, than of actual experience.

The apparatus of the game does not much matter, not its abacuslike physical structures, or its formulas, or its mathematical operations. It presents to us a monasticism of the intellect, in a community that abstracts – from various idealizations of the life of mind, spirit, meditation – the discursive processes of human interiority pursued in a kind of unsettled quiet. The first appeal of the game is to those who, like mathematicians, could play it "with a virtuosity and formal strictness at once athletic and ascetic." But this becomes only too easily, in this world of some unspecified future looked back upon from the year 2400, an institutionalized egoism, insufficiently responsive to Knecht's daimon, which had played such a large part in his being attracted to the game, or to the moving of "the inner self and the outer world" toward each other, or to that mixture of "the antipodes of this life, its Yin and Yang," which bring together "unstinting service of the hierarchy" and self-awakening "toward advancing, toward apprehending reality."[43]

The points of book and author cannot be made tersely. They need the large, solid, but not too heavy structure of the book, of its Kantian, Nietzschean, Burckhardtian, Jungian tensions and distensions, and the paraphernalia of Hesse's own journeyings. His other works – novels, poetry, critical musings – all are vital if one wants to accom-

[43]See Hermann Hesse, *Magister Ludi*, trans. Richard and Clara Winston (New York: Bantam, 1970), pp. 68, 24, 36–37, 47, 251.

pany him where he leads. Miguel Serrano, the Chilean writer and diplo-
mat, in his little book on Hesse and Jung, quotes himself as saying to
Jung that for Hesse "the right road is simply one which is in agreement
with nature." Jung agrees; that is also his philosophy. "Man should live
according to his own nature," Jung says; "he should concentrate on
self-knowledge and then live in accordance with the truth about himself. What would you say about a tiger who was a vegetarian? You
would say, of course, that he was a bad tiger." That is a suitably
gnomic utterance, amplified just enough with the injunction to live in
accord with one's nature, "both individually and collectively." Better
still is a passage in a long letter from Jung to Serrano, which although
not directly about Hesse was occasioned by comments about him and
by thought related to his. It is Jung near the end of his life, saying a
great deal in a few words, toward the end of a fine long letter, speaking
about things which are enduring in his thought and Hesse's:

> *To be is to do and to make.* But as our existence does not depend
> solely upon our Ego-will, thus our doing and making depends
> largely upon the dominant of the unconscious. I am not only will-
> ing out of my Ego, but I am also made to be creative and active. To
> be quiet is only good for someone who has been too or perversely
> active. Otherwise it is an unnatural artifice, which unnecessarily
> interferes with our nature.[44]

That is, it seems to me, a splendid addendum to *The Glass Bead Game,*
if not a summation of the book, and a fair indication of the influence of
Jungian thought and analysis upon the best work of Hermann Hesse.

Jung is in constant attendance in Hermann Broch's astonishing
novel *The Death of Virgil,* in which death and life face each other at the
supreme moment in the experience of the epic poet, his last twenty-
four hours. Transformation has never had a more precise text. Virgil is
struggling somehow, as life surrenders to death, to articulate the experience of death in what remains to him of life. He fails, he must fail, he
does not entirely fail, something comes through "the ever denser mist
. . . he, the man, having remained human notwithstanding his con-
course with the uncreated. . . ."
There is nothing like it in our literature, except perhaps the voy-
age beyond earthly boundaries of Dante. "No longer as an earthly face,
but just as a beholding tree-top, he gazed upward to the stars, into the
face of heaven which had gathered into itself the lineaments of all
creatures and had transfigured them. . . ." The sentence, God's sen-

---

[44]See Miguel Serrano, *C. G. Jung and Hermann Hesse: A Record of Two Friend-
ships,* trans. Frank MacShane (New York: Schocken, 1966), pp. 91, 87.

tence, man's sentence, a death-sentence, a life-sentence, goes on for more than a page and a half, and does so clearly, richly, magically, before reaching the "boundary of plant-life," then "Primal darkness," and finally the movement through an ever-enlarging brightness into "a breath-stripped universal day." Virgil – and the writer and the reader – experience unity, where there is "neither direction nor beginning nor end." But where, Virgil asks himself, is "his own face in this universe?" And again, "was he, who was no longer even floating, no longer held by any hand, actually here at all?"

There are answers of a sort, some beholding "in the middle of the world-shield, in its infinite depth," some response to "the summons of the word." There is a great "rumbling," a tumultuous "breaking forth as a communication beyond every understanding. . . ." There is the conviction that "nothing could be lost, because end was joined to beginning. . . ." The word hovers "over the universe, over the nothing, floating beyond the expressible as well as the inexpressible," and Virgil floats "on with the word" and is "enveloped" by a "roaring," by a "flooding sound and . . . penetrated by it . . . incomprehensible and unutterable for him: it was the word beyond speech."[45]

Not even a Virgil can capture this. This is the epic man experiences but is given no time as we understand time to explain it, to transcribe it. Broch comes close. Working his way somehow, somewhere into the archetypes of transfiguration, living what we cannot live until we cease to live, he brings death alive in this long, captivating account of the ultimate individuation.

It is, as Aniela Jaffé suggests in her study of *The Death of Virgil* in the Festschrift presented to Jung on his eightieth birthday, a significant contribution to our understanding of individuation. It is appropriately summarized by Ernestine Schlant in her fine crisp book on the writer: "Brochian mythologizing mixes the Jungian archetypal myth of consciousness with the Judaeo-Christian covenant and presents them in the antithetical relation between ethics and aesthetics."[46] But suggestions and summaries can deliver us only to what Broch, in his Virgilian persona, calls "the fore-court of reality." For the rest we must

---

[45]See Hermann Broch, *The Death of Virgil*, trans. Jean Starr Untermeyer (New York: Pantheon, 1945), pp. 467, 469, 473–475, 477–482.

[46]See Ernestine Schlant, *Hermann Broch* (Chicago: University of Chicago Press, 1986), p. 108. The Jaffé study of Virgil's individuation process, "Hermann Broch: 'Der Tod des Vergil': Ein Betrag zum Problem der Individuation," appears in *Studien zur analytischen psychologie C. G. Jungs. Festschrift zum 80. Geburstag von C. G. Jung* (Zurich: Rhein-Verlag, 1955), II, pp. 288–343. Also worth looking at for the treatment of Broch's relationship to Jung is Peter B. Waldeck, *The Split Self from Goethe to Broch* (Lewisburg, Pa.: Bucknell University Press, 1979).

work and play as Broch worked and played, must join him as he joined Jung in trying to construct an epistemology of the collective unconscious, a ritual, however brittle and incomplete, for wrestling the archetypes into conscious awareness.

In a number of handsomely cadenced passages, which Jean Starr Untermeyer has made into a strong free verse, Broch as Virgil brings us, in the fore-court of reality, to his theory of knowledge of the unconscious, collective and personal. It is "the necessity inherent in the universe," where perception discovers itself and turns toward itself "as if for the first time," where "man is held into his task of knowing" and nothing will turn him away from it, "not even the inevitability of error." This is the way into knowledge, into being, no less. It has such strength, such power, as it moves beyond an earth-bound sham-infinity, that even the fear of death can be faced, and thus life can be lived in its fullness:

> . . . through such conscious assimilation
> the dread might be expunged,
> only thus might one pass through the horny portal of dread
> and achieve existence;
> this was the reason why man was held into the space of
>   incertitude. . . .

What reason? This reason, that he, that we, all of us, can be "held into space after space" of our "own awareness," as we move "into the spaces" of the "self-realizing self, self-realization—fate of the human soul."[47]

"It is a queer business, being an author, and I do not fit into any of the well-known categories." So says Robertson Davies about his work. But the judgment is wrong, I think, whether one interprets it as a kind of boasting or diffidence. Davies fits into a number of categories. He is knowledgeable about the theater, having worked in it in several capacities, and he writes well about it. He is a good critic, even a literary theorist of sorts, although he approaches theory obliquely, in

---

[47]*The Death of Virgil*, pp. 99–103. Broch knew Jung—he was introduced to him by Jolande Jacoby at about the time he was finishing his other great novel, *The Sleepwalkers*, in 1932—and there are frequent references to Jung and Jungian ideas in Broch's letters. There are Jungian textures in the stories that make up *The Guiltless* (Boston: Little, Brown, 1974), and there are in the various versions of the unfinished *Mountain Novel* (*Der Bergroman*)(Frankfurt: Suhrkamp), as in the stories, anima/animus speculations, presented through narrative and characterization. For all his ease with literary devices, it is clear in his late work that Broch was moving farther and farther away from any trust in the conventions of literature, or even in the enduring strengths of the art, but not, it is equally clear, from his preoccupation with human interiority and the archetypal forces alive in it.

asides in his engaging essays. In these essays he shows the good effects of a late career as a university professor, as he also does in his work as a novelist. That is, of course, his most considerable category, one he fits securely. In all these categories, he writes with the confidence and grace of one who has pursued – and gained – psychological understanding.

Davies is not shy about his understanding. "When I am asked why I have spent so much time, over the past twenty-five years, in the study of the work and thought of Dr. C. G. Jung, I reply that it is because Jung's discoveries and speculations throw so much light on my work as a student and teacher of literature." Jung's psychology, as compared with Freud's, has the advantage of being "much more aesthetic and humanistic in its general tendency . . . not so Procrustean in its effect on artistic experience." Perhaps its summary virtue for a novelist is that it "is not a system of dogma, and it is no enemy to common sense. It does, however, try to persuade common sense to venture into paths which are not commonly explored, though they are not new, and many people before Jung called attention to them."

And so with archetype and dream in hand and with a notable freedom from jargon and dogma, Davies ventures into the paths of the novelist, some reasonably well known, some quite uncommon to fictional exploration. Those ventures have led to two trilogies with unmistakable Jungian textures and convictions, gatherings of novels that have almost seemed to demand their own literary and psychological form, as Davies makes clear in talking about the first of them, *The Deptford Trilogy*. It was not planned as a trilogy and it does not read as a trilogy, but it all hangs together, for there was always more Davies wanted to say about materials uncovered in each of the volumes. And so *Fifth Business* led to *The Manticore* and that in turn – because its "matter . . . was still troubling" the writer – led to *World of Wonders*.[48]

Village and theater struggle for allegorical roles in this trilogy. Deptford is an Ontario village which yields the opening movements of the story and its movers. The voice we hear in the first volume quickly invokes the theater. "I have been cast by Fate," says Dunstan Ramsay, "and by my own character for the vital though never glorious role of Fifth Business!" He looks, the schoolmaster Ramsay is telling us, as if he were a supernumerary in the drama but he is in fact, although neither hero nor villain nor confidante, "nonetheless essential to bring about the Recognition or denouement." Ramsay's further comment is disingenuous: "Who could not, indeed, comprehend what Fifth Busi-

[48]See Robertson Davies, *One Half of Robertson Davies* (New York: Penguin, 1978) pp. 14, 143, 126, 192, 15–16.

ness is, even if he should meet the player of that part in his own trivial life-drama!" What gives *Fifth Business* its hold on the reader is that we never fully understand what that part is, although we would like to do so, because of Ramsay's own qualities and those—all over the lot psychologically—of the people whose lives intersect with his. In a sometimes tantalizing way, Davies has insinuated himself into the persona of the schoolteacher-narrator: "The business of getting used to myself as a hero was only part of the work I had on hand. . . ." The kind of life I wanted to live—yes, but I was not at all sure what it was. I had flashes of insight and promptings, but nothing definite." There is a mixture of transference and countertransference here, from character to author and from author to character, that seems tutored by the relationship between analyst and analysand. It adds a pleasing irony to events and keeps them from turning into melodrama as major figures replace minor ones at center stage and the mystery of the death of a Toronto financier, Boy Staunton, star of the show, gives way at the last moment to the pyrotechnics of Magnus Eisengrim, an "illusionist" whose turn on stage will be the leading one in the last volume of the trilogy.

About two-thirds through *Fifth Business*, the narrator, speaking in both his voices, Ramsay's and Davies's, admits that "by this time I was myself much concerned with that old fantastical duke of dark corners, C. G. Jung. . . ." The remark is very much in passing, but it suggests the magic of the writer's preoccupation with the psyche, as he moves from fictional events well under way to the sensibilities taking them in—his own, his Fifth Business recitalist's, and ours, his readers', all indebted one way or another to the "old fantastical duke" for shedding light on the dark corners, or at least providing the candle-power.[49]

There is much more of Jung in *The Manticore*, which is really a case history shrewdly pasted together from a brief narrative in conventional first-person recital by the "case" of David Staunton, lawyer son of Boy Staunton, from his Zurich notebook which records his experience of analysis with a Jungian analyst, Johanna von Haller, and a final tidying up through a week of his diary pages. The title is explained in mid-analysis, after David has dutifully, classically, fallen in love with Dr. von Haller. It is a dream image in which a smiling, sibylline Johanna, dressed "in a white robe with a blue mantle," holds a lion on a chain. The lion has a man's face, David's, and a tail that ends in "a kind of spike, or barb." The creature is quickly identified as the manticore of fable, with lion's body, man's face, and a tail that stings.

---

[49]See Robertson Davies, *Fifth Business*, in *The Deptford Trilogy* (New York: Penguin, 1983), pp. 19, 91, 121, 186.

By association it is also an image of David's undeveloped feeling function. Touchy, as undeveloped feelings will be, dangerous in its barbs, like the lawyer Staunton in court, "The Unconscious chooses its symbolism with breath-taking artistic virtuosity."[50]

The story lines in the last volume reach back to the village in which, as we are reminded very strongly at the end of this novel, Boy Staunton threw a snowball with a stone in it, on a fateful day in 1908, that hit Mary Dempster, large with the child that was to become, after a suitable name change, Magnus Eisengrim. Magnus was born prematurely because of the explosive event and his mother was maddened. He blamed Boy for both. The *World of Wonders* that Eisengrim enters soon enough in boyhood is a carnival show, scene of multiple initiations for him, into sodomizing homosexuality, into the magic of mind and machine, into enchantments harmless and harmful. The occasion of the making of a film about a legendary French illusionist for the BBC, with Magnus playing the part of the conjuror, becomes the opportunity for a book-length conversation in which Eisengrim tells all.[51]

The Jungian lines are perhaps more obscure in the second trilogy than in the first, but they are unmistakable once one sees how they turn up, in refraction and obliqueness rather than open adoption. No therapy sessions in *The Rebel Angels*, *What's Bred in the Bone*, or *The Lyre of Orpheus*, but a plenitude of archetypes, of Gnosticism, of alchemy, of mythic truth and daimonic presence, and by the last pages of the last volume an open acknowledgment of Jung, even if by ironic inversion. The rebel angels—straight out of the Gnostic gospels—are translated into an odd lot of professors at the College of St. John and the Holy Ghost (Davies's little joke with refractory spirits) at the University of Toronto. Their function, as one of the two narrative voices in the first book explains it to one of them, was not to be "soreheaded egotists like Lucifer. Instead they gave mankind another push up the ladder, they came to earth and taught tongues, and healing and laws and hygiene—taught everything—and they were often special successes with 'the daughters of men.' " The woman doing the explaining is such a daughter—and more. She is Maria Theotoky, daughter of a gypsy and a Pole, a student of Rabelais, a master of languages. Her names associate her with the mother of God. Her skills, real and imagined, justify her being called Sophia, after the incarnation of wisdom.[52]

[50]See Robertson Davies, *The Manticore*, in *The Deptford Trilogy*, pp. 428–432, 544–549.

[51]See Robertson Davies, *World of Wonders*, in *The Deptford Trilogy*, pp. 844–864.

[52]See Robertson Davies, *The Rebel Angels* (New York: Viking, 1982), p. 257.

The title of volume two is half of a medieval proverb, "What's bred in the bone will come out in the flesh," an adaptation of the Latin *Naturam furca expellas, autem usque redibit*: what is in us cannot be repressed. And so it is that Frank Cornish, through school and sexual initiation, and betrayal by his cousin-wife and the multiple treasons of the modern world, is led to perform his own acts of misrepresentation as a counter-intelligence agent and, as both an authority on art forgery and a painter who produces his own counterfeit masterpieces. He is watched over by two spritely presences. One is his daimon, Maimas, whose hermaphroditic authority helps him to grope, as he-she-it says, "for the Mystical Marriage, the unity of the masculine and the feminine in himself, without which he would have been useless in his future life as an artist and as a man who understood art." The other is the Lesser Zadkiel, the Angel of Biography entrusted with recording the facts of his life. Their dialogues, presented in some twenty italicized interventions, add zest to a book and a figure that occasionally all but cry out for supernatural help. We need to know not to take quite so seriously this making of a life, even so distinguished a life. Here we have no such agreeable mediatrix as Maria proves to be in *The Rebel Angels*, or as her fellow narrator, a professor who adopts the persona of a New Aubrey, in ironic imitation of the seventeenth-century author of *Brief Lives*, John Aubrey. Lacking such mediation, we are grateful for the puncturings of pomposity the two spirits provide alongside their confirmation of Francis Cornish's large achievement and the paradoxical forces in his life that shape it and assure it – Masters and Sibyls, saturnine and mercurial presences, archetypal Mothers. There is even a place for an oddly deformed, early dead half-brother, hidden away in the attic of the Cornish home, who proves to be, in the daimon's words, Francis's "Dark Brother," providing him with security in his drawing hand and in "his artist's sensibility."[53]

Nothing in *The Lyre of Orpheus* quite matches the splendor of the achievement of Francis Cornish, his own as an artist in painting that work which demonstrates his genius, *The Marriage of Cana*, and that of Davies as a novelist in creating and making us believe in the psyche and spirit of genius. Everything in the last book of the trilogy reminds us of the greater accomplishment of the second. The Cornish Foundation, which bankrolls the Hoffmann reconstruction, in doing so constantly arouses memories of Francis which make small what it is doing with his money. The working out of the opera, *Arthur of Britain, or The Magnanimous Cuckold*, is a student effort, skillfully done, which earns its composer her Ph.D., but is scarcely of the significance of the Cor-

---

[53]See Robertson Davies, *What's Bred in the Bone* (New York: Viking, 1985), pp. 3, 398–399, 434–435, 147.

nish painting, which we can believe can be attributed to a sixteenth-century artist, named after his magnum opus, The Alchemical Master. Nothing in the protracted *Sturm und Drang* episodes that surround the composing and performance of the opera can hold the mind or stir the feelings as the events in Francis's life and the comments upon them by his attending spirits do. The art historian responsible for the mis-identification of the Cornish painting makes his reputation and the beginnings of a great career upon it and then understandably takes his life when his mistake is revealed in *What's Bred in the Bone*. The scale is entirely different in the *Lyre*, little more than some desultory pluck-ings on romantic strings.

In the Dickensian epilogue which brings us up to date on people, places, and things at the end of *The Lyre of Orpheus*, we are told, anent the response of "critics of culture" to the biography of Francis Cornish written by one of the rebel angels, that "several of these were tarred with the recently fashionable Jungian brush, and had even read some of the writings of Jung." That is fair comment upon Davies, whose reading of Jung has clearly been wide and searching. He is instructed by Jung in his writing, not hypnotized. He uses concept, not jargon; tutelary guidance, not dogma. And so we see some irony in the use of Jungian terms and ideas by an agreeable and even wise young woman, Francis's fellow snoop in counter-intelligence, summing up Francis: "Of course you're a Canadian. Do you know what that is? A psychological mess. For a lot of good reasons, including some strong planetary influ-ences, Canada is an introverted country straining like hell to behave like an extravert. Wake up! Be yourself, not a bad copy of something else!"[54] This grandiloquent application of introvert-extravert typology to countries, coupled with astrological determinism is surely meant to be funny—Canadian introverts made into extravert mimics of the United States and its people, famous for not being introspective. Strong planetary influences, don't you know? A light use of Jung, one might conclude; Davies speaking some small truths with ironic exaggeration.

Unhappily, Davies seems to make this sort of application of Jungian typology to nations quite seriously. Using the Free Trade agreement between Canada and the United States as his excuse, he offers in a lecture, abridged for publication in the London *Times Liter-ary Supplement*, the diagnosis he earlier assigned his young woman in *What's Bred in the Bone*. Without a trace of irony and only the barest suggestion that there might be something questionable about it—"Is it fanciful to ascribe a psychological character to a country?"—he gets

---

[54]See Robertson Davies, *The Lyre of Orpheus* (New York: Viking, 1988), pp. 41–42, 268, 332, 295, 277, 355, 463.

right to it. How would we know the French, the Germans, and the
Scots for what they are except by such ascription? Canada may
present a problem in its lack of outward marks, but its "inward character is something very clear, when you know what you are looking for."
Davies knows: "Canada is very much an introverted country and it
lives cheek by jowl with the most extraverted country in the world,
and indeed the most extraverted country known to history." He
explains the terms, and then quickly instructs us. Extraversion to the
south: the United States "assumes that it must dominate, that its
political and moral views are superior to all others, and that it is
justified in its interference with countries it thinks undemocratic,
meaning unlike itself." All evil is outside its borders, is this extravert
country's sense of itself. Resisting such evil is for the United States a
"primary national duty." The Soviet Union, always an introverted
state, must necessarily find itself in opposition, the resulting conflict
intensified by "assertions of moral superiority on both sides."[55]

Surely, this is carrying generalization about collectivities too far,
even for one so well schooled in analytical psychology and so determined to carry that schooling wherever his convictions lie, or more
exactly, so overdetermined. This, it seems to me, is the sort of characterization of countries, cultures, and peoples which we associate with
the perversion and misshaping of the disciplines of learning of the
Third Reich and which, whether in oblique support or in direct attack,
drew Jung himself into his most questionable assertions about peoples
and cultures. A novelist and teacher of Davies's sensibility, with such
clear psychological gifts, should know better.

Of course, Davies does know better, as his novels make clear in
their tracings of individuation aspired to, moved toward, and even on
occasion achieved. In the two trilogies, in the elegant "extended plea
for imaginative sympathy toward the theatre of the nineteenth century" which he makes in *The Mirror of Nature*, in his occasional essays,
and in interviews, he shows himself open-minded, generous, and
unwilling to fall into easy generalization. He sees, with the accommodating psyche and spirit we expect in those who have more than passing knowledge of Jung, persons, not a national character, not large
groups of unspecified think-alikes.

He says, for example, about the plays of Ibsen, after brisk, intelligent discussions of *The Master Builder* and *John Gabriel Borkman*,
"We look at mankind now in quite a different way, and our ideas about
the conditional nature of truth and the psychological complexity of
human action have been immeasurably extended." We see in the "mir-

---

[55]See Robertson Davies, "Aca Nada?" in the *Times Literary Supplement*, September 30–October 6, 1988, pp. 1070, 1080.

ror of nature" that is the theater, even in the posturings of melodrama, "not quite ourselves, but rather what we think of ourselves, which is surely the very age and body of our time, its form and pressure. And as we in our time shall be judged, let us be as understanding as we know how in our judgment of the century gone."

The same fighting free of the rhetoric of abstraction and generalization turns up in a television interview. There Davies deals scornfully with the simplistic critical reduction, as "for instance, that Dostoyevsky has analyzed the Russian character. I'm sure Dostoyevsky would be horrified by any such suggestion. Because inevitably what he sees in the Russian character is reflected through his own personality. . . ."[56] And so it is with Robertson Davies as with the other novelists who for any reason can be associated with Jungian insights. We see in him not a representative of the culture of an introverted country, but a writer in whose works, as he said of Ibsen, "our ideas about the conditional nature of truth and the psychological complexity of human action have been immeasurably extended." Complexity remains the identifying mark.

[56]See Robertson Davies, *The Mirror of Nature: The Alexander Lectures 1982* (Toronto: University of Toronto Press, 1983), pp. 115, 120; and *Conversations with Robertson Davies*, ed. J. M. Davis (Jackson, Miss.: University Press of Mississippi, 1989), p. 132.

CHAPTER 8
POETRY

S ymbols are not allegories and not signs: they are images of contents which for the most part transcend consciousness." That bold statement in *Symbols of Transformation* suggests the appeal of Jung for poets, that and the sentence that follows: "We have still to discover that such contents are real, that they are agents with which it is not only possible but absolutely necessary for us to come to terms." From this discovery, Jung says, we learn "what dogma is about, what it formulates, and the reason for its existence."

A footnote to this last assertion, quoting from a letter of Seneca, translates dogma into terms a modern poet might well seize: "God is near you, he is with you, he is within you. This is what I mean, Lucilius; a holy spirit indwells within us, one who works our good and bad deeds, and is our guardian. As we treat this spirit, so we are treated by it. . . . In each good man 'a god doth dwell, but what god we know not.'"[1]

The seizings of poets influenced by Jung are unmistakable, their chronicling of good and bad deeds, their insistence on the reality of a contents that transcend consciousness. Theirs is a remarkable access to the world of the unconscious, of dream, of shadow. They seem to feel almost as urgently as Jung did the necessity of coming to terms with the agents of the unconscious.

As poet, as critic, as novelist, Edwin Muir had remarkable access to dreams, not only his own dreams but the dreams of what Jung would have called the race. It took a while to get to this point of easy, almost triumphant access. It required psychoanalysis with a Jungian inflection. That opened much to Muir in 1919, when he was just into his thirties, just securing a hold of sorts on life in London, just putting behind him a difficult and often depressing life in Glasgow. The analysis was far from complete, but it established ties to the world of the unconscious and the primordial and reinforced the great strengths of

[1]See C. G. Jung, *Symbols of Transformation*, *CW*, vol. 5, pp. 77–78, par. 114.

his early life in the Orkney Islands, brought up, as he says he was in the diary which concludes his autobiography, "in the midst of a life which was still co-operative, which had still the medieval communal feeling."[2] The reach back, all the way back, as a way of coming forward is what counts when we read Muir. Where he came from, where we may go with new experiences of the old, can be gathered from the fine, clear opening lines of "The Window."

> Within the great wall's perfect round
> Bird, beast and child serenely grew
> In endless change on changeless ground
> That in a single pattern bound
> The old perfection and the new.[3]

There was always a kind of innocence in Muir that remained for the most part untarnished although not always serene through a distinguished career as a translator with his wife Willa, also from the islands, in her case the Shetlands, through a late but splendid flowering as a poet, into a never quite easy life as a literary figure. Not even the terrors he witnessed in his years before the second world war in Prague when the Nazis took over or after the war in the same city when the Communists succeeded to power could altogether disturb that innocence, that sharp-eyed island view crafted, as he himself says, in the preindustrial world. He knew about that innocence, although he would never claim it in so many words for himself, out of the early Jungian encounter. "There is one region in Man where innocence and a good conscience still reign," he wrote in 1920, in his first considerable book, *We Moderns.* Where? "In the unconscious." There we find love and its special joy, "the joy of unconscious Man, still innocent as before the Fall, with a good conscience enjoying the anticipatory rapture of new life."[4]

The terror that cast its shadow over the joy of love was for Muir well named Original Sin. He had no satisfactory explanation for the shadow – "I am not a good theologian, and the existence of evil remains

---

[2]See Edwin Muir, *The Story and the Fable* (Boston: Rowan Tree Press, 1987), p. 264. See also Muir's *An Autobiography* (New York: William Sloane, 1954), which carries the story forward beyond World War II, deepens the Jungian associations, though not by direct citation, and ends with these memorable words: "As I look back on the part of the mystery which is my own life, my own fable, what I am most aware of is that we receive more than we can ever give; we receive it from the past, on which we draw with every breath, but also – and this is a point of faith – from the Source of the mystery itself, by the means which religious people call Grace" (p. 281).

[3]Edwin Muir, *Collected Poems: 1921–1951* (London: Faber, 1952), p. 115.

[4]Edwin Muir, *We Moderns: Enigmas and Guesses* (New York: Knopf, 1920), p. 187.

a mystery to me; I prefer that mystery to any explanation of it that I know"—but he had an ample poetry for it when he came again to write poetry in middle age.[5] There is perhaps a greater innocence in the heart that can accept the mystery of evil, describe it, find its multiple guises and plots, and thus live with it, than in the head that can account for it but not accept it, not live with it, but only rail against it. Muir faces it, knows its horrors, names its sources, finds alongside it, and against it, its compensations. Even more remarkably, he discovers that the compensations for evil and its opposition come from the same starting place. It is his version of the *complexio oppositorum*.

Muir does all of this elegantly, with a fullness of symbol and allegory, in a language and verse forms of the utmost straightforwardness and accessibility to the reader, in the simplicity and clarity of dream and the larger, more obscure, inner meanings as well. Eden is the strongest of his dream verse centers, lucidly presented, instructive, open to the drama of active imagination.

> One foot in Eden still, I stand
> And look across the other land.
> The world's great day is growing late,
> Yet strange these fields that we have planted
> So long with crops of love and hate.

He, first translator with his wife of Franz Kafka into English, close observer of the totalitarian terror, knew well enough how much we continue to live in the shadow world, the too often unclaimed shadow world. But he remembered that in this world, where there still

> burns the archetypal leaf
> To shapes of terror and grief

it must be said with an equal certainty that

> still from Eden springs the root
> As clean as on the starting day.[6]

Muir is attentive to the images, the sounds, the oblique meanings of the archetypal shadows. In one of his most startling and moving evocations of the unclaimed world of those shadows, "The Horses," he reminds us how much we have lost and continue to lose because of our denials of what is there. We think to give up only the evil that must be there, but the symbolic drama of the poem insists that we relinquish

---

[5]Edwin Muir, *The Story and the Fable*, p. 262.
[6]Edwin Muir, *One Foot in Eden* (London: Faber, 1956), p. 46.

much that is good as well and most important lose touch with reality. The horses, "strange horses," came

> Barely a twelvemonth after
> The seven days war that put the world to sleep.

Afraid, unguided, we turned away, the world turned away. No sound, no sign of life; everything, even the radios, "dumb." But the horses have staying power. "Stubborn and shy," they waited

> as if they had been sent
> By an old command to find our whereabouts
> And that long-lost archaic companionship.

The horses of the great barely touched reservoirs of the unconscious are constant visitors in Muir, although in so many different guises we may miss them and the obscure but not unobtainable wisdom that they bring. "There is no trust but in the miracle," he says in his quickly, shrewdly reasoned "Dream and Thing." But we turn away from miracle, even the recurring one of dreams, even the most plentiful reminders of human possibility.[7]

At the end of his autobiography, Muir proclaims that "the only justification for society is that it should make possible a life of the imagination and the spirit, or, for those who are not troubled by the spirit, a life at least of the senses, since even that is infinitely above the life of routine, which is a sort of no-life." He had come, he says, to some imaginative understanding of his own life, had begun "to understand human life not as a life of routine and machinery, but as a fable extending far beyond the experience given to us by our senses and our practical reason." Thus the title of his autobiography, *The Story and the Fable*. Thus the appearance of terms like "racial memory" and "racial unconscious" in his critical writing and in his reminiscences. Thus his move away from what he calls his "infatuation with Nietzsche" into the speculative textures of Jungian thought and Christian belief.[8] There is no fixed alliance or reasoned movement back and forth between the religious and the psychological in Muir's work, but a more and more felicitous understanding, through the imagination, of how they come together.

Charles Olson was a large man, just three and a half inches under seven feet, and his poetry is large on the page, as if to make us focus quickly and come inside his running commentary on what the world

---

[7] Ibid., pp. 73-74, 67.
[8] See *The Story and the Fable*, pp. 236, 199-200.

really amounts to, his eager transcriptions of reality. Reality and its process make up the subject matter of Olson's sprawling *Maximus* poems. He kept a dream journal and, we are told, "consulted his Jung volumes almost daily in analyzing his dreams."[9] He fought his way as a poet and theorist and teacher and doyen of the Black Mountain College writers to what he called "composition by field." He speaks for open form, for "projective verse," against the closed structures of fixed meter, stanzaic form, anything that takes selection away from the poet or keeps content from finding its own form.

Olson learned much about alchemy from Jung, and to make sense of *Maximus* is to move toward its energies, toward energy itself. A poem, Olson proposes to another poet, Robert Duncan, is "the issue of two factors, (1) heat, and (2) time. . . . And time is, in the hands of, the poet. For he alone is the one who takes it as the concrete continuum it is, and who practices the bending of it (as others do, say, aluminum, to make the rockers, say, of a hobby-horse)." If we master the flow of time, "we invoke others." There the alchemical change occurs. "Because we take time and heat it, make it serve our selves, our form."

The ego is the enemy. "Wash the ego out," Olson commanded, but the *Maximus* poems, for all their courting of alchemical change and determination through "the projective act" to lead to "dimensions larger than the man," rest almost entirely, as readers of the poems know only too well, upon Olson's out-sized sense of himself. He has an explanation.

> It comes to this: the use of a man, by himself and thus by others, lies in how he conceives his relation to nature, that force to which he owes his somewhat small existence. If he sprawl, he shall find little to sing but himself, and shall sing, nature has such paradoxical ways, by way of artificial forms outside himself. But if he stays inside himself, if he is contained within his nature as he is participant in the larger force, he will be able to listen, and his hearing through himself will give him secrets objects share.[10]

Olson's verse does sprawl, even as he works heroically to stay away from artificial forms outside himself. But it also preserves the heat of the time he spends swimming inside himself, inside the unconscious which he defined as "the universe flowing-in inside."[11] Everywhere in *Maximus*, he follows Jung's psychology and the form of Ezra

[9]See Robert von Hallberg, *Charles Olson: The Scholar's Art* (Cambridge, Mass.: Harvard University Press, 1978), p. 234, n.35.

[10]See Charles Olson, *Human Universe and Other Essays*, ed. Donald Allen (New York: Grove Press, 1967), pp. 70, 60.

[11]See Don Byrd, *Charles Olson's Maximus* (Urbana, Ill.: University of Illinois Press, 1980), p. 71.

Pound's *Cantos*, as in his critical writings he imitates Pound's collo-
quial tone and falls into a kind of pretentious unpretentiousness. But
he has his own vitality, his own charm, his own vigor, his own being,
found as he says one finds the right proper noun, " 'tested' by one's own
experience (out plus in)" – that is, the outside world and one's inner life,
bringing together the "phylo-line," the history of the race, and "what
one oneself can know," the ontogenetic, one's personal history.[12] Ontogeny recapitulates phylogeny – it is a formula well known to Jung and
Jungians.

So it is that the large, long, sprawling poem begins.

> *I, Maximus of Gloucester, to You*
> Off-shore, by islands hidden in the blood
> jewels & miracles, I, Maximus
> a metal hot from boiling water, tell you
> what is a lance, who obeys the figures of
> the present dance

To achieve the merging of all, the instruction of all, the poet turns
gnostic, becomes, courtesy of Jung the Monogene, "the only begotten."
In Olson's words in *Maximus* IV, he is "the original unit" who "survives
in the salt."

The Jungian textures remain strong right to the end of the *Maximus* poems and give them, for some of us, their largest and most
enduring identity. He says in the last book of the work what is surely
true of himself in all of it, that he is

> Wholly absorbed
> into my own conduits to
> an inner nature or subterranean lake
> the depths or bounds of which I more and more
> explore and know more
> of.

"And the Place of it All?" Maximus/Olson asks in the last lines of the
poem. He answers, with suitable spacing between the words, "Mother   Earth   Alone."[13] That is his "stance toward reality outside a poem as well as a new stance towards the reality of the poem
itself," his definition of what the projective involves.[14] It is a fair

---

[12]*Human Universe*, p. 97.

[13]See Charles Olson, *The Maximus Poems* (New York: Jargon/Corinth, 1960),
Maximus Poems IV, V, VI (London: Cape Goliard/Grossman, 1968), and *The
Maximus Poems, Volume Three*, ed. Charles Boer and G. F. Butterick (New
York: Grossman, 1975). See also, G. F. Butterick, *A Guide to the Maximus
Poems of Charles Olson* (Berkeley: University of California Press, 1980).

[14]*Human Universe*, p. 59.

description, too, of what he attempted in his *Maximus* poems and what makes his work of continuing interest, and not only to Jungians.

Robert Bly is well known in Jungian circles as a lecturer, as a reader of his own poems and those of others, and as author of the well-made *Little Book on the Shadow*. He is a composer of mosaiclike verses with clean, sharp images drawn from his native Minnesota landscape and the nearby Dakotas, from the world around him and the world inside him. He has also made over into finely responsive and responsible poems in English the images and the logic of the poets he has translated, Jiménez, Neruda, Lorca, and Vallejo from the Spanish; Hölderlin, Novalis, Trakl, Rilke, and Hesse from the German; Baudelaire and Ponge from the French.

Bly is not a self-conscious rhetorician nor systematic in any precise way about bringing into the light the world beneath the surface, the inner world, where sixteenth-century German mysticism and modern depth psychology seem often to have been his guides. He is a poet attentive to inner voices, often highly politicized ones. When he rails against the establishment and its "executives" in his political poetry, it is because they are deaf to inwardness, conspirators against its rough graces. In the poems he wrote against the conduct of the Vietnam War, his derision and mockery were as strong as he could make them, bitter caricatures of Lyndon Johnson and Dean Rusk, rescued from the sour duty of propaganda by their supporting images. What may last longer than the poems themselves is his insistence that the sharp divide between politics and human interiority is false to the poet, false to the reader, false to all of us. "The life of the country," he wrote in an essay on political poetry, "can be imagined as a psyche larger than the psyche of anyone living, a larger sphere, floating above everyone. . . . In that sphere he finds strange plants and curious many-eyed creatures, which he brings back with him. This half-visible psychic life he entangles in his language."

That is the content, in effect, of the anthology he put together for the Sierra Club, *News of the Universe: Poems of Twofold Consciousness*. It ranges over several centuries, contrasts old and new ways of articulating consciousness, has everywhere a meditative texture, a reflection of the governing consciousness, Bly's. Nature is large in the collection – plant, animal, human – in a wide range of examples, from that narcissism that Bly sees as "an elegant form of the Old Position" to the "object poem, or thing poem," where "it is as if the object itself, a stump or an orange, has links with the human psyche, and the unconscious provides material it would not give if asked directly." Bly's editing, his translations, his short essays, gather to a conclusion: "Literature and art that attempt to reopen channels between human

beings and nature, and to make our fear of her dark side conscious, help us to see her without fear, hatred, or distance. . . ."
Among the strong little volumes of verse Bly has published in recent years, the Taoist reflections in *Jumping out of Bed* seem to me the most compelling, fitted out as they are with woodcuts. It is full of poetry about writing poems, about not writing poems, about the strengths of nature and of solitude in nature. Everywhere there is connection to everything:

> you open your mouth, I put my tongue in,
> and this wild universe-thing begins!

But there is also "a fierce intent that nature does not know of" that "drives inside the poem"; Bly identifies it as "something dense, a human madness."[15] Short poems, larger pictures, a spacious domain— multiple refractions of the collective and the personal, of the conscious and the unconscious.

Ted Hughes is the poet of the Shadow, his own shadow, civilization's shadow. He is also the Poet Laureate of England, charged with writing ceremonial poems, required to perform a verse ritual in which somehow the throne will be served, ordinary readers or listeners will find sense in his words, and Hughes will not seem either to be condescending to the Queen and her subjects or to be compromising his own integrity. Can he reconcile the ritual violence of the poetry which made

[15]See Robert Bly, *Selected Poems* (New York: Harper and Row, 1986); "On Political Poetry" (*The Nation*, April 24, 1967); *Forty Poems Touching on Recent History* (Boston: Beacon Press, 1970); *Jumping out of Bed*, with woodcuts by Wang Hui-Ming (Fredonia, N. Y.: White Pine Press, 1987), pp. 39, 41; and *News of the Universe: Poems of Twofold Consciousness*, ed. by Robert Bly (San Francisco: Sierra Club Books, 1980), pp. 127, 212–213, 285. See also, *Leaping Poetry: An Idea with Poems and Translations Chosen by Robert Bly* (Boston: Beacon Press, 1975), the informing idea of which is that "a great work of art often has at its center a long floating leap, around which the work of art in ancient times used to gather itself like steel shavings around the magnet." It need not be just the one long leap; it could be many short ones. "The real joy of poetry is to experience this leaping inside a poem. A poet who is 'leaping' makes a jump from an object soaked in unconscious substance to an object or idea soaked in conscious psychic substance" (pp. 3–4). The anthological note is struck again by Bly in his *Iron John: A Book About Men* (Reading, Mass.: Addison-Wesley, 1990), where he attempts through argument, citation, and ritual to counteract the bad effects, as he sees them, of the depleted "images of adult manhood given by the popular culture." His own translations of a Grimm fairy tale, which gives the book its title, and of poets from several literatures, as well as plentiful use of Jungians of many sorts and his own verses give the work a myth-tinctured flavor, but something less than the conviction of the enduring strengths of religious myth of Jung himself.

him his reputation and a (just barely) plausible choice for Laureate with the ritual benevolence which his royal role demands? Reconciliation is not Hughes's great interest. Rather the disastrous course of the modern world is – seen, felt, tasted in a drama of the senses in which the governing insights are drawn from Jung. "Yes," he wrote in 1977 to a critic engaged in writing a book about him, "I met Jung early, and though I think I have read all the translated volumes, I've avoided knowing them too well, which no doubt frees me to use them all the more."[16] It is a freedom which led him, with whatever fullness or incompleteness of understanding of Jungian thought, to chronicle the eruptions of the unreconciled Creator-God and his creatures. No, he tells us in his finely compressed "Theology," a twelve-line retelling of the crucial moments in Genesis, the serpent did not lure Eve to eat the apple. Adam did it. Then Eve ate Adam and the serpent gobbled Eve – "This is the dark intestine." As for the rest –

> The serpent, meanwhile,
> Sleeps his meal off in Paradise –
> Smiling to hear
> God's querulous calling.[17]

Hughes's drama, just this poetic side of a fever-pitch melodrama, in which an event may go in any of a series of contradictory directions, is almost all, to use a consecrated Jungian term, *enantiodromia*. Everything is caught in opposition. Even while praising a book on *The Environmental Revolution* and looking forward to the possibility, however remote, that "the earth can be salvaged," the prevailing tone of his review is the familiar one in this poet of the shadow: "The subtly apotheosised misogyny of Reformed Christianity is proportionate to the fanatic rejection of Nature, and the result has been to exile man from Mother Nature – from both inner and outer nature." The conservationist, working with the extraordinary resources given us in the technology of the computer, may be able to restore some primordial balance to a wasted world. It is a fine irony, recalling "the old-fashioned dynasties of the gods." Science destroys Nature, but then, "on its half-destroyed mother's body, begets the Computer, a God more powerful than its Father or its Grandfather, who reinstates Nature, its

---

[16]See Ekbert Faas, *Ted Hughes: The Unaccommodated Universe* (Santa Barbara, Calif.: Black Sparrow Press, 1980), p. 37. See also the essays in *The Achievement of Ted Hughes*, ed. Keith Sager (Manchester: Manchester University Press, 1983), and Leonard M. Scigaj, *The Poetry of Ted Hughes: Form and Imagination* (Iowa City: University of Iowa Press, 1986).

[17]Ted Hughes, "Theology," in *Wodwo* (London: Faber, 1967), p. 149.

Mother and Grandmother and Great-Grandmothers, as the Holy of Holies, mother of all the gods."

Violence is always on Hughes's mind. It permeates his feelings and fills his poetry, because it is the spirit of the time, or rather is what has all but extinguished the spirit: "We are dreaming a perpetual massacre." There are no easy ways out, no panaceas. Socialism won't do; it is only an arrogant attempt to mute the "elemental power circuit of the universe," which we all know "produces terror, illness, death."

Against all of this, there is the ancient way, the way of primitive societies which took up the energies and ritualized them: "The old method is the only one." It is a way of renewal, Hughes saw, and in his own way preached, after he had perfected the instrumentation of his verse and found a voice which was altogether his own, drawn from the materials of folktales, from a kind of personalist anthropology, and a reading of the works of Jung. Secure in his craft, he could move with assurance into the realm of the shadow, into conflicts of ego and alter ego and self, into shamanistic narratives in which he himself played the roles of priest, analyst, sacrificial victim, and bewildered onlooker.[18]

One can draw a line between the works written before the suicide in February 1963 of Hughes's wife, Sylvia Plath, from whom he was separated, and those that came after, and commentators have not been slow to do so. But the violence and pain which characterize the best of the later work were clearly there before the terrible event, anticipated or fully present. Hughes offers some direction to our understanding in the note that prefaces *Wodwo*, the volume in which stories, a play, and poems written before and after Plath's death signal the great change in his work: "The stories and the play in this book may be read as notes, appendix and unversified episodes of the events behind the poems, or as chapters of a single adventure in which the poems are commentary and amplification."

The speaker in the soliloquy called "Snow," challenged by "infiltrations of snow, encroachments of this immensity of lifelessness," offers some sense of what must be brought together: "My mind is not my friend. My support, my defence, but my enemy too – not perfectly intent on getting me out of this." At the end of *Wodwo*, in the title poem, the speaker asks, "What am I?" He enters the water of his meditations, wonders whether the weeds around him know him and name him to each other, recognizes that he has "been given the freedom of this place" and the question that goes with the freedom, "what am I

---

[18]See Faas, pp. 186–187, 198, 66, 68.

then?" In the last lines, he thinks if he sits still, everything will stop to watch him:

> I suppose I am the exact centre
> but there's all this what is it roots
> roots roots roots and here's the water
> again very queer but I'll go on looking[19]

Hughes did go on looking and what he saw he made into personifications of flora and fauna, into a drama bringing together Aeschylus and Calderon and fragments of myth gathered around the figure of Prometheus, into a version of Seneca's *Oedipus*, into enactments of the treasure trove of myth, sometimes softly performed for children, more often played in a broken and bloodied theater of the unconscious for adults. The most quickly accessible of the adult performances, perhaps, is *Crow*, "a sequence of poems relating the birth, upbringing and adventures of a protagonist of that name." It is a witty work and a frightening one, in which the primordium lives in human colors and in a bird's feathers. It is black in its humor, bleak in its wisdom, noisy and cheerful in its constant assertion that "Truth Kills Everybody."

"In the beginning was Scream," we are told. God tries to teach Crow to talk. " 'Love,' said God. 'Say, Love.' " Crow's response each of the several times God repeats his request is to gape at God. Out of the gapings come a white shark, a bluefly, a tsetse fly, a mosquito – the pests and predators of our fleshly existence. With a last "try," man's "bodiless prodigious head" comes vomiting forth from Crow, and then

> Crow retched again, before God could stop him.
> And woman's vulva dropped over man's neck and tightened.
> The two struggled together on the grass.
> God struggled to part them, cursed, wept –
>
> Crow flew guiltily off.

The world of Crow is a world of punishing solipsism. It is also a world in which the terror of myth-ordained, experience-confirmed solitariness is sometimes abrogated. Then something better, if only for a moment, wells up from the human interior. When darkness began to seem universal, "as if the soul were not working," just then, "At that very moment the smile arrived" –

> for a moment
> Mending everything

---

[19]See "Snow," "The Harvesting," *The Wound*, and "Wodwo," in *Wodwo*, pp. 71–92. There are useful discussions of *Wodwo* in Faas, Sager, and Scigaj; Scigaj is notably attentive to Jung and Jungian ideas in Hughes.

Finally, we are left with a hymn to a modicum of being which rests within us, everyone, somewhere far inside,

> hiding from the mountains in the mountains.
> Wounded by stars and leaking shadow
> Eating the medical earth.[20]

The same desperate attempt to get to some elusive and yet necessary center persists in *Gaudete*, Hughes's most ambitious, most substantial, most crowded work. It is a work that started to be a film scenario and has been acted on the stage, but it is most alive perhaps on the printed page. Its tortuous plot hangs on the fate of an Anglican priest, who has been spirited away from earth into some other world, to be replaced by an oak log infused with life and made into his replica. His replica's destiny, which seems to be to beget the Messiah, requires his trying to accomplish that heavenly end by impregnating the women of his parish in an entirely earthly way. The changeling fails. The women's husbands discover what has been happening and kill him. The original clergyman returns then, to wander about the west of Ireland hymning some unnamed goddess.

To encompass such a mad fullness of plot, there are many scenes, a blunt verse, and an extraordinary set of poems to make up an epilogue, where the goddess is addressed with a sexual and spiritual urgency that recalls the Song of Songs and its Eastern double, the *Gita Govinda*. There are Great Mother inflections. There is a deep penetration of collective shadows, and apocalyptic visions in which all possible Jungian tones seem to be sounded and imaged—subjective, objective; personal, collective; good, evil; defiling, saving.

At the end, we are told, out of the wandering minstrel-priest's "diary of coming to his senses, or of trying to come to his senses," that every day the world is getting both bigger and smaller, more beautiful and uglier, that the goddess's comings are coming closer and that her goings are getting "worse." The very last lines identify priest and poet, man and goddess, everything that stands against anything, all that must be reconciled, in the poet's being, in the human world:

> So you have come and gone again
> With my skin.[21]

After *Crow* and *Gaudete* there is a quieter poetry, a more personal vision. The world seems to have fewer comings and more goings, at least as notated by this diarist of the unconscious. What one remem-

---

[20]See Ted Hughes, *Crow* (New York: Harper and Row, 1971), pp. 71, 2, 8, 52, 84.
[21]See Ted Hughes, *Gaudete* (London: Faber, 1977), p. 200.

bers vividly of his meticulously observed nature is a river that alternately sings as it "walks in the valley" and saunters into "a long stillness." He presents us with a God who accepts the pain of crucifixion but cannot "understand what had happened / Or what he had become."[22]

Two last little volumes press upon us notations from a life of turbulent interiority. One, *Moortown Diary*, is a culling of poems from the splendid 1979 volume, *Moortown*, ten years later, reprises aimed at "excluding everything . . . that might be pressing to interfere with the watching eye," even including "the poetic process." The other, *Wolfwatching*, again stresses content over form. There are unmistakable awkwardnesses, rhythmic falterings, but rarely a weakening vision. He remains the preeminent poet of the Shadow. Like his Prometheus he will not

> Be let stir.
> The man I fashioned and the god I fashioned
> Dare not let me stir.[23]

One can read Peter Redgrove as a poet or a novelist, a teacher or a philosopher of science and the imagination. He may seem an orthodox card-carrying Jungian. Certainly he makes abundant use of Jung. Unmistakably he is at ease in all the genres he has attempted. One sees these things, one recognizes the achievement, but that is not enough, for Redgrove is so much himself, so much an amalgam of all that he has done, that no one title is good enough, although "poet" comes close. If, however, one means by that simply the practice of the art in its acknowledged forms, then one may miss the sharp intelligence that bursts through his collaborations with Penelope Shuttle, especially *The Wise Wound*, their book on menstruation, and the great grasp of the unconscious which his *The Black Goddess and the Unseen Real* promises to be in its bookjacket subtitle, "Our Unconscious Senses and Their Uncommon Sense," and then remarkably enough actually becomes.

Jungian orthodoxy is not Redgrove's shibboleth, either to accept or reject, although he is clearly at ease with the psychology and makes constant use of it, sometimes critically, often provocatively, almost always to deepen his and our penetration of the unseen, the too little heeded powers of the world of which he has made himself a votary. The epigraph of *The Black Goddess* is from the seventeenth-century *Reli-*

---

[22]See Hughes, *Selected Poems 1957–1981* (London: Faber, 1982), pp. 230, 231.

[23]See Ted Hughes, *Moortown* (London: Faber, 1979); *Moortown Diary* (London: Faber, 1989); *Wolfwatching* (London: Faber, 1989); and *Selected Poems 1957–1981*, p. 200.

gio Medici of Sir Thomas Browne: "In brief, conceive light invisible, and that is a spirit. . . ." The book's bias and freshness spring from an exchange Redgrove reports in his introduction, quoted from his beginnings with John Layard, the magisterial English Jungian with whom he analyzed. At one point, Layard said of himself that he was "a *sineater* and that was why his mouth watered." Redgrove "protested in the name of common-sense; he replied, 'We've had enough of that. What we need is uncommon sense.' "[24]

Why Jungian psychology? For its uncommon sense: "it seemed to explain things about poetry or the experiences I had better than any other philosophy or psychology that I had encountered." The high place accorded the imagination in Jungian thought is its special attraction for Redgrove. But he has his quarrels with Jung. The four functions make good sense to him, especially as they move one toward "completion, individuation, a creative self-revolutionary instinct." But the redeemer as a figure in Jungian work is uncomfortably drawn in terms of "the Christian Christ." For Redgrove, Jung's figure would be better described as "Mercurius, which is the infinitely creative variable stream of images or similes . . . one of the stages in the alchemist's work."

He defines an artist as "a man who is able to move around his psyche rather than get stuck in one portion of it." Thus art is therapy, whatever Jung's or others' disclaimers, and in Redgrove's reading of Jungian psychology, "the end of analysis or the purpose of analysis is to live in a continual state of active imagination. In other words, to see the correspondences." He does not find those correspondences in the Bible: "I cannot approach a Bible which has a male supremo as God or as a male savior. It is not Jesus but his sister that I am interested in, and there is no such Bible." A religious symbol, to be useful to Redgrove, he explains, has to "be reversed into a feminine or physiological context. . . ."

Everything in Redgrove presses toward the feminine, to the point of identification with it. He cites Jung's distinction between the masculine and feminine spirit approvingly, the first seeking perfection but not completeness, the second exactly the other way around. For Redgrove, this supports his "interest in breaking down categories and boundaries." He is also clear about his element among the primordial four elements – water, "the feminine element." One would not need his

[24]See Peter Redgrove, *The Black Goddess and the Unseen Real* (New York: Grove Press, 1987), pp. xiii–xiv.

testimony here; his poetry is awash in that element and very much in the feminine mode, "urethral," he says, as against phallic.[25]

To pursue water in Redgrove's poetry is a rewarding enterprise as long as it does not exclude other textures, other topics and themes, other elements. In the title poem of *Dr. Faust's Sea-Spiral*, for example, the old savant and would-be seer is frightened and frustrated, as in Marlowe and Goethe and Mann and all the other tellings of the Faust story.

There is a grand storm in this Faust that does bright, clear, loud things and brings with it images of a restored androgynous nature. Its strength is the secret of sexuality:

> When men and women embrace
> They impersonate it
> They are a cone of power
> An unbuilt beehive

And it is not simply a collectivity but gatherings of empowered pairs, as the next lines make clear:

> We two are a brace of them behaving as one
> We invaginate, evaginate,
> Time stops inside us.

The central poem of this volume, in a sense the initiatory statement in Redgrove's work, is "The Idea of Entropy at Maenporth Beach." It is a reply of sorts to Wallace Stevens's "The Idea of Order at Key West," where Stevens seems to identify order with the woman who sings the song of poetic order, starting at line one. She is the "maker," the poet, the order. In Stevens, the "tragic-gestured sea / Was merely a place by which she walked to sing." For Redgrove, the sea is so much alive in Stevens's poem that the poem itself contradicts the poet. In the entropy – the disorder or degradation – at Maenporth in Cornwall, a woman in a white dress covers herself with mud, "baptizes herself" in Redgrove's summary of his poem. The dress is not right, the woman says to herself; her "smooth white body" is not right either. She wants no smoothness, no slickness, but the spattering of mud "with rich seed and ranging pollens." Is this right, she asks herself, "As the fat, juicy, incredibly tart muck rises / Round her throat and dims the diamond there?" She changes, caparisoned now "like a mound of lickerish earth." She becomes a black woman, covered with mud and rejoicing in it. She is jubilant in her blackness and vows always in future to have some-

---

[25]See "Scientist of the Strange: An Interview with Peter Redgrove," in *The Manhattan Review*, vol. 3, no. 1 (Summer 1983) pp. 8, 19, 31, 30, 29, 33, 39.

thing black with her – "A snotty nostril, a mourning nail will do." But this is no simple-minded conversion, turning in white for black. "Mud is a good dress, but not the best." Her run slows down to a walk, where she shows in "streaky white." Collisions, contrasts, new colors spring to life. The song we hear is of the "shrugged up riches of deep darkness. . . ."[26]

It is a handsome poem and a moving gathering-in of the magnetic forces and coincidences of opposites which water has particularly seemed to incarnate for Redgrove. It is a poem understandably dedicated to his Jungian master, John Layard, and equally understandably the poem is assigned to one of the two central characters in his novel, *The Beekeepers*, and reproduced entire in that book as the character's creation. The two figures, Guy and Matthew, become dowsers. Finding water in all its guises and implications is an answer of sorts to the intrigues – sinister, suggestive, murderous, freeing – which animate and deepen the suspenseful story. After the poem is gathered into the story, the reflection in Guy's mind explains the verses and his and Redgrove's preoccupation: "Finding a lady in the water and the earth: that was the image. It could be that it was telling him . . . that dowsing was one of his explorer's paths. After all, one dowsed with one's whole body; it was the natural reaction of one's tissues to the presence of water in the earth."[27]

In his devotion to the watery element, this poet, novelist, and metaphysician of the unconscious, trained as a scientist and resident at a school of art, has found a freeing imagery to which almost everything that exists can be attached. The movement that opens the title poem of *From Every Chink of the Ark*, for example, has the excuse of Noah's passengers, all the phyla of animal creation, to link images with the sea, but the water of Noah's ocean is not simply the biblical flood; it is the majestic element that presides over being.

In Redgrove's poems, waters "veil themselves," a well is "grateful" for stars that the sky has lost, a river is charged with electricity, a dream is made "marvellous" with "drenched sportswomen." A "Woman Bending in a Field" is "The queen of the wet dust." With her "mantle" comes "An erotic, ghostly atmosphere." Onto her – and onto us reading the poem – "Water pours down, like life that has suddenly undressed." The images are surrealist, Jungian, deliquescent. Water, water everywhere and endless drops to drink. In bed, "Under the Duvet," beneath "the sleep-feather," a child meets "the water / of the mountain's grey brain ever-distilling. . . ." An archetypal woman "is the hole in the

---

[26]Peter Redgrove, *Dr. Faust's Sea-Spiral Spirit and Other Poems* (London: Routledge, 1972), pp. 71–80, 20–21.

[27]Peter Redgrove, *The Beekeepers* (London: Routledge, 1980), p. 71.

water / That ascends gasping," like someone out of Henry Moore's garden of holey delights. A mother willing her child out of her belly wills her own birth, which occasions a further stripping and emergence, "So that, undressing, she forgets to say her prayers. . . . " That becomes the occasion for connection with the presiding deity again, the water that "forgets and reflects / The beauty above her."

The message is clear. It is proclaimed again and again, with increasing mastery of cadence and image and all the elements of narrative that can be made compact without losing either the characterization or the suspense-tinged plotting of good story-telling. We want to know what happens. We care about these people, the girls and women especially, but also the poet himself in his various personae. Why we care and what we care about are the bold points of the poetry, the content, the leaping about in the waters, the feeling that catches fire and that the water never douses. We join in this poetry a watery communion.[28]

Time in Redgrove's life is marked by "an immense sea-clock." In a bright daylight, in "The Big Sleep," he is visited by waves that glitter and hum like "bees of the sun." He is describing, in terms of his place at the sea-end of southwest Britain, a repose that recalls that archetypal poem of repose, Andrew Marvell's "The Garden," where the seventeenth-century poet makes use of the great Renaissance and medieval conceit that everything that is to be found on earth has its counterpart in the seas and the fullness of the ocean stands for the happiness of the contemplative mind.

For Redgrove, "Ever-living, moving, salt sleep" offers an oceanic fullness like Marvell's mind. In it, the sleeper has the stability and strength of a "sleepy warm rock in the earth centre" and the blinding powers of the sea lead us to confront the archetypal Dreamer. When their time comes, "in their season," the women of Redgrove's seashore world stroll about, a large drop "of the Dreamer in their bellies. . . ." "The Big Sleep" is a strong poem, another of the poet's brisk metaphysical outings. It gains something, too, from its title, with its oblique connection with a classical private-eye detective story, Raymond Chandler's 1939 novel of the same name.[29]

There is suspense and there is detection in all of Redgrove's writing. There is also a kind of guilt if we fail to track down the

---

[28]See Peter Redgrove, *From Every Chink of the Ark* (London: Routledge, 1977), pp. 9, 209, 103; *The Apple-Broadcast* (London: Routledge, 1981), pp. 63, 98, 99; *The Man Named East* (London: Routledge, 1984), 16, 35, 79; *In the Hall of the Saurians* (London: Secker and Warburg, 1987), pp. 41, 27.

[29]*In the Hall of the Saurians,* pp. 53–54. One hopes this little book, the archetypal slim volume of verse, will not be lost from view on the shelves.

great truths of the unconscious presence, needless to say a female one, for which so many clues have prepared us. That is the bustling content of *The Black Goddess* and its appeal to an epistemology of Extra-Sensuous Perception, so-called in a play on ESP, "because the word 'sensuous' (as opposed to the word 'sensory') implies a certain gusto." And gusto there is aplenty.

Take the Black Goddess. She may be "identical" with the Holy Ghost. She may be the figure of Wisdom in the hymn that opens Chapter VII of the Book of Wisdom or the Black Shulamite of the Song of Songs. "We have also met her as the Sphinx rejected by Oedipus, as the Dark Girl of the Eastern Love-Books, the Queen of Sheba . . . and the Fallen Daughter or Animal Soul." We see her as a tree. We sense her "living perfume." We feel her touch.

Redgrove reminds us of all the feminine appropriations of the Holy Spirit – the dove, which he sees as a yoni-image; the *Ruach*, the breath, mind, and spirit of the Old Testament, hovering, brooding "over the waters as a creative mist." As *Ruach* she is as well "air, gas from the womb." As Sophia she is as Jung saw her in *Psychology and Religion*, the Holy Spirit "enabled by Job's soul in his dialogue with the frenzied Hebrew male God to enter human history once again." She is "the night-demoness, the succubus-incubus, the left-hand wife-husband who consorts with those who sleep alone and who blesses or curses them with nocturnal orgasms and erotic dreams (glorified as Madame St Urzulie in voodoo, which calls her to heal people by means of these same nocturnal experiences)." She is Adam's Lilith, she is an almost endless series of emanations reaching back beyond recorded time to the primordium. She is the Great Earth Mother who "presides over the meditations of this book." We must know her mode as analogue, as opposed to the " 'no' of the yes-no digital" mode of Oedipus, know her enigmatic presence, feel her tentacles as "strangleress, which is the meaning of the Greek word Sphinx."

The pre-Oedipal Sphinx is what is constellated here, "that part of the mother we do not see, but which haunts us all our lives." She – the Black Goddess, our neglected senses, our lost animal strengths – not only gives us birth but promises rebirth. "The Sphinx is truly answered: humans are born for rebirth." In the housing of a woman's body, we do not have the dream-body that Freud saw but a fully fleshed "out" place – a temenos or moon-place – in which we can make our way out of the helpless state of our first years and "continue to develop, as though we were still womb-creatures, possessed of womb-plasticity, under our mother's influence in the home."[30]

---

[30]*The Black Goddess*, pp. 45, 115–116, 70, 116–118, 108, 114, 117, 8, 186, 68.

Redgrove has made a compelling case for Everywoman in his poetry, in his story-telling, in his readings of the myths. He joins Jung in a kind of Olympian view of womankind, both of women in themselves and of the woman in men, echoing Jung in that search for wholeness which the reawakened images of alchemy in the dreams of people in this century seem to suggest. As he and Penelope Shuttle summarize them in *The Wise Wound*, those dreams sometimes articulate that "quest for wholeness . . . as a search for the red 'philosopher's stone' which is a grail or uterus, whose touch turns the world to 'gold'—that is, turns it to vivid, shining value." It is to repair the "wound," to find the value in the so-called Curse of Eve, that Redgrove's and Shuttle's investigation of menstruation is dedicated.

The investigation succeeds. The sacrifice of the blood becomes a blessing rather than a curse, whatever physical or spiritual or psychological hardship may be associated with it. We are reminded, not simply that "without menstruation there is no ovulation, and therefore no people," but that everything that clusters around it may be looked at as revivifying. The moon-tides, for example, the moon-cults, mooning, need not be reduced to a crazy abstraction or lopsidedness. Basic measurements are drawn there; the very idea of measurement or proportion can be traced to the menstrual cycle: "What we are trying to show is that basic to our language and our thought is an idea of measurement or proportion, originally associated with the measured return of the moon each month, and that many of the words we use for rational science and its measurements are 'lunatic' words."

Whether or not Redgrove and Shuttle "have shown that the 'Fall,' the evolutionary step that made humankind, can be seen as menstruation itself," they have done much to reassert the primordial strengths of woman as shaman, artist, keeper of the cycles, luminous center of proportion in human society. They have made us look more closely at many texts and reminded us with assistance from Esther Harding, Emma Jung, and Ann Ulanov what "new and relevant life" may be found in Jung's work when examined with a woman's eye. Witches, pop-culture products like Dracula and *The Exorcist*, whole and half worlds of occult phenomena are rescued from a cultural climate which has too often read its own temperature incorrectly because it has been so unwilling to take women's measured readings seriously.[31]

In a poem called "The Moons of Scilly," describing the skies and what they reveal of the land in the islands that congregate off the southwestern tip of England, Redgrove talks of

---

[31]See Penelope Shuttle and Peter Redgrove, *The Wise Wound: Eve's Curse and Everywoman* (New York: Richard Marek, 1978), pp. 31, 61, 135, 227.

Grounded moons, a scrapheap
Of discarded moons, every one a beauty.

He tells of cliffs "full of . . . pictures" and filled, too, with the best accounts we have of the tumults of our history. The relics are of a great collectivity, cracked, seamed, even fractured, but with the promise of wholeness brought by the shape history has impressed on the stone, where Redgrove finds again his prime figuration of the feminine, the sphinx, now displayed in "rucked stone and closed eyes."[32]

Redgrove is not simply a poet speaking in figure when he invokes this most compelling of his deities. She is alive to him, positive, real, accessible in ways that Yeats's sphinx, that famous "rough beast" slouching "towards Bethlehem to be born," is not. We understand something new about the *conjunctio* experience out of Nathan Schwartz-Salant's emendation of Jung that Redgrove cites. It is not just an "unconscious ordering factor" that one discovers by going backward in time in analyzing dreams, but an unmistakable presence, "an imaginal experience *between two people in the here and now.*" Redgrove italicizes the last eight words to stress his understanding of "imaginal" as " 'imagination' in the sense of a perceptive faculty." He is persuaded – and he persuades us – that anyone who comes to his work with any sympathy for Jungian thought, and the barest tutelage in it, is bound to find a deepening of his or her own experience of the imagination and its "never-failing abundance."[33]

---

[32]*In the Hall of the Saurians*, pp. 33–34.

[33]*The Black Goddess*, pp. 156, 185. The Schwartz-Salant citation is to an article in the 1984 issue of *Chiron: A Review of Jungian Analysis*.

CHAPTER 9

THE OTHER ARTS

The reach of the Jungian imagination is handsomely demonstrated in arts other than literature. It turns up in film and theater and related criticism. It hangs loosely in the work of some painters, as an informing presence; it makes itself the center of events in at least one notable case. It is very much alive in the music of one of the most resourceful and inventive composers of this century and skirts several dance stages as well.

No more than the people who have used a Jungian content in their music, painting, dance, drama, or film should we try to hold that content to easy, quick definition. We are in and out of levels of consciousness and the unconscious. We touch the edges of tragedy and comedy, where they fall off into each other. Transformative textures abound. Alchemy plays its part. Systematic analysis of the materials of these worlds of the arts of the unconscious can be useful, as the first entry in this chapter indicates. So can a presumptive movement into allegory, almost in defiance of Jung's understanding of symbol. The point is that there is not any fixed landing place. We entrust ourselves again to an informing complexity, to that spirit that Seneca invoked which works our good and bad deeds from a place deep within us.

In his introduction to Bettina Knapp's *Theatre and Alchemy*, Mircea Eliade notes the achievement the book represents:

> In her competent and meticulous analysis of nine dramas selected from the universal history of theatre—from *Shakuntala* to Claudel's *Break of Noon*—Professor Bettina Knapp did not look for the actual familiarity of their authors with an alchemical tradition. (As a matter of fact, only Strindberg was deeply involved in alchemical experiments.) She chose a more promising approach, namely the path opened by C. G. Jung when he noticed that the unconscious undergoes processes which express themselves in alchemical symbolism and which bring forth a psychic renewal corresponding to the results of hermetic operations.

He ends his tribute by underscoring the fact that no one before Knapp had "envisaged a systematic analysis of the alchemical process underlying the entire dramatic literature," and in terms even more important, that her book "discloses a deep and hidden spiritual dimension of the theatre in world literature."

It is a rich book, reaching across many literatures to make its Jungian points. In *A Dream Play*, "Strindberg's subtle alchemical transmutations have succeeded in stilling time, stretching space, illuminating darkness, and sensing the darkness of matter." The king in Ghelderode's *Escurial* is looked at as "a God-Father-Senex figure." In Claudel's *Break of Noon*, "The leaden atmosphere ushers in feelings of death, decay, and darkness." Yeats's *The Only Jealousy of Emer* yields shadow and anima figures and "alchemical operations which take his protagonists from a state of primal oneness to *separatio* and *coagulatio*." An obscure play for non-Polish readers, Witkiewicz's *The Water Hen* is seen as offering "a new theatrical language" and a compelling example of the *puer aeternus*. Villier de l'Isle-Adam's *Axël*, made famous as a defining work of modernist literature in Edmund Wilson's *Axel's Castle*, is celebrated for its dramatization of "a transformation process: man's ascension from his leaden condition to his Golden Essence." Ansky's *The Dybbuk* is both "a religious mystery" and "the paradigm of a 'spagyric marriage': an inner psychic union which takes place beyond the physical realm, in a retort, as a projection." A Japanese Noh play, *Matsukaze*, "combines *solutio* and *sublimatio* operations," with water as the dominating image. Finally, in Kalidasa's *Shakuntala*, that centerpiece of the Indian theater, "The 'inner heat' produced via tantric techniques coincides with the 'mystical heat' of the alchemists," and a union which is both of man and woman and of alchemical elements, which can be described as a *complexio oppositorum*, produces a son who assures the future of the human race.

As she has done in so many of her books of Jungian studies of the arts, Bettina Knapp uses analytical psychology as a critical tool, not as a reductionist solution. She says as much about alchemy here. It can deepen our experience of a play, as actor, director, reader, or critic, and if looked at "as operational alchemy," as Artaud saw "the principle of theatre," can push us beyond our "limited field of vision." But, she reminds us, quoting Jung, alchemy "was one of the great human quests for the unattainable."[1] And so we find life in the theater this way, but no end to mystery.

<hr />

[1] See Bettina L. Knapp, *Theatre and Alchemy* (Detroit: Wayne State University Press, 1980), pp. x-xi, 40, 47, 80, 110, 132, 137, 154, 201–202, 230, 248, 1, 257.

Eugene O'Neill was loath to give credit to psychoanalysis or psychoanalysts for such psychological insights as his plays might contain. He was "no great student" of the subject, he wrote to the critic Joseph Wood Krutch, who was sympathetic both to O'Neill and to depth psychology, responding to Krutch's criticism of *Strange Interlude*. He admitted that he did "know quite a bit about it, without ever having gone in for a complete analysis. . . ." He had never thought of the characters of the play as possessed by "complexes," at least not "in any Freudian sense. . . ." In sum, although *Strange Interlude* "is undoubtedly full of psycho-analytic ideas, still these same ideas are age-old to the artist and . . . any artist who was a good psychologist and had had a varied and sensitive experience with life and all sorts of people could have written *S.I.* without ever having heard of Freud, Jung, Adler & Co."

Four years later, writing to the critic and editor Barrett Clark, he was moved to an even stronger protest. Critics, he complained, "read too damn much Freud into stuff that could have been written exactly as is before psycho-analysis was ever heard of. Imagine the Freudian bias that would be read into Stendhal, Balzac, Strindberg, Dostoevsky, etc. if they were writing today!" The O'Neill play under discussion here is *Mourning Becomes Electra* and the terms are just about the same as with *Strange Interlude*: "I think I know enough about men and women to have written *Mourning Becomes Electra* almost exactly as it is if I had never heard of Freud or Jung or the others." He insists again that writers were psychologists long before the advent of depth psychology, "and profound ones. . . ." And again he stresses the fact that he is "no deep student of psycho-analysis." But then he adds something new.

> As far as I can remember, of all the books written by Freud, Jung, etc., I have read only four, and Jung is the only one of the lot who interests me. Some of his suggestions I find extraordinarily illuminating in the light of my own experience with hidden human motives. But as far as influence on my work goes he has had none compared to what psychological writers of the past like Dostoevsky, etc. have had.

That says a lot, both the denial and the affirmation. That he can put an exact number to the books by depth psychologists that he has read suggests he is much more conscious of his indebtedness to psychoanalysis than he is willing to acknowledge. His singling out of Jung points to sympathies that help define the psychological textures of his plays. Certainly, with or without benefit of Jung, he was fascinated by persona rituals in modern life and went as far as he could to dramatize them, with masks, as in the Easter parade of *The Hairy Ape* or the

THE OTHER ARTS 187

picking up and doffing of identities through masks in *The Great God Brown*, or the elaborate program of asides in *Strange Interlude* to indicate the difference between the personae offered in open meetings and conversations and the feelings and thoughts hidden beneath the maskings. In the last plays, especially *Long Day's Journey into Night*, he concentrated on the drama of individuation. It is almost always individuation foiled or individuation in the breach, but the yearning is unmistakable and the terms in which it is expressed are unmistakably tutored by a conscious psychology, even if the tutor is often Dostoevsky and Strindberg rather than Jung.

While he was still working on *Journey*, he explained to the critic George Jean Nathan that it was "a deeply tragic play, but without any violent dramatic action. At the final curtain, there they still are, trapped within each other by the past, each guilty and at the same time innocent, scorning, loving, pitying each other, understanding and yet not understanding at all, forgiving but still doomed never to be able to forget." The "they" of the play is his family, the O'Neills, just barely disguised as the Tyrones, the archetypal family cast in theatrical terms with an aging Irish-American actor at its head. Its violences are entirely psychological. They are not only more persuasive but more sharply dramatic than the murders and suicides of the American Civil War trilogy O'Neill made of Aeschylus's *Oresteia*, his *Mourning Becomes Electra*. Something of the same richness pervades *A Touch of the Poet* and *More Stately Mansions*, designed as two of the works in a projected eleven-play cycle which was to mark out the fortunes, interior and exterior, of an American family over many generations. More of it is to be found in *A Moon for the Misbegotten*, which takes up the plight of O'Neill's older brother, the James Tyrone of *Journey*, in his hapless journey in search of a woman to mother him.

O'Neill thought that there was "a fine unusual tragic comedy" in the play about his brother, but he had other work to do. He had finished rewriting *A Touch of the Poet* and wanted to get on to " 'The Last Conquest' (the World-Dictator fantasy of a possible future, and the attempted last campaign of Evil to stamp out even the unconscious memory of Good in Man's spirit . . .)." He was sure he would not be understood. He felt that "until this war, which must be won, is won, people should concentrate on the grim surface and not admit the still grimmer, soul-disturbing depths." But very much like the Jung of *Answer to Job*, O'Neill was haunted by the "soul-disturbing depths" and by a kind of gnostic deity that seemed to be responsible for them, or if not responsible, to have turned away from them and their terrible effect upon humanity. The best he could do was to "censor" himself, "and with this shackle added to recurring spells of illness and mental depression – In short 'The Last Conquest' remains for the most part in scenario, although it haunts me."

He reproached himself, again in words that suggest Jung. He knew this was "no way for the free creative spirit to act. Its answer to war should be that of Archimedes: 'Get out of my light. Your shadow is disturbing my problem.'" O'Neill made every attempt to claim his shadow, even the world's shadow. The late plays are an endless grappling with shadows, his family's, the American family's, the Irish-American family's. His personal shadows were lengthening in his last years. His younger son was on drugs, had tried suicide, had lost his own infant son to crib death. His older son, a sometime scholar, a drinker, succeeded in killing himself. His daughter Oona had married Charlie Chaplin when she was only eighteen and Chaplin three times her age. It was a marriage he strongly opposed, that brought new publicity for him, which he detested. He and his wife were gravely ill; his hands trembled so from Parkinson's disease, he could not write, could not return to "The Last Conquest." But he had done enough, enough to warrant the Nobel Prize in 1936, enough in the plays that came after the Prize to beggar the earlier ones. Only William Faulkner and T. S. Eliot among American writers had dealt so courageously with a beleaguered interiority. O'Neill had "heard of Freud, Jung, Adler & Co." He had shown in ways which we may just be beginning to understand what he found in Jung so "extraordinarily interesting in the light of [his] own experience with hidden human motives."[2] With those late plays, and especially *Journey*, he joined Strindberg in the making of new dramatic myth of the ancient archetypal family.

An equally bold foray into archetypal worlds distinguishes much of the choreography of Martha Graham. One sees it in the dances themselves. One knows it beyond argument in the notebooks of the dancer-thinker-choreographer. There stand revealed sources. There one sees the movements of the dances drawn deep down into myth and legend, woven in and through the collective unconscious and the personal. In her "Preliminary Studies for Clytemnestra," she moves meditatively around materials from the Eranos volume on the Mysteries – "From all the things that life offers we have spun a net, a necessary cause that chains & enslaves us." In her notes for her "Mary Queen of Scots," she ransacks T. S. Eliot, St. John Perse, Tennyson, ancestral images. Ritual, mystical initiation, dream confessional alternately light up and darken the pages of these notebooks.

The Jungian presence is most pronounced in the forty pages of

---

[2]See *Selected Letters of Eugene O'Neill*, ed. Travis Bogard and J. R. Bryer (New Haven, Conn.: Yale University Press, 1988), pp. 247, 386, 506–507, 538.

notes on "The Dark Meadow of the Soul." There we have Jung himself, such archetypalists as John Layard and Maud Bodkin, and others conjured up by Jung, by musings on Jung, by a constant restless reconnoitering of the rituals of interiority. The arresting quotation from Jung comes quickly—"If the ego arrogates to itself power over the unconscious, the unconscious responds with a subtle attack." St. Augustine, filtered through Jung, sums up the abiding texture of this masterful dance drama—"I will raise myself over this force of my nature, step by step ascending to Him who has made me. *I will come to the fields & spacious palaces of my memory."*

One can gather from these pages some of what one feels in the direct experience of the dances. "Psychic energy is contained in archetypal dance—in the transpersonal images it conveys," Bettina Knapp writes. We are all caught by it when it is as alive as it is in Graham's "Dark Meadow." There is, as Knapp says, a "specific electric charge" ignited, and more, "a 'living-ness'—a numinosity in the performer and observer." That is the "Contemplation of the Inner Image" brought into bodily movement, onto the stage, that Graham talks about in her notes for "The Trysting Tent," where she moves from a place of shadows to a place where love has become a fortress, through classical worlds and romantic and pop modern, plotting her "tryst" in a tent that she designates "the tabernacle of our own being." It is a rich researching of the "primordial figures of the far night," which others in the modern dance have also done, but none with such open and moving acknowledgment of sources. Here we know with inner and outer eye the meeting of Jung's inside and outside worlds.[3]

A Jungian inflection is sometimes urged upon Jackson Pollock's painting, especially in the years from 1938 to 1941. It is, I think, a dubious viewing, which rests largely on the fact that he moved from treatment of his alcoholism with an eclectic psychiatrist to work with two distinguished Jungian analysts, Joseph Henderson and Violet de

---

[3]See *The Notebooks of Martha Graham* (New York: Harcourt Brace Jovanovich, 1973), pp. 212, 311-317, 167-206, 217-240; and Bettina L. Knapp, *Archetype, Dance, and the Writer* (Troy, N. Y.: Bethel, 1983), pp. 7-8. The Hubbard Street Dance Company of Chicago, which offers work not unlike that of Paul Taylor in its range of dance and musical styles and sources, does a set of tangos which, according to the explanatory program note, "represent a journey toward the 1068 of the anima . . . the feminine principle." Margo Sappington, the choreographer of this work, *Cobras in the Moonlight*, cites Esther Harding's words in the program: "For no individual is entirely male or entirely female. Each is made up of a composite of both elements, and these two constituents are not infrequently in constant conflict within the psyche." As with the Jungian material in the Graham *Notebooks*, the invitation to dance movement is unmistakable—at least to the choreographic temperament.

Laszlo. Pollock's own statement to Seldon Rodman, that he had been "a Jungian for a long time," suggests something about the works he prepared for his analysts, his so-called "psychoanalytical drawings," and the early paintings that show an egregious mythological or anthropological concern. It is a concern much more than it is a content. Elizabeth Frank's comment on the 1938–1941 paintings, works that "teem with serpents, skulls, female images, and plant and animal forms," seems just right: "It is as if Pollock vacuumed up whatever he saw – Jungian symbols, American Indian motifs, whatever shapes and images that sifted through his memory – with a mighty suction that fused them with his own incessant creation of images."

Pollock's Jungian analysts did indeed work to put the painter at ease with his unconscious. It was not a simple process, nor was it directed by any urge on the analyst's part or the painter's to "portray" the unconscious. There was, as Henderson explains, no free association, no examination of responses. Pollock "was much too close to the symbolism of the drawings to tolerate any real objectivity toward them." They were "a bridge to communication, and . . . gave him the assurance that at least one other person understood something of their abstruse language."

Henderson found "archetypal symbolism" in Pollock's drawings. He also discovered, in the work that followed, the product of "a prolonged period of representing human figures and animals in an anguished, dismembered or lamed condition," something close to "the dissociation of schizophrenia" and more, a state of mind that Henderson compares to "a shamanistic trance state." Henderson sees Pollock in these drawings as reflecting an experience like that of "the novice in a tribal initiation rite during which he is ritually dismembered at the onset of an ordeal whose goal is to change him from a boy into a man."

Certainly he changed as an artist, if not from boy to man, then from a painter of tentative advances into what might be called the world of the unconscious or of dream and fantasy, and finally to the firm assurance of the world of swirl and drip which fills his great oversize paintings from the early forties to his death in 1956. He moves from wounded animals and "totem lessons" through *Alchemy* and *Sea Change* to paintings he is content to call simply by number, *7, 10, 12, 25*. Titles turn up again in the paintings of the last years – *Blue Poles, The Deep, White Light, Search* – but they do not direct us to a theme or topic. The perambulations through his own interiority of the seasoned painter show an extraordinary strength in that "halfway" form that in 1947 he announced himself as working toward, away from the "dying form," the easel picture, and "towards the wall picture or mural." The strength is that of an intuitive artist, but also an inventive one, who has discarded easel for floor, who as Jack the Dripper, as a wit of the 1950s dubbed him, could make exterior drips, drops, and splashes into a persuasive calligraphy of interior states. In the conversation with Rodman in which he called himself a longtime Jungian, Pollock disclaimed the movement name under which his work was more and more being categorized, abstract expressionism. He also wanted no part of terms like *nonobjective* or *nonrepresentational*, which to a painter so clearly possessed of his own imagery and figural language are as foolish as the classification of "atonality" for composers like Schönberg or Berg. "When you're painting out of your unconscious, figures are bound to emerge," Pollock told Rodman. He saw painting as "a state of being," as "self-discovery. Every good artist paints what he is."[4]

If we could say exactly what Pollock "is," we would not need his paintings. Surely we know that in his most assured work, modern painting reaches at the very least one important exclamation point. Freedom is a declarable content here, and it is clear that it springs from a preoccupation with the unconscious, opened, besieged, held in place, with knife and stick and hardware-store paint and movements more and more controlled and organized, movements of body and of spirit. To try to translate these into a particular psychoanalytic vocabulary, even one so generously accommodating to the contradictions and conflicts of human interiority as the Jungian, is, it seems to me, a fruitless task. There is some painting with a demonstrable Jungian content, openly proclaimed and easily identifiable, although not to be reduced any more than Pollock's total accomplishment as a painter to a series of psychoanalytical equations. What there is of Jung in Pollock is much more in his biography than in his painting.

Jackson Pollock claimed a longtime preoccupation with Jungian ideas. He is only one of many artists who have had some experience of Jungian analysis or have been caught, for a moment or longer, with the possible application of Jungian concepts and constructs as a way of explaining or of motivating the art process. Sam Francis is not only a distinguished painter long associated with the abstract expressionists, but a publisher of an impressive list of books by Jungians at The Lapis Press in his native state, California. But the artist in whom Jung figures openly in the works themselves, not simply in words about her paintings or sculpture, is none of these. It is Ann McCoy, a woman learned in things Jungian, splendidly articulate in discussing them,

---

[4]See Elizabeth Frank, *Jackson Pollock* (New York: Abbeville Press, 1983), pp. 27, 41, 63. See also, B. H. Friedman, *Jackson Pollock: Energy Made Visible* (New York: McGraw-Hill, 1972); and *Jackson Pollock: A Catalogue Raisonné*, ed. F. V. O'Connor and E. V. Thaw (New Haven, Conn.: Yale University Press, 1978).

but more important, eloquent in her translation of her learning into line and color and texture, into an iconography of the inner life.

Ann McCoy's Jungian understanding is supported by a long-lived experience of analysis with, among others, Hans Dieckmann, James Kirsch, and C. F. Meier, the last of whom remains a major resource. She keeps track of her dreams, in the Jungian manner, catalogues them, looks for personal and collective associations, moves comfortably from a dream fragment to a mythological symbol system. She speaks, in an essay about her paintings, of gathering her images through "incubation" or a "sleeping in," an ancient practice that can be traced to the Egyptians. She finds signifying materials in American Indian culture, where, as she says of the Chippewa, dreams "are still acknowledged to be the realm of revelation and transformation." For her, alchemy is not a historic curio, but a continuing Great Work that survives in the modern world in forms manifestly connected with the early alchemists. Their "phantasies," she says, "express symbolically occurrences in the deepest layers of the psyche, and provide a language for the steps in the inner transformation process. The goal of the individuation process is the conscious realization of the Self. Alchemical processes, *mortificatio, solutio, coniunctio,* etc., have their parallel in the dream world and in the life of the psyche."

That parallel is visible in a work like her *Coeur de Lion,* where lions and wolves act out the meeting of light and dark, the devouring of a royal figure, and then, behind the violence, a sequential "sublimation of the *prima materia* [the devouring wolf] and rebirth of the king." She says that her own dreams are "filled with dismemberment and the dissection of the body" and supports her understanding of what this means with a reference to the alchemist Robert Fludd, who "felt the body to be a reflection of God's cosmos in its organs." She knows those organs well. She has attended and participated in autopsies. The discourse of the blood, which so much of her work bespeaks, has a precise and all but palpable presence in the bodies, open and closed, of her art. It is not a detached ethereal symbolism, but something that moves from the flesh, living and dead, into the resurrections of pencil lines and paint, a world meticulously inspected and reproduced.

There is a whole gallery of interiority in Ann McCoy's art. The *Magna Mater,* a temple of Isis, a *Daemon* as *Deus Inversus,* a pyramid, sacred and profane figures, human and animal – all come together in a figurative art which at all points displays an extraordinary drawing skill. A similar fullness of detail makes her sculpture into a kind of liturgy of interior experience. People, animals, and objects stand or move in dream and mythological enactments – an *Isis Processional,* a *Lion Goddess Barque,* a *Barque for Isis and Hathor.* All are fleshed out in an insistent testimony to an "obsession with transcendence."

The "physical man precedes the spiritual"; that is always clear, but not in a destructive combat, even when there is a great blood-letting. Both survive. In the flesh and the spirit in this art the miraculous is always possible. Death contains the seeds of resurrection – or at least the possibility of a Dantean visitation. The guide here is not Virgil, but C. G. Jung, and when it is time for Jung to make way for a supernatural replacement, as Virgil gives way to Beatrice in Dante's *Commedia*, it is one of the great ladies who takes over – Isis, or the Great Mother, or the Virgin Mary.[5]

Henry Moore's maternal figures really are *great* mothers, not because of any open alliance to the archetype, but simply because of their palpable size, very large indeed physically, and even larger psychologically. Mother fixation? Regressive orality or anality? Reductions to jargon simply will not do. It is not a reduction, however, to speak of "the archetypal world of Henry Moore," as Erich Neumann does in the book of that title, nor is it questionable, I think, to use a Moore Madonna and Child as illustration of the primordial goddess, as Neumann does in his archetypal study, *The Great Mother*. But we must accept, as Herbert Read tries to make us do in his fine clear treatment of the sculptor in *The Forms of Things Unknown*, that "Moore's symbolism is completely unconscious, and is not dictated by any priesthood, or dedicated to any ritual."

Moore's use of a Mayan reclining figure is an interesting case in point. He assured Read that when he first came to know the Mexican figure, it was not with any awareness of "its ritualistic or archetypal significance – to him it was just a piece of sculpture which attracted him by its formal qualities as a work of art." What is archetypal in the Mayan figure is, in a sense, almost exactly what is archetypal in Moore's use of the form, allowing for all the differences in time and culture. "What we must admire, in the modern artist," Read sensibly concludes, "is the confidence with which he accepts as a gift from the unconscious, forms of whose significance he is not, at the creative moment, precisely aware."

Moore was himself very much aware of the need to stay free of analytical vocabularies and critical systems. He found his clearest ties with the world of nature, human, animal, vegetable. Even architecture was a problem. The connection did not come naturally: "Unless there are so many buildings there already that it doesn't matter – nothing

---

[5]The Ann McCoy quotations are from catalogue essays written for exhibitions in San Francisco and Edinburgh and from her "Meditations on the Red Mass," in *Bomb* Magazine, December, 1985. See also her conversation with Claudia Gould, "Mythologizing the Feminine," in *Arts* magazine, February 1989.

can be done about it," he said of commissions that "had to do with architecture." Nature was something else for Moore, free of the "disadvantages" of architecture: "Nature is asymmetrical and its scale is a human one, even when there are mountains. But architecture can be so brutally big that the humanity drops out of it."

When Moore was sent a copy of Neumann's *Archetypal World of Henry Moore*, he stopped reading after the first chapter, "because it explained too much about what my motives were and what things were about. I thought it might stop me from ticking over if I went on and knew it all. . . . If I was psychoanalysed I might stop being a sculptor." That may not be quite fair to Neumann, but it is the necessary stance of an artist like Moore. One does not have to agree with Read that the work of artists such as Picasso and Moore is "not significant of any expressible ideas," to recognize the good sense in what follows in Read's rumination about art of this kind: "It gives concrete existence to what is numinous, what is beyond the limits of rational discourse: it brings the dynamics of subjective experience to a point of rest in the concrete object. . . . In this sense the artist has become the alchemist, transmuting the *materia prima* of the unconscious into those 'wondrous stones,' the crystal forms of art."

How proper is it, then, to associate Moore's world and Jung's, inside or outside? Clearly, Moore was not a registered Jungian. But equally clearly he provided endless illustration – in drawings as well as sculpture – of that process in which art and archetype descend upon the artist, who, like the poet in Jung's words, is "himself conscious of the fact that he stands as it were underneath his work, or at all events beside it, as though he were another person who had fallen within the magic circle of an alien will."[6]

It is not a matter then of claiming Moore for Jungian performance but of understanding Moore and Jung better through the association of art and idea. Read's various writings about his friend Moore are helpful and so is the Neumann book, but the most persuasive demonstration of the conjunction of the work of the artist and the psychologist seems to me to be in the large permanent exhibition of the maquettes – the models, some small, some large – on which Moore based his sculpture, or from which it was cast, at the Ontario Art Gallery in Toronto. There, mostly in plaster, one meets what seems like

[6]See Herbert Read, *The Forms of Things Unknown* (New York: Horizon Press, 1960), pp. 71-75; and Geoffrey Shakerley and Stephen Spender, *Henry Moore: Sculptures in Landscape* (New York: Clarkson Potter/Crown, n.d.), pp. 30, 34. See also, Erich Neumann, *The Great Mother*, trans. Ralph Manheim. (Princeton, N. J.: Princeton University Press, 1955), and *The Archetypal World of Henry Moore*, trans. R. F. C. Hull (Princeton, N. J.: Princeton University Press, 1959).

the *Urstoff* of the archetypal worlds of Moore and Jung, and the appropriate word to describe what one meets is *numinous.*

The place of Jung in the work of the composer Michael Tippett is so clear that some may be tempted to look for a specific musical content that reveals the influence. It would be a mistake. The Jungian presence is strong and open in the libretti Tippett wrote for his operas, in the texts around which he constructed his oratorio and a set of songs enlarging a character drawn from one of his operas, and in his writing about his music. But all one can do when it comes to the music itself, whether written around a text or purely instrumental, is to speculate about the psychological accents one may find in this or that figuration, in the rhythmic intensity, in the many dramatic strengths of this modern British composer.

Just before the concluding spiritual of the oratorio *A Child of Our Time,* the solo tenor sings, "I would know my shadow and my light, so shall I at last be whole." Tippett has said that a great deal in his music comes from this material. The operas show it. His cantata, *The Vision of St. Augustine,* reflects it. His tumultuous *The Mask of Time* reads and sounds like an elaborate commentary on Jung's *Modern Man in Search of a Soul,* updated by a half-century, with emphasis, as always in Tippett where there are words to guide us, on the experience of shadow and light and the possibility of achieving wholeness.

The oratorio is the fitting introduction to this material. It presents the terrible events that followed the shooting of a Nazi official in Paris by a young Jewish refugee, a boy hiding out with his aunt and uncle. It is not a violent work but a contemplative one, alive to Nazi atrocities and their consequences, softly, philosophically responsive to the transformative powers of such events, for good as well as evil, as we do or do not take them into our psyches, into our spirits. Negro spirituals—"Nobody Knows the Trouble I Seen," "Go Down, Moses," "Deep River"—mix with jazz textures, recitatives, arias, dramatic choruses, to tell a scapegoat story, to elicit a meditative feeling. It is an arresting experience, a splendid preparation for the work that follows.

In *The Midsummer Marriage,* Tippett plays with feelings, forms, characters, and plottings that suggest, as he himself has indicated, the plays of T. S. Eliot, Shakespeare's *A Midsummer Night's Dream,* and Mozart's *The Magic Flute.* But, the composer said, more to his purpose was Shaw's *Getting Married.* In that remarkable one-act comedy which is nonetheless a full-length play, a young man and woman contemplating marriage are made to look hard at themselves, to try to find themselves, to see if in fact there are selves to find. Tippett explains: "I *saw* a stage picture (as opposed to hearing a musical sound) of a wooded hill-top with a temple, where a warm and soft young man was being rebuffed by a cold and hard young woman (to my mind a very common present situation) to such a degree that the collective magical archetypes take charge – Jung's *anima* and *animus* – the girl, inflated by the latter, rises through the stage, flies to heaven, and the man, overwhelmed by the former, descends through the stage floor to hell." There are theatrical pyrotechnics, a large reach into several mythologies, a vivid set of modern musical textures, and a sprightly set of names – Mark and Jenifer (as "the Cornish variant of Guinevere") from the "Celtic world of romance," King Fisher (the royal title "like Duke Ellington"), and a clairvoyant, Sosostris, the last two clearly with a bow to the Eliot of *The Waste Land*.

Words and names mean a great deal to Tippett. He sees his visions of wholeness, of light drawn from the shadows, through them and the music he composes to support and amplify them. In a brief commentary on *The Vision of St. Augustine*, he acknowledges the "visionary element" in his music, tells us that it found "its first full flowering" in *The Midsummer Marriage*, and quotes from *King Priam*, the work that stands between *Marriage* and *Vision*. In that operatic transfiguration of the Trojan War, where names like Achilles and Hector bring such visionary splendor even before words and music have been supplied, "the hero comes to the 'loop in time,' and with eyes shut to the outside world murmurs," Tippet says, quoting his hero and himself and, in effect, Homer and Greek tragedy and all who have made use of them:

> I see mirrors
> Myriad upon myriad moving
> The dark forms of creation.

Vision "is a special case of the same expressive need."

What it is, in fact, is a gathering of Latin texts, from Augustine's *Confessions* and the Vulgate Bible, with interjections of glossolalia to convey the ecstasy of religious conversion, and moments of penetration of the mystery of time. It is written for baritone, chorus, and orchestra, with an eloquence which springs from the elegant Latin and a crackling modern musical style. The ear is filled but not overwhelmed, for like Augustine's our vision must be auditory and after all the words and names, all the handsome sounds, have passed by, we must be able to contemplate the *complexio oppositorum* of the words whispered in Greek by the chorus which say everything about *Vision*: "I count not myself to have apprehended."

The same teetering-tottering, resolute-irresolute moving in the shadows, finding light in darkness, falling from the light into the dark, energizes *The Knot Garden*. It is a comedy, but not a comic opera. Its names are allegorical, some of them anyway. The central couple are Faber (Homo Faber, man the maker) and Thea (the goddess), his wife. The other couple, in this set of variations on the mixing of pairs in Mozart's *Così fan tutte*, is homosexual – a black writer, Mel, and a white musician, Dov (the bird of peace). The other characters are Faber and Thea's ward, Flora, who, pointedly, has not yet been deflowered; Denise, Thea's sister, a "freedom fighter" whose body is broken, the result of torture; and Mangus, an analyst who, in trying to bring order into others' lives, must realize the disorder in his own. There is no mistaking the closeness in plot and characters to Eliot's *The Cocktail Party*. Although nothing like the apparatus of the guardian angels, which gives Eliot's play its religious wit and power, enters here, the work does offer its own kind of faith and hope. They lie in an acceptance, very much tutored by Jungian doctrine, of resolution in irresolution. The faltering love of the married couple must accept the confusions and involutions that the title and the setting illustrating it represent: the knot garden, which is to say a tricky and even frightening labyrinth, can at any moment become a rose garden, like that of Eliot's "Burnt Norton," where we discover and lose and find again our beginnings and ultimate purpose.

There are flattenings of feeling, intentional or not, in the snatches of popular music, of blues and spirituals, and the use of measures from "We Shall Overcome," no doubt with lofty purpose. But Tippett is not without his ironies. He plays engagingly with the world of Shakespeare's *The Tempest*, Mangus as Prospero, Mel as Caliban, Dov as Ariel, Flora as Miranda, Faber as Ferdinand, in the "charade" of Act III, in roles that "are never absolute." They move from acting out to standing aside as spectators, with Thea and Denise remaining themselves, anima figures, the one (Denise) to say, "I do not understand confusion," the other to pronounce, "In love the purities are mixed."

The final ironies turn around a series of inconclusive departures. Mel and Denise go off together. Flora goes "to her 'brave new world.'" Dov is left alone. Mangus "disappears," but not before his sharp observation,

> We look in the abyss.
> Lust for Caliban will not save us.
> Prospero's a fake, we all know that.

Thea and Faber play out the briefest of epilogues. They proclaim a transcending of their "enmity . . . in desire." They give over to the moment, in which, as Thea says, memory recedes, and Faber can vow that he is "all imagination." As they move to each other and the curtain is about to descend, they chorus, "The curtain rises." It is the paradox of *Waiting for Godot*, where the tramps say at the end of each act, "Let's go," and do not move. It is the Jungian paradox.

There is something like a tightening of that paradox in the three *Songs for Dov*, for tenor and small orchestra. Dov is less an Ariel figure here, of the kind he was in *The Knot Garden*, than a variously open and guarded voice for the composer. He comes out into the garden again; he reprises the famous "Kennst du das Land" lines from Goethe's *Wilhelm Meister* which Tippett uses in the opera. He is, like Goethe's young man, in his *Wanderjahre*, but grown now, the composer says, "a creative artist struggling with the intractable problems of 'poets in a barren age.'" He joins Pasternak's Dr. Zhivago on his Siberian journey, looking to accomplish, for himself, for Tippett, a set of variations on a theme pronounced by Pasternak – "The living language of our time is urban" – and with the Russian poet and novelist's suggested tool, the pastoral metaphor. To make city over into country, to make the land a lively reality for concrete-bound city people – that is a worthy paradoxical enterprise. It joins "The live horse / The iron horse, / Pegasus, the flying horse," Wagner's *Flying Dutchman*, and the horses riding off into the sunset of Western films. It brings harp, lute, and guitar together in the words and a bold, percussive, swinging orchestral sound that almost overwhelms the voice of Dov, but leaves him, like the chorus in *Vision*, the last whispered words, alone, unaccompanied. The tenor says, "Sure, baby." It is a banality that some have found embarrassing – there are others – in this work. But it fits, I think, as do the words of Duke Ellington, "It don't mean a thing if it ain't got that swing," quoted without Duke's music. Westerns, electronic sounds, banalities, and an urge to timeless pastoral all remind us of a truth invoked by John of the Cross, by T. S. Eliot, and by Jung: that one has to go through time, one's own time, to get beyond time.

Time is the fixation of Tippett in *The Mask of Time*. As its title indicates, it is a pageant of sorts, like an Elizabethan masque. It is also a work preoccupied with the disguises of time, both those things which time conceals and those that mask time. It is written very much to the meditative ear, "explicitly concerned with the transcendental," says the composer, a depiction of the world "of plurality, diversity and abundance," says Meirion Bowen, the composer's appointed commentator. It achieves its vocal and instrumental richness through a handsome deployment of parts, voices above all, full of quotations, allusions, and influences, philosophical, literary, musical, Western, Eastern. For all the citation and invocation of Yeats, Eliot, Shelley, Milton, Rilke, Akhmatova, the *I Ching*, Zen Buddhism, and the like, the abiding impression is one of sound, not of particular words. We gather verbal meanings when we read the text, but listening to the music we hear

Sound, a word intoned with its own identifying motif in the first of the ten sections that make up the two parts of the *Mask,* and then repeated a number of times later on.

It is fitting that a work so filled with ideas of polarity and polarization, of conflict between stated meaning and gathered understanding, should settle finally into a rhetoric of sound, not of words. What we hear is the differentiation of feeling that the words simply point to and the music completes as it moves around reasonably familiar styles and textures – Monteverdi and Dowland from the Renaissance, Stravinsky, Schöenbergian *sprechstimme,* jazz, a full panoply of orchestral and vocal devices from the moderns. We also hear, and with understanding that needs no large articulation in words, that careful winding in and out of the psyche which this composer manages so well. "In some contexts in the work," he says, "I have utilised the idea of *reversal,* a term that has many overtones and connotations." He explains that he has "encountered it in the *I Ching,* in Heraclitus, in Jung – who preferred the Greek-derived *enantiodromia* – and in modern physics, e.g. the mechanics of the pendulum or the satellite that reverses its course; I have found 'reversal psychology' suggestive." We hear this, whether we should use such words or not, as we hear translated into sound the great open spaces of the American Southwest and Mexico and Tippett's fears about nuclear violence. It is not a program we get here, however, but a psychology, an archetypal psychology.

Tippett is clear that in the writing of his four symphonies he was following "an archetype not a form." That is why for him to speak of the death or "twilight" of the symphony is unacceptable. He is not pursuing a form, although he started comfortably enough with patterns "following Beethovenian precedent" as he began to plan his First Symphony in prison in 1942, serving a three-month sentence as a conscientious objector to the war. His authority as a symphonist is unmistakable, in the symmetries of the First Symphony, in the motoric drive and other rhythmic strengths of the Second, in the inexorable progress of the Fourth, which like the great cadences of Johann Sebastian Bach gives the impression of being one long protracted melodic line buttressed by a series of supporting statements from the orchestral choirs. The Third is the most richly varied, ending with a bold finale in blues. A soprano sings slow and fast blues, built around Tippett's lines, verbal and musical, a touch of bop in a flügelhorn obbligato, a triumphant concluding portion echoing the harsh opening of the last movement of Beethoven's Ninth, the "Ode to Joy," an echo in fact of an echo, for that is the way the whole blues section begins.

In the words of the four sets of blues, there are suggestions of *Answer to Job* doctrine –

Ah, merciful God, if such there be
. . . .
But if the cherub stands b'fore God,
Let him demote himself to man,
Then spit his curses across the celestial face
Though he be answered (Answered?)
With annihilation from the whirlwind.

There is also, in a musical setting dense with whoops and jazz pulse and instrumental anxiety, another kind of answer. "We fractured men," the soprano sings, "Surmise a deeper mercy." It is the mercy of the dream, a feeling, even though dreams may "crack," that all is not threat, all is not terror. It is a *complexio oppositorum.*

We sense a huge compassionate power
To heal
To love.

It would not be unfair, I think, to say that Tippett works in his purely instrumental music merely to give voice to whatever he senses, whatever he can articulate of that "huge compassionate power." In the mid-1940s, when he completed the revised version of the first of his four string quartets, his experience working with the unemployed and their hungry children in the North of England "made him determined," Meirion Bowen says, "that his own music should reflect 'the compassion that was deep in my heart.'" There is also, in the same music, the contrary force, the threat of "annihilation from the whirlwind," that demands from Tippett an answering compassion. The epigraph from Blake's *The Marriage of Heaven and Hell* which stands above the finale of the First Quartet reflects the contrary motion: "Damn braces. Bless relaxes."

It would be wrong to ascribe a precise program to the quartets, to the three piano sonatas, and the other instrumental music, but there is no mistaking the rhythms and textures of contrariety, the struggle and merging of opposing forces, the psychological reach again of Tippett's music. The breaking of fixed pulse is one way he does this, in "additive" rhythms that recall Stravinsky, the jazz pianist Lennie Tristano, and the poet Gerard Manley Hopkins's "sprung" rhythm. Another, closely related, is by a constant confrontation between "arrest" and movement. The music seizes up, and so does the attentive listener. Even more arrestingly, the voices of solo instruments, as in the Triple Concerto, move against each other, join, and separate, in meetings of the collective and the individual which seem to give musical diction to the Jungian vocabulary. Inevitably, the commentator on this work speaks of Tippett presenting "his three instruments like archetypes" and of their preserving "their essence the more for the contrast of their shared music."

Because there is so much that links the instrumental works — quotation, paraphrase, parallel treatment — to the music written in support and elaboration of words, it is not difficult to hear a precise echo in the Piano Concerto or the Fantasia Concertante on a Theme of Corelli of *The Midsummer Marriage* and its content, or in the Second Piano Sonata of *King Priam*, or in the Third Symphony of *The Knot Garden*. Nor can one miss the constant presence of a restless spirit, a bustling psychic energy, a temper remarkably like that of an immensely assured improvising jazz musician or a well practiced devotee of self-analysis. Like a cultivated jazzman, Tippett has apparently found more and more ease in transcribing affect and emotion into music. Like a devoted self-analyst, one particularly instructed by Jungian ideas, he has kept a close watch on his interior life and on its interweavings with the outside world and found ways to make his vigilance into music. The result, especially for those of us to whom access to feeling and human interiority is an incomparably engaging subject, is very good indeed.[7]

The reach of Jung into film is not very large or marked, except perhaps in the case of Federico Fellini's autobiographical masterpiece *8½*. Some have speculated, as Fellini's biographer Hollis Alpert reports, that the director was himself in Jungian analysis at the time of his making of the film. In fact, as Alpert was able to determine, Fellini was engaged in conversations with a leading Jungian analyst in Rome, Ernst Bernhard, but was not actually *in* analysis. As a moment of magic in the film, involving a mind reader and a child's language game in which every syllable of a word is framed by the letter *s*, sets loose a spate of memories like a Proustian teacake, so a kind of telephone magic brought Fellini and the analyst together. In *8½*, the language game produces the words *asa nisi masa*, which without the framing *s*'s is revealed to be *anima*. In the telephone experience, a kind of reaching out from the unconscious, Fellini was trying to reach, so he thought, "a very beautiful lady." Instead he got a man who said, "This is Bernhard," not the beautiful lady — as the analyst he had actually reached quickly made clear — but "an old man," perhaps the old wise man of Jungian lore. Coincidence? Deliberate misdialing? It is the kind

---

[7]The quotations from Tippett, like the selections from the libretti, are from the notes accompanying recordings of his music on Argo, EMI (Angel), London, L'Oiseau-Lyre, Phillips, and RCA. See also, *The Operas of Michael Tippett* (New York: Riverrun Press, 1985); and Meirion Bowen, *Michael Tippett* (London: Robson, 1981).

of intervention, deliberate or not, which constantly slows up, almost breaks apart, and then, at the very end, makes it possible to produce the film within the film which is the point of *8½*, the whole number and fraction standing for its place in the Fellini *oeuvre*, the eighth of his films plus a half.

Marcello Mastroianni's is the persona Fellini selected for himself in *8½*, not too fanciful an image for the director, whose life and readings of life in his films constantly bring fantasy and reality into something like contemplative perspective. Alpert quotes him as saying, "I have complete faith in Jung, and total admiration for him," and remarks on a "fascination with Jung" that led Fellini to visit Bollingen, to get to know Jung's son, and to read Jung at some length. The reading, for Fellini, was a way of opening himself to his own world of fantasy and of getting beyond the constriction he felt in himself at "not having general ideas about anything. Reading Jung has freed me from the sense of guilt and the inferiority complex this limitation gave me."[8]

Certainly fantasy plays its part in the films that preceded *8½*, with particular persuasiveness in *I Vitelloni, La Strada,* and *La Dolce Vita.* But for those of us who see Fellini's work as moving with more and more security into realms of symbol and fantasy after *8½*, it is what he accomplishes with the world of interiority, even when he is most dispirited, in his *Amarcord* and *Satyricon, Juliet of the Spirits, City of Women, And the Ship Sails On,* and *Ginger and Fred* that makes him so provocative and so gratifying a film director and thinker. It is not necessary to draw constant or precise parallels between Jungian ideas and Fellini's to see how vigorously and with what imagination the filmmaker pursues the truncations of individuation that are everywhere achieved in the waste lands of the late twentieth century, or how, in a world of absurd and degrading apes and stereotypes, such as the television jungle of *Ginger and Fred,* it is possible for person to emerge from persona and the grace of true individuation to transform an awkward mimicking into a largeness of character. That is the achievement of both the conception of the role of Amelia, the Ginger Rogers dancer in the film, and the playing of it by Fellini's wife, Giulietta Masina. It may be too much to call this a Jungian allegory, but it is not far short of that.

One of the powerful holds of film on its audiences is its closeness to dream. Robert T. Eberwein develops this experience, known to many of us consciously, into a substantial theory of film. He argues, following the poet Wordsworth's description of birth as "a sleep and a

[8]See Hollis Alpert, *Fellini: A Life* (New York: Atheneum, 1986), pp. 167–170, 177.

forgetting," that "our experience of film permits us to return to the state of perceptual unity that we first participated in as infants and that we can know as dreamers." In that experience, there is the promise of a psychic totality, of a return to "the integrative vision" of infancy and childhood.

In the unfolding of his theory, Eberwein makes effective use of Jung. As against Freud's idea that "a dream is ultimately an infantile wish that emerges during sleep," Jung is presented as arguing that "the dream is a compensatory activity on the part of the individual. . . . Dreams themselves emerge from the buried psychic life of the dreamer as well as of the human race and display in their content archetypal elements common to all cultures." The film *Spellbound*, which its director Alfred Hitchcock shrugged off as "just another manhunt story wrapped up in pseudo-psychoanalysis," has been much discussed as a Freudian outing, simple-minded or complex. Eberwein cites a reading by Royal S. Brown, for whom the pivotal figure of the psychiatrist in the film – the Ingrid Bergman role – "in the course of her adventures as a Freudian sleuth . . . passes through all the stages outlined by Jung and his disciples for the so-called 'process of individuation.' " For Brown, the film is "consciously Freudian and unconsciously Jungian."

There is more of Jung, although less than one might hope for, in Eberwein's treatment of Ingmar Bergman's *Persona*. If this is, as many have insisted, "a film about film making," it is even more a deliberate use of film as the dream screen, drawing audiences into the forgetting, the reminding, the reawakening that the film-dream experience quickens in its viewers. Its special strength is in what Bergman makes of the intertwinings of its two central women: "The interpenetration of their psyches and mutual absorption of each other's Jungian 'shadows' defy ordinary means of representation; these can only be manifested in film, where the very nature of the medium is used to imitate the interaction of their shadows." The convoluted psychodrama reaches particular intensity when one of the women, Alma (Bibi Andersson), attacks the other, Elisabet (Liv Ullmann), for her mistreatment of her son, the unwanted but physically present child who stands in taunting contrast to the child Alma aborted when she became pregnant after an orgy. "In attacking the actress for having a son she did not want, Alma seems to be projecting her own feelings of guilt and shame by casting onto Elisabet what Carl G. Jung calls the shadow." She is certainly doing that, and more. As Eberwein properly reminds us, "the self-reflexive nature of *Persona* is in some ways its message. We watch, and must be content with, images projected onto surfaces."[9] Must we? Bergman is not. He teases us by the merging of the images of the two women, by cutting in which it is impossible to tell which body parts belong to whom, by literal shadows to suggest figurative ones. Either woman could be the other at crucial moments. Bergman himself, in his treatment of the women, seems to feel himself now this one, now the other, now both, making himself as he almost always does in his films the ultimate dream screen, making the women his anima enactments, asking us in the audience to accept them for the duration of the film as ours perhaps as well. This is where further Jungian speculation seems to me to be called for, but even without it, the materials for it are all there. They give Eberwein's thesis great plausibility.

It is surely not wrong to make some use of the insights of Jung and even of Jungian language in looking at and judging films and attempting to construct a critical apparatus with which to make sense of the film experience. But an egregious use of Jungian terminology can only be maddening, to the user in the end as well as to those confronted with it. It is all too easy in this central popular art of the twentieth century to find the spoors of the archetypes and the tracks of the functions, dramatized as they are not only in the figures enacted but in the captivating actors. There they are, old sensation-type Cary Grant, thinking-type Greta Garbo, intuition-type Gérard Philipe, feeling-type Charlie Chaplin. What a wonderful game, especially if we add to the players the great directors and then, in the spirit of Jung, make countless combinations of the function types. No, we would be wiser here to remember that Jung was offering his categorical terms as a means of understanding the multiplicity of ways different kinds of human beings perceive and evaluate the world around them, objects, subjects, themselves. Some are, on the whole, systematic, some unsystematic, some committed to rule and reason, others satirical or offensive, rude or violent against them. The insights are real enough, the terms useful in modest display. Once again, complexity is the point, a *coincidentia* or *coniunctio oppositorum*, not a simplistic reduction.

---

[9]See Robert T. Eberwein, *Dream Screen: A Sleeping and a Forgetting* (Princeton, N. J.: Princeton University Press, 1984), pp. 4, 12–149 104–105, 129. See also, Ingmar Bergman, *The Magic Lantern: An Autobiography*, trans. Joan Tate (New York: Viking, 1988), where there are no explicit references to Jung, even in discussions of films where Jungian inflections are unmistakable, such as *Persona*, *Cries and Whispers*, *Hours of the Wolf*, and *Scenes from a Marriage*, but there is a clear attraction to what might be called Jungian issue and psychic event. See too, Bergman's "Film Has Nothing to Do with Literature," in *Modern Culture and the Arts*, ed. J. B. Hall and Barry Ulanov (New York: McGraw-Hill, 1972).

CHAPTER 10

PHILOSOPHY

If we understand philosophy as a systematic seeking after wisdom or the general principles of a theory of knowledge or a disciplined approach to something that might be called ultimate reality, then each of the large figures looked at in this chapter might well be called a philosopher. They are all more or less systematic in their approaches, all highly skilled, learned, lucid, and provocative in their use of Jung. Their skills, their learning, and their lucidity are also tutored by disciplines other than philosophy.

Jean Gebser would be thought of by some as a sociologist. Gaston Bachelard was trained as a chemist, a fine preparation for the philosopher of science he became en route to his work as a phenomenologist of poetic reverie, of dream, of the ancient elements of physical and psychic being. Rodney Needham is a distinguished anthropologist and philosopher both. Arnold Toynbee is a historian captivated by the place of religion, understood in dramatic Jungian terms, in what might be called both a philosophy and psychology of history. The last of the group, R. C. Zaehner, was a historian of religions, a philosopher of religion, a bustling, bristling, eloquent comparativist whose Gifford lectures, *Concordant Discord*, deserve a place beside James's *Varieties of Religious Experience* in that monumental series of two-year explorations of the world of human interiority that Lord Gifford chose to call "natural religion."

A monumental work in which Jungian thought figures in odd and significant ways is Jean Gebser's *Ursprung und Gegenwart*, translated as *The Ever-Present Origin*. It is a history of evolving consciousness, a theory of transformation, a response to a world in crisis, a world "headed toward an event," as Gebser says in his preface, "which, in our view, can only be described as a 'global catastrophe.'" Gebser offers his readers the possibility of "a transformed continuity where mankind and not man, the spiritual and not the spirit, origin and not the beginning, the present and not time, the whole and not the part become awareness and reality." In the original two-volume work and in the emendations in the editions that followed it, including the English translation, what develops is something like a thirteenth-century *Summa*. As with Thomas Aquinas and Albert the Great and the other summists, the work presents itself as an objective exposition of ideas, but never, not for a moment, loses contact with its shaping consciousness, Gebser's. Since the consciousness is that of a poet, a cultural historian, a social philosopher, and a wanderer across cultures, forced by wars and the violent eruptions of our time to move from Germany to Spain to France to Switzerland, the encounter between objectivity and subjectivity is always lively, on many levels of understanding, and with that urgency that those who have been made into displaced persons by the Nazis and the Spanish Civil War and World War II are bound to feel and then to make us who have escaped such displacement feel too.

Jung's place in this extraordinary undertaking is indeed an odd one. In Switzerland – where Gebser arrived in August 1939, just two hours before the borders were closed by the war – he taught for some years at the Jung Institute. His preoccupation with structures of consciousness and their primordial sources was bound to find deepening support in Jung's thought. His strong belief in the possibility of movement from an unbalanced rational consciousness to an "arational" and integral one, from egocentricity to ego-freedom, echoes Jung at many turns. But what Gebser constructs is very much his own. It is deliberate, systematic, often organized in ways foreign to Jung, and although it owes much to him in its psycho-historical and psycho-philosophical textures, it owes as much again to physicists such as Einstein, Heisenberg, and Weizsäcker, to the poets Rilke, Hölderlin, Mallarmé, and T. S. Eliot, to the philosophers Plato and Aristotle and Heidegger, to composers and painters, especially Picasso, and to others across the arts and sciences too numerous to mention here but much more than passing names in a vast sea of footnotes. There are, in fact, two kinds of footnotes, those that support quotation and paraphrase in the conventional manner, with exact citation, and those that go well beyond the convention with supplementary discussion and digression, occasionally approaching although never matching in length or enterprise the great seventeenth-century master of the extended footnote, Pierre Bayle.

It is in these discussions and digressions, whether in the body of the text or the notes, that one sees the closeness to Jung. For example, in the 117 footnotes that accompany chapter 6 of Part II, in which the "sciences of the mind," psychology and philosophy, are examined as manifestations of the "aperspectival world," Gebser moves from conventional citation a half-dozen times. He expatiates on prefigurations of modern psychology in the Renaissance and Enlightenment years, on

the inadequacy of "ambivalence" as a psychoanalytical term, on therapy "from the side of the spiritual," on synchronicity, on "the rational
as a deficient form of the mental structure," and on quantum logic, or
the logic of complementarity, as it has been called. In the body of the
text, there are corresponding moments where Gebser, without forsak-
ing his systematic exposition, has some provocative things to say
about archaeology and its contribution to our understanding of the
"pre-temporal" or "time-free," about Jung and "quaternity constellations," about Jung's help in freeing archetypes "from biological determinism," Heidegger's exhausting and driving "to its limits the assertions of speculative private philosophy" and the parallel weakening of
philosophy as a discipline by the introduction of "psychological factors
(as opposed to Heidegger)" in the work of Jaspers and Sartre.

This is a discussion, in all its parts, of particular significance for
Jungians. It may require some schooling in Gebser's special vocabulary, but he himself provides that in the early pages of his book, and his
constant use of such terms as *aperspectival, arational,* and *diaphainon*
makes them not only familiar but something like the last of these
three, diaphanous, translucent at the very least, and ultimately open,
clear, transparent.

Like Jung, Gebser is caught by the persistence of the primordial
and the special awareness of *Ursprung,* the ever-present origin, in
Gegenwart, the present time, the modern world. Thus he divides the
two parts of his Summa: I, the foundations of the aperspectival
world – the world of wholeness – in earlier structures of consciousness:
the archaic, where it all begins to evolve; the magical, where experience
is added to instinct in a one-dimensional structure of consciousness;
the mythical, where differentiation is stirred in an awakening consciousness; the mental, where directed thought and an immoderate
rationalism predominate; the integral, distinguished by a concretion of
time and a movement toward a diaphanous present. These structures
lead Gebser to a discussion of mutations "as an integral phenomenon,"
the "space-time constitution of the structures," and then through consideration of the "phenomena" of soul and spirit and "previous forms of
realization and thought" to the barest presentation of the foundations
of that world he will take up in Part II, what he calls the aperspectival.
In II, the subjects are time and an awakening consciousness of the
possibility of freedom from it, new mutations, creativity, new concepts
of the modern age, and then the particularization of these things in the
arts and sciences.

Wholeness is Gebser's aim, hope, and daring prediction: "The
undivided, ego-free person who no longer sees parts but realizes the
'Itself,' the spiritual form of being of man and the world, perceives the
whole, the diaphaneity present 'before' all origin which suffuses every-

thing." For all the fullness of organization with which he has presented his hopeful Summa, Gebser disclaims, in the last paragraphs of his book, any attempt at developing a thesis or a synthesis: "Theses are parts of rigidifying, perspectival thought." Gebser looks instead to bring us face to face with "the new reality and its corresponding mode of realization, 'verition' or 'a-waring' which is made possible by the new consciousness structure." Rather than synthesis, he has offered to our view his "discovery of the basic concern of our epoch." An increase of consciousness, and more particularly, "our conscious participation in the construction of a new reality," is what he sees as a way out of the abundant suffering of the West "from scepticism and suspicion" and of the Soviet bloc "from ideological anxiety."

The terms remain tied, deliberately or not, to the vocabulary of transformation we associate with Jung. Those "for whom the present . . . is no more than a time-bound moment" will have no part in "the emerging transformation." Success will come only for those who understand the present as "a time-free origin, a perpetual plenitude and source of life and spirit from which all decisive constellations and formations are completed." To come to such an understanding requires a shock to one's psyche and spirit, a series of major changes in the way one sees and feels. Those changes, that shock, amount not to a systematic move toward the aperspectival, but an asystematic one, using the Greek prefix "a-" in the way Gebser does, not as a negation of the systematic, but as a liberation. That freeing may come from any of the disciplines, arts, or sciences, or emerge from some combination of them. Three examples make this particularly clear.

The first is from the cubists. Gebser learned much from his association with Picasso, Braque, and others who accomplished the great revolution in seeing in our time, moving us at the very least to accommodate a two-dimensional picture plane, flattened to the dimensions of surfaces in order to take in everything that is there and to accommodate the two-dimensional flattening alongside the three-dimensional perspective which since the Italian Renaissance we have come to take for granted. He recognizes in cubism the attempt "to see things not only from above or in profile but also . . . to penetrate them." There are swift changes of viewpoint and with each one the grasp of "a new fragment" in a "dynamic, continuously changing process" in which the "relationship between form and space" is revealed as the fourth dimension.

The second example is from Robert Musil. The author of that "immense novel," *The Man Without Qualities*, indicates "with the precision that is his hallmark his aperspectival concerns." It comes in a prefatory note to the third volume of the great unfinished work: "Some will ask what is the standpoint of the author, and what are its results?

I cannot vindicate myself. I treat the object neither from all sides—
which is impossible in a novel—nor from one side, but rather from
various sides which belong together."

The third and last example is from Jung, to whom Gebser gives
the largest portion of his treatment of psychology. He sees Jung as
limited by the "inherent weakness of his discipline—namely, the lack of
any spiritual moment. . . ." He criticizes him for his inadequate differentiation "between trias (triadicity) and trinity. . . ." But he finds what
might be called a compensating balance in Jung's quaternities,
whether the filling out of the trinity is accomplished by a shadow
figure, a Satan, or woman. It is an "attempt at a 'totality' beyond
dualism. . . . an attempt to overcome the three-dimensional paternal
world. . . ." He likes Jolande Jacobi's enunciation of Jung's differentiation of the "totally other," and Jung's incorporation of it in a four-
dimensional psychology, the fourth dimension being time, as in modern physics.

Gebser says flatly that "Jung's later research is definitely not
directed toward the perception of the spiritual," which I think is quite
against the facts. But he does see in "one of his earlier basic concepts,
that of 'archetypes,'" something "definitely arational in nature." That,
from Gebser, is high praise. But we must remember that the structural
concepts that Jung presents in his discussions of archetypes would be
inconceivable "without the merging effectivity [*Wirksamwerden*] of
four-dimensionality." Furthermore, we must understand the concept of
the archetype "as an incipient manifestation of the aperspectival
world, for despite its psychological determination, it is ultimately
apsychic." It is only in the way they appear that archetypes can be
considered "psychic phenomena." Since they are eternally present, they
are time-free and "lacking a material existence," they act to "preform
the psyche." They are not only immaterial, but amaterial; not only
irrational, but arational. "They point to a rationally unrealizable 'state'
before time and space, and indeed before space-timelessness." Know-
ingly or unknowingly, Jung has stumbled on ultimate truth, even if he
has insisted on a vocabulary focused on the psyche.[1]

Jungians would be wise, I think, to make greater use of Gebser's
work, both where it complements Jung and where it extends his ideas,
to recognize the similarities and dissimilarities of temperament, of
vocabulary, or conviction, but above all to see how both men in their

---

[1] See Jean Gebser, *The Ever-Present World*, trans. Noel Barstand and Algis Mick-
unas (Athens, Ohio: Ohio University Press, 1985), pp. xxvii, 8, 411–417, 5, 23, 35,
42, 85, 117, 2–3, 543, 546, 545, 495–496, 396–397, 399–402.

assiduous pursuit of understanding of the structures of consciousness were constructing a vocabulary and imagery of wholeness.[2]

Gaston Bachelard made his first reputation as a philosopher of science and ended up as an epistemologist of fire and space and reverie, as the philosopher of dream. More precisely, he began as a postman in a small French town, the son and grandson of shoemakers, then became a student of chemistry and physics. Even as a philosopher of science, his impulse was to a kind of "objective meditation," to the constant extension of the possibilities of human experience and human sympathy, even in the laboratory. Understanding, for him, had "a dynamic dimension . . . a spiritual élan, a vital élan."[3] The philosopher's "job . . . is to find primary truths within himself. . . ."[4]

Bachelard was an anima naturaliter Jungiana. Latent in all his speculations about the sciences was the stirring of the psyche, the archetypes, the complexes. Northrop Frye, in his introduction to the first of the books in which Bachelard moved into his new territory, *The Psychoanalysis of Fire*, suggests that what he calls a complex "might better be called something else, to avoid confusion with the purely psychological complexes of actual life." Frye suggests myth, because myth is "a structural principle in literature." I respectfully disagree. While he gives the word his own inflection, Bachelard means something like Jung's "complex." Myth is in fact complex, highly complicated, and it does join the complexes of "actual life" with those of literature and religious experience and anywhere else that the human imprint can be found. Not the least of these are the places, as Frye describes the complexes of Bachelard's *Fire*, "at which literary myth becomes focussed on its cardinal points of creation, redemption and apocalypse."

Fire is Bachelard's starting point. He is embarked, by way of the four elements of the medieval and ancient world—earth, air, fire, water—on a journey through the territory of the imagination. He proposes, he says, "as did C. G. Jung, to seek out systematically the component elements of the Libido in all primitive activities." The Libido, he tells us, is the "source of all the works of *homo faber*," that is, of man the builder, man the maker, man the poet. The image he associ-

---

[2]See George Feuerstein, *Structures of Consciousness: The Genius of Jean Gebser—an Introduction and Critique* (Lower Lake, Calif.: Integral Publishing, 1987). A useful book by the co-director of the California Center for Jean Gebser Studies.

[3]See Gaston Bachelard, *The New Scientific Spirit*, trans. Arthur Goldhammer (Boston: Beacon Press, 1984), pp. 170–171, 177.

[4]Gaston Bachelard, *The Philosophy of No: A Philosophy of the New Scientific Mind*, trans. G. C. Waterston (New York: Orion Press, 1968), p. 8.

ates with this builder-maker-poet is the definition somebody once made of man as a hand and a language. He reconstructs fire in human experience through its sexual significance and its chemistry, its association with the ancient temperaments and its idealization. Fire in principle is "the male activity and . . . this wholly physical activity, like an erection, is the principle of life. . . ." Clearly, "all Alchemy was penetrated by an immense sexual reverie," one of wealth and power and rejuvenation. Bachelard wants to show that the sexual reverie is a fireside one, and that "*Sexualized fire* is preeminently the connecting link for all symbols." He finds his chemistry in alchemy, his lasting typology in the relationship of the ancient elements and the temperaments, what he calls "a tetravalent doctrine of poetic temperaments," which is less a fixed psychology of types than a joining of worlds through the mediation of the masters of the past—alchemists, poets, scientists in both the ancient and modern senses of the word. We end where we began, in Jungian territory, that earth from which Bachelard proceeds to make his own province:

> To seize fire or to give oneself to fire, to annihilate or to be annihilated, to follow the Prometheus complex or the Empedocles complex, such is the psychological alternation which converts all values and which also reveals the clash of values. What better proof can there be that fire, in the very precise sense of C. G. Jung, is the point of departure "for a fertile archaic complex," and that a special psychoanalysis must destroy its painful ambiguities the better to set free the lively dialectics which bestow on reverie its true liberty and its true function as a creative mental process?[5]

The fertility of the archaic fascinated Bachelard in his study of the imagination, but never at the cost of insensitivity to the immediacy of the image as it comes to poets, philosophers, whomever. We must be receptive to it when it arrives, he says in the magnificent opening paragraph of his *Poetics of Space*, for the "poetic image is a sudden salience on the surface of the psyche. . . ." First of all, we must respond to that, not in principle, not as an effect we can trace to a cause, but as the product of that "major power of human nature," the imagination. It is the ontology of the imagination that Bachelard proposes to study in his poetics of space, and again in his elaboration of related material in his *Poetics of Reverie*, as earlier he had dealt with fire, with *Water and Dreams* in an "Essay on the Imagination of Matter," *Air and Dreams* in an "Essay on the Imagination of Movement," *Earth and Reveries of Will* in an "Essay on the Imagination of Power,"

---

[5]See Gaston Bachelard, *The Psychoanalysis of Fire*, trans. A. C. M. Ross (Boston: Beacon Press, 1964), pp. vii–viii, 30, 49, 51–52, 55, 89–90, 112.

and *Earth and Reveries of Repose* in an "Essay on the Imagination of Intimacy." In these essays on the ancient elements and the imagination and in short reviews, introductions, and the like, written from 1939 to 1960, he demonstrates meticulous attention to the image rising up in its "sudden salience," breaking through all walls of separation, pronouncing its immediacy and, in the very nature of its being, "relation . . . to an archetype lying dormant in the depths of the unconscious."

In his responses to the immediacy of the poetic image, to its roots in matter, its narrative content, and its lyric pulse, Bachelard is drawn to what he calls its "reverberation" of its archetypal nature. "In this reverberation, the poetic image will have a sonority of being." Once more he stresses that "the poetic image is independent of causality," for he is not looking to "explain" the image, whether through psychoanalysis or philosophical argument or any other procedure associated to cause and effect.[6]

As the poet Paul Claudel compares a human breast to the geographical design of the rounded delta of a river and its milk to the river's water, so Bachelard speaks of "the liquid of organic psychoanalysis." We learn from the thing in itself as we experience it, in that kind of alchemy which characterizes the prescientific mind's way explaining of the chemical through the biological, rather than the other way around, the way of the modern scientist. "The prescientific mind thinks concretely about images that we take for mere metaphors. It really thinks that the earth *drinks* water." Bachelard, gifted with the immersion in being of an alchemist, and trained in the distancing perspective of the modern chemist and physicist, can bring us now "once more" to "see that all great substantial values, all valorized human movements, rise without difficulty to the cosmic level."[7]

The classical statement of that vatic seeing is in *The Poetics of Space*, where Bachelard starts his study of the images of intimacy with the poetics of the house as a fitting way of presenting "the topography of our intimate being." His guiding metaphor springs directly from Jung's comparison of the soul with a building of two stories, a cellar

---

[6]See Gaston Bachelard, *The Poetics of Space*, trans. Maria Jolas (New York: Orion Press, 1964), pp. xi, xxx, xii–xiii. For Bachelard, the imagination, as Etienne Gilson notes in his splendid introduction, "is a most secret power that is as much of a cosmic force as of a psychological faculty." Gilson hails "the striking originality of a man so deeply rooted in the soil of everyday life, and in such intimate relation with the concrete realities of nature, that after carefully scrutinizing the methods whereby man achieves scientific cognition, he yielded to an urge personally to communicate with the forces that create it" (pp. ix–x).

[7]See Gaston Bachelard, *Water and Dreams: An Essay on the Imagination of Matter*, trans. E. R. Farrell (Dallas: Pegasus Foundation, 1983), pp. 123–124.

and a filled-in cave beneath it. Up above, we have a sixteenth-century main floor and a nineteenth-century second one. Below, built over relics of the stone age and glacial life, are Roman "foundation walls." Bachelard's questions are crucial: "can we not find within ourselves, while dreaming in our own modest homes, the consolations of the cave? Are the towers of our souls razed for all time?" And his answer, which becomes by elaboration the body of this book and its sequel on reverie, is decisive: "Our soul is an abode. And by remembering 'houses' and 'rooms,' we learn to 'abide' within ourselves. Now everything becomes clear, the house images move in both directions: they are in us as much as we are in them and the play is so varied that two long chapters are needed to outline the implications of house images."

Space surrounds us. Space reflects us. If we go beyond metaphor, beyond simply giving "concrete substance to an impression that is difficult to express," we discover in our space those images that reflect us back to ourselves. The image, "pure product of absolute imagination, is a phenomenon of being. . . ." It speaks to us of us in the drawers, chests, and wardrobes, the nests, shells and corners of our world, the miniatures and intimate immensity which when mediated to us by a poet make little ordinary things huge in their extension of our "intimate space."

Bachelard has recourse to Jung on alchemy and Erich Neumann on the "force" of the Mother-Earth archetype. He asserts his own obligation "to establish the actuality of archetypes." He makes the instrumentation of dream as tangible as the strings and horns and woodwinds of a symphony orchestra. He gives a psychic breadth to phenomenological philosophy which enlarges the method of the school, but more important shows us where its substance really lies. What he is doing, he explains in a splendid chapter on "the Dialectics of Outside and Inside," is affirming the principle of examining and testing "the psychological being of an image, before any reduction is undertaken."[8] It is a concretizing of the experiences of the imagination he achieves, even at his most airily speculative, rather than an abstract conceptualization which gives us everything about the imagination except the thing itself. He returns us to the experience of the image, which is to say poetry at the source – the poetry inherent in things, in their immediacy, in their archetypal immensity. We seize these things. We experience the houses and drawers and shells and nests of our world, the earth, air, water, and fire of our being, in our intimate spaces, "following 'the path of reverie,' " discovering, detailing, annotating "a growth of awareness in every instance of awareness." That is the burden and

8See *The Poetics of Space*, pp. xxxii–xxxiii, 74–75, 199, 188, 219.

the weightlessness – the flight away from anything that will hold us down to destructive ambiguity and insensitivity – of *The Poetics of Reverie.*

In another ample introduction, Bachelard acknowledges the primary source of his reasoning – the "psychology of the depths," by which he means the work of Jung and in particular the "profound duality in the human Psyche" which comes to us "under the double sign of an *animus* and an *anima.*" Bachelard anticipates here what has become a major position for many Jungian revisionists.

Anima and animus inhere in all of us, says Bachelard, both of them in both men and women, "sometimes cooperating, sometimes in dissonance." Each has its function, dream issuing from the animus, reverie from the anima. On that basis, Bachelard distinguishes the dream – *rêve* in the French – "which is so often marked by the hard accents of the masculine," from the feminine textures of reverie, which "conducted in the tranquility of the day and in the peace of repose – truly natural reveries – is the very force (*puissance*) of the being at rest." What Bachelard is moving toward in this book is his hope "to indicate the force of coherence which a dreamer feels when he is really faithful to his dreams" and his conviction "that his dreams take on coherence precisely because of their poetic qualities."

Words have a solemn importance in this attempt to discover the basic elements of a philosophy of repose: they can effect a poetic coherence. So do Bachelard's meditations on childhood, not an attempt to forge a child psychology but rather an effort to make sense of the dramas of childhood and of their lasting effects. In the world of reverie, analysis is constantly at the disposal of the conscious dreamer, who unlike the night dreamer has a *cogito*, an "I," for whom the images that come in reverie may, like "the images of the poet's reverie dig life deeper, enlarge the depths of life." Finally, it must be noted that one breathes well in the great complementarities of poetic reverie; there one can experience "the triumph of calm, the summit of confidence in the world. . . ." Images in reverie can grow as large as the cosmos. We "inhabit a world." The dreamer of reverie has "the impression of a *home* (*chez soi*) in the imagined universe," where "one is always departing; one lives in the *elsewhere* – in an elsewhere which is always comfortable." The abiding mark of this dream world is happiness.

What is essential to Bachelard's reading of sexual identity, or what he calls in his movements through words "a harmonics of sexuality," is what comes to us in "solitary reverie," where he says "we know ourselves in the feminine and masculine at the same time." In reverie dream-object and dreamer come together in a dualism that matches the meeting of masculine and feminine, which at once is "concrete and limitless." A highly virile man is "too simply characterized by a strong *animus*," but is not to be thought of as without that archetypal presence. In all of us, male or female, "when the reverie is truly profound, the being who comes to dream within us is our *anima*."

Bachelard is uneasy with an anima/animus dialectic that depends on "injured psychisms." He prefers rather the contemplation of the "great cosmic reveries of alchemy" that he finds in Jung and looks through dream to find the principles of a *"studious animism."* Complexity is again the governing texture and the relations of two persons hang upon as many combinations and permutations as can be performed upon the "keyboard of four beings in two persons," in which animas and animuses meet each other in endless combinations and permutations within themselves and with others. These multiple conjunctions reflect the complex joinings of substances in alchemy, joinings which are always conjunctions of "the forces of the masculine and feminine principles." In support of the wide range of "this psychological explanation of man by the world worked on by androgynous reveries," Bachelard offers Jung's presentation of the twelve engravings of man from the *Rosarium Philosophorum.*

Bachelard is not fazed by the difficulties of Jungian alchemy. His philosophy of reverie is up to all sorts of objections as the dreamer of reveries must be up to the doubts and shadows that confront him. The shadow that the dreamer meets wherever he is less than fully himself is a "rich being. . . . a more penetrating psychologist than the psychologist of everyday life. . . . the being which doubles the being of the dreamer through reverie." In reverie, we meet the I-dreamer, a "projected being," who is double as all of us are, and like each of us, possesses an anima and animus. Conclusion? "Here we are at the knot of all our paradoxes: the " *'double' is the double of a double being."* When we are alone – any one of us – there are in fact four of us.

Bachelard's variations on alchemical themes are full of odd glints and deep surroundings, constantly moving from nuance to something that promises permanence. The largest of his insights, one both motivated by Jung and shared with him, is that the idealization of the masculine and feminine transforms them into values, quadripolar values. And if they are not idealized? Then, asks Bachelard, "are they anything more than poor biological servitudes?"

Let us remember that Bachelard is a trained scientist and philosopher as well as a poet of space and reverie. For all the elements of the rhapsodic that infuse these pages, he never loses sight of reasonable procedure, of something like systematic analysis. And so, in good reason, we are asked to look at the other side, again with reference to Jung, when dreams dissipate and energies falter and the remaining virtues are middle-class. At that point anima/animus becomes animosity. In a poor married life as Jung describes it in *Psychology and*

Religion, the "*anima* gives rise to illogical outbursts of temper; the *animus* produces irritating commonplaces." We are reduced in such circumstances to "parcellary personalities" which assume "the character of an inferior man or woman."

Before he is finished with this meditation, Bachelard takes something like Dantesque flight. Dante's Beatrice is for him "a synthesis of the greatest idealizations: for a dreamer of human values, she is the erudite *Anima*. She radiates by the heart and the intelligence." To do her justice, a whole book would be required. Such a book exists, he says, Etienne Gilson's *Dante and Philosophy*. So does Bachelard's own extraordinary matching of poetic insight and systematic definition. Here is what reverie brings the dreamer; here are its graces and life-filling repose:

> The *anima* is always the refuge of the simple, tranquil, continuous life. Jung was able to say: "I have defined the *anima* very simply as the Archetype of life." It is the Archetype of the immobile, stable, harmonious life well accorded to the fundamental rhythms of an existence devoid of drama. Whoever dreams (*songe*) of life, of the simple life without looking for knowledge (*savoir*) inclines toward the feminine. By being concentrated around the *anima*, reveries help the dreamer find his repose. In each of us, man or woman, the best of our reveries come from our feminine element. They bear the mark of an undeniable femininity. If we did not have a feminine being within us, how would we rest ourselves?[9]

As philosopher and poet Bachelard is Jung's collaborator, but not his mirror. He learns from the analytic psychologist, he draws deeply from his works, but ultimately keeps his own counsel, finding for himself and sending us to find for ourselves such marvels as the rediscovery in the "depths" of sleep of a "formative carnal space" and in the images that meet us "as the moment of waking approaches" a new order of dreams, "dreams of will, schemes of will." What he finds at that moment, in "the oneiric space of dawn," is "a sudden *inner* light." In that instant everything is straight for the sleeper-dreamer-waker. "Day breaks even within the waking mind. The imagination of concentration is replaced by a will to irradiation."[10]

Bachelard is a servant of the roots of things, an explorer of the archetypes "buried in the unconscious of all races." He deliberately chooses the alchemist's role. He knows, with Jung as his authority,

---

[9]See Gaston Bachelard, *The Poetics of Reverie*, trans. Daniel Russell (New York: Orion Press, 1969), pp. 5, 18–19, 15–16, 155, 182, 58, 62, 69–70, 74, 76, 80, 84, 87, 95, 92.

[10]See Gaston Bachelard, *The Right to Dream*, trans. J. A. Underwood (New York: Orion Press, 1971), pp. 174–175.

that "the alchemist *projects* on patiently worked substances his own unconscious, which accompanies and parallels sensory knowledge." He remembers Jung's warning "against assuming the unconscious to be located beneath consciousness," but as he understands the alchemist's unconscious, it "projects itself into material images as *a depth.*" What the alchemist projects is his depth. From this perception, in his poetic-scientific way, Bachelard draws a conclusion: "Dreaming depth, we dream *our* depth. Dreaming of the secret power of substances, we dream of our secret being. But the greatest secrets of our being are hidden from ourselves, they are hidden in our depths." He is indeed Jung's collaborator, if not his mirror.[11]

Those interested in these materials should not miss the sinuous way Jungian terms and ideas move through the writings of the English anthropologist and philosopher Rodney Needham, whose work as an anthropologist has large philosophical underpinnings and whose philosophical speculation is constantly deepened by the knowledge of man brought by anthropology. Some sense of the lines of Needham's capacious thought may be gathered from his dedication of *Belief, Language, and Experience* to the memory of the anthropologist Lucien Lévy-Bruhl—to whom Jungians are indebted for the mass of meanings gathered in the phrase *participation mystique*—and of the philosopher Ludwig Wittgenstein. In examining "the topic of belief," he says, quoting and paralleling Wittgenstein, that he has "been concerned methodologically with 'fundamental principles of human enquiry.'" It is necessary in such an inquiry to "implicate in common a number of what are otherwise academically discriminated as separate disciplines." Philosophy is for Needham first among these and under it whatever might make easier some attempt at a definition of man, its "categories of thought, laws of logic, and innate ideas. . . ." To this he adds Jung's urging of "the recognition of archetypes," such other "psychic syndromes" as the Oedipal, and his own term, "natural symbols," to describe "certain phenomenal and conceptual vehicles of meaning that seem to exert an intuitive influence on man's psyche and the regulation of his thoughts."[12] Although he uses the term somewhat differently from Jung, he does make substantial use of the concept of the archetype, as for example in his lectures on "Primordial Characters." There he explains that he is "concentrating on the principles of

[11]See *On Poetic Imagination and Reverie: Selections from the Works of Gaston Bachelard*, ed. and trans. Colette Gaudin (Indianapolis: Bobbs-Merrill, 1971), pp. 84, 53-54. The excerpts are from *La Terre et les rêveries du repos (Earth and Reveries of Repose).*

[12]See Rodney Needham, *Belief, Language, and Experience* (Chicago: University of Chicago Press, 1972), pp. 216-217.

synthesis that constitute primary factors into archetypes and that discriminate one archetype from another. . . ."

Needham believes that "the imagination can be studied in positive terms, by means of a comparison of collective representations from around the world and in the records of history." His method of study, he is persuaded, makes possible "the isolation of primary factors, synthetic images, and standard operations" which are neither invented nor willed, but are the "properties of the unconscious." It is a range of human experience that "is not entirely dark and inaccessible" as Freud thought, but one that "can be investigated in empirical terms, through collective representations and social forms, exactly like any social facts. . . ." The unconscious "can be investigated in this way because it is, as ethnographic comparison proves, a genuinely collective unconscious." Properly managed, it would show "the cogency of Jung's assertion that the original structural components of the psyche are of no less surprising a uniformity than are those of the human body." Strong words, these, important ones, that, as Needham himself makes clear, diverge "widely from the intellectualist bent of modern anthropology, with its concern for questions of cognition and rationality." He is not speaking against this concern, but simply "urging . . . that manifestations of the imagination, under its most general and specific aspects, can be recognized and can be studied comparatively as social facts."[13]

It is an important change of emphasis that Needham is speaking for, not to unseat anything but to awaken a larger sensitivity than has been usual in the study of man, in anthropology and sociology and elsewhere. Thus in *Reconnaissances*, he explores "the notion that certain images and ideas and cerebrational vectors have an archetypal character." He is moved again by his conviction that certain "distinctive features of . . . collective representations are products of the unconscious," and more particularly in this little book to investigate Morris Philipson's contention that "for the Jungian thesis" of the universality of the collective unconscious "to be tested for anything like" such "validity, the anthropologist's work is indispensable." One of his conclusions is that the archetype, "especially in Jung's resort to this notion . . . cannot be identified with particular manifestations but can only be discerned through them. . . ." It is not through the associations of the archetype, in minute particulars, that we discern its character, but "for its distribution, its stability, and its recurrent emergence through great disparities of social settings, collective representations, and fantastic fictions."

[13]See Rodney Needham, *Primordial Characters* (Charlottesville, Va.: University Press of Virginia, 1985), pp. 46, 65–66.

Is this not enough? Consider, Needham says, "the range of social facts in question," and then ask "by what reason a primordial image stands in need of better testimony." It will seem, he muses at the end of the book, that in analytical outings like his, "proceeding from collective representations to mental operations we are on increasingly shaky ground." That is simply the nature of such undertakings, moving "from the known to the unknown," recognizing that "even in a formal sense we have no clear idea of what features to seek."[14] But that is what his brand of social anthropology, or social philosophy, to use an ancient but still appropriate term, is about. One makes what many might find daring or even questionable associations, such as the one he postulates between physiology and symbols in *Circumstantial Deliveries*. His investigation of physiological symbols there is brief, handsomely articulated, and provocative in the way that St. Augustine's setting forth the connections between signs and things is in his *De doctrina Christiana*. One statement seems to me crucial for an understanding of Jung's metapsychology and the way we choose to live with the psyche, either as a theoretical construct or a living reality. Why, Needham asks, do we use symbols at all? The physiology of symbolism does not seem to offer an answer. He proposes something else.

> There is a bolder alternative, namely, to contend that we do not need to account separately for the way in which a connection is made between physiology and symbol. The symbolic vehicles in question can be viewed as testifying to natural proclivities of thought and imagination; their distribution, constancy, and persistence accord them that designation. Under this aspect they can be said to possess an archetypal character, and a phrase of Jung's then comes to bear: "the archetype does not proceed from physical facts but describes how the psyche experiences the physical fact."[15]

It may be that the "psyche"—the quotation marks are Needham's—is to be understood simply in terms of the kind of connections he has been investigating with the aid of his disciplines and the associations Jung has been defining and exemplifying with the help of his. There are no fixed definitions or notions in these disciplines that are allowed easy rule in Needham's approach to collective experience. In his appealingly testy set of essays, *Against the Tranquility of Axi*

[14]See Rodney Needham, *Reconnaissances* (Toronto: University of Toronto Press, 1980), pp. 13–14, 39, 105.

[15]See Rodney Needham, *Circumstantial Deliveries* (Berkeley, Calif.: University of California Press, 1981), p. 51. See also pp. 26 and 43, where Needham raises questions on "the organic basis of the collective unconscious" and "certain symbolic forms as archetypal predispositions" that arise from Jung.

oms, he associates himself with "the designations of a number of the books of Sextus Empiricus," the second-century physician whose writings are the source of most of what we understand of the classical skeptics and the special resource of Montaigne's Pyrrhonist probing. What is so refreshing about Needham's informed questioning is that it is not presented in order to deny the possibility of knowledge, but rather to increase both knowledge and understanding by making us less quick to accept as established, or worse, as axiomatic, methods and ideas that are no more than conjectural. As we have seen, this has particular importance for our reading of the collective unconscious and related Jungian speculation. Tempered by Needham's kind of skepticism, we neither accept nor reject so easily; we inquire more, we decide less. In the world of the psyche, that can only be a gain.[16]

Arnold Toynbee was criticized, sometimes severely, for giving too much attention to the unconscious, and in particular to Jung's idea of the collective unconscious, in his twelve-volume *Study of History.* He himself notes the criticism in the final volume of the series, one devoted to "reconsiderations." He has been censured for not offering a reasoned explanation for "the rhythm of conflicting and alternating order and disorder, stability and explosion" which his massive study of the major civilizations of the world describes and supports through endless witness, through fact and theoretical speculation and strong assertion. But the rhythm "cannot be elucidated by reason," Toynbee says, "because it is one of the *a priori* categories through which reason operates." Where he finds "undesigned regularities and recurrences in the ascendant in human affairs," he looks for their understanding "in the medium of the subconscious," and he is not then "surprised to find them particularly clearly pronounced in periods of social disintegration, since these . . . are the periods when consciousness, will, and purpose are least, and the subconscious most, in the ascendant."

Toynbee is not greatly dismayed by criticism of his psychologizing, although he is attentive to it. The rhythm of order and disorder, of creativity and decay, is to be found as much in the psychological alternations and conflicts of the life of a historian as in the history he

---

[16]See Rodney Needham, *Against the Tranquility of Axioms* (Berkeley, Calif.: University of California Press, 1983), pp. 47 and 52, for the discussion of archetypes, and pp. 93-120, on reversals and transformation, a fascinating commentary on his epigraph for the chapter, from Wittgenstein: "We predicate of the thing what lies in the method of representing it. Impressed by the possibility of a comparison, we think we are perceiving a state of affairs of the highest generality." The few pages of mathematical notation are worth whatever struggle may be necessary for those who are interested in translating symbolic experience, ritual, and the like into any form of useful representation.

studies. As the "disciple" of Jung he has been called, Toynbee is well aware of this. The temperament of the historian inevitably reflects relativity of analysis and judgment which characterizes the study of human affairs, for everyone's genetic heritage is subject to "Nature's mathematical game of permutations and combinations." We are "allotted" our "actual temperament almost casually by a biological mechanism which, from the human product's standpoint, is a blind throw of the dice; and it has been singled out of a host of various possibilities ranging, perhaps, over most of the gamut of Theophrastus's characters and Jung's psychological types."[17]

It is typical of Toynbee to combine references to an ancient Greek philosopher and a modern psychologist to make his point. His is a temperamental inclination like Jung's, far-ranging, caught by the ancient world, still alive to the modern. He is himself very clear about how much he owes to Jung. In the tenth volume of his *Study of History*, he offers a kind of intellectual autobiography to explain the circumstances in which he found his own "angle of vision" and the shaping forces which aroused his curiosity about history. His "awakened curiosity," after a remarkable movement across civilizations, ancient, medieval, and modern, "led him to widen his range" between the world wars, "by taking into his cognizance the general course of current international affairs, and to add a new dimension to this mental universe by transshipping, with C. G. Jung as his navigator-psychopompus, from a surface-craft to a submarine in order to sound the Psyche's subconscious abyss." In his copious Edwardian way, the historian is declaring a great indebtedness to the psychologist.

In his expressions of gratitude to the psychologist, Toynbee is offering a thoughtful illustration and defense of his use of Jung and also producing something like the explanation he is not sure can be made of his philosophy of history: it is, perhaps, less a philosophy than a psychology with theological overtones.

To begin with, Toynbee acknowledges his gratitude to *Psychological Types*, which opened up for him "a new dimension in the realm of Life." He is grateful for a catholicity and diversity of materials which permitted him to find his "way into the *terra incognita* of the Psyche's subconscious abyss by proceeding from the known to the unknown." He was fascinated to see "the same primordial image coming to light in a familiar myth and in some *rebarbatif* clinical case . . . which might have repelled my mind if my interest in the analysis of the myth had not drawn me on to take a consequent interest in the myth's clinical counterpart." It became for him a major insight: "I found here the

[17]See Arnold J. Toynbee, *A Study of History, Vol. XII: Reconsiderations* (London: Oxford University Press, 1961), pp. 241 n.3, 241–242, 61–62.

equivalents, in the experience of the Soul, of a number of phenomena that I had already experienced for myself in the experience of Society." He gives a series of arresting parallels: "The polarization of the *libido* (psychic energy) when it strikes an obstacle . . . the schism in the Body Social (mirror of the Soul) after a failure to respond to a challenge. The depression of subordinated functions into the Subconscious . . . the estrangement of a proletariat from a dominant minority. The explosive discharge of obstructed *libido* . . . a Völkerwanderung of barbarian war-bands when the *limes* [the fortified boundary] behind which they have been pent up at last gives way in a collapse that had been symbolized for me in the bursting of the Dam of Ma'rib." And so he goes through other examples to conclude: "The projection of elements of the Subconscious upon external objects was the equivalent of the radiation of elements of the life of a disintegrating civilization into its external proletariat."

Toynbee is not optimistic about the disorder of our world. There remains in us some possibility, perhaps, of a religion that possesses universal appeal from which appropriate spiritual development might follow, something not unlike the discovery he himself made through Jung, which his second acknowledgment notes. Plato had encouraged him "to part company with an early-twentieth-century Western Zeitgeist whose oracles were scales and dividers because, in this Geist's self-blinkered eyes, the only realities were those that could be weighed and measured." Enter Jung: "I have now lived to see the subconscious well-spring of Poetry and Prophecy restored to honour in the Western World by the genius of C. G. Jung. . . ."[18]

In the course of the provocative fifth volume of Toynbee's *Study*, devoted to the nature and process of the disintegration of our civilization, Jung appears in support of Toynbee's psychology of history. Toynbee finds a "fitting epitaph" for the last of the Neoplatonists – and "also for his Buddhist and Taoist and Confucian counterparts" – in one of the handsome passages in *Modern Man in Search of a Soul* in which Jung accounts for major eruptions and major "innovations" in history. They come from "below," never from "above," burstings forth of consciousness in which the human spirit looks for some way of answering the fears and anxieties which beset it, creating for the purpose treaties and pacts and rearrangements of society in the form of democracy, dictatorship, capitalism, "bolshevism." What is most significant, most attuned to the upheaval in the world, is the response of "the lower social levels who follow the unconscious forces of the Psyche; it is the much-derided, silent folk of the land – those who are less infected with

[18]Ibid., vol. X, pp. 1, 3, 7, 19–20, 225–226, 228.

academic prejudices than great celebrities are wont to be," and Jung
salutes them and so does Toynbee after him. "All these people, looked
at from above, present mostly a dreary or laughable comedy; and yet
they are as impressively simple as those Galileans who were once
called blessed."[19]

Toynbee has frequent recourse to Jungian categories, with or
without credit to Jung. His interior monologue – and dialogue, too, as
ego moves to meet self or self mediates to ego – is so dense at times
that one must sometimes pause long over his extensive parenthetical
fillings and footnote elaborations. A good case in point is a note in the
eighth volume that starts out to deal with the "spiritual malaise which
is the occupational disease of an intelligentsia," moves to the "psychological tension" in modern Hindus who have been "Westernized intel-
lectually while remaining Hindu in feeling, intuition, and sensation (to
use C. G. Jung's categories)," and caps the observation with the
example of nineteenth-century Russians in which the tension was less
severe because the conflict between Slavic tradition and Westernizers
was not so deep. The Russian intelligentsia of the period were also
"gifted with a power of artistic expression and . . . moved to use this
gift as a vent for relieving their spiritual malaise by discharging their
feelings in works of literature. This literary secretion from a culturally
sick body social was a pearl of great price for the historian as well as
the psychologist and the man of letters."[20]

The odds and ends of this restless historiographer's mind are
worth pursuing, especially as they move around Jungian categories. In
volume IX, Toynbee gathers from the German of Ernst Robert Curtius
the fascinating matter turned up in the exchanges of the philosopher
Mikhail Gershenson and the poet, classicist, and critic Vyacheslav
Ivanov from corner to corner of the common room of a convalescent
home "for scientific and literary workers" in Soviet Russia in 1920.
This *Correspondence from Two Corners*, as the published dialogue is
called, shows Gershenson weighed down by the decay of civilization
and longing for a Lethean bath that would wipe out ugly memories
while Ivanov speaks for an understanding of culture as an altogether
appropriate "recollection, not only of our forefathers' terrestrial form
and outward appearance, but also of their spiritual achievements in
dedicating Mankind to ideals." For Ivanov, "recollection is a dynamic
principle, in contrast to an oblivion that signifies lassitude, cessation
of movement, decline, and regression to a condition of relative
torpidity."

---

[19]Ibid., vol. V, pp. 567-568. The quotation from *Modern Man in Search of a Soul*
(New York: Harcourt, Brace, 1933) is on p. 211.

[20]Ibid., vol. VIII, p. 207 n.1.

Ivanov's words galvanize something in Toynbee. What Ivanov is doing, the historian says, is "diagnosing the nature of 'the Antaean rebound' " – that is, the spring with which the mythological Antaeus rebounds from the bosom of "a motherly Earth" when he lights on it – "in terms of Socrates' doctrine of *anamnesis* and Jung's concept of Primordial Images." If we are to achieve self-possession, says Toynbee, echoing Curtius, we must dig down in "the very innermost depths." And when we spring up again, we must resist the opposite temptation, the Atlantic, associated with the figure of Atlas, who when he "touches a step-fatherly Heaven . . . clamps the load down upon his head." But that is "to become identified with the archaic image" that we may have "retrieved from the Abyss. . . ." What we must do instead is to work toward some imaginative expression of the unconscious.

The subtlety and fullness of Toynbee's handling of the Antaean-Atlantean opposition can only be gathered from the most careful reading of these pages. They say a great deal about culture and religion and the importance of the psyche in the orders and disorders of both. He speaks with particular feeling of the dangers involved in bringing back materials from the past by identifying with them. He sees such possession by the renascent materials as a kind of cancer against which only a spiritual initiative will work: "The better the spiritual health of the victim of a renaissance at the time of his self-inflicted ordeal, the better his chance of metabolizing the uncanny treasure that he has wrested from the coffers of Hades, and in metabolizing it, constraining it to serve his weal as an elixir instead of working his woe as a cancer."

For Toynbee, as he never tires of saying, Jung and a few others had made clear "that the subconscious abyss on whose surface each individual human personality's conscious intellect and will were afloat was not an undifferentiated chaos but was an articulated universe in which one layer of psychic activity could be discerned below another." We are, in a sense, caught in a sea of psychic energy, which, although it can be seen as possessing an "irreducible minimum" of its precious stuff, must also be understood as having a "maximum limit" to its quantities, from which "it follows that, if a reinforcement of energy is required for putting a greater drive into one activity, the requisite additional supply will have to be obtained by making economies in other quarters."

There may be a maximum limit to psychic energies, but there is a constant replenishing and extending of the *materia prima* of the arts. It is not the fund of human experiences, even over millennia. It is not "the speculative adventures of the Intellect," to use the words of the historian J. B. Bury, "but 'the Eternal Deep' from whose Primordial Images Wordsworth derived his intimations of Immortality." What the poets constantly discover and rediscover "is the glow of a spiritual fire fed by mighty coal-seams that have been slowly compacted in the womb of Mother Earth out of the debris of forests deeply buried there countless ages ago." This is the "visionary gleam" that artists discern in nature. For Toynbee it is in the empirical order; it is scientific fact. For him, "Jung had demonstrated that the Fine Arts draw their inspiration from creative depths of subconscious experience at which, on the Intellect's Lilliputian scale of time-reckoning, there 'is no variableness, neither shadow of turning' [James 1:17], in the ageless presences of the Primordial Images."[21]

One may think Toynbee too much carried away with his desire to make empirical fact of Jungian theory, but surely it is undeniable that he makes better sense of the randomness, the confusion worse confounded, of human history this way than others have with their inflexible determinisms or all too flexible relativisms. One sees this most clearly in the intricately wrought discussions, over nearly 200 pages of chapter VII of volume VII, on the universal churches. There he deals with churches as "cancers," as "chrysalises," which is to say as "secondary and transitional phenomena," serving "as egg, grub, and chrysalis between butterfly and butterfly," and as "a higher species of society." He examines civilizations as "overtures" and "regressions" in the lives of churches. He describes, dramatically, the "challenge of militancy on earth," when a church becomes aggressive "for the purpose of winning, or recapturing, This World for the *Civitas Dei* not by extinguishing life on Earth but by transfiguring it. . . ."

Religion, or the opening to spiritual initiative, must face diversity, diffraction, the "hard way" which is the way of life, where "the stepping-stones are stopping-places and the pilgrim's progress is a *tour de force*." Toynbee is moved by the Jungian H. G. Baynes, writing in his *Mythology of the Soul* about Prometheus, "the cultural innovator who stole the fire of the Gods, as the prototype for all time of the daring hero-criminal who challenges the primordial images, the immemorial gods of the Unconscious, in order to place more power–i.e. knowledge–in the hands of Consciousness. . . ." Prometheus's guilty act was to steal from Heaven, "the realm of primordial images," energy which had been concealed in the unconscious from the beginning of time and to bring it "under the control of Consciousness." The paradoxical result for Toynbee is "that some of the greatest advances in the Soul's approach to God," those of saints and seers, have been condemned as "appalling backslidings–and this in good faith–by men of

---

[21] Ibid., vol. IX, pp. 144-147, 165-166, 328, 639, 697, 703-704. See also V. I. Ivanov and M. O. Gershenzon, *Correspondence Across a Room*, trans. Lisa Sergio (Marlboro, Vt.: Marlboro Press, 1984), p. 27, where "recollection" is translated as "memory."

common clay" who could not themselves "make the grade." So Pompey was aghast at not finding any material object of worship in the Temple at Jerusalem. So Christians were called, by different people in different places, atheists and libertines.

The diffractions and the distortions are almost endless. Among them is one that Toynbee sees issuing from depth psychology. It could be predicted, he suggests, that "the Modern Western scientific mind, after having followed the Hellenic school of philosophy for three Cartesian centuries in mistakenly identifying God with the conscious rational superstructure of the Psyche, might be led astray by its portentous discovery of a psychic underworld into exchanging an Hellenic error for an Indic one and following in turn the Indic school in mistakenly identifying God with the Psyche's subconscious irrational abyss." That warning, made at mid-century, is one that Jungians at the end of the century should surely take seriously. We are too quick, Toynbee is telling us, as Man always has been, to "identify with God Himself any work of God that Man, in the exercise of his puny prowess, has newly discovered or newly mastered. . . ."

That precise caution should accompany the reading of what is perhaps the most considerable Jungian tour in Toynbee's volumes, an examination of the "higher religions" in terms of "the psychological types into which Human Nature appears to be differentiated." No matter what the claim to catholicity on the part of these religions, they must move to the ebb and flow of human history and of human types within that history. No single religion can accommodate all. The claim of any one of these to an all-embracing faith is "tacitly refuted" by syncretistic practices in which ardent attempts are made to assuage and reconcile beliefs long defined as incompatible with the religion. Toynbee proposes that we see universality, not in any one of these religions but in all, gathered together under the categories of introvert and extravert, of thinking, feeling, intuition, and sensation types.

In a "classification by attitudes," the inward-turning religions "of Indic origin," Hinduism and Buddhism, might be seen as introvert and "the two religions of Judaic origin," Christianity and Islam, which lead their communicants to turn outwards to meet God, might be called extravert. A further separation is made, between "the rationally discriminating pair of faculties . . . represented by Hinduism and Christianity, and the irrationally perceptive pair by Islam and Buddhism." The "predominant faculty" in Hinduism is thinking, with its emphasis upon "the comprehension, by the Consciousness, of its psychic antithesis the Subconscious"; in Christianity, it is feeling, "proclaimed in the three words 'God is Love,' . . . the heart of the Christian revelation." In Islam, the predominance of sensation, "in the Jungian meaning of an uncritical apprehension of matters of faith," is clear in the "confession of faith — 'There is no god but *the* God, and Muhammad is The Apostle of *the* God,'" and in the required five hours of prayer each day and pilgrimage to the holy cities. Buddhism exhibits the leading role of intuition in the "sudden flash of enlightenment in the soul of the Founder" and attempts of the Zen school to duplicate the experience.

Toynbee's is not a reductionist reading. He shows the interplay of "introverted" thought, sensation, and intuition in Hinduism, finds a matching pairing of feeling and sensation in Christianity, with an "auxiliary" role for intuition, and discovers the important place of the thinking faculty in Islam and in Buddhism, with countless variations among the "sister" faculties. The experience in "the four living higher religions" is, as in the individual, one of a range of faculties and attitudes "that are, all alike, importunate in seeking vent." Always, there is a tension between the conscious and the unconscious. Ever, "each religion was . . . seeking, like the psychological type which it served, to achieve the impossible feat of ministering to the whole gamut of the Psyche's elemental needs for expression." The best any one of the great religions can hope for is a limited part, joining with the others, not in a flattening syncretism, but in the fulfillment of "their common purpose of enabling every human being of every psychological type to enter into communion with God the Ultimate Reality."

Toynbee comes as close here, I think, as possible to articulating the view, always implicit, occasionally explicit, of religion held by Jung. "In the orchestra of Religion, does one psychic faculty count for more than another?" Toynbee asks. The answer rests on "our view of the nature and destiny of Man." He then suggests, as Jung's treatment of the different religions in different psychological contexts does as well, the higher place of one or the other as we elect to go with the faculty of feeling, say, toward the "enjoyment" of God, or with the intellect "at a discount when it is 'introverted' for service as the predominant faculty" in religion, or "more profitably employed when it is 'extraverted' for secular purposes."[22] It is an imaginative speculation, Jungian in tone and direction, open to correction, fixed only in the conviction that without psychological understanding we will make as

---

[22]Ibid., vol. VII, pp. 393, 545, 442–443, 462–463, 497, 722–735. William McNeill's biography of Toynbee, *Arnold Toynbee: A Life* (New York: Oxford University Press, 1989) offers a generous appraisal of one distinguished historian by another, not hesitating to place him in the company of Herodotus. Unfortunately, for all McNeill's sympathy for Toynbee's historiography, he misses entirely the psychological element in his thinking which, for me at least, translates what sometimes seems like self-indulgent vision-making into serious thought. McNeill does not deal with Toynbee's use of Jung, in religious subject matter or any other.

little sense of the nature of the religions and their place in civilizations as we do of the rise and fall of the civilizations themselves.

Jung's presence in another person's work is nowhere more moving
or impressive, it seems to me, than in the books of R. C. Zaehner. The
late Spalding Professor of Eastern Religions and Ethics at Oxford
University conducts what amounts to a running dialogue with Jung,
over many volumes, agreeing, disagreeing, translating terms from
ontology or cosmology into those of Jungian psychology that seem
appropriate to him, or even better, elucidating Asian religions, bringing Eastern concepts and religious experience into Western focus. In
his *Mysticism Sacred and Profane*, where Zaehner's aim is "to separate
out the varying phenomena that appear in praeternatural and 'mystical' experiences," he has constant recourse to Jung. He has "drawn
widely" on Jung's ideas, he explains in his introduction, because they
"seem to illumine much in Oriental religion that had previously been
obscure."

Zaehner's *Mysticism* is famous in its field for its distinctions
between what he calls "nature mysticism" and the "mysticism" of monists and pantheists, on the one hand, and the practice and experience of
theists on the other. The monism of Eastern religion in practice means
"the isolation of the soul from all that is other than itself." The "three
distinct mystical states which cannot be identical," of theist experience, he defines as "the pan-en-henic where all creaturely existence is
experienced as one and one as all; the state of pure isolation of what we
may now call the uncreated soul or spirit from all that is other than
itself; and thirdly the simultaneous loss of the purely human personality, the 'ego,' and the absorption of the uncreate spirit, the 'self,' into
the essence of God, in Whom both the individual personality and the
whole objective world are or seem to be entirely obliterated." He under-
takes to duplicate Aldous Huxley's experiment with the hallucinogen
mescalin, to test the assertion that all preternatural experiences "must
be basically the same" and what the historian of Eastern religions A. J.
Arberry says has "become a platitude," namely that everywhere, even
in the most unpropitious circumstances, "mysticism is essentially one
and the same, whatever may be the religion professed by the individual
mystic: a constant and unvarying yearning of the human spirit for
personal communion with God."

Nothing that Zaehner finds in the texts he examines, or the drug
experience he himself took on, justifies for him such a conclusion of
oneness among theist mystics, monists of the "nature mysticism"
kind or any other, and users of drugs. Superficial resemblances are
the best one can discover. Among those who turn to drugs what one
may find is both hallucination and the manic phase of the manic-

depressive psychosis. In a passage in William James, where James identifies a "great subliminal or transmarginal region" from which, as Zaehner says, he "seems to derive all mystical experience," Zaehner sees instead "an adumbration of what Jung now calls the collective unconscious. . . ." He makes Jung's term his own, comparing the collective unconscious "to a vast sea of common race experience from which the individual consciousness sticks up like the top of an iceberg . . . the submerged and much larger portion of the iceberg would be the personal unconscious. To achieve equilibrium between the three is to achieve sanity, integration, wholeness, salvation." When modern man tries to live without any attention to the unconscious, he courts disaster, "for the unconscious which is irrational and 'bestial' in the sense that it recognizes neither good nor evil . . . cannot be disregarded, but must be acknowledged and controlled. The wild discrepancies that exist between 'natural' and 'diabolical' mystical experiences, between the 'manic' and the 'depressive' states of the manic-depressive psychosis, between the glory and the terror experienced by Huxley under the influence of mescalin, are not explicable in terms of union with the Deity or unity in the Absolute or even of union with Nature."

Zaehner examines the experiences of a number of nature mystics, often with effective use of Jungian language. There is Richard Jeffries, absolutely "opposed to any form of mysticism that is based on asceticism," but fated never to reach the "higher than deity" at which he aimed. There is the novelist Proust, whose "glimpses of eternity" do not take him beyond the "natural bounds" of personality: "In his experience there is no merging into Nature, there is only a complete realization of self. It is not what Jung calls a case of inflation, but a genuine case of 'integration.' " The poet Rimbaud's route to the unknown took him by way of "the short cut of drugs and debauchery." What he discovered – something "utterly incalculable . . . irrational . . . beyond or below good and evil" – he called the "universal mind" or "universal soul." Zaehner calls it "in fact nothing other than the 'collective unconscious' of Jung. . . ." On the positive side, Rimbaud's ecstatic experience brought him through "Hell" to what he thought could be described as his lost innocence. "On the debit side it had also brought him to the confines of madness, to what Jung calls 'positive inflation,' the megalomania characteristic of the manic and the drug-addict." He had perhaps communed with Nature; "he had failed even to approach God Who is worshipped 'in spirit and in truth.' "

The experience of John Custance, a man highly familiar with Jung, is not unlike Rimbaud's, although it produced no poetry, only a set of testimonies to the delights of manic states. Zaehner is, I think, very fair to his witness and to the interpretation he draws from his reading of Jung, but he finds his claim to mystical experience "an over-simplification." There may be some good reasons for associating what Custance underwent with the collective unconscious, but not with the mysticism of the spirit of John of the Cross and Teresa of Avila: "St. Teresa's experience differs fundamentally in this, that it effected a total transformation and sanctification of character which no merely praeternatural agency could bring about." Jung would surely not disagree.

In the remaining half of this seminal work, Zaehner draws upon his own familiarity with Jung many times. He finds in the "integration which, according to Jung and *The Secret of the Golden Flower*, represents the union and reconciliation of the male and female principles in the psyche," the explanation of much in the Upanishads. He is touched rather than persuaded by that response to the definition of the dogma of the Assumption of Mary which made Jung propose a swelling of the Trinity to a Quaternity. For Zaehner, the "symbolical significance of the dogma . . . is not the deification of the 'eternal feminine,' *anima*, collective unconscious, or whatever it may be, but the deification of the human soul as represented by Mary who in common with all human beings is the daughter of the One Father, and is, in her own right, the spouse of the Holy Ghost and Mother of the Son."

Zaehner moves from this discussion into what becomes, over a series of volumes, a protracted examination of Jung's understanding of evil, of the shadow, of the alchemical *conjunctio oppositorum*, of the bringing together in one way or another of the "seamy side" and the "positive side" of the human person. For Zaehner, the Augustinian and Thomist readings of evil as the privation of being "seem to make sense. If we adopt Jung's premise that integration is the final cause or good of human beings on the purely natural plane, then, obviously, the seven deadly sins are, each and all of them, a privation of some essential element in the integrated whole." Sin is what twists and makes the person small, "for, theologically, sin is what deflects a man away from his final cause, therefore from integration necessarily since this must be an essential stage on man's painful journey towards God. Thus to speak of integrating the 'shadow' either into the 'individuated' psyche or into the Deity is nonsense, if by the shadow is understood evil in the sense of a privation of some good, a maiming of oneself." If all it means is "untamed instinct," then to bring it "out into the open will mean, in practice, its taming." The differences here between Jungians and Christians, then, "may be little more than a matter of terminology."

Whatever Zaehner's discomfort or even strong disagreement with Jung, he is clearly pleased to find in his work illumination, as he says, of "so much that was dark before," as for example the under-

standing that "what is usually called the natural mystical experience
may be nothing more than an uprush from . . . the collective unconscious," or in another way of putting it, that "the natural mystical
experience [is] a reversion to a primitive state of affairs when consciousness had not yet separated itself from the unconscious." He is
not at ease with the discovery of God or the God-archetype "at the
bottom of the collective unconscious. Between Him and the conscious
mind, then, will be found Jung's various, and excessively amorphous,
archetypes; the shadow or dark side of the human psyche described in
religions as the Devil; the *anima* and *animus* representing the complementary sexual side of men and women; the Great Mother representing Mother Nature, the *prakrti* of the Samkhya or the *maya* of
the Vedanta." We would, then, in Zaehner's speculation, be faced with
descents, where the conscious mind is seeking "to merge and lose
itself in the unconscious." We would dive down to where the Great
Mother sits, be overcome by the shadow ("the Devil"), or perhaps
"plunge triumphantly past all these nightmare horrors" and at bottom find "the God who makes his dwelling in our inmost depths, just
as the Incarnate God chose to reside in the womb of a Jewess, 'a
narrow and filthy place' as a Zoroastrian polemist observes." No, says
Zaehner to his Jungian fancy. He has no doubt about the reality of
the collective unconscious, "but that God is one of its constituents
awaits more convincing proof."

Zaehner answers his own questions about the God-archetype in
the course of a chapter setting "Theism *Versus* Monism." The fact that
for Jung the God-archetype is "the most powerful constituent in the
collective unconscious, and the one which can develop into the most
formidable 'autonomous complex,' does not, of course, mean that God
exists only in the collective unconscious and is therefore only a *psychological* as opposed to an ontological reality." The point is, as eminent
authority makes clear, that "God is our eternal exemplar; and, being
the ground of the human soul, it follows that, according to Christian
dogma, this exemplar must be the heart and centre of the human
psyche." Zaehner is prepared, however, to accept the "God-archetype"
as a description of the "image of God" that "is in all of us, for it was in
this image that Adam was created." Obviously, it is an image that "can
never appear perfectly in a mere human being since it must be distorted by original sin." We see not only through a glass darkly, but in a
rusty mirror, which, "as the Sufis never tire of pointing out," cannot
present us with a true image. "The purpose of asceticism is to polish
the mirror so that the reflection or image of God may perfectly
emerge." For most of us, most of the time, "the mirrors, which are our
souls, are . . . distorting mirrors. . . . Thus the God-archetype is liable to

appear in mythology, as in the visions of neurotics, in an often absurdly distorted form." We can, however, take in the God who "condescends to manifest Himself in human form. And if He does this, then this Man-God must be what Jung calls psychologically true as well as morally true."

Thus it is in this remarkable dialogue with Jung that Zaehner comes around to something like a full acceptance of Jung's terminology, if not to all of the reasoning that lies behind it. It is as if Jung were always with him in the writing of the book, pressing him to look again at his objections, to see if he had not missed something. It is especially clear in the problem that more than any other was to consume Zaehner in the last years of his life, the problem of evil. At first he is content to put Jung's understanding of evil aside, if not altogether to dismiss it, as a "crypto-Manichaeanism, the *pessima haeresium*, and does to some extent account for the extreme confusion of Jung's pandaemonium of the collective unconscious." It would be better to accept the Zoroastrian understanding of evil, not as the privation of a good of Christian theology, but as "a separate *spiritual* principle, hostile to God and to the material universe which God creates as a bastion against Ahriman, the eternal substance of evil, who is the author of death. . . ." By the end of his book, Zaehner is more tentative. He hopes it will not be "unfair" to say that Jung is not certain about his theological position, since it is not the God of any theology that directs his work but the God-archetype he encounters in his patients, an archetype that "appears in protean and ambivalent forms." That leads him to take another look at Jung's "attitude towards evil."

What we have gathered from the animals, Zaehner says in this last recension of Jung, is the "dark, feminine" side, the instinctive one, of human nature, which is "neither good nor evil, but has, as Jung has demonstrated, great potentialities for both." It makes good sense to integrate this part of our nature into the "total psyche," but not as "moral evil," with which Jung seems to confuse the shadow. "What Jung appears to mean," says Zaehner in this summation, "is that the material, instinctive, and non-rational side of our nature must be given its proper place in the integrated psyche." In the interest of our greater understanding, he offers Al-Ghazali comparing "the relationship between the rational soul and the twin faculties of lust and anger to a man, his pack-animal, and his dog, the proper place of the two latter being that of an obedient servant," and the Hindu idea of "taming" the passions. Separation may follow integration, "the separation of the immortal soul from all its mortal trappings, of *yang* from *yin*, of *purusa* from *prakrti*." This would occur, in the normal ordering of things, "in the second half of life when the instincts lose much of their force and the isolation of the spirit seems less 'unnatural.' "[23] Whether deliberately or not, Zaehner once again is invoking the presence of Jung, who never tired of stressing the centrality of religion in the later years, not as something necessarily either desirable or undesirable, but as a clinical fact, something he had learned from working with his patients.

Zaehner's sensitivity to the presence of the psyche in religious affairs is itself a commanding presence in the books that follow *Mysticism Sacred and Profane*. In his "essay in the comparison of religions," *At Sundry Times*, explaining that Buddhism contains nothing that can be called revelations, he describes the Buddha's discovery of "the true view of life" and his proclamation of it as that of "one who has 'awoken' from the bad dream of phenomenal existence." Zaehner sees the Buddha as "a psychologist rather than a founder of religion," which, he says, "may well explain Jung's interest in the many religions that sprang from his teaching." In the same instructive way, commenting on the *Rig-Veda* hymn (X.129) famous for "its obscure groping after the One, which, it felt instinctively, must underlie all the diversity of an everchanging world," Zaehner makes a specifically Jungian connection: "the author, throughout his changing terminology, seems to conceive of primal existence as a formless and moving mass (water, darkness, the Void, or Not-being) – the *materia prima* or female principle of alchemy and Jungian psychology."

In Jung's use of ancient Indian religion, Zaehner finds corroboration of his assertion that Buddhism and Samkhya-Yoga are not "interested primarily in the nature of God but in the nature and immortality of the human soul." That is not to say that the Indian systematization of "an experience which may occur to anyone," the feeling of possessing a second self apart from the ego and immortal, represents the integration of the personality in the Jungian sense, or even the possibility of it. What is involved is release "from the embrace of the phenomenal world and the ego." This is the center of religion for Indians, not the being of God.

The "intimations of a 'cosmic consciousness' " in the Upanishads Zaehner insists on separating, at least in language, from "what Jung perversely persists in calling the collective *un*conscious." The quality that defines so much in these religious writings, the "merging into the infinite," is not, he thinks, a return to "a state of undifferentiated oneness," with the mother of the child discovering its separateness for

---

[23]See R. C. Zaehner, *Mysticism Sacred and Profane: An Inquiry into Some Varieties of Praeternatural Experience* (Oxford: Clarendon Press, 1957), pp. xvii, 165, 168, xi, 43–44, 82, 90, 105, 115, 121, 124, 148, 144, 150, 148–149, 193–194, 123, 202–203.

the first time, as Jung suggests in his *Psychology of the Unconscious*, but rather what Jung calls the integration of the personality – "the subsuming of the purely mortal parts of the psyche – ego, feeling, thought, etc. – into the immortal self or *atman*." There follows from this a handsomely sustained discussion of the way a soul reflects or becomes one with existing things, "in a certain sense," at least, as Aristotle qualifies the experience, understanding existing things as "either objects of sense or objects of intellection." For the Hindu, the "categorizing function of the intellect" is divisive; he reacts "against what Jung calls the male principle in the human psyche." The Hindu looks for that experience and those ceremonies in religion that "release psychic energy, to use the Jungian phrase."

Our understanding, inclined perhaps to the orderly and categorical, requires more than the rhetoric of identification with the eternal essences of Eastern religious monism. Jung, says Zaehner, "like Aristotle before him, has helped to throw light on the nature of these monistic utterances by translating them from the realms of ontology and cosmology, where they make little or no sense, to that of psychology." Again, Jung is useful as a way of understanding the Hindu and Buddhist attitude toward the problem of evil: "Like Jung Hindus were prepared to accept it as the 'negative' side of either the human or the divine personality." In the Upanishads, for example, ideas of good and evil mean nothing "once an eternal mode of existence has been realized."

In the opening paragraphs of the eloquent last chapter of *At Sundry Times*, Jung has his most significant moment. Zaehner is arguing that it makes more sense to look for the *praeparatio evangelica*, those things that prepared the way for the Christian gospel, in Asia rather than ancient Greece. He is not speaking of the processes of reason, of scientific inquiry, or even of metaphysical speculation. These are European enough. But religion, "as distinct from theology," says Zaehner, is something else.

> It is concerned not with any metaphysical system, not even with what some modern esoteric writers would call 'metaphysical truth,' but rather with the deep-down places of the human soul which metaphysics and psychology can rationalize but can neither reach nor understand, the non-rational sub and super-structure of the human psyche which normally adopts a defiantly hostile attitude towards the rationalizing ego and which Jung has conveniently labelled the 'collective unconscious.'[24]

---

[24]See R. C. Zaehner, *At Sundry Times: An Essay in the Comparison of Religions* (London: Faber, 1958), pp. 22, 33–34, 42–43, 52–54, 57, 78, 150, 165–166.

In the lectures which became the book *Hindu and Muslim Mysticism*, Zaehner argues with Jung's statement that "we cannot distinguish between the archetype of the self and the God-image, by which he means God as he makes himself known in mystical experience," distinguishing in his argument two types of religious experience. In one, where God and the soul remain separate, the relationship is "always one of love." In the other, found in Yogic mysticism and the first six chapters of the *Bhagavad-Gita*, there is not a love between persons, but that asceticism of integration and realization of self that looks for "the extrication of an eternal element in the soul from all that is not eternal." This is not union "of one with another," for "yoga is the realization of a single spiritual essence and in the Gita means exactly what Jung means by integration (the word *yoga* itself means 'joining'), whereas mystical union in the Christian sense is the union of one spiritual essence with another, the most natural simile for which is sexual union."

The distinction is particularly clear, with the help of Jungian language, in setting off the meaning of Yoga in the *Gita*, the best known and most read work of Asian religion in the West, from its place in Buddhism and the Samkhya system. For Buddhists, the word *Yoga* means "conjunction" and more particularly the enchainment of the immortal spirit to the body and the world through "the four fetters of craving, false views, becoming and ignorance." In Samkhya-Yoga, the word stands for the "dis-joining or dis-uniting . . . of the eternal soul from the psycho-physical apparatus to which it is temporarily attached." In the *Bhagavad-Gita*, when the word is used to describe a spiritual exercise, it "means almost exactly what Jung calls 'individuation' or 'integration of the personality': the *yoga-yukatma* is the integrated personality, the man who has subjected his senses, conquered desire, subjected his mind to the atman or permanent spiritual essence and thereby brought it to rest." It is not the radical disjunction of classical Samkhya-Yoga: "it is a true integration, not a total isolation of the soul from matter." It is indeed what Jung means by individuation.

Individuation is a subtext in *Matter and Spirit* rather than a proclaimed theme or topic. Jung, too, surfaces rarely by name in this elegant little treatise on the "convergence" of the physical and the metaphysical in Eastern religions, Marx, and Teilhard de Chardin. But when Zaehner confronts the central issues of his discipline, comparative religion, his ongoing dialogue with Jung is bound to make its appearance, and so it does. Out of a discussion of "the birth of consciousness" and the emergence of an androgynous first man, Zaehner draws the "vision of innocence which Jung symbolizes as the archetype of the *puer aeternus*" and its quite "extraordinary hold on men's minds." Out of a discussion of ego and self, defined in Jungian terms, he brings us to the soul—that "something that appeared to be immortal" which Jung had "stumbled onto" in his work with his patients. Thus do we arrive at individuation, the integration of the personality: Jung's "aim and that of every psychoanalyst who knows his job must be first to make the patient whole and then to return him to society, so that he may be integrated again in and with society as such." Using the example of a patient of Jung, and with the help of some well-chosen words from the Taoist Chuang Tzu, Zaehner defines the role of the self as an integrating power. The patient had emerged from "acute neurosis," determined to be "receptive to whatever comes . . . good or bad, sun and shadow . . . accepting [her] own nature with its positive and negative sides." Zaehner sums up:

> To allow the self to take over the control of the whole psyche is equivalent to "allowing the nature with which one is endowed to have its free course" [Chuang Tzu]. It is to allow the immortal substrate of the soul, which, having its habitat outside time, must therefore be static, to regulate one's purely secular affairs in time. This is Yoga applied to practical life; it is to integrate ego, intellect, will, and emotions around the immortal center of the psyche; and the latter, if it has already been purged of sin as Yoga requires that it should be, will itself benefit and increase by the association.[25]

It is a dazzling vision, this integration of all one's sides, but to be dazzled is at least in part to be confused, in this case by an excess of light or of a claim to light. Zaehner looks at the claims, so often dazzling, of religion, East and West, of Teilhard de Chardin, of Marx. Marxism promises the possibility of justice in the "industrialization of underdeveloped countries," but it is without that "sense of purpose," that vision, in which the "free development of each will be the condition for the free development of all." Teilhard de Chardin's understanding of the way "God works through matter itself for our common sanctification" is what remains for Zaehner the ideal, "a final spiritualization of all human matter."[26]

Zaehner is caught by the vision, dazzled for a moment, for some pages, but not seriously confused. He has seen the light, or what looks as if it might be the light. He has also seen the darkness and been deeply troubled by it. For much of the rest of his life, he worked to

---

[25]See R. C. Zaehner, *Hindu and Muslim Mysticism* (New York: Schocken, 1969), pp. 89, 135.

[26]See R. C. Zaehner, *Matter and Spirit: Their Convergence in Eastern Religions, Marx, and Teilhard de Chardin* (New York: Harper and Row, 1963), pp. 53–57, 102–106, 207–210.

make some sense of the ways light and darkness act in our lives, to suggest under a number of different rubrics, in procedures both scholarly and unscholarly, the possibility of what he called *Concordant Discord*, the title of his Gifford lectures on "the interdependence of faiths."

Zaehner means many things by his happy title. He means that introduction of "unity into diversity" that St. Francis de Sales speaks of in the opening of his *Treatise on the Love of God*, which he uses to open his lectures. It amounts to a bringing of order into things, and from it, harmony, proportion, and the integrity that "begets beauty." He means also that the rearranging of ideas, words, and arguments is all that we can hope to accomplish, in this metaphysical area: "All that we normally do is to reword and rearrange the ideas of others in our own concordant discord. It is good to realize that we can rarely hope to do more than this." He is particularly successful, I think, in his rearranging and rewording of Jung to achieve some of that consonance amid dissonance which is his aim.

Jung defines for him "what Lord Gifford would have understood as 'natural religion' which, like the indwelling God himself, seemed, in the words of C. G. Jung, to have 'no knowable boundaries and to encompass me on all sides, fathomless as the abysms of the earth and vast as the sky.' " And Jung also puts best for him the loss of credibility of the "ancient God" of vengeance and the growth of understanding of the God we meet as an interior presence. The quotation is from *The Secret of the Golden Flower*: "If I accept the fact that a god is absolute and beyond all human experience, he leaves me cold. I do not affect him, nor does he affect me. But if I know, on the other hand, that God is a mighty activity in my soul, at once I must concern myself with him; he can then become even unpleasantly important, and in practical ways, too." The God who stirs "a mighty activity" is for Zaehner the one that accounts for the interest in Zen and in drugs. Jung's understanding of the collective unconscious and the two selves in man — the ego as center of the conscious mind and "the 'self' as he calls it, borrowing the Sanskrit term *atman*, which is the centre of the total personality, both conscious and unconscious" — is a help, too, in diagnosing the temper of the time. It is a not-too-difficult language in which to discuss the sense of "a connecting link between all things which the Hindus call Brahman and Jung called 'God's world.' "

For Zaehner, Jung is a very special witness, for he "more than anyone else . . . has familiarized the intelligent reader in the West with Eastern mysticism." What led Jung to that understanding, which he articulated so persuasively, was the experience of a God in Nature "so different from the God his Protestant upbringing had proposed for his earnest consideration that the latter had to be put in inverted commas." And then, as Jung reports in his autobiography, he "always knew that he was two persons." One was the well-behaved schoolboy of 1890; the other was the one who "knew God as a hidden, personal, and at the same time suprapersonal secret." But this world in which personality No. 2 has its being does not support, Zaehner warns, either a monist reductionism or a simplistic ecumenism in which all religions and religious experience become one. That is true neither for Zaehner nor for Jung. Zaehner's last acerbic comment in this vigorous discussion is very much to the point. It is a quick gloss on a text in the *Bhagavad-Gita*, where Krishna, the personal God, speaks, saying, "Attach your mind to me: engaged in Yogic exercise put your trust in me" (7:1). Zaehner comments: "For Krishna, being God, knew that to become one with Nature or the universe is not the same as becoming one with himself in the bond of love. Did we really need a God to tell us this?"

The answer to Zaehner's question is, as is so often true in this danger zone, both Yes and No. We do have intermediaries. We have the explanations of what it means to achieve that peace that transcends temporal limitations, what for Hugh of St. Victor in the twelfth century was the equivalent of the *Gita's* "standing on a peak," what his brother in religion, Richard of St. Victor, describes as the movement of "the liveliness of the intelligence in the soul of the contemplative," which "sometimes comes and goes with wonderful quickness, sometimes . . . circles around, sometimes . . . draws itself into a point and remains motionless." The peak, Zaehner explains, is "what Jung calls personality No. 2, the *atman* or 'self' of the Bhagavad-Gita." We are in the world of the prayer of quiet or recollection of the sixteenth-century Carmelite mystics, Teresa of Avila and John of the Cross, or of "the 'self' of the Hindus, the 'buddha-nature' of the Mahayana," says Zaehner, "the still apex or ground of the soul of the Christian mystics, the unsullied image of God." That is true if we think of the peak "as some existent thing," like personality No. 2. If we think of it "as a state of being, then it is Nirvana, the 'fixed, still state of Brahman,' the 'immortal, devoid of fear.' " Its graces, however one thinks of it, are many, but so are its dangers. One may "remain fixed and, as it were, frozen on the frosty peak of solitude . . . tempted to rest here for ever as the Buddha would have done had he followed his own inclination." How do we escape? Through divine intervention, as for example, in "the astonishing words, '*Attach your mind to me*' " of the *Gita*.

To discover divine intervention it is not enough to accept the Muslim consolation, "Who knows himself, knows the Lord." It calls for a constant vigilance, a working at the discovery of one's own self, as Zaehner puts it, which is "hard enough in itself since it runs wholly counter to the habits of 'natural' man born of the flesh."

We need time, we need to be alert, we need to face with honesty and courage the deceits and embroilments of what Zaehner calls "the serpent's gift"–reason. In pursuing the abuses of reason, Zaehner to some extent aligns himself with Rousseau, who as he shows "aligns himself with Catholic tradition" in asserting that it is not the product of the forbidden fruit of Eden, knowledge, that is evil, but rather man's use of it. In a series of closely *reasoned* steps, Zaehner uses Rousseau to make the point that "reason comes first, and like the serpent, it is neither good nor evil but at the disposal of both. Conscience comes second, and it is of God." That leads him in turn to the inevitable colloquy with Jung on the mystery of evil.

He takes up the rest of the statement from *The Secret of the Golden Flower*, quoted above. Jung, it will be remembered was left cold by the god beyond human experience, but still concerned, of necessity, with the God who might be met as "a mighty activity in his soul." What follows is in effect a forecasting of the harsh meditations on evil of *Answer to Job*: "he"–that is, God, Yahweh–"can then become even unpleasantly important, and in practical ways too, which sounds horribly banal, like everything appearing in the sphere of reality."

Zaehner goes quickly enough to *Answer to Job*, where Jung tells us that "God is not only to be loved, but also to be feared." Into our hands, the "dark God" has given the atom bomb and chemical weapons. Jung's God here is man's moral inferior, a figure like the dark deity of the Gnostics. Jung's aim is "nothing less," says Zaehner, "than to psychoanalyse God out of savagery ('the paragon of all creation is not a man but a monster') into sanity." Job is the example *par excellence* of the good man "subjected by God to the most fearful testing at the hands of his son, Satan." Zaehner takes on the savage God and savaging he is given in Jung's book. He does so, not lightly, but with some sympathy for the "thesis that Yahweh is an irrational savage who, though ceaselessly talking of justice, is not just himself."

It is important to Zaehner to remind us that in the Book of Job, Yahweh "is very much more 'conscious' than Jung would have us believe." Job's pride must be "shattered," and he must prove that there is "more to him than a pious landowner, rich, respectable, and self-assured," to be acceptable to God. He is too much taken with his own innocence; he is contemptuous of the poor. Job must learn, in his severely chastening experience, what is proclaimed in the Book of Proverbs, the first revelation according to Jung of "the 'feminine' aspect of the Deity . . . that 'the fear of Yahweh is the beginning of knowledge.' " He must learn in some detail from "the young man Elihu who speaks–and Jung seems not to have noticed this–in the name of Wisdom, Yahweh's feminine counterpart." From Elihu, a remarkable figure who speaks just this once, he must gather that "God does not fit man's measure." Elihu asks the crucial question: "Could an enemy of

Justice ever govern?" And he answers that Yahweh "can tell kings that they are good for nothing, and treat noblemen like criminals . . . [He] shows no partiality to princes and makes no distinction between the rich and the poor, all alike being made by his own hands." No, Zaehner concludes, "Jung is entirely wrong"; Job is not the "moral victor" of the story, but rather stands "convicted of self-sufficiency, rebelliousness, and pride. . . ." He is more an AntiChrist than a Christ figure. "Job is the man who will not accept suffering: Christ is the God who did."[27]

In spite of his resounding "No!" to Jung's picture of a sometimes morally inferior and too often frightening God, Zaehner in his last books could not leave the subject alone. Jung's characterization of the deity pursues him through *Zen, Drugs and Mysticism* and *Our Savage God*. In the first book, he attacks the mixing together of a kind of maddened "unbelief," drug-induced ecstasies, and Eastern religion. In the second, he confronts evil firsthand in the delusions and depravities of Charles Manson and his followers, with corollary examples drawn from *A Clockwork Orange*, in its film version, and from the diabolist Aleister Crowley, whose reconciliation of good and evil finds its governing principle in the words "Do what thou wilt shall be the whole of the law." In all this, Jung plays a significant role.

Much of what Zaehner has to say in these searing volumes is gathered for contemplation in the quotation from Georges Bernanos that opens *Zen, Drugs and Mysticism*: "The old house has collapsed behind our backs and when we came to take our place in the homes of the young, they hadn't yet found out how to build their own, and we found ourselves in an indeterminate sphere, among the stones and rafters, in the rain." We may indeed be "trapped," as so much evidence and so many commentators on the evidence seem to insist, appalled like Pascal by the eternal silences of the infinite spaces that science has opened up for us. But where Pascal and Bernanos found, even in the appalling silence and indeterminate wandering in the rain, occasion for faith, only too many find the meaningless operations of "pure chance" and a frightening unanswering darkness. In this setting, Zaehner reminds us again of Jung's "pantheism," of the "absolute god" that leaves him cold, of the mixing of good and evil that Jung finds in the Old Testament, of the conflict between personalities 1 and 2 in "God's world," and of the great difference between individuation and the integration of the personality that it bespeaks and the extinction of the ego in the enlargements of "positive inflation" or the diminution amounting to annihilation of the ego in "negative inflation."

---

[27]See R. C. Zaehner, *Concordant Discord: The Interdependence of Faiths* (Oxford: Clarendon Press, 1970), pp. 1, 8, 30, 46, 100, 131, 294–301, 307–308, 312–313, 319, 323, 322, 334–335, 341–342, 344, 346, 349–354.

The way out is not to be found in the nostrums of drugs or even in a less threatening kind of pursuit of cosmic consciousness. We need guidance. A few saintly people, such as Pope John XXIII, who have "lost their ego and therefore all egoism," may have the necessary qualifications, being "holy and sane" and with "experience of both religious contemplation and the religious experience LSD is alleged to provide." Such people are rarely encountered. Those with any qualifications are "exceedingly few and far between – perhaps one in a thousand psycho-analysts, of whom Jung was certainly one. . . ." We must, Zaehner insists, deal with the God Jung makes us confront, a God "beyond good and evil, and the author of both. This, for Jung, is a fact that has to be faced; and in this he differs greatly from the fashionable 'Eastern' mysticism of today." It takes, he says, "the insight of a Jung and the faith of a deeply convinced Christian like Bonhoeffer to see the wrath of God as the necessary obverse of his grace."

Jung is one of four modern "prophets" who can offer guidance to our sick society, and have the qualifications to do so. Teilhard de Chardin, Georges Bernanos, and Dietrich Bonhoeffer are the others. Of them, we are told, "it was only Jung and Bonhoeffer who showed real compassion for 'the poor, the lame, the twisted, the plain stupid,' because for both of them God was a living and ever present reality – quite as terrible as he was lovable, but known and experienced as the ultimate Good that is beyond all good and evil."

It is a remarkable reading of Jung, setting him beside three men of such open religious sensibility and the supporting schooling, and finding in him a compassion comparable with that of Bonhoeffer, the victim of the Nazis toward whom Jung is thought by some to have been too forbearing if not something worse. Zaehner understands, too, in Jung, an awareness of the divine presence that aligns him with Pascal in the famous phrase of the *Mémorial*, noting Pascal's experience of the reality of God, the "God of Abraham, God of Isaac, God of Jacob, not the God of the philosophers and scientists."[28] There is no comparable document in Jung's hand, and there seems to be no matching experience, but there is an intensity of pursuit and directness of understanding that suggest something close enough, something very far from unbelief mixed with drug-induced ecstasy and Eastern religion, something with its own commanding and commendable certitude, as Zaehner sees it.

It is more and more a nervous certitude for Zaehner, as he moves into his examination of the terrors of a world presided over by *Our Savage God*. The immediate occasion, as he explains in the opening

---

[28]See R. C. Zaehner, *Zen, Drugs and Mysticism* (New York: Vintage, 1974), pp. 22, 41–42, 56, 59, 96–97, 99, 101, 133, 141, 171, 176–177, 184, 189.

sentences of the book, is the arrival by chance "or what C. G. Jung would have called 'synchronicity,'" of a letter and some pieces by an American academic, one of which points to "how dangerous" the *Bhagavad-Gita* might be "if literally interpreted." A principal example is Charles Manson, the grim eminence behind the Sharon Tate murders in 1969. Again the lethal combination: drugs combined with "some experience of what Manson took to be 'enlightenment' as preached by the religions of Indian origin." Is it possible, Zaehner asks, that some kinds of "mystical experience" could produce not "holy indifference but . . . a diabolic insensitivity which was experienced as being beyond good and evil?"

Jung again provides a governing insight: "the God of 'revelation,' whenever and wherever he reveals himself, *is* terrible. As Jung saw, though it may be true that all opposites are reconciled in him, they are still there in all their uneasy tension." We can deny this and become Zoroastrian dualists, but "the human spirit seems to yearn for a single principle which harmonizes justice and strife into an Absolute which is beyond all change." Zaehner's psychological preoccupation is identical with Jung's now. Like Jung before him, he is giving "expression to the shattering emotions that the unvarnished spectacle of divine savagery and ruthlessness produces in us."

There is no dismissal here of Jung's anguished response to the Book of Job and the God of confounding aspects, savage, tender, unspeakable at either end, the terrible or the grandly good. Zaehner remains a Christian of strong conviction, but one now also of strong enough stomach to admit to the contradictions in the deity that the modern world seems determined to act out and, what is more, he is prepared to admit to them in Jung's words. He offers, finally, a comfort that some may see as small: "when our turn comes to die, we shall see, as Bernanos saw, that any pathetic little effort we may have made to obey his impossible commandment will be gratefully and graciously accepted by that savage God who yet pities us with an everlasting love." It is a considerable consolation if we can go as far as Bernanos and Zaehner go, a consolation and an answer to Jung's answer to Job that accepts almost all the terms of Jung's creed. We must recognize, the tough-minded argument insists, that we really want what God wants, "our sorrows, our sufferings, and our loneliness, although we fondly imagine we only want our pleasures. . . . We do not know ourselves. Sin makes us live on the surface of ourselves: we only go back into ourselves to die – and it is there that He is waiting for us."[29]

Zaehner rehearses some of the same arguments and answers, and

[29]See R. C. Zaehner, *Our Savage God: The Perverse Use of Eastern Thought* (New York: Sheed and Ward, 1974), pp. 9–10, 16–17, 219, 224–226, 229, 231, 307.

with many of the same resources, in the posthumous collection of his lectures and papers, *The City Within the Heart*. Jung is again a major exhibit of religious disappointment and religious experience, one who has given eloquent witness to the hiddenness of the deity and the gathering in the Godhead of "a totality of inner opposites . . . the indispensable condition of his tremendous dynamism." Again, in Jungian language, we are asked to move from the suppression of "the everyday 'ego' " to the point where it can be "replaced by the absolute Self (which is the real you)." Finally, in the passionate essay which reconnoiters so much of this territory, "The Wickedness of Evil," Zaehner quotes lines from the Hindi poet Kabir, "claimed as a saint," he tells us in *Our Savage God*, "by Hindus, Muslims, and Sikhs alike." God is characterized in these lines as a Thug, one of those votaries of the fearful goddess Kali who felt directed by her to mug and to murder by any means those selected by her as victims. A few of those are worth repeating as Zaehner repeated them from book to essay. They gather up much that is in Jung's doctrine of God and in Zaehner's appropriation of that doctrine. They also, in an assured way, turn contradiction into mystery and mystery into peace.

> God is a Thug: and Thuggery's what he has brought to the
> world!
> Yet how can I live without him, tell me, my motherly friend.
> Who is the husband? Who is the wife of whom?
> . . .
> Who is it who dies? Who is wracked with torment?
> Says Kabir: 'What of it? I'm pleased with the Thug as he is:
> For once I recognized the Thug, the Thuggery vanished away.'[30]

---

[30]See R. C. Zaehner, *The City Within the Heart* (New York: Crossroad, 1981), pp. 5-8, 29-31, 35, 44. The matching passage in *Our Savage God* is on p. 217.

CHAPTER 11

COMPLEXIO OPPOSITORUM

We find Jung by losing him. He is the historian of the collective unconscious, the narrator of the life of the symbol and defender of its integrity. He is the collator of dreams, the typologist of human personality in its dartings in and out of consciousness, its maskings and unmaskings, its free and unfree associations. He makes the case for the claims of the shadow at one end of our experience and of the numinous at the other, and links those extremes, and sorrowfully notes their unnecessary separation. He is present in all of his work, on the page, in the analytical session, in the conference, present and unabashedly, speaking often in the first person, adding his own experiences to those of his patients, supplementing the observations of his colleagues, summoning evidence from a past that stretches into the primordium to deepen and extend and confirm what he has seen, what he has thought, what he has felt. He is a constant presence but always in the service of something much larger than himself, that which really abides. It is that Jung, it seems to me, to whom the people brought together in this book testify, the Jung who is most present when he is most absent.

What these witnesses tell us about in their scholarship, their works of art, their theology, their philosophy is a world awash in complexities. Opposites conjoin. Archetypes as ancient as the human race still offer useful models, whether for action or inaction, to encourage or to caution us. "Tell it slant," Emily Dickinson advised, and these witnesses follow the poet and Jung in doing just that. They do so not simply as a reflection of a method, but as a working through, in their different modes, of a theory of knowledge and an approach, however oblique, to a metaphysics of individuation. But theirs is individuation as self-realization, not as self-creation, and it finds its being in a complex world of contingency whose roots reach back to the primordial.

There is, we learn from them who have learned from Jung, no simple reduction possible in a world so filled with chance and archetypal destiny. The psyche resists such reduction. The spirit rebels. We may talk as if such simplification were possible and even try to live that way, but our being insists on its complexity and will not or cannot accept the repression of its multivalent reality. With a fine metaphysical irony, neurosis may come then not from a failure to observe rational modes of thought and behavior but from a refusal to recognize the place of the nonrational and the irrational alongside the rational.

The significations of our complexity are endless and persistent in making their claims. We can suppress them or at least think we do, by denying their existence. But they are irrepressible and will come back to haunt us in soft reverie, or roaring fantasy, or perhaps unhappy somatization, in a tic, an ache, a major contraction of our physical being. What Jung, that nosy polymath, did was to push his way through the arts and sciences, the disciplines of human knowledge, to track the significations of our complexity in their psychic haunts. He offended against staked claims as he made new appropriations, struck at new orthodoxies with ancient demonisms, insisted on the high place of multiple magics as guides to the mechanics of the symbol. Myth, alchemy, medieval mysticisms, Oriental asceticisms – all had their rings in the circus of the psyche. But these were reflections, recordings, speculative pathways, not end places. Neither Jung nor any of his followers ever recommends our settling down in a culture, a shamanism, a religion demonstrably far removed from our own. On the contrary, as Jung never tired of saying, we must be on guard against that kind of transplanting, and as we see in the work of those in the outside world who have been influenced by him, insights that come to us from some considerable cultural or psychic distance are most beneficial when we stress the distance they have traveled and our necessary separation from their sources.

What we get, then, from Jung in the outside world is not a palliating ecumenism. We do not efface differences; we celebrate them. We look backward to look forward. We look outward to see inward. We know that not all can be clear; we recognize that a certain fuzziness may sometimes bring us closer to reality than a laying on of scientistic rhetoric, but we do not therefore underestimate or relinquish the resources of close reasoning or scientific method. We accept the *complexio oppositorum*. Do we have any other choice? Do we want any other?

INDEX

Abraham, Lyndy, 116n.
abstract expressionism, 191
active imagination, 35, 151–153, 166
Adams, Henry, 111
Adler, Alfred, 17, 186, 188
agriculture, 62
Akhmatova, Anna, 198
Albright, W. F., 22, 43, 45n.
alchemy, 25, 31, 50, 60–61, 91, 116-117n., 125, 128, 159, 168, 182, 184–185, 192, 194, 211–213, 215-217, 245
allegory, 164, 166, 184, 202
Alpert, Hollis, 201–202
analytical psychology, 2, 29–30, 68, 100, 119, 185
    language of, 84
Andersson, Bibi, 203
Andreyev, Leonid, 92
androgyny, 59
anima/animus, 47–48, 59, 66, 75, 92, 114–117, 121, 124–125, 133–137, 147, 185, 196–197, 204, 214–216
anima hominis, 99
anima mundi, 5, 61, 82, 97–99
Ansky, S., 185
anthropology, 91, 217–219
apocalypse, 72–73
Appignanesi, Lisa, 135n.
Aquinas, Thomas, 98, 102–103
Arberry, A. J., 228
archaeology, 207
    biblical, 22
archetypal feminine, 87
archetype, 4, 11, 16, 19, 23–25, 27–28, 34, 36, 44, 50, 54–55, 61, 65–66, 74–75, 77, 82, 87, 90–92,

94, 96–99, 101, 104, 105n., 106, 110–111, 114–116, 128–129, 133, 140, 156–157, 159, 196, 199, 201, 207, 209–210, 217–218, 244
    anima, 113
    God, 32–34, 231
    of Mother Earth, 213
    of the child, 66, 68
    of the collective unconscious, 14, 24
    of the father, 9
    of the Great Mother, 50, 193
    of the quest, 53
    of the Self, 49, 57
    of the wise old man, 111, 135
    of transfiguration, 155
    of wholeness, 8
    sexual, 9, 66
architecture, 109, 193–194
Aristotle, 64, 89, 206, 234
Aronson, Alex, 114–116
art, 34, 82–83, 87–88, 91–92, 96, 101, 106n., 107–109, 112–113, 125
    modern, 85, 89, 99
Artaud, Antonin, 185
artist, 3, 65, 74, 82, 85–87, 90, 108–109, 129, 151–152
ascesis, 52
asceticism, 50, 51n.
atonality, 191
Austen, Jane, 93–95
autobiography, 5–9, 64–65, 103, 167

Bach, Johann Sebastian, 199
Bachelard, Gaston, 114, 205, 210–217
Bachhofen, Johann, 96, 148

Bair, Deirdre, 141-142
Baird, James, 109-112
Balzac, 59, 186
Barzun, Jacques, 17
Baudelaire, Charles, 170
Bayle, Pierre, 206
Baynes, H. G., 225
Beckett, Samuel, 92, 141-147
Beethoven, 199
Berg, Alban, 191
Bergman, Ingmar, 203-204
Bergson, Henri, 88
Bernanos, George, 240-242
Bernhard, Ernst, 201
Bhagavad Gita, 132
Bharati, Agehananda, 24-25
Bible, 87, 125, 132, 177, 196
biology, of religion, 28
Bion, Wilfred, 141
bios, 66-67
Blaga, Lucian, 56
Blake, William, 93n., 117-118,
    119n., 125, 200
Bly, Robert, 170-171
Bodkin, Maud, 110, 189
Boff, Leonardo, 45n.
Bonhoeffer, Dietrich, 241
Borelli, John, 50n.
Bovet, Theodor, 14
Bowen, Meirion, 198, 200, 201n.
Braque, Georges, 208
Brivic, Sheldon, 140n.
Broad, C. D., 104
Broch, Hermann, 154-156
Brown, Royal S., 203
Bryant, Christopher, 29-30
Buber, Martin, 18, 71-72, 79n., 89
Bucke, R. M., 58
Buddha, 150
Buddhism, 47-49, 149, 226-227,
    233-234
    see also Tantric Buddhism,
    Tibetan Buddhism, Zen
    Buddhism
Budgen, Frank, 138
Bullock, Alan, 25-26
Bultmann, Rudolf, 25
Burckhardt, 153
Bury, J. B., 224
Bush, Douglas, 93-95, 98

Cahill, Joseph, 20

Campbell, Joseph, 52, 57, 60n.,
    76-78, 79n., 91
cannibalism, 129
Carus, Paul, 96
Cassirer, Ernst, 108
Cezanne, Paul, 86
Chandler, Raymond, 180
Chaplin, Charlie, 188, 204
character, 14
characterology, 81, 121
Charon, Jean E., 105n.
chemistry, 211-212
childhood, 39
Christ, 18-19, 31, 58, 61, 73, 112,
    118, 125
Christianity, 31, 35, 40, 42-43, 53,
    59, 61, 71, 226-227
Church, Richard, 8
Cioran, E. M., 63, 64n.
Clark, Barrett, 186
Clark, Stephen, 102-103
Claudel, Paul, 185, 212
Clift, Wallace, 30-32
Cockshut, A. O. J., 8n.
Coff, Pascaline, 47, 48n.
coincidentia oppositorum, 58-59,
    119, 137, 151-152, 204
Coleridge, 12, 88-89
collective superconscious, 21-22
collective unconscious, 5, 9, 11, 14,
    16, 19-22, 25-27, 34-35, 39-41,
    44, 47, 54-58, 61-62, 68, 75,
    78-79, 81-83, 87, 90-91, 97-99,
    105n., 106, 108-110, 120,
    121-122, 125, 132, 138, 140-141,
    150, 156, 188, 219n., 229-233,
    244
collectivity, 55, 83-84, 126, 128-129,
    131, 162, 171, 178, 183, 218-219
Colmer, John, 132n.
Colum, Mary, 136
comedy, 184, 195, 197
Comfort, Alex, 27-29, 98
communism, Marxist, 59
complex, psychological, 141, 210
complexio oppositorum, 31, 43, 58,
    117, 121, 152, 166, 185, 196, 200,
    244-245
complexity, 2-4, 43, 84n., 163, 245
coniunctio oppositorum, 204
conjunctio, 183
conjunctio oppositorum, 230

Conrad, Joseph, 111, 121
conscience, 38
consciousness, 3, 6-7, 12, 16, 20-21,
    26-17, 31-34, 36, 40, 44-45,
    49-50, 54, 59, 69-71, 75-76, 82,
    84-86, 88-90, 100, 106, 109,
    115-117, 138, 145, 148, 150-151,
    155, 164, 171, 184, 207, 217, 225,
    244
    dream-, 141
    ego-, 5, 7, 140
    God-, 35
contrasexuality, 125
Corbin, Henry, 57, 60n., 68-70, 71n.,
    75
cosmology, 28
    Babylonian, 57
Cott, Jonathan, 105n.
countertransference, 158
Coward, Harold, G., 50n.
creativity, 106
cubism, 208
Curtius, Ernst Robert, 223-224
Custance, John, 229-230

dance, 184, 188-189
daimon, 6, 37-39, 60, 71, 74-76, 99,
    147, 150, 153, 160
Danielou, Jean, 60n.
Dante, 64, 154, 193, 216
Darwin, Charles, 6
Davies, Robertson, 156-163
death, 154-156
de Lisle, Leconte, 111
demon, 92, 103
    see also daimon
depth psychology, 1, 3, 15n., 16-17,
    22, 24, 36, 41, 75, 79, 98, 110,
    115, 121, 170, 186
    as art, 1
    as religion, 1
    as sceince, 1
    see also analytical psychology,
        psychoanalysis, psychology
Descartes, René, 142, 146
Dickinson, Emily, 244
Dieckmann, Hans, 192
dogma, 164
Doll, Mary A., 142n.
Donceel, J. F., 29
Doran, Robert M., 18, 19n.

Dostoevsky, F., 121, 148, 163,
    186-187
Douglas, Mary, 46
Dowland, 199
drama, 184
    see also theater
dreams, 3, 11, 49, 54-56, 58, 60-63,
    73, 77, 85-86, 90-91, 101, 103,
    105-106, 117-118, 124-125,
    137-140, 148, 157, 164, 166,
    167-168, 190, 192, 202-204, 205,
    210, 214, 244
    millennial, 9
    of children, 142
drugs, 240-242
Duncan, Robert, 168
Durand, Gilbert, 52
Durkheim, Emile, 25
Dyson, A. E., 111n.

Earle, William, 8n.
Eastern tradition, 11
Eastern religion, 46-51
Eaton, Gai, 11-13
Eberwein, Robert T., 202-204
Eden, 128
Edwards, David L., 27, 30
ego, 25, 32-34, 48, 75, 115, 118, 141,
    168, 189, 240-241, 243
Ehrenzweig, Anton, 96, 98
Einstein, Albert, 65, 206
Eisner, Robert, 74-76
Eliade, Mircea, 3, 52-53, 56-64, 68,
    71, 75, 105n., 110, 184-185
Eliot, T. S., 6-7, 82-85, 127, 188,
    195-198, 206
Ellington, Duke, 198
Ellmann, Richard, 136n., 139n.
Emerson, R. W., 82
emotion, 20-22
empathy, 35
empiricism, 25, 30
enantiodromia, 114, 118, 172
engrams, 109
enthousiasmos, 37
Erikson, Erik, 95
ESP, 104
eudaimonism, 38-39, 75
evil, 19n., 31, 50, 59, 71, 118

Faas, Ekbert, 172n.

faith, 18-19, 21, 30, 43, 53, 60, 76,
     84, 126
fantasy, 11, 202
father-imago, 9
Faulkner, William, 122, 188
Fellini, Federico, 201-202
feminine, 177-178, 181, 183,
     214-215, 230
Fenollosa, Ernest, 111
Feuerstein, George, 210n.
filius macrocosmi, 61
film, 184, 201-204
Finney, Brian, 8-9
Fitch, Raymond E., 113
Fludd, Robert, 192
Fodor, Nandar, 55
Fox, George, 6
Francis, Sam, 191
Frank, Elizabeth, 190
Fraser, J. T., 54, 66, 91, 96, 109
Freedman, Ralph, 151n.
Freud, Sigmund, 1, 8-9, 11-12, 17,
     23, 28, 41-42, 44, 74-75, 82-83,
     85, 91, 96, 98, 106-107, 109, 121,
     132-133, 135-136, 138-139, 148,
     157, 181, 186, 188, 203, 218
Friedman, B. H., 191n.
Frye, Northrop, 90-93, 110-111,
     210
Fujiyoshi, Jikai, 25
fundamentalism, 43

Garbo, Greta, 204
Gauguin, Paul, 111
Gay, Peter, 17
Gebser, Jean, 54, 205-209
Genet, Jean, 92
Gershenson, Mikhail, 223
Geulincx, Arnold, 142
Ghelderode, Michel de, 185
Gill, Brendan, 79n.
Gilson, Etienne, 212n.
Girard, René, 53
gnosticism, 25, 51n., 61, 71-72,
     147-148, 159, 169, 239
God (Godhead), 31-35, 41, 43,
     53-54, 58, 61, 71n., 74, 77, 79n.,
     101, 117-118, 119n., 125, 164,
     174, 176-177, 225-228, 231-232,
     235, 237-243
     -imago, 110
gods, 14, 67

Goethe, J. W. von, 59, 89, 93n.,
     96-97, 114, 178, 198
Goldbrunner, Josef, 14-15
Gould, Alan, 104
grace, 31, 36, 128
Graham, Martha, 188-189
Grant, Cary, 204
Graves, Robert, 96
Gray, Effie, 112
Great Mother, 129
Greece, 123

Hagstrom, Jean H., 118-119n.
Hamlet, 121
Harding, Esther, 182
Hart, Clive, 140, 141n.
Hartmann, Eduard von, 96
Hartmann, Nicolai, 26
Hearn, Lafcadio, 111
Hegel, 19n., 26, 114
Heidegger, Martin, 25, 40, 79-80,
     206-207
Heiler, Friederich, 60n.
Heisenberg, Werner, 206
Henderson, Joseph, 50-51n.,
     189-190
Heracleitus, 6, 99
hero, 74, 78, 116
     Jesus as, 32-34
Hesse, Herman, 111, 147-154, 170
Hickman, Hannah, 135n.
Hillman, James, 18
Hinduism, 24-25, 226, 234, 237,
     243
history, 220, 222
Hitchcock, Alfred, 203
Hitler, Adolph, 125
Hölderlin, Friedrich, 170, 206
Holy Spirit, 181
Homer, 77, 123
homosexuality, 123-124
Hopkins, G. M., 6, 200
Horia, Vintila, 62-63
Hough, Graham, 97-98, 102
Hughes, Ted, 171-176
Hui-chao, Lin-chi, 48
Hulme, T. E., 85, 88
Hume, Kathryn, 111n.
Huxley, Aldous, 228-229

Ibsen, Henrik, 162-163
Ignatius Loyola, 33

image, 213
imagination, 59, 61, 70, 88, 90, 97,
    100-102, 105, 111-112, 115, 118,
    120, 121, 123, 133, 151, 213, 218
    literary, 140
    moral, 134
imago dei, 101
incest, 133
individuation, 5-6, 12, 18, 19n.,
    21-22, 25, 30, 42, 47-49, 52, 54,
    59, 61-63, 68, 70, 72-73, 75,
    114-115, 117, 119, 148, 155, 177,
    187, 202-203, 235-236, 240, 244
Ionesco, Eugene, 92
Isherwood, Christopher, 9
Islam, 226-227
Ivanov, Vyacheslav, 223-224

Jacoby, Jolande, 156n., 209
Jaffe, Aniela, 155
James, Henry, 8
James, William, 17, 95, 104
janusian thinking, 105-106
Jaspers, Karl, 207
Jeffries, Richard, 229
Jesus, 87, 118
    see also Christ
Jimenez, 170
Jones, Ernest, 138
Jordens, J. F. T., 50n., 71n.
Joyce, James, 76, 82, 85, 92,
    121-122, 128, 135-141, 145, 148
Joyce, Lucia, 136
Judaism, 72, 132
Jung, C. G.,
    as mystic, 3, 64
    at his death, 64
Jung, Emma, 182

Kabbalah, 72
Kafka, Franz, 93-95, 121, 166
Kahler, Erich, 83-84
Kain, Richard M., 138n.
Kalidasa, 185
Kant, Immanuel, 22, 153
Kaufman, Walter, 26, 27n.
Keaton, Buster, 142, 144-145
Kelsey, Morton, 18
Kerenyi, C. J., 11, 57, 60n., 65-68,
    75
Kermode, Frank, 117n.
Kierkegaard, 63, 75

Kirsch, James, 192
Klages, Ludwig, 132
Klee, Paul, 23-24, 86
Klein, Melanie, 96
Knapp, Bettina, 184-185, 189
koan, 13
Kohut, Heinz, 1
Krutch, Joseph Wood, 186
Kuryluk, Ewa, 111n.

Lahr, Bert, 145
Lang, Joseph B., 147-149
language, 109, 141
Larkin, Philip, 52
Lascaris, Manoly, 123
Laszlo, Violet de, 189-190
La Touche, Rose, 112
Lautréamont, 110
Lawrence, D. H., 89, 111, 121-122
Layard, John, 60n., 177, 179, 189
Lee, Laurie, 8
Leitch, Vincent B., 111n.
Levin, David Michael, 79-80
Levi-Strauss, 52, 75
Lévy-Bruhl, Lucien, 217
libido, 47, 51n., 110, 138, 210, 222
l'Isle-Adam, Villier de, 185
literary criticism, 91, 93, 99, 102,
    121
literary theory, 81-120, 121
Lonergan, Bernard, 19n.
Longfellow, H. W., 109
Lorca, F. Garcia, 170
Loti, Pierre, 111
love, 103, 127, 131, 235
Luft, David S., 135n.

Maeterlinck, 92
Magalaner, Marvin, 138n.
Mallarmé, Stéphane, 110, 206
Malraux, Andre, 106, 142
mandala, 18, 47, 62-63, 80, 114,
    122, 124, 127
Mann, Thomas, 83, 121-122, 148n.,
    178
Manson, Charles, 240, 242
Marcel, Gabriel, 25
Marlowe, 178
Marvell, Andrew, 19, 116-117n.,
    180
Marx, Karl, 235-236
masculinity, 27, 214-215

materialism, 110
Mayans, 193
Mazzeo, J. A., 111n.
McCormick, Edith, 136
McCormick, John, 134n.
McCormick, Mrs., 138
McCoy, Ann, 191-192, 193n.
meditation, 48-49
Meier, C. F., 192
Meister Eckhardt, 12
Melville, Herman, 93-94, 109,
    111-112
Memories, Dreams, Reflections
    (Jung), 5, 8, 18, 37, 65
menstruation, 176, 182
Merleau-Ponty, Maurice, 79
metaphor, 23-24, 36, 55-56, 83, 100
    of self, 5, 9
Mill, John Stuart, 6
Milner, Marion, 96
Milton, John, 198
Miyuki, Mokusen, 48-49
Moacanin, Radmila, 49-50
Molnar, Thomas, 52-53
Mondrian, Piet, 86
monotheism, 28, 53
Montaigne, M. E. de, 5-7, 220
Monteverdi, Claudio, 199
Moore, Henry, 90, 180, 193-195
mother, 9
Moyers, Bill, 77
Mozart, W. A., 151, 195
Muir, Edwin, 9, 121-122, 164-167
music, 82, 184, 195-201
Musil, Robert, 132-134, 208
Muslims, 243
mysterium coniunctionis, 58
mystic, 3, 64-65
mysticism, 61, 64, 82, 228, 230, 235,
    245
myth, 27, 33, 52-80, 87, 91-92, 94,
    96-98, 109, 113, 119, 124, 138,
    210, 245
    personal, 5, 7-9, 25, 140n.
mythology, 11, 34, 87

Nag Hammadi texts, 72
Nathan, George Jean, 187
Nature, 61
Needham, Rodney, 205, 217-220
Neruda, 170

Neumann, Erich, 50, 60n., 67, 79,
    87, 193-194, 213
neurosis, 13, 15, 29n., 30
Newman, John Cardinal, 5-6
Nietzsche, Friedrich, 26, 75, 78, 96,
    153, 167
nihilism, 80n.
Noh, 185
Nolan, Sidney, 122
Norton, David L., 37-39
Novalis, 170
novel, 121-163, 208-209

objectivity, 69
Oedipus, 74
O'Flaherty, Wendy, 54-56
Olney, James, 5-7, 8n., 99-102
Olson, Charles, 167-169
O'Neill, Eugene, 111, 186-188
O'Neill, Timothy, 119-120
ontogeny, 22
opposites, 151-152
opus alchymicum, 61
Osborne, John, 9
Ostow, Mortimer, 22-23
ourobouros, 29
Ovid, 76-77

paganism, 52, 72
painting, 184, 189-192
Parmenides, 99
participation mystique, 102, 108,
    217
Pascal, Blaise, 63, 240-241
Pasternak, Boris, 198
Pauli, William, 11
Payne, Richard, 47
perennial philosophy, 99-100
Perse, St. John, 188
persona, 92, 114, 202
personality, 95
Peters, Frederick G., 135n.
Philipe Gerard, 204
Philipson, Morris, 106-108, 218
Philosopher's Stone, 64
philosophy, 70, 205-243
Philp, H. L., 59
phylogeny, 21
Picasso, Pablo, 74, 85, 194, 206,
    208
Pinter, Harold, 92
Pirandello, Luigi, 92

Plath, Sylvia, 173
Plato, 26, 64, 75, 89, 99, 206, 222
pleroma, 100–102
poemagogic, 96, 98
poet, 83, 86–87
poetics, 102, 211–214, 216, 229
poetry, 82, 99, 122, 142, 164–183
    political, 170
    primitive, 127
Pollock, Jackson, 189–191
Polonius, 99
Ponge, 170
Popper, Karl, 1
pornography, 89
Portmann, Adolph, 60n.
positivism, 3, 16, 62, 101
Pound, Ezra, 168–169
Powell, Anthony, 139n., 140n.
Protestantism, 111–112
Proust, 86, 229
psyche, 2–3, 5, 7, 9, 13, 15n., 16–17,
    19n., 20–23, 26, 29n., 32–34, 36,
    39, 42, 48, 53, 57, 59–60, 66–67,
    69–70, 78, 80, 82–83, 86,   88,
    107, 115–116, 119, 121–122,
    141–142, 144, 170, 210, 214, 219,
    221, 226–227, 234, 245
psychoanalysis, 28, 69, 82, 96, 132,
    136, 140–141, 186
psychobiology, 27
psychology, 34, 45n., 91, 96, 99, 119,
    140
    Jungian, 101, 177
psychosis, 49, 136, 229
Pythagoras, 99

quaternity, 68, 119
Quispel, Gilles, 60n., 71–73, 74n.

Raglan, Lord, 91
Rahner, Hugo, 60n.
Raine, Kathleen, 117
Rand, Ayn, 79n.
Rank, Otto, 1, 96, 148–149
rationalism, 53
Read, Herbert, 8, 82, 84–90,
    193–194
reality, 11, 26, 40, 64, 69, 73, 83, 89,
    103, 155–156, 168.
    psychic, 30
    ultimate, 33, 205
Redgrove, Peter, 176–183

Reid, Forrest, 9
reincarnation, 105n.
religio, 67
religion, 10–45, 52, 60, 63, 70, 109,
    126, 225, 233–234
    Eastern, 13, 52
    see also Eastern tradition,
        Eastern religion
Ricoeur, Paul, 53–54
Rieff, Philip, 75
Rilke, R. M., 170, 198, 206
Rimbaud, Arthur, 110–111, 229
ritual, 91
Robinson, Henry Morton, 76
Rodman, Seldon, 190–191
Rollins, Wayne, 35–36
Rosarium Philosophorum, 215
Rosen, J. N., 55
Rothenberg, Albert, 105–106
Rousseau, J. J., 239
Ruskin, John, 112–113

Sainte-Beuve, C.-A., 81
Sandulescu, C. George, 141n.
Sanford, John A., 18
Sartre, J. P., 207
Satan, 118
satori, 13, 48
Scharfstein, Ben-Ami, 22–23,
    64–65
Schiller, 149
Schlant, Ernestine, 155
Schoenberg, Arnold, 86, 191, 199
Schrodinger, Erwin, 60n., 65
Schuon, Frithjof, 19–20
Schwartz-Salant, Nathan, 183
science, 11, 14, 21, 34, 83, 92
scientific method, 101
scientists, 65
Scigaj, Leonard M., 172n.
scripture, 35–37, 92
sculpture, 193–194
self, 6–9, 19n., 21, 24–25, 32, 37, 40,
    48–49, 52, 57–59, 61, 66, 68–70,
    71n., 73, 79, 80n., 86, 88–89, 101,
    114–115, 117–120, 149, 151, 236,
    243
Seneca, 164, 174, 184
Senne, René Le, 81
Serrano, Miguel, 154
sexuality, 124, 129–132, 178, 211,
    214

shadow, 42, 92, 103, 113-117, 152,
  164-166, 171, 176, 185, 188, 203,
  230-231, 244
shadow self, 9
Shakerley, Geoffrey, 194n.
Shakespeare, William, 114-117, 195,
  197
Shaw, G. B., 195
Shelley, P. B., 97, 198
Shinichi, Hisamatsu, 25
Shuttle, Penelope, 176, 182
sign, 15, 32, 83, 107, 164
sin, 36, 63, 118
Sitwell, Osbert, 9
Slusser, Gerald H., 32-35
Smart, Ninian, 46
Smith, M. Brewster, 24
Socrates, 64, 75-76, 224
Sophocles, 64
soul, 5, 9, 15, 33, 35, 41, 61, 69-71,
  97, 110
space, 89, 91
speleology, 58
Spender, Stephen, 194n.
Spiegelman, J. Marvin, 48, 49n.
Spinks, G. Stephens, 10-12, 15
spirit, 5, 14-15, 30, 32, 39-41, 44,
  45n., 58
spirituality, 45n.
spiritus mercurius, 61
spiritus mundi, 5, 97
Stein, Gertrude, 114
Stelzig, Eugene, 151
Stendhal, 186
Stevens, Wallace, 109-110, 178
Stevenson, R. L., 111
Stewart, Allegra, 114
Stoppard, Tom, 92
Storr, Anthony, 94-95
Stravinsky, Igor, 86, 199-200
Strenski, Ivan, 56, 57n.
Strindberg, August, 92, 185-188
subconscious, 20n.
subjectivism, 87
sublimation, 149
superego, 38
superrealism, 85, 88
surrealism, 85, 88
symbolism, 34, 46, 57, 60, 82, 93n.,
  97, 108, 125, 193
  archetypal, 190
symbols, 7, 11, 15, 23-24, 27, 31, 32,

  36, 42-45, 46-47, 50, 53, 55, 58,
  61, 68-70, 73, 75, 78-80, 83,
  87-88, 90, 95, 97, 99, 195n.,
  107-109, 112-113, 139, 141, 147,
  164, 166, 184, 190, 192, 211, 217,
  219, 244
  alchemical, 91
  of transformation, 131
  religious, 41, 44-45
synchronicity, 68, 104-106, 207,
  242

Tacey, David J., 132n.
Talmud, 132
Tantric Buddhism, 47, 49-50,
  50-51n.
Taoism, 12, 33, 58
Tavistock Clinic, 141, 145
Teilhard de Chardin, 21, 235-236,
  241
temenos, 114
Tennyson, 188
theater, 184-185
  of the absurd, 92
Thomas Aquinas, 41, 206
Tibetan Buddhism, 50
Tillich, Paul, 25, 40-45, 52, 60n.,
  79n.
time, 89, 91, 101
Tindall, William, 135, 137-138
Tippett, Michael, 195-201
Tolkien, 119-120
Tomlin, E. W. F., 15-16
totality, 48, 58-59, 61, 68
Towers, Bernard, 20-22
Toynbee, Arnold, 205, 220-227
tragedy, 184, 187
Trakl, 170
transcendence, 15, 24, 51n.
transference, 158
transformation, 154, 184-185, 205
  personal, 150
Tristano, Lennie, 200
Troy, William, 111n.
truth, 11, 24, 27, 30, 32, 53, 73, 89,
  100, 103
typology, 6-7, 9, 14, 17, 81, 89, 94,
  99, 121, 150, 161-152, 204, 244

UFO, 103, 105n.
Ulanov, Ann, 48, 182
Ullmann, Liv, 203

unconscious, 1, 3, 5-6, 9, 12, 23,
   29n., 36, 41, 45, 48, 55-56, 59-61,
   69, 71, 73-74, 77, 80, 83-86,
   88-89, 97, 99-101, 104, 106-107,
   110, 114, 116-117, 119, 122, 125,
   131, 133, 137, 141-142, 144-148,
   150, 156, 164-165, 168, 171,
   175-176, 181, 184, 189-191, 194,
   201, 217-218, 220, 222, 224-225
   existential, 84
   generic, 83-84
Untermeyer, Jean Starr, 156
Upanishads, 12, 51n., 230, 234

Vallejo, 170
Vedas, 87
violence, 125, 128, 131, 187
   in poetry, 171-173
Virgil, 64, 154-156, 193
von Hartmann, Eduard, 12

Wagner, Richard, 198
Waldeck, Peter B., 155n.
Waveren, Erlo van, 105n.
Weaver, Harriet, 138
Weigel, Gustave, 43-44, 45n.
Weiss, Ottocaro, 136, 138
Weizsäcker, C. F., 206

Wellek, René, 81-82
Welling, Georg von, 61
Wheelwright, Philip, 110
White, Patrick, 121-129, 131-132
White, Victor, 15, 59
Whitman, Walt, 110
Wilson, Edmund, 185
Wilson, F. A. C., 111n.
Winnicott, D. W., 1
Winter, Gibson, 23-24
Witkiewicz, 185
Wittgenstein, Ludwig, 217, 220n.
Wolfe, Peter, 132n.
Wolff-Salin, Mary, 45n.
Wordsworth, William, 12, 86, 110,
   202, 224

Yeats, 5, 9, 82, 97-103, 183, 185,
   198
yin/yang, 48
yoga, 51n.

Zaehner, R. C., 205, 228-243
Zen, 237, 240
Zen Buddhism, 13, 25, 48, 132, 198
Zimmer, Heinrich, 57, 60, 77
Ziolkowski, Theodore, 150
zoe, 66